Thank you for picking up
Haikyu!! volume 1! I hope
you like it. For those of you
who are like, "Volleyball?
Never played it. I don't even
know the rules!"...I hope
to make this a story full of
fun and great characters
you'll enjoy and who will
make you want to say,
"I want to root for these guys!"

Hey!
★

Uh...

HARUICHI FURUDATE began his manga career when he was
25 years old with the one-shot Ousama Kid (King Kid), which
won an honorable mention for the 14th Jump Treasure
Newcomer Manga Prize. His first series, Kiben Gakuha, Yotsuya
Sensei no Kaidan (Philosophy School, Yotsuya Sensei's Ghost
Stories), was serialized in Weekly Shonen Jump in 2010.
In 2012, he began serializing Haikyu!! in Weekly Shonen Jump,
where it became his most popular work to date.

W0007759

HAIKYU!!

VOLUME 1
SHONEN JUMP Manga Edition

Story and Art by
HARUICHI FURUDATE

Translation **1** **ADRIENNE BECK**
Touch-Up Art & Lettering **2** **ERIKA TERRIQUEZ**
Design **3** **FAWN LAU**
Editor **4** **MARLENE FIRST**

HAIKYU!! © 2012 by Haruichi Furudate
All rights reserved.
First published in Japan in 2012 by SHUEISHA Inc., Tokyo.
English translation rights arranged by SHUEISHA Inc.

The stories, characters and incidents mentioned
in this publication are entirely fictional.

No portion of this book may be reproduced or transmitted
in any form or by any means without written permission
from the copyright holders.

Printed in Italy

Published by VIZ Media, LLC
P.O. Box 77010
San Francisco, CA 94107

10
First printing, July 2016
Tenth printing, April 2021

VIZ MEDIA
viz.com

RATED
T
TEEN
ratings.viz.com

PARENTAL ADVISORY
HAIKYU!! is rated T for Teen and
is recommended for ages 13
and up for mild language.

SHONEN JUMP

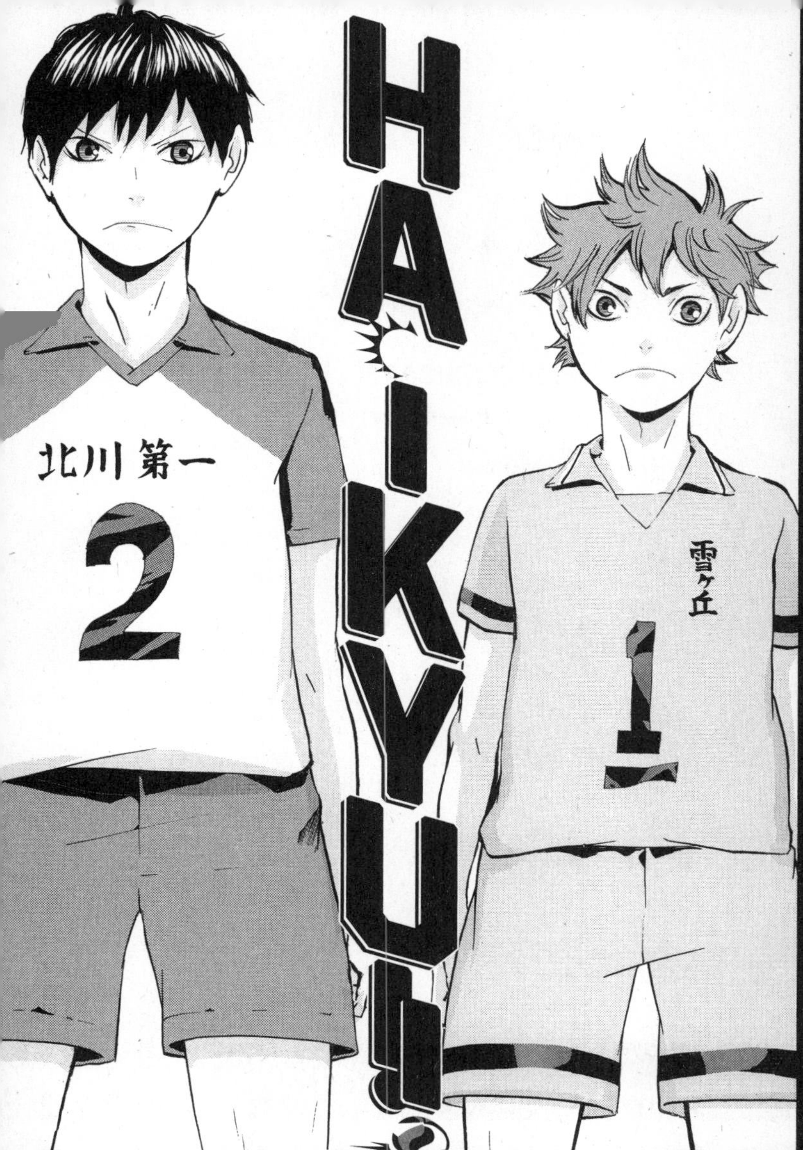
HAIKYU!!
北川第一
2
雪ヶ丘
1

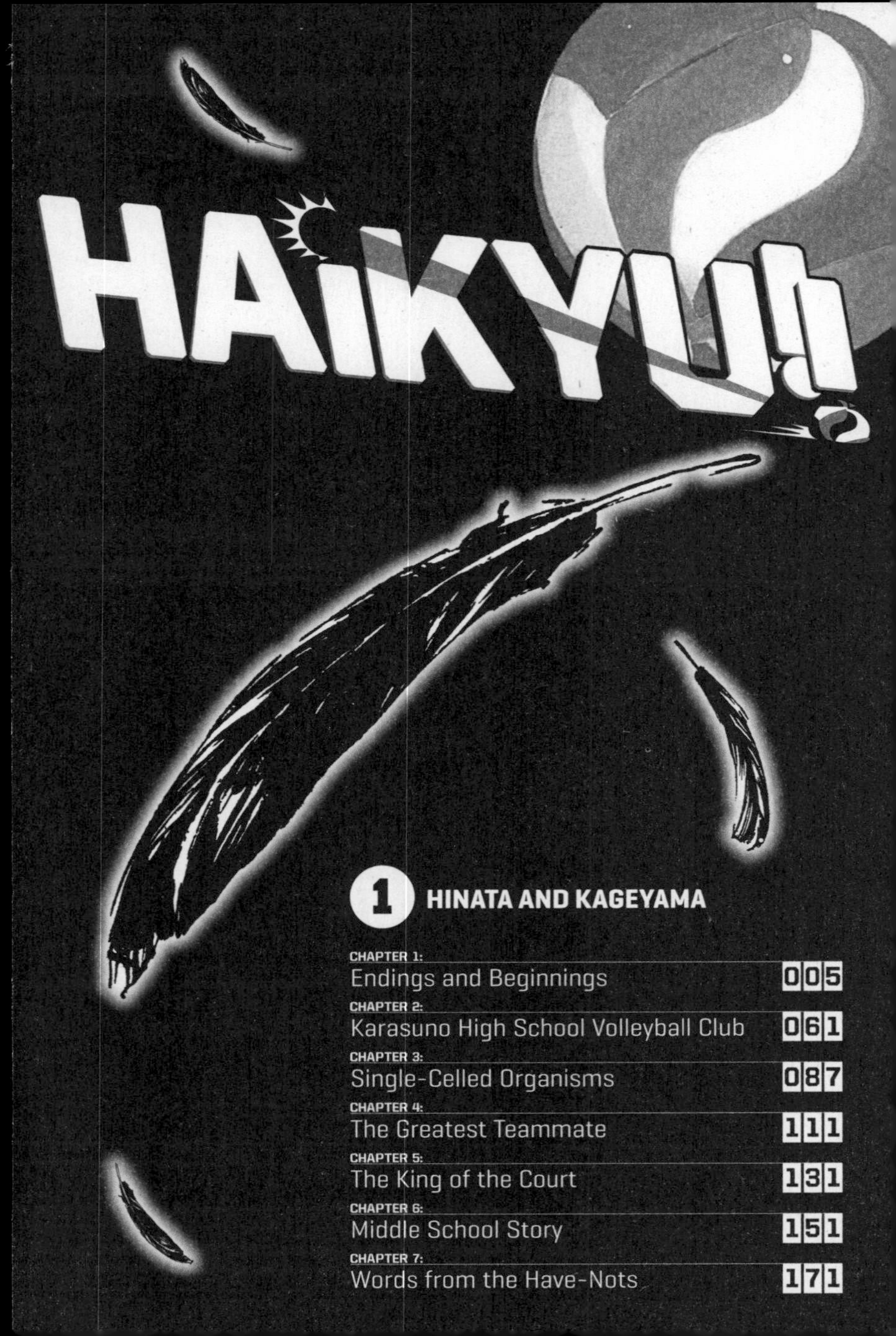
HAIKYU!!

1 HINATA AND KAGEYAMA

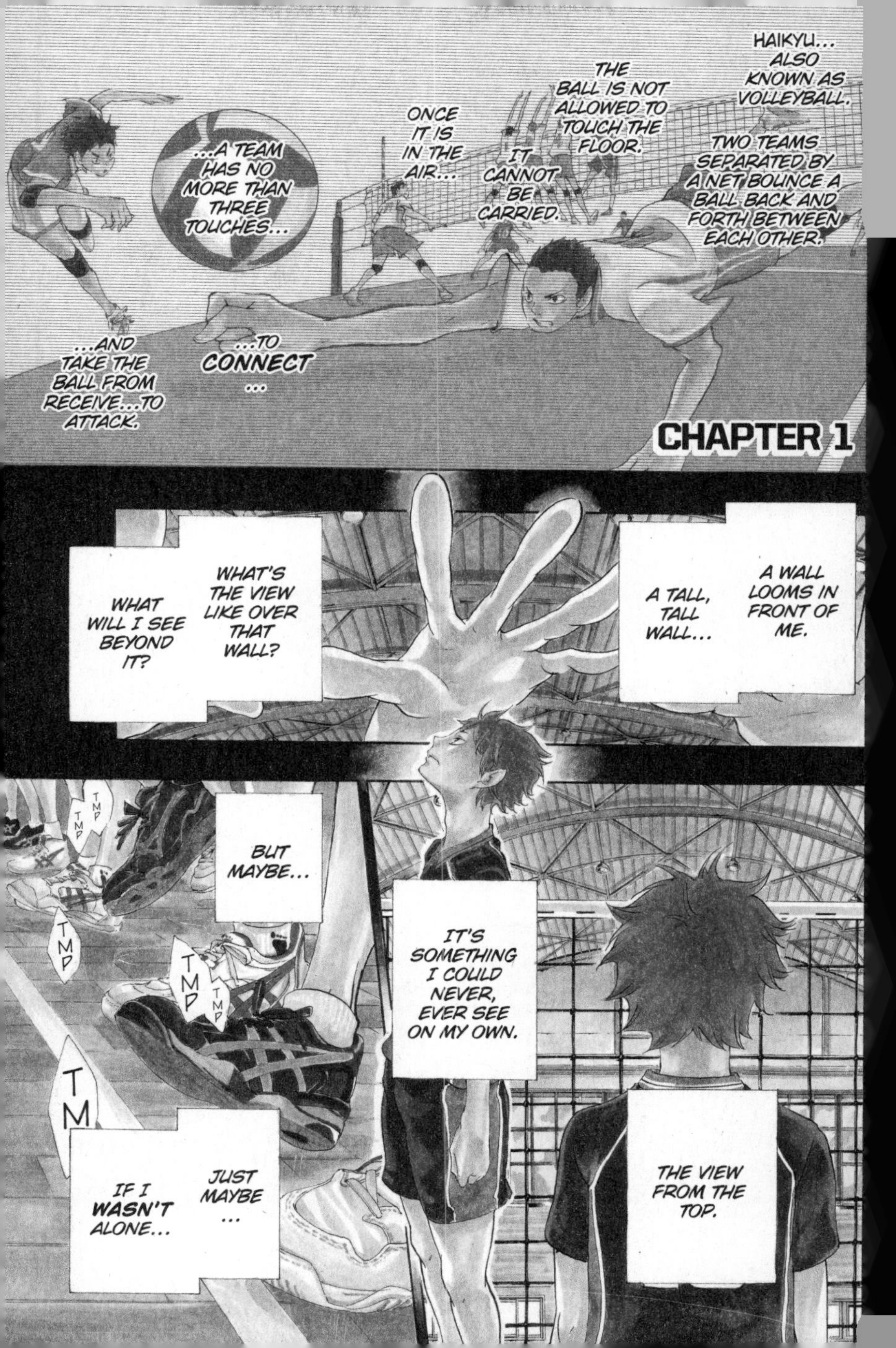
HAIKYU... ALSO KNOWN AS VOLLEYBALL.
TWO TEAMS SEPARATED BY A NET BOUNCE A BALL BACK AND FORTH BETWEEN EACH OTHER.
THE BALL IS NOT ALLOWED TO TOUCH THE FLOOR.
IT CANNOT BE CARRIED.
ONCE IT IS IN THE AIR...
...A TEAM HAS NO MORE THAN THREE TOUCHES...
...TO CONNECT ...
...AND TAKE THE BALL FROM RECEIVE...TO ATTACK.
CHAPTER 1
A WALL LOOMS IN FRONT OF ME.
A TALL, TALL WALL...
WHAT'S THE VIEW LIKE OVER THAT WALL?
WHAT WILL I SEE BEYOND IT?
IT'S SOMETHING I COULD NEVER, EVER SEE ON MY OWN.
THE VIEW FROM THE TOP.
TMP TMP
BUT MAYBE...
TMP
TMP TMP
TM
JUST MAYBE ...
IF I WASN'T ALONE...

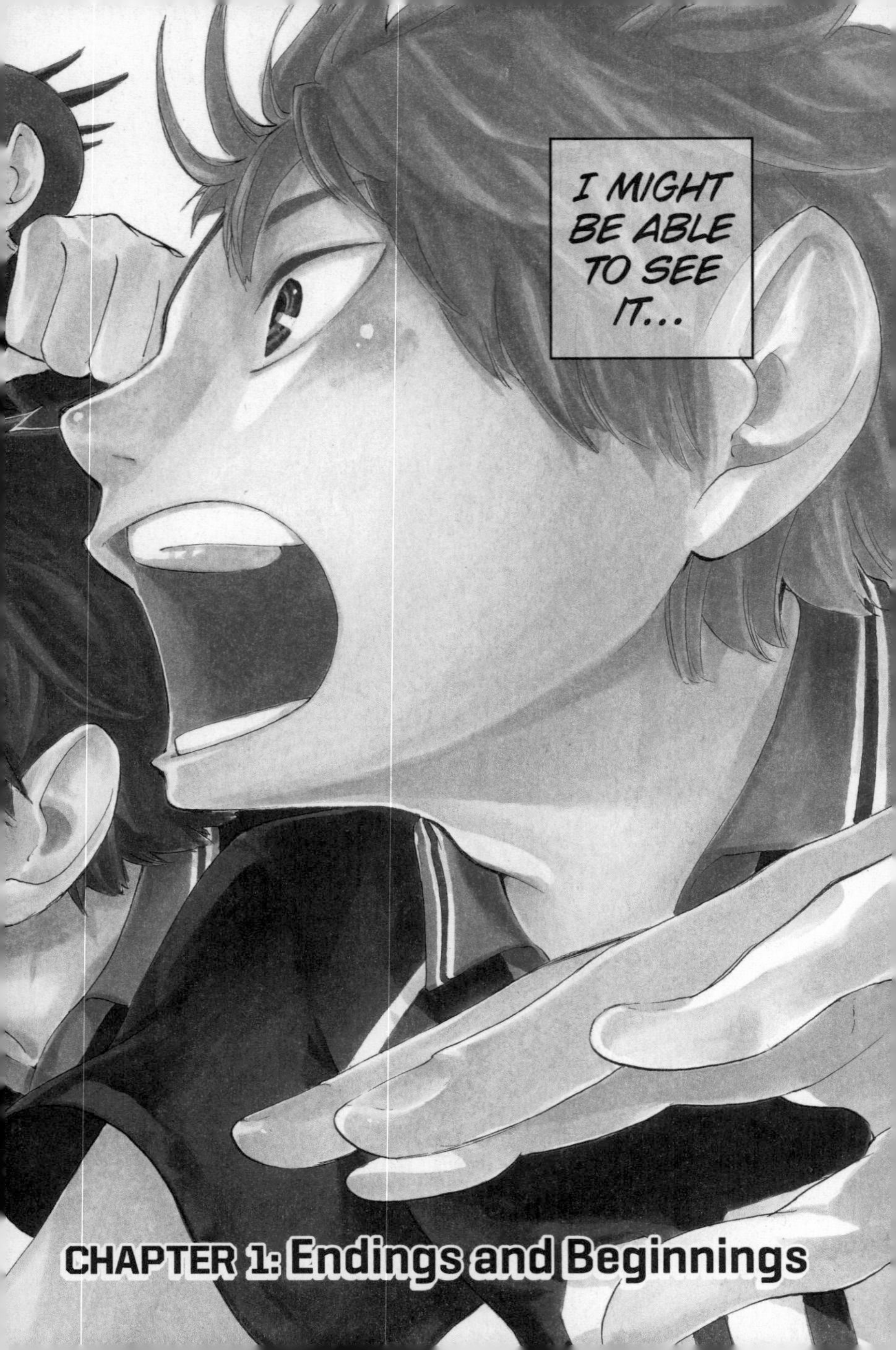
I MIGHT BE ABLE TO SEE IT...

CHAPTER 1: Endings and Beginnings

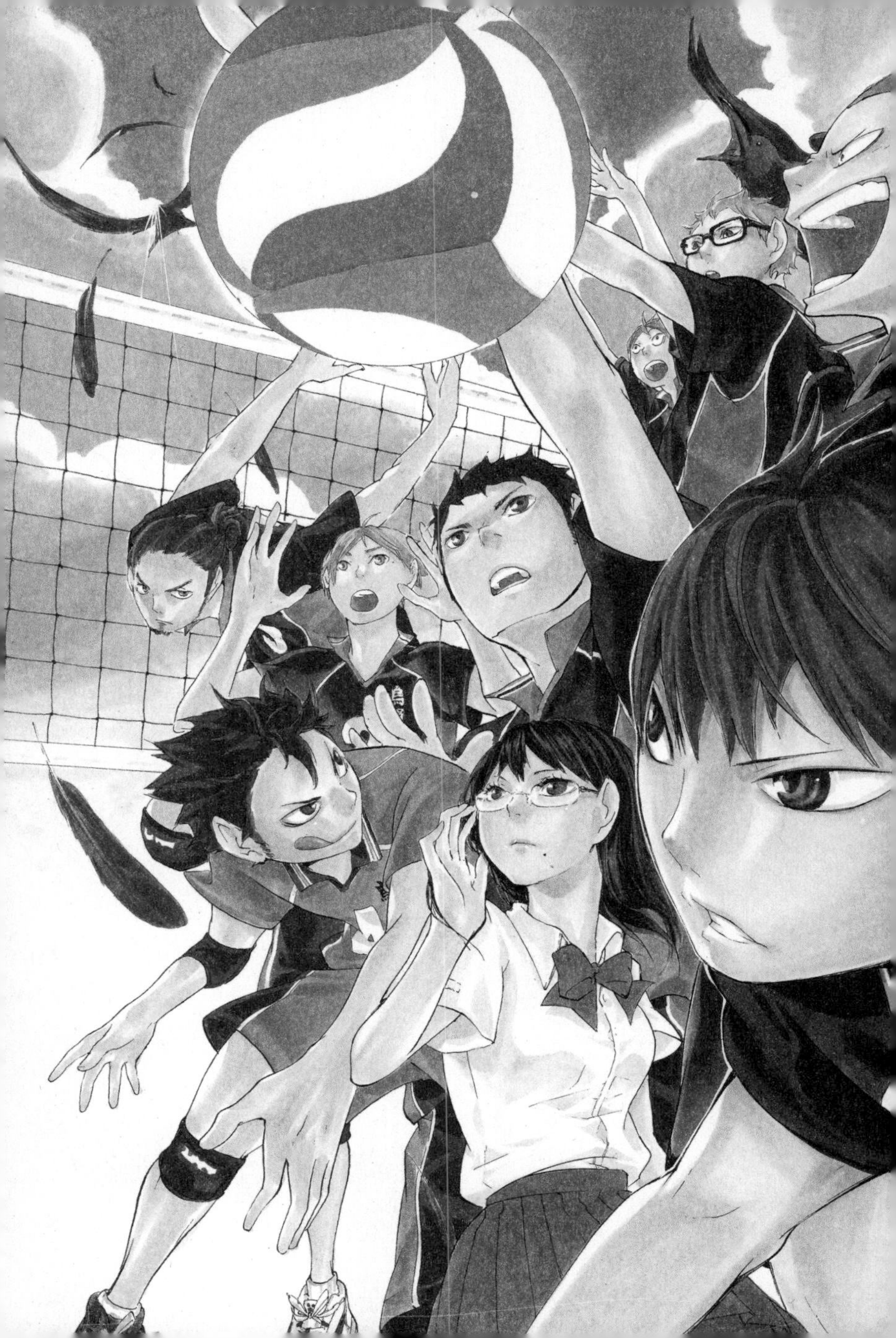

HAIKYU!!

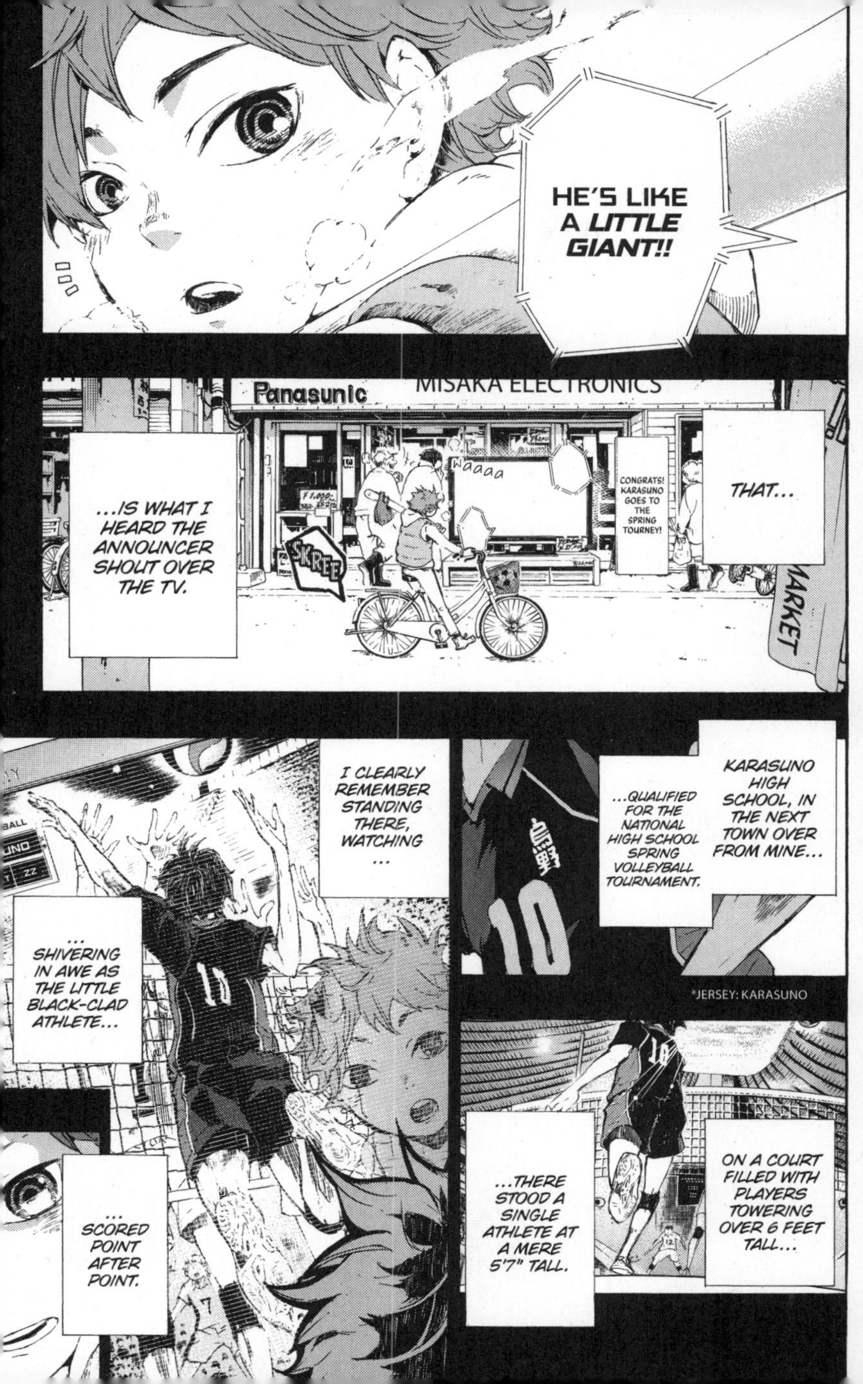
HE'S LIKE A *LITTLE GIANT!!*
Panasunic
MISAKA ELECTRONICS
THAT...
CONGRATS! KARASUNO GOES TO THE SPRING TOURNEY!
Waaaa
SKREE
...IS WHAT I HEARD THE ANNOUNCER SHOUT OVER THE TV.
MARKET
KARASUNO HIGH SCHOOL, IN THE NEXT TOWN OVER FROM MINE...
...QUALIFIED FOR THE NATIONAL HIGH SCHOOL SPRING VOLLEYBALL TOURNAMENT.
*JERSEY: KARASUNO
ON A COURT FILLED WITH PLAYERS TOWERING OVER 6 FEET TALL...
...THERE STOOD A SINGLE ATHLETE AT A MERE 5'7" TALL.
I CLEARLY REMEMBER STANDING THERE, WATCHING...
...SHIVERING IN AWE AS THE LITTLE BLACK-CLAD ATHLETE...
...SCORED POINT AFTER POINT.

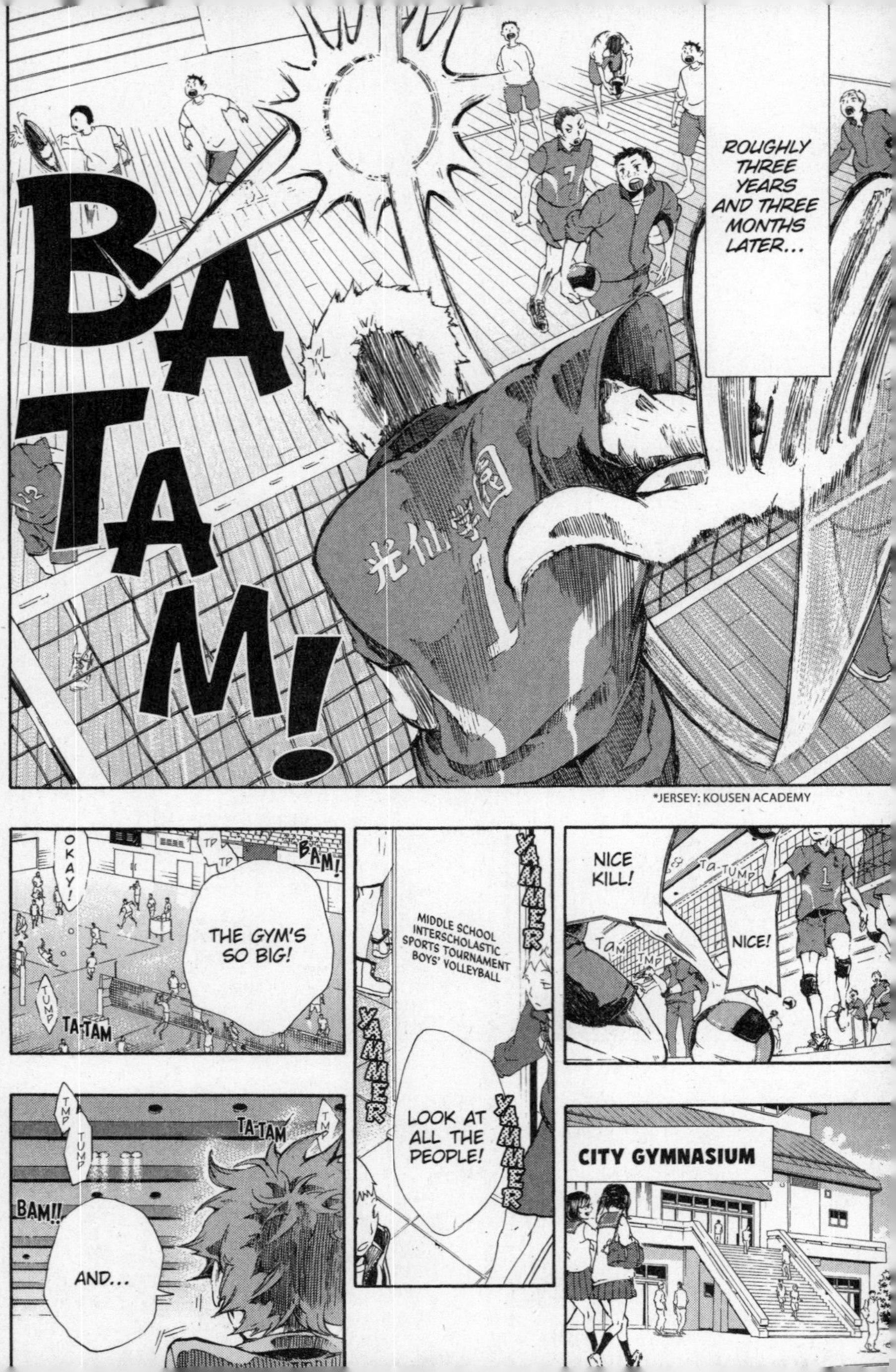
ROUGHLY THREE YEARS AND THREE MONTHS LATER…
BATAM!
光仙学園
*JERSEY: KOUSEN ACADEMY
NICE KILL!
Ta-TUMP
NICE!
Tam
TMP
CITY GYMNASIUM
YAMMER
MIDDLE SCHOOL INTERSCHOLASTIC SPORTS TOURNAMENT BOYS' VOLLEYBALL
YAMMER
LOOK AT ALL THE PEOPLE!
YAMMER
OKAY!
TP
TP
BAM!
THE GYM'S SO BIG!
TUMP
TA-TAM
TMP
TMP
TA-TAM
TUMP
BAM!!
AND…

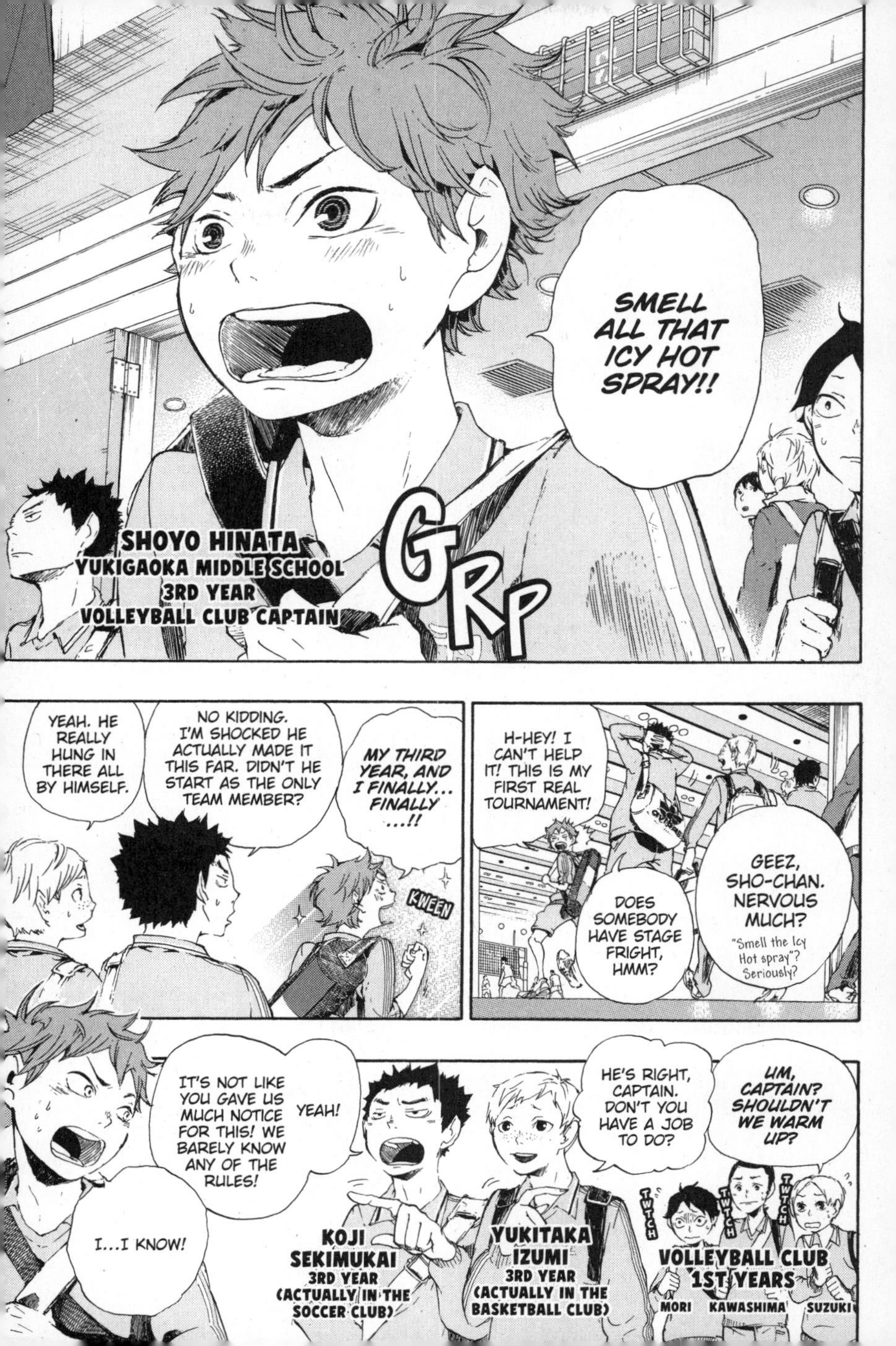
SMELL ALL THAT ICY HOT SPRAY!!
GRP
SHOYO HINATA
YUKIGAOKA MIDDLE SCHOOL
3RD YEAR
VOLLEYBALL CLUB CAPTAIN
H-HEY! I CAN'T HELP IT! THIS IS MY FIRST REAL TOURNAMENT!
GEEZ, SHO-CHAN. NERVOUS MUCH?
"Smell the Icy Hot spray"? Seriously?
DOES SOMEBODY HAVE STAGE FRIGHT, HMM?
MY THIRD YEAR, AND I FINALLY... FINALLY ...!!
KWEEN
NO KIDDING. I'M SHOCKED HE ACTUALLY MADE IT THIS FAR. DIDN'T HE START AS THE ONLY TEAM MEMBER?
YEAH. HE REALLY HUNG IN THERE ALL BY HIMSELF.
UM, CAPTAIN? SHOULDN'T WE WARM UP?
HE'S RIGHT, CAPTAIN. DON'T YOU HAVE A JOB TO DO?
TWTCH
TWTCH
TWTCH
VOLLEYBALL CLUB 1ST YEARS
MORI KAWASHIMA SUZUKI
YUKITAKA IZUMI
3RD YEAR
(ACTUALLY IN THE BASKETBALL CLUB)
YEAH!
KOJI SEKIMUKAI
3RD YEAR
(ACTUALLY IN THE SOCCER CLUB)
IT'S NOT LIKE YOU GAVE US MUCH NOTICE FOR THIS! WE BARELY KNOW ANY OF THE RULES!
I...I KNOW!

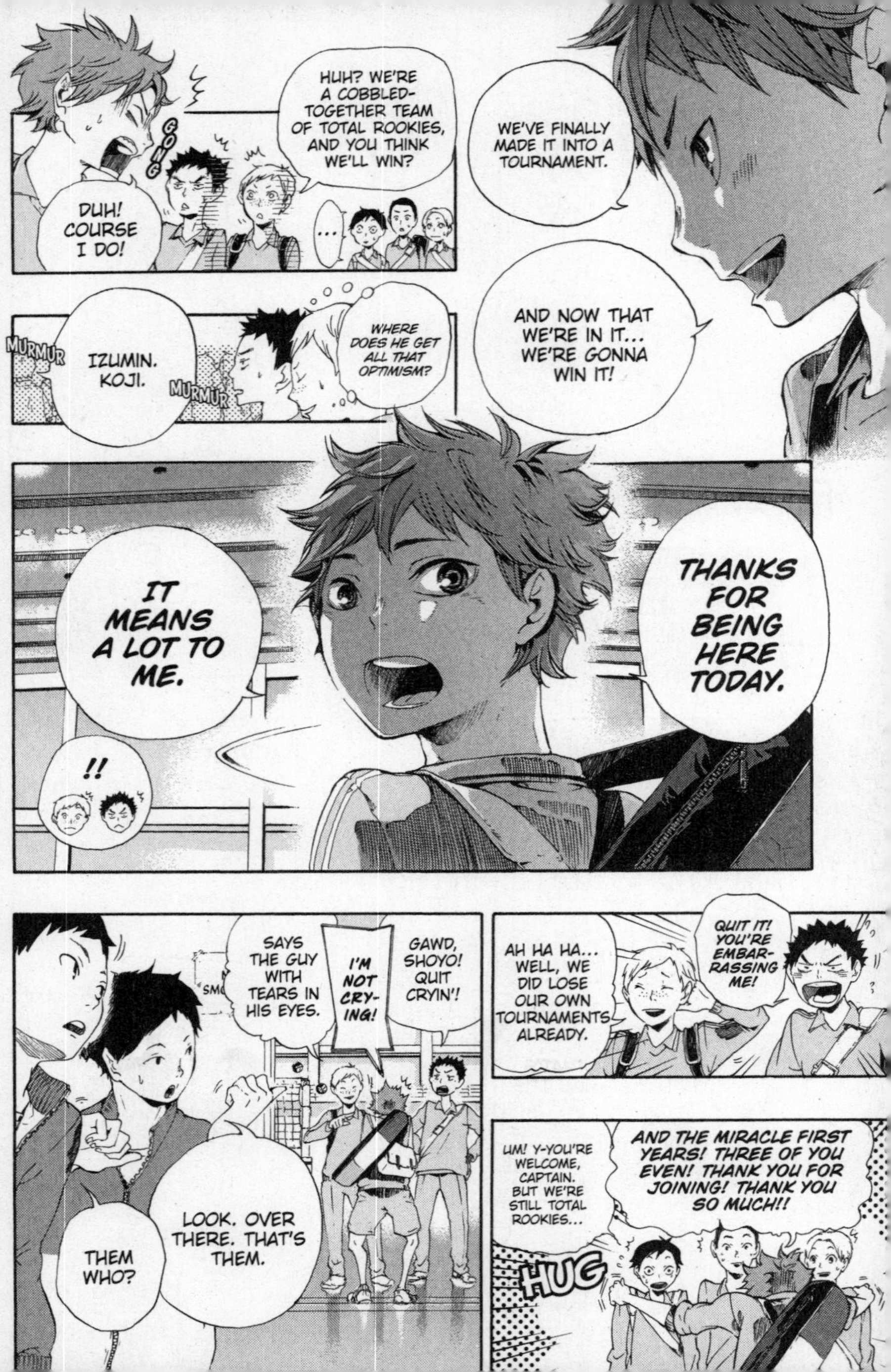
WE'VE FINALLY MADE IT INTO A TOURNAMENT.
AND NOW THAT WE'RE IN IT... WE'RE GONNA WIN IT!
HUH? WE'RE A COBBLED-TOGETHER TEAM OF TOTAL ROOKIES, AND YOU THINK WE'LL WIN?
GONG
DUH! COURSE I DO!
...
WHERE DOES HE GET ALL THAT OPTIMISM?
MURMUR
IZUMIN. KOJI.
MURMUR
THANKS FOR BEING HERE TODAY.
IT MEANS A LOT TO ME.
!!
QUIT IT! YOU'RE EMBARRASSING ME!
AH HA HA... WELL, WE DID LOSE OUR OWN TOURNAMENTS ALREADY.
AND THE MIRACLE FIRST YEARS! THREE OF YOU EVEN! THANK YOU FOR JOINING! THANK YOU SO MUCH!!
UM! Y-YOU'RE WELCOME, CAPTAIN. BUT WE'RE STILL TOTAL ROOKIES...
HUG
GAWD, SHOYO! QUIT CRYIN'!
I'M NOT CRYING!
SAYS THE GUY WITH TEARS IN HIS EYES.
LOOK. OVER THERE. THAT'S THEM.
THEM WHO?

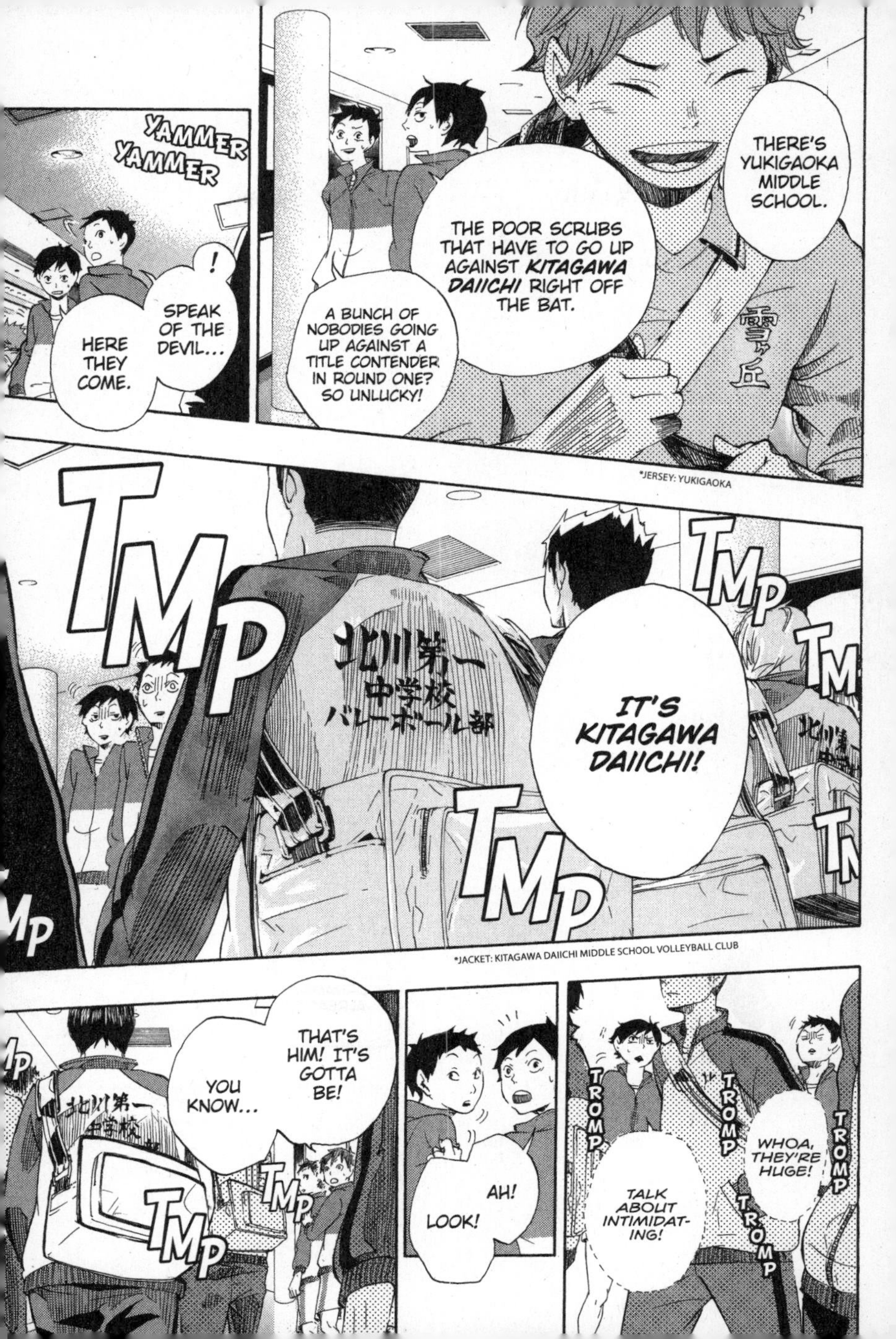
THERE'S YUKIGAOKA MIDDLE SCHOOL.
THE POOR SCRUBS THAT HAVE TO GO UP AGAINST KITAGAWA DAIICHI RIGHT OFF THE BAT.
A BUNCH OF NOBODIES GOING UP AGAINST A TITLE CONTENDER IN ROUND ONE? SO UNLUCKY!
雪ヶ丘
YAMMER YAMMER
!
SPEAK OF THE DEVIL...
HERE THEY COME.
*JERSEY: YUKIGAOKA
TMP
TMP
TM
IT'S KITAGAWA DAIICHI!
TMP
北川第一中学校バレーボール部
TMP
*JACKET: KITAGAWA DAIICHI MIDDLE SCHOOL VOLLEYBALL CLUB
TROMP
WHOA, THEY'RE HUGE!
TROMP
TROMP
TALK ABOUT INTIMIDAT-ING!
TROMP
AH!
LOOK!
THAT'S HIM! IT'S GOTTA BE!
YOU KNOW...
TMP
TMP

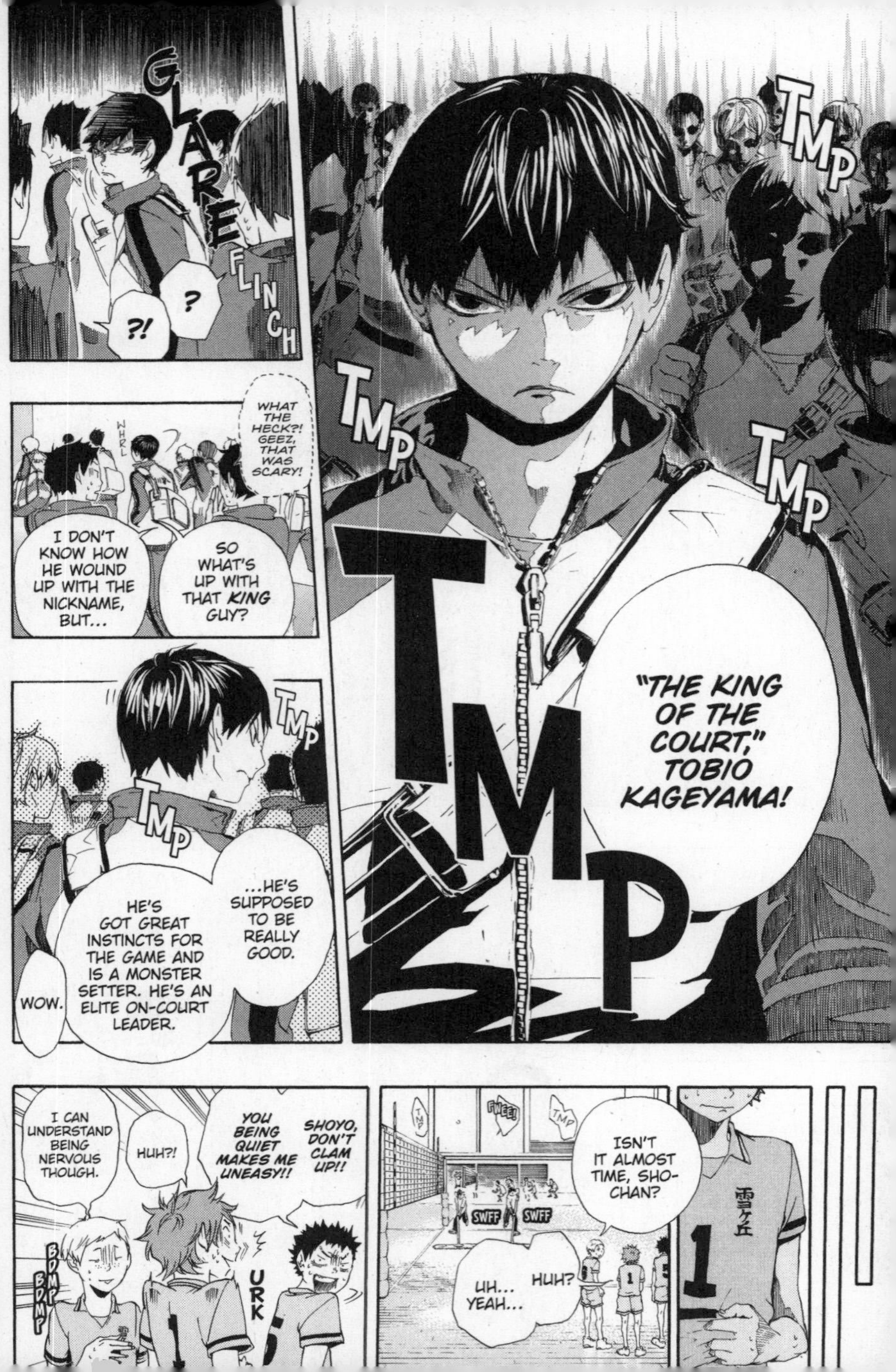
TMP
TMP
TMP
TMP
TMP
"THE KING OF THE COURT," TOBIO KAGEYAMA!
GLARE
FLINCH
?
?!
WHAT THE HECK?! GEEZ, THAT WAS SCARY!
WHRL
SO WHAT'S UP WITH THAT *KING* GUY?
I DON'T KNOW HOW HE WOUND UP WITH THE NICKNAME, BUT...
TMP
TMP
...HE'S SUPPOSED TO BE REALLY GOOD.
HE'S GOT GREAT INSTINCTS FOR THE GAME AND IS A MONSTER SETTER. HE'S AN ELITE ON-COURT LEADER.
WOW.
雪ケ丘
TMP
FWEE!
TMP
ISN'T IT ALMOST TIME, SHO-CHAN?
SWFF
SWFF
HUH?
UH... YEAH...
SHOYO, DON'T CLAM UP!!
YOU BEING QUIET MAKES ME UNEASY!!
HUH?!
I CAN UNDERSTAND BEING NERVOUS THOUGH.
URK
BDMP
BDMP

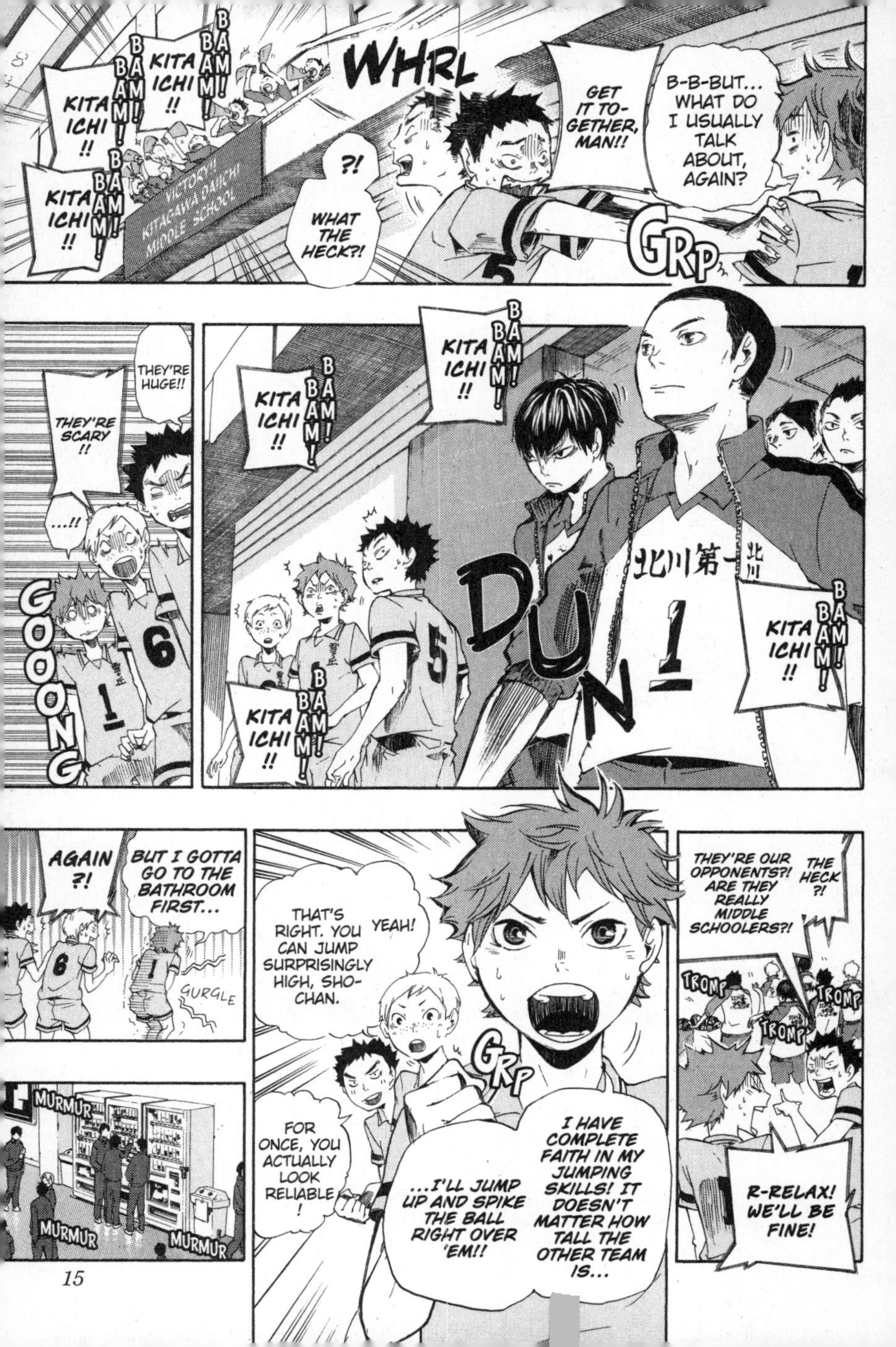
B-B-BUT... WHAT DO I USUALLY TALK ABOUT, AGAIN?
GET IT TO-GETHER, MAN!!
WHRL
GRP
?!
WHAT THE HECK?!
KITA ICHI!!
BAM BAM!
KITA ICHI!!
BAM BAM!
KITA ICHI!!
BAM BAM!
KITA ICHI!!
VICTORY!! KITAGAWA DAIICHI MIDDLE SCHOOL
KITA ICHI!!
BAM BAM!
KITA ICHI!!
BAM BAM!
北川第一
DUN
KITA ICHI!!
BAM BAM!
KITA ICHI!!
BAM BAM!
THEY'RE HUGE!!
THEY'RE SCARY!!
...!!
GOOONG
THE HECK?!
THEY'RE OUR OPPONENTS?! ARE THEY REALLY MIDDLE SCHOOLERS?!
TROMP
TROMP
TROMP
R-RELAX! WE'LL BE FINE!
YEAH!
THAT'S RIGHT. YOU CAN JUMP SURPRISINGLY HIGH, SHO-CHAN.
GRP
I HAVE COMPLETE FAITH IN MY JUMPING SKILLS! IT DOESN'T MATTER HOW TALL THE OTHER TEAM IS...
...I'LL JUMP UP AND SPIKE THE BALL RIGHT OVER 'EM!!
FOR ONCE, YOU ACTUALLY LOOK RELIABLE!
BUT I GOTTA GO TO THE BATHROOM FIRST...
AGAIN?!
GURGLE
MURMUR
MURMUR
MURMUR

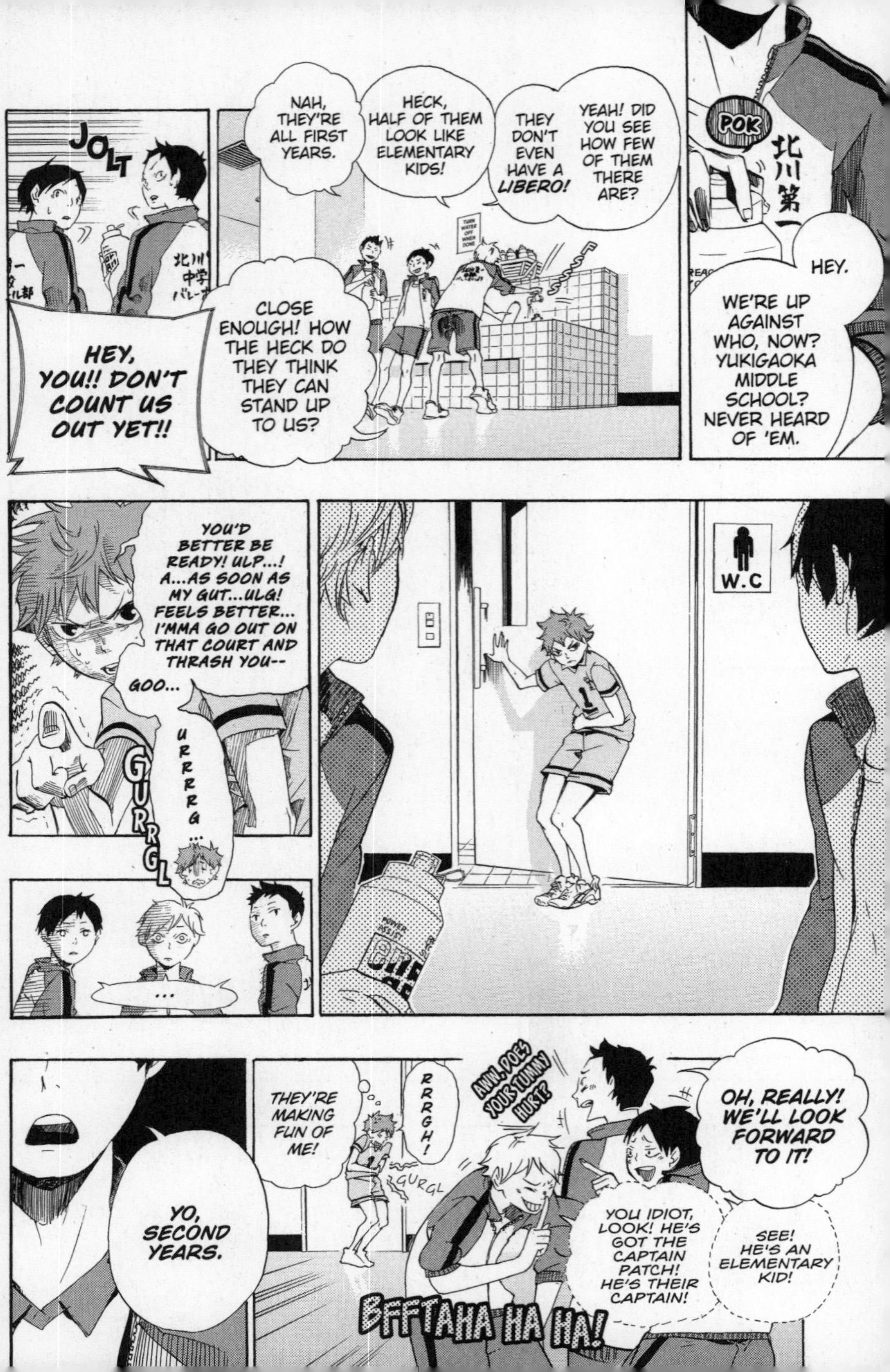
POK
北川第一
HEY.
WE'RE UP AGAINST WHO, NOW? YUKIGAOKA MIDDLE SCHOOL? NEVER HEARD OF 'EM.
YEAH! DID YOU SEE HOW FEW OF THEM THERE ARE?
THEY DON'T EVEN HAVE A *LIBERO!*
HECK, HALF OF THEM LOOK LIKE ELEMENTARY KIDS!
NAH, THEY'RE ALL FIRST YEARS.
TURN WATER OFF WHEN DONE
CLOSE ENOUGH! HOW THE HECK DO THEY THINK THEY CAN STAND UP TO US?
JOLT
HEY, YOU!! DON'T COUNT US OUT YET!!
W.C
YOU'D BETTER BE READY! ULP...! A...AS SOON AS MY GUT...ULG! FEELS BETTER... I'MMA GO OUT ON THAT COURT AND THRASH YOU--
GOO...
URRRRG...
GURGL
...
OH, REALLY! WE'LL LOOK FORWARD TO IT!
AWW, DOES YOUR TUMMY HURT?
RRRGH!
THEY'RE MAKING FUN OF ME!
GURGL
SEE! HE'S AN ELEMENTARY KID!
YOU IDIOT, LOOK! HE'S GOT THE CAPTAIN PATCH! HE'S THEIR CAPTAIN!
BFFTAHA HA HA!
YO, SECOND YEARS.

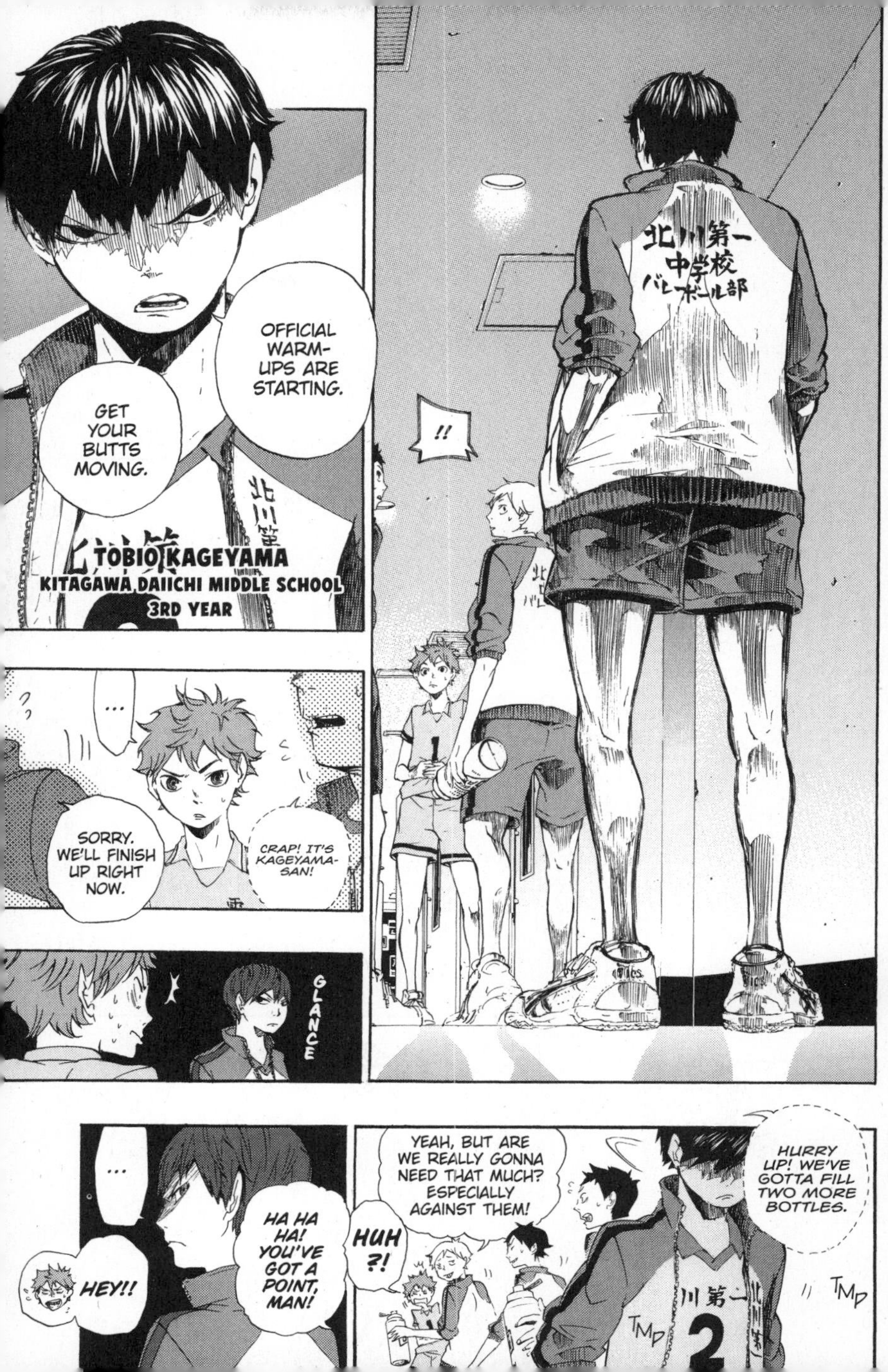

!!
北川第一
中学校
バレーボール部
OFFICIAL WARM-UPS ARE STARTING.
GET YOUR BUTTS MOVING.
TOBIO KAGEYAMA
KITAGAWA DAIICHI MIDDLE SCHOOL
3RD YEAR
...
CRAP! IT'S KAGEYAMA-SAN!
SORRY. WE'LL FINISH UP RIGHT NOW.
GLANCE
HURRY UP! WE'VE GOTTA FILL TWO MORE BOTTLES.
YEAH, BUT ARE WE REALLY GONNA NEED THAT MUCH? ESPECIALLY AGAINST THEM!
HUH ?!
TMP
TMP
...
HA HA HA! YOU'VE GOT A POINT, MAN!
HEY!!

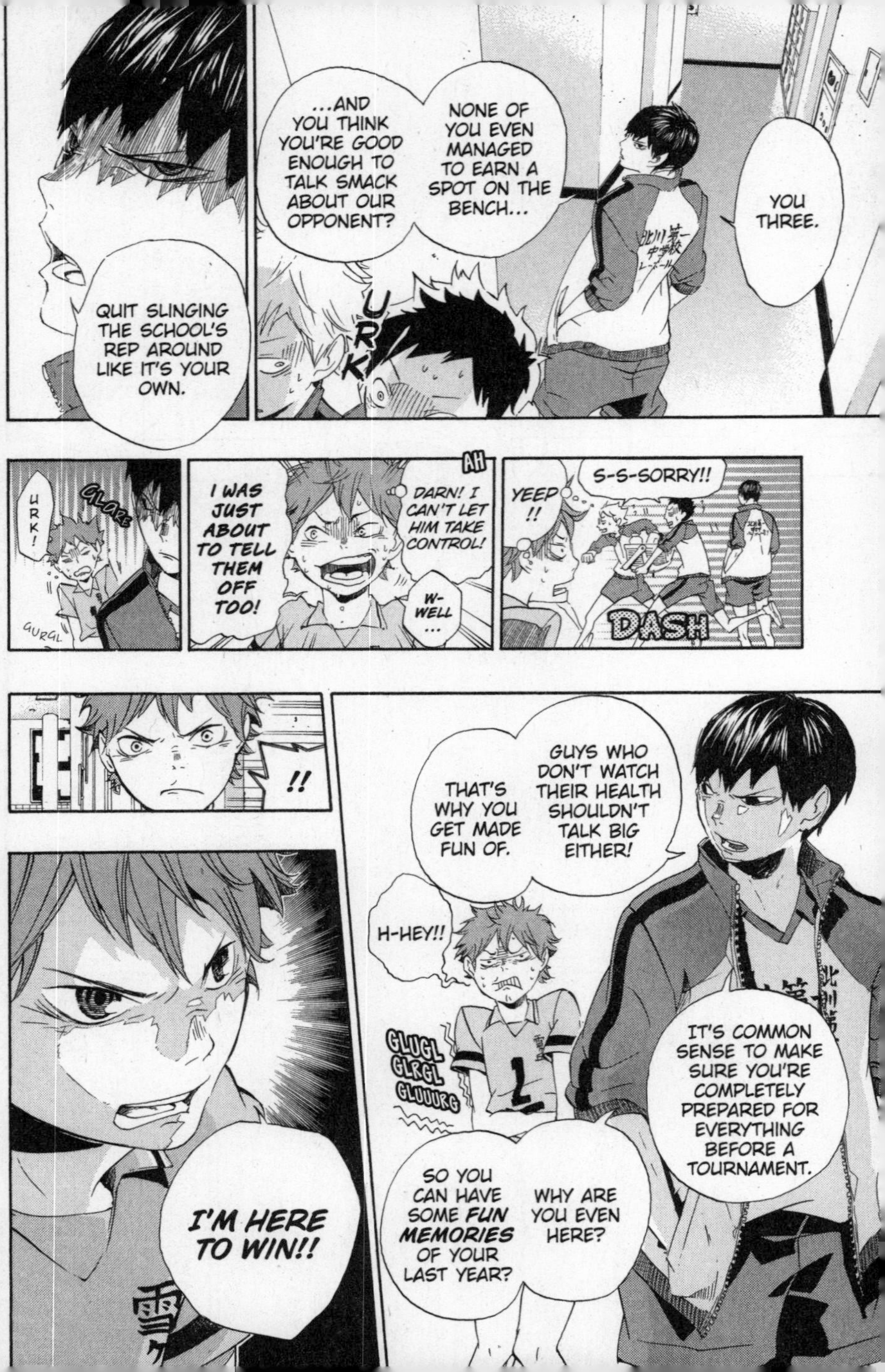
YOU THREE.
NONE OF YOU EVEN MANAGED TO EARN A SPOT ON THE BENCH...
...AND YOU THINK YOU'RE GOOD ENOUGH TO TALK SMACK ABOUT OUR OPPONENT?
URK
QUIT SLINGING THE SCHOOL'S REP AROUND LIKE IT'S YOUR OWN.
S-S-SORRY!!
YEEP !!
DASH
AH
DARN! I CAN'T LET HIM TAKE CONTROL!
I WAS JUST ABOUT TO TELL THEM OFF TOO!
W-WELL ...
URK!
GLARE
GURGL
GUYS WHO DON'T WATCH THEIR HEALTH SHOULDN'T TALK BIG EITHER!
THAT'S WHY YOU GET MADE FUN OF.
H-HEY!!
GLUGL GLRGL GLUUURG
IT'S COMMON SENSE TO MAKE SURE YOU'RE COMPLETELY PREPARED FOR EVERYTHING BEFORE A TOURNAMENT.
WHY ARE YOU EVEN HERE?
SO YOU CAN HAVE SOME FUN MEMORIES OF YOUR LAST YEAR?
!!
I'M HERE TO WIN!!

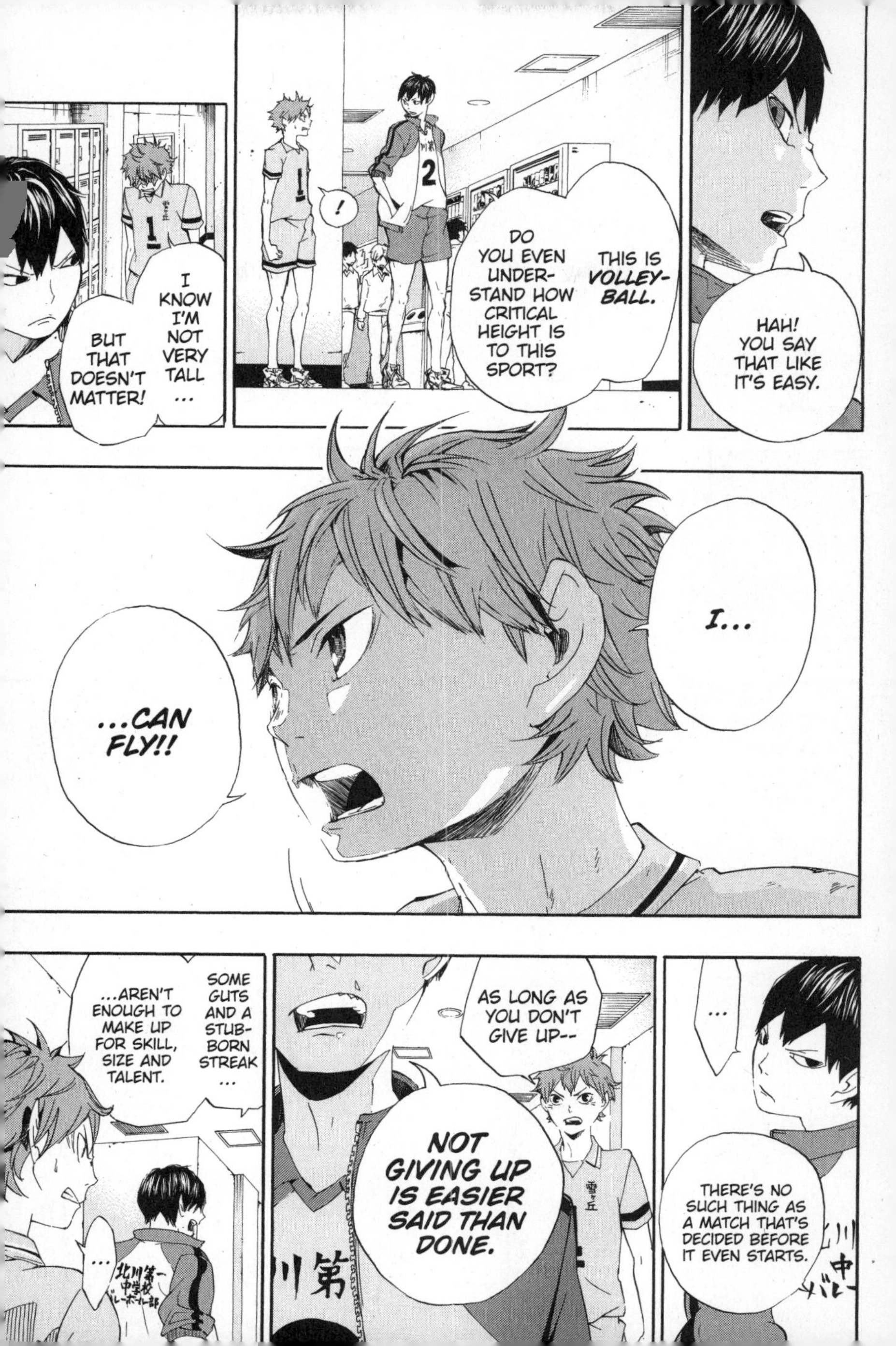
HAH! YOU SAY THAT LIKE IT'S EASY.
THIS IS VOLLEY-BALL.
DO YOU EVEN UNDER-STAND HOW CRITICAL HEIGHT IS TO THIS SPORT?
!
I KNOW I'M NOT VERY TALL ...
BUT THAT DOESN'T MATTER!
I...
...CAN FLY!!
...
THERE'S NO SUCH THING AS A MATCH THAT'S DECIDED BEFORE IT EVEN STARTS.
AS LONG AS YOU DON'T GIVE UP--
NOT GIVING UP IS EASIER SAID THAN DONE.
SOME GUTS AND A STUB-BORN STREAK ...
...AREN'T ENOUGH TO MAKE UP FOR SKILL, SIZE AND TALENT.
...
北川第一中学校バレーボール部

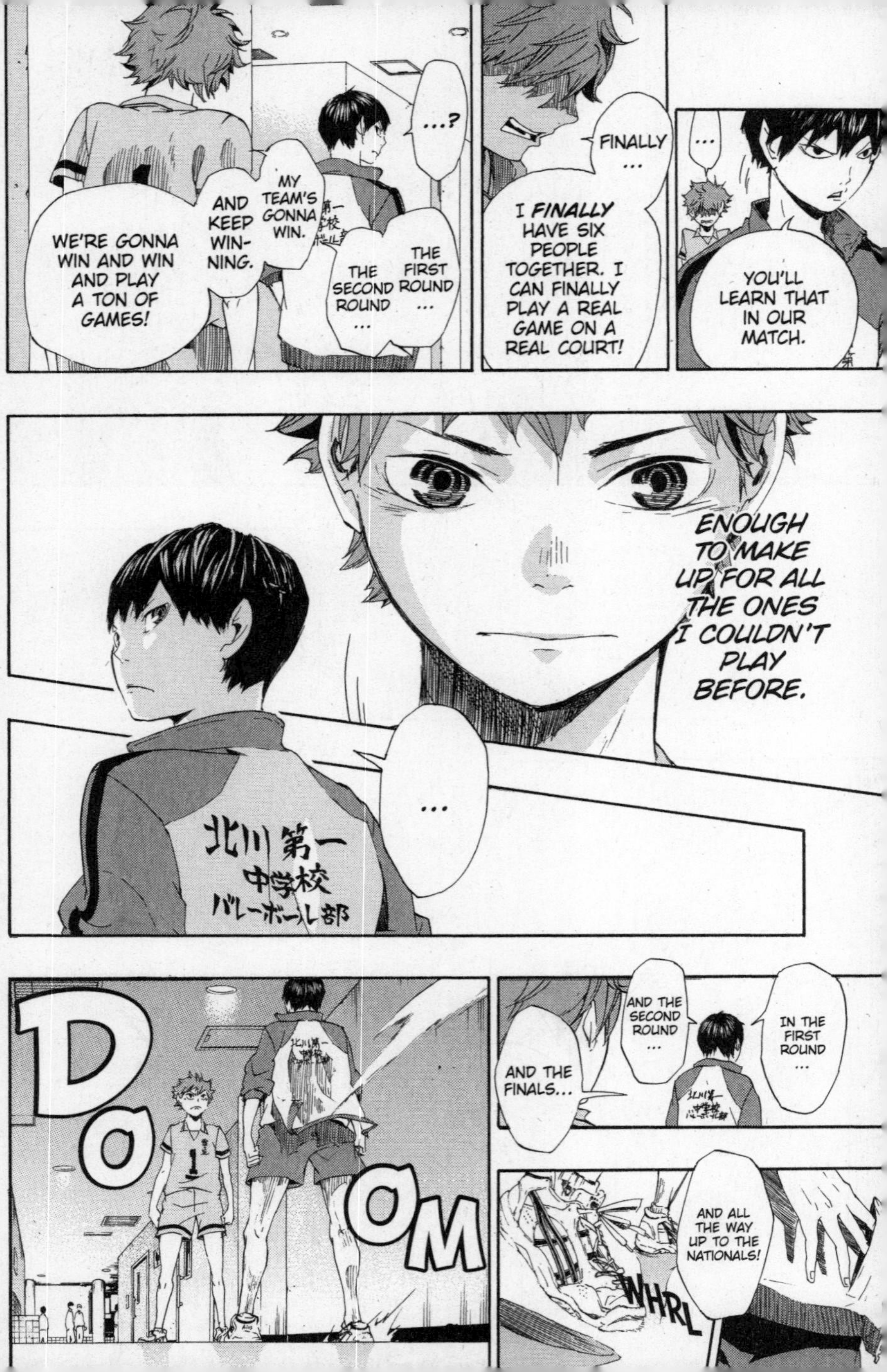
...
YOU'LL LEARN THAT IN OUR MATCH.
FINALLY ...
I *FINALLY* HAVE SIX PEOPLE TOGETHER. I CAN FINALLY PLAY A REAL GAME ON A REAL COURT!
...?
THE FIRST ROUND ...
THE SECOND ROUND ...
MY TEAM'S GONNA WIN.
AND KEEP WIN-NING.
WE'RE GONNA WIN AND WIN AND PLAY A TON OF GAMES!
ENOUGH TO MAKE UP FOR ALL THE ONES I COULDN'T PLAY BEFORE.
...
北川第一
中学校
バレーボール部
IN THE FIRST ROUND ...
AND THE SECOND ROUND ...
AND THE FINALS...
AND ALL THE WAY UP TO THE NATIONALS!
WHRL
DOOM

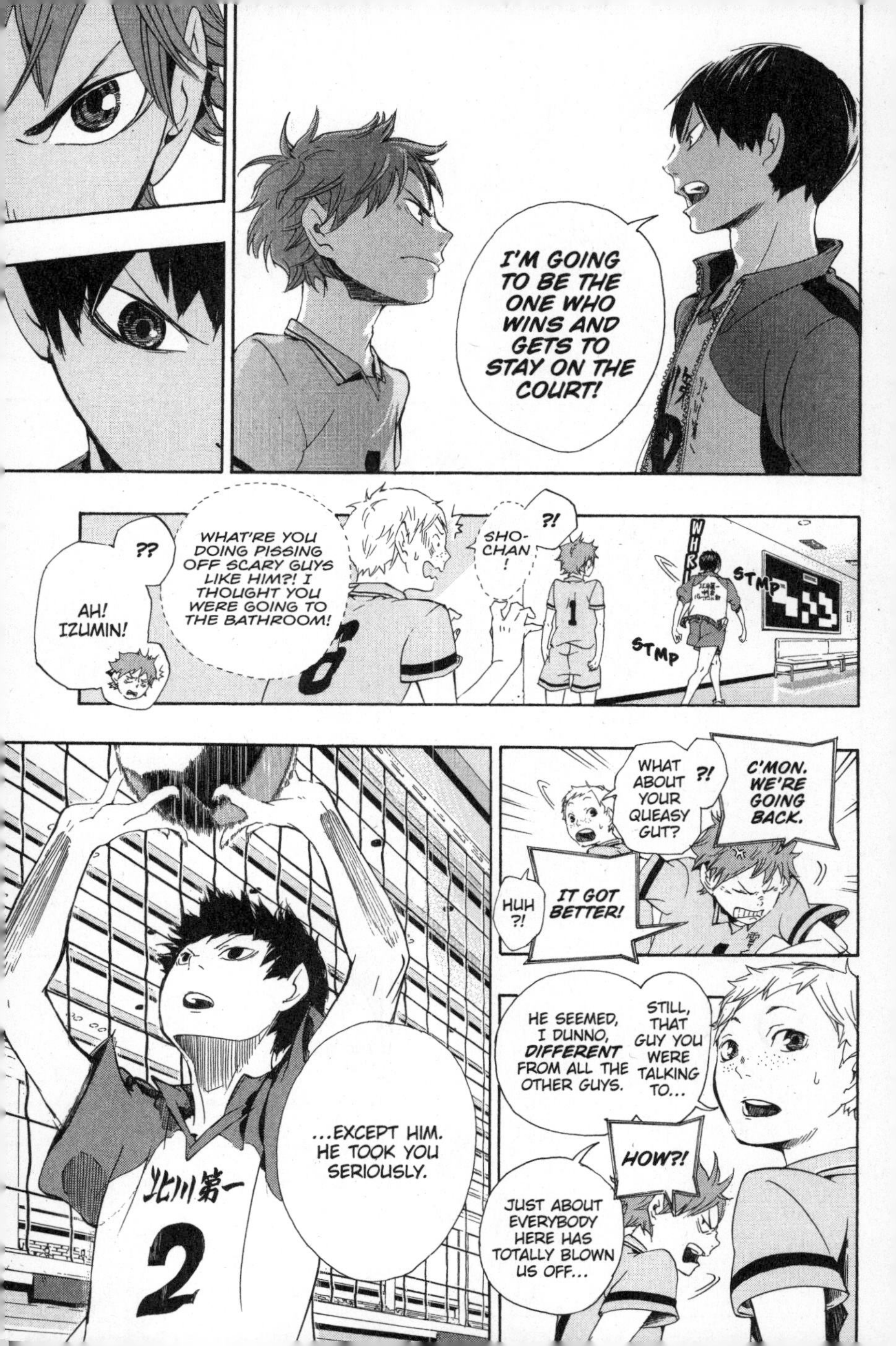
I'M GOING TO BE THE ONE WHO WINS AND GETS TO STAY ON THE COURT!
WHR
STMP
STMP
?!
SHO-CHAN!
WHAT'RE YOU DOING PISSING OFF SCARY GUYS LIKE HIM?! I THOUGHT YOU WERE GOING TO THE BATHROOM!
??
AH! IZUMIN!
C'MON. WE'RE GOING BACK.
?!
WHAT ABOUT YOUR QUEASY GUT?
IT GOT BETTER!
HUH?!
STILL, THAT GUY YOU WERE TALKING TO...
HE SEEMED, I DUNNO, *DIFFERENT* FROM ALL THE OTHER GUYS.
HOW?!
JUST ABOUT EVERYBODY HERE HAS TOTALLY BLOWN US OFF...
...EXCEPT HIM. HE TOOK YOU SERIOUSLY.
北川第一
2

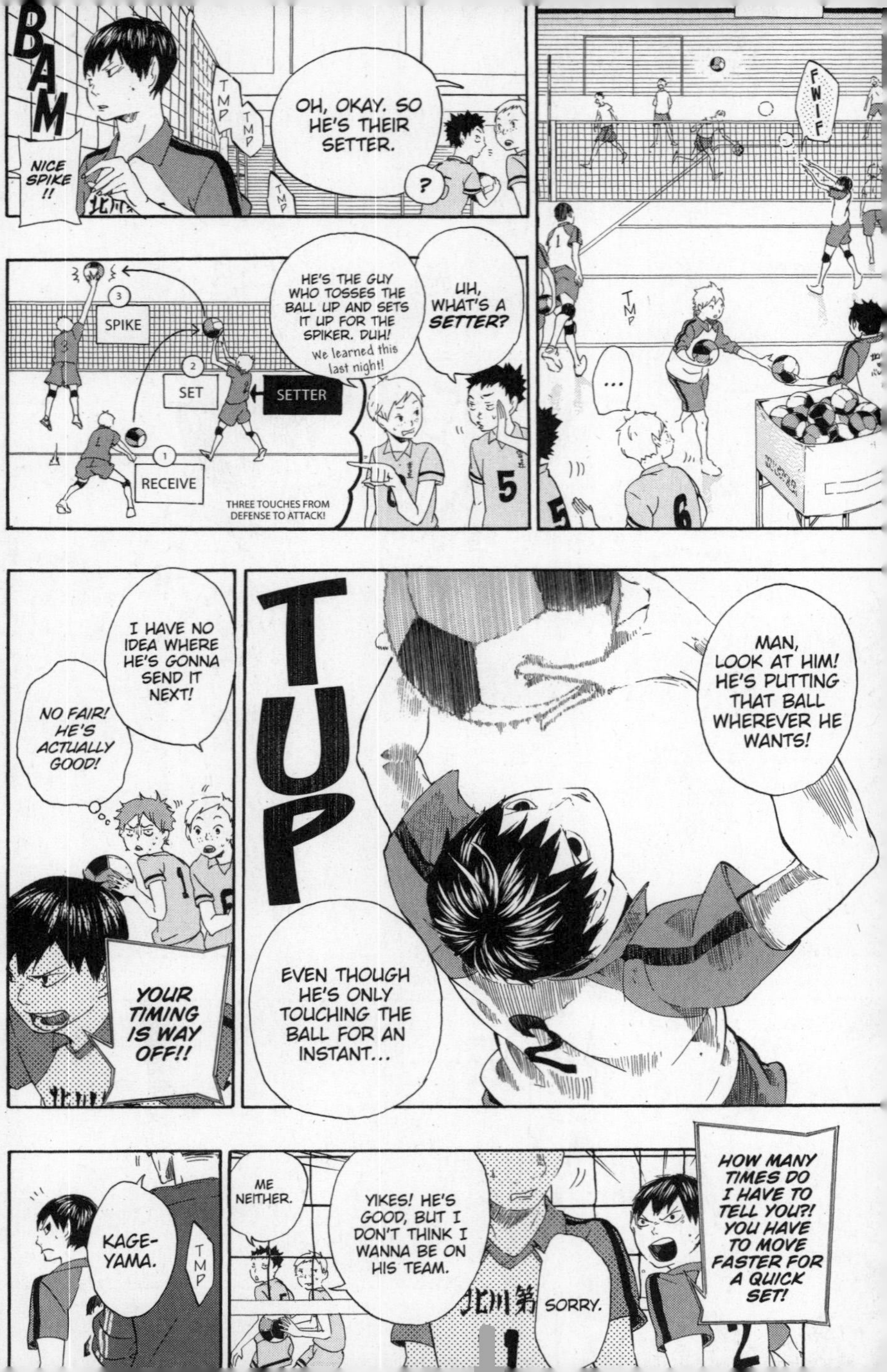

FWIF
TMP
...
OH, OKAY. SO HE'S THEIR SETTER.
?
TMP
TMP
TMP
NICE SPIKE!!
BAM
UH, WHAT'S A SETTER?
HE'S THE GUY WHO TOSSES THE BALL UP AND SETS IT UP FOR THE SPIKER. DUH!
We learned this last night!
3
SPIKE
2
SET
SETTER
1
RECEIVE
THREE TOUCHES FROM DEFENSE TO ATTACK!
MAN, LOOK AT HIM! HE'S PUTTING THAT BALL WHEREVER HE WANTS!
TUP
EVEN THOUGH HE'S ONLY TOUCHING THE BALL FOR AN INSTANT...
I HAVE NO IDEA WHERE HE'S GONNA SEND IT NEXT!
NO FAIR! HE'S ACTUALLY GOOD!
YOUR TIMING IS WAY OFF!!
HOW MANY TIMES DO I HAVE TO TELL YOU?! YOU HAVE TO MOVE FASTER FOR A QUICK SET!
SORRY.
YIKES! HE'S GOOD, BUT I DON'T THINK I WANNA BE ON HIS TEAM.
ME NEITHER.
TMP
KAGE-YAMA.

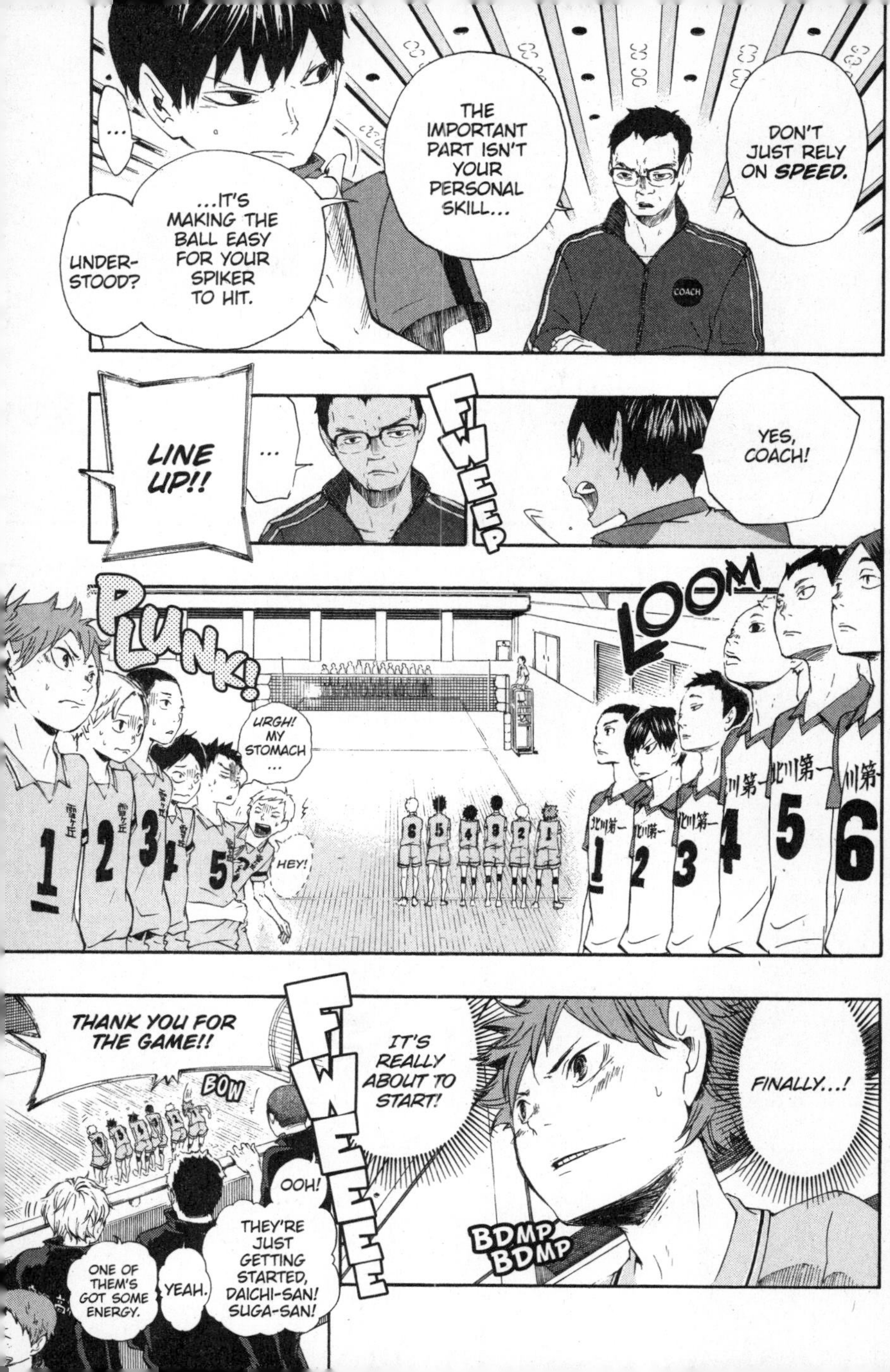
DON'T JUST RELY ON **SPEED.**
THE IMPORTANT PART ISN'T YOUR PERSONAL SKILL...
...IT'S MAKING THE BALL EASY FOR YOUR SPIKER TO HIT.
...
UNDER-STOOD?
COACH
YES, COACH!
FWEEP
...
LINE UP!!
LOOM
HEY!
URGH! MY STOMACH ...
PLUNK!
FINALLY...!
BDMP BDMP
IT'S REALLY ABOUT TO START!
FWEEEE
THANK YOU FOR THE GAME!!
BOW
OOH!
THEY'RE JUST GETTING STARTED, DAICHI-SAN! SUGA-SAN!
YEAH.
ONE OF THEM'S GOT SOME ENERGY.

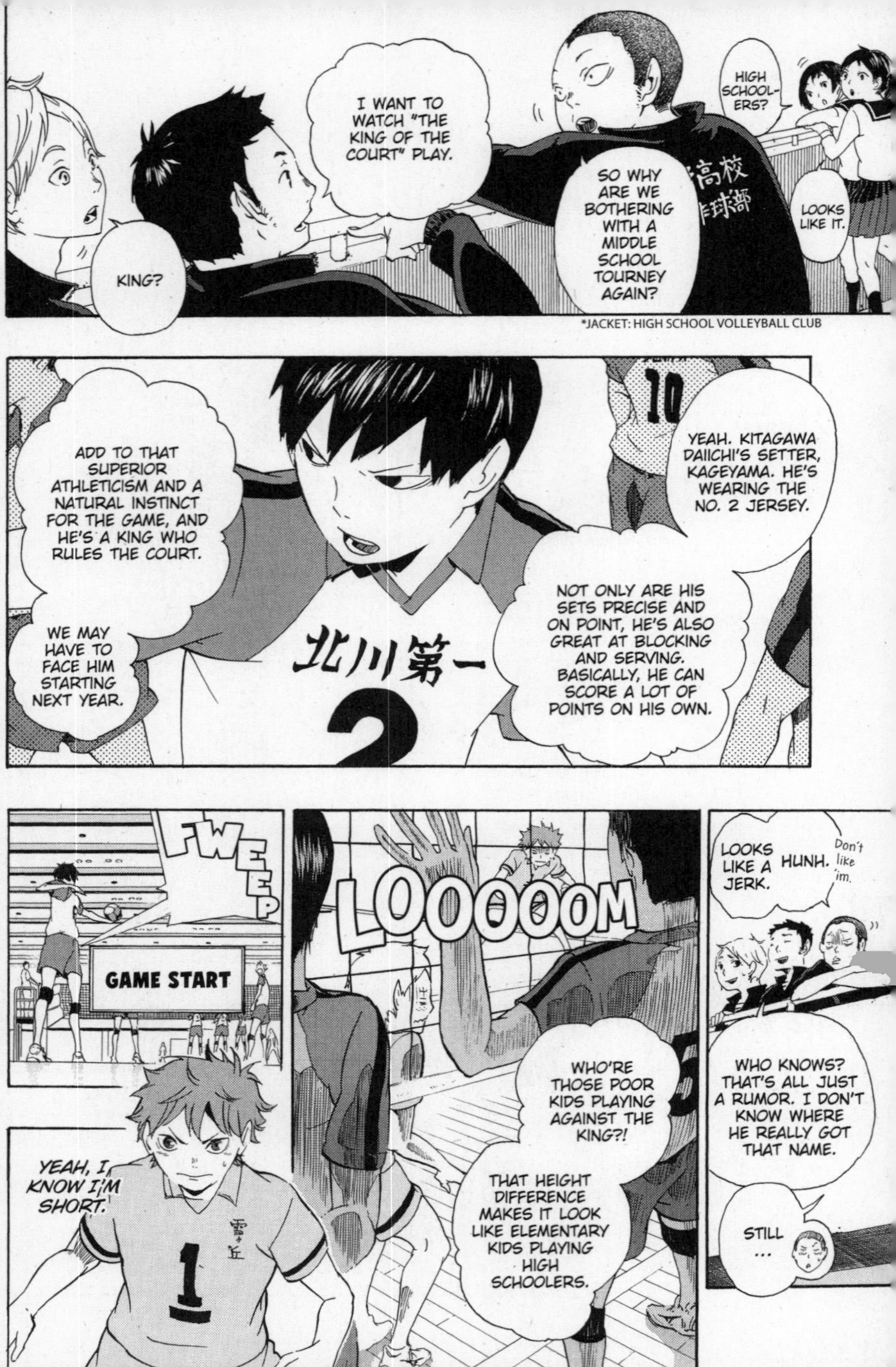
HIGH SCHOOL-ERS?
LOOKS LIKE IT.
SO WHY ARE WE BOTHERING WITH A MIDDLE SCHOOL TOURNEY AGAIN?
I WANT TO WATCH "THE KING OF THE COURT" PLAY.
KING?
*JACKET: HIGH SCHOOL VOLLEYBALL CLUB
YEAH. KITAGAWA DAIICHI'S SETTER, KAGEYAMA. HE'S WEARING THE NO. 2 JERSEY.
NOT ONLY ARE HIS SETS PRECISE AND ON POINT, HE'S ALSO GREAT AT BLOCKING AND SERVING. BASICALLY, HE CAN SCORE A LOT OF POINTS ON HIS OWN.
北川第一
2
ADD TO THAT SUPERIOR ATHLETICISM AND A NATURAL INSTINCT FOR THE GAME, AND HE'S A KING WHO RULES THE COURT.
WE MAY HAVE TO FACE HIM STARTING NEXT YEAR.
LOOKS LIKE A JERK.
HUNH.
Don't like 'im.
WHO KNOWS? THAT'S ALL JUST A RUMOR. I DON'T KNOW WHERE HE REALLY GOT THAT NAME.
STILL ...
LOOOOOM
WHO'RE THOSE POOR KIDS PLAYING AGAINST THE KING?!
THAT HEIGHT DIFFERENCE MAKES IT LOOK LIKE ELEMENTARY KIDS PLAYING HIGH SCHOOLERS.
FWEEP
GAME START
YEAH, I KNOW I'M SHORT.
1

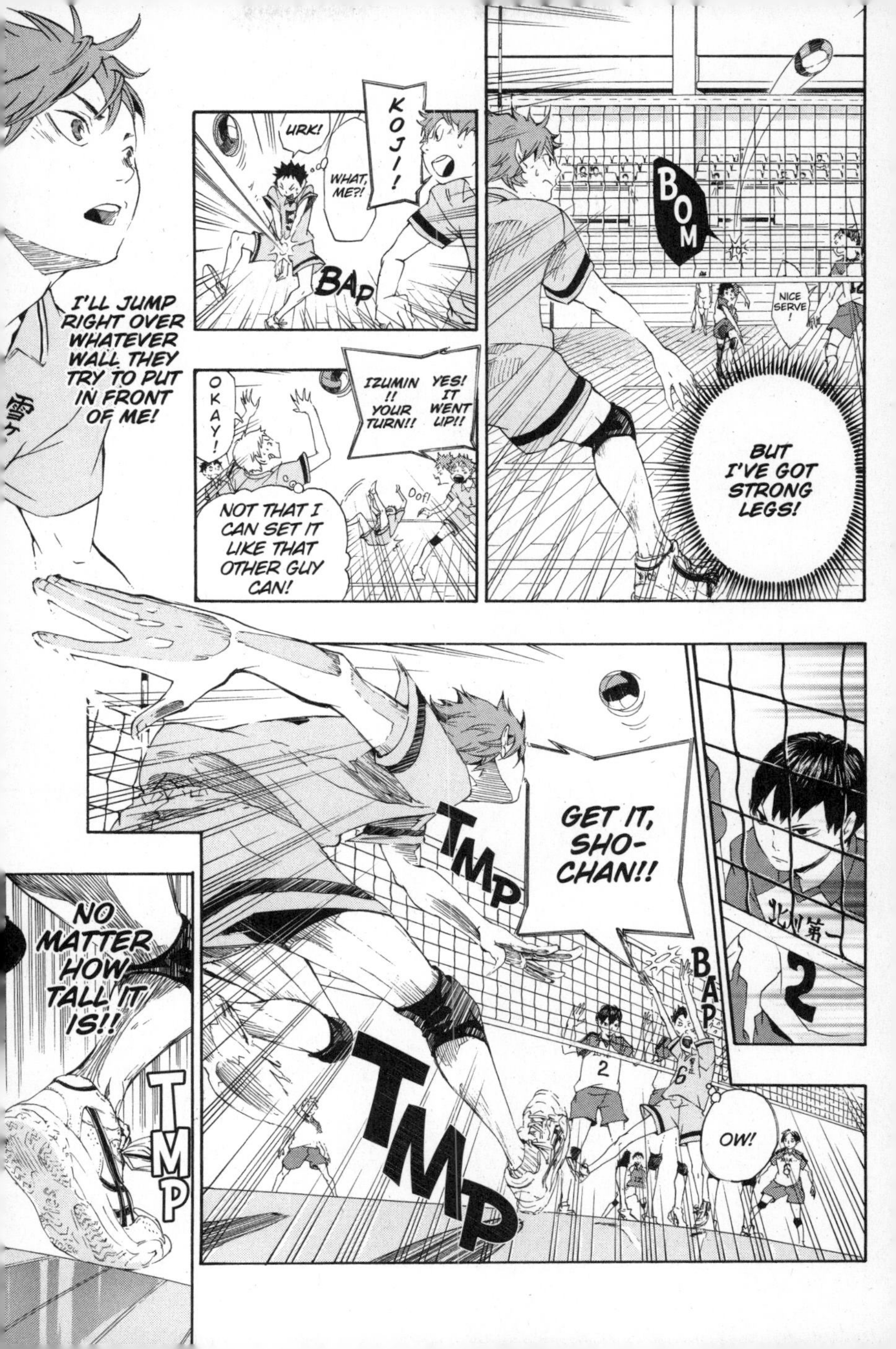
BOM
NICE SERVE!
BUT I'VE GOT STRONG LEGS!
KOJI!!
URK!
WHAT, ME?!
BAP
YES! IT WENT UP!!
IZUMIN!! YOUR TURN!!
OKAY!
Oof!
NOT THAT I CAN SET IT LIKE THAT OTHER GUY CAN!
I'LL JUMP RIGHT OVER WHATEVER WALL THEY TRY TO PUT IN FRONT OF ME!
北川第一
2
GET IT, SHO-CHAN!!
TMP
BAP
TMP
OW!
NO MATTER HOW TALL IT IS!!
TMP

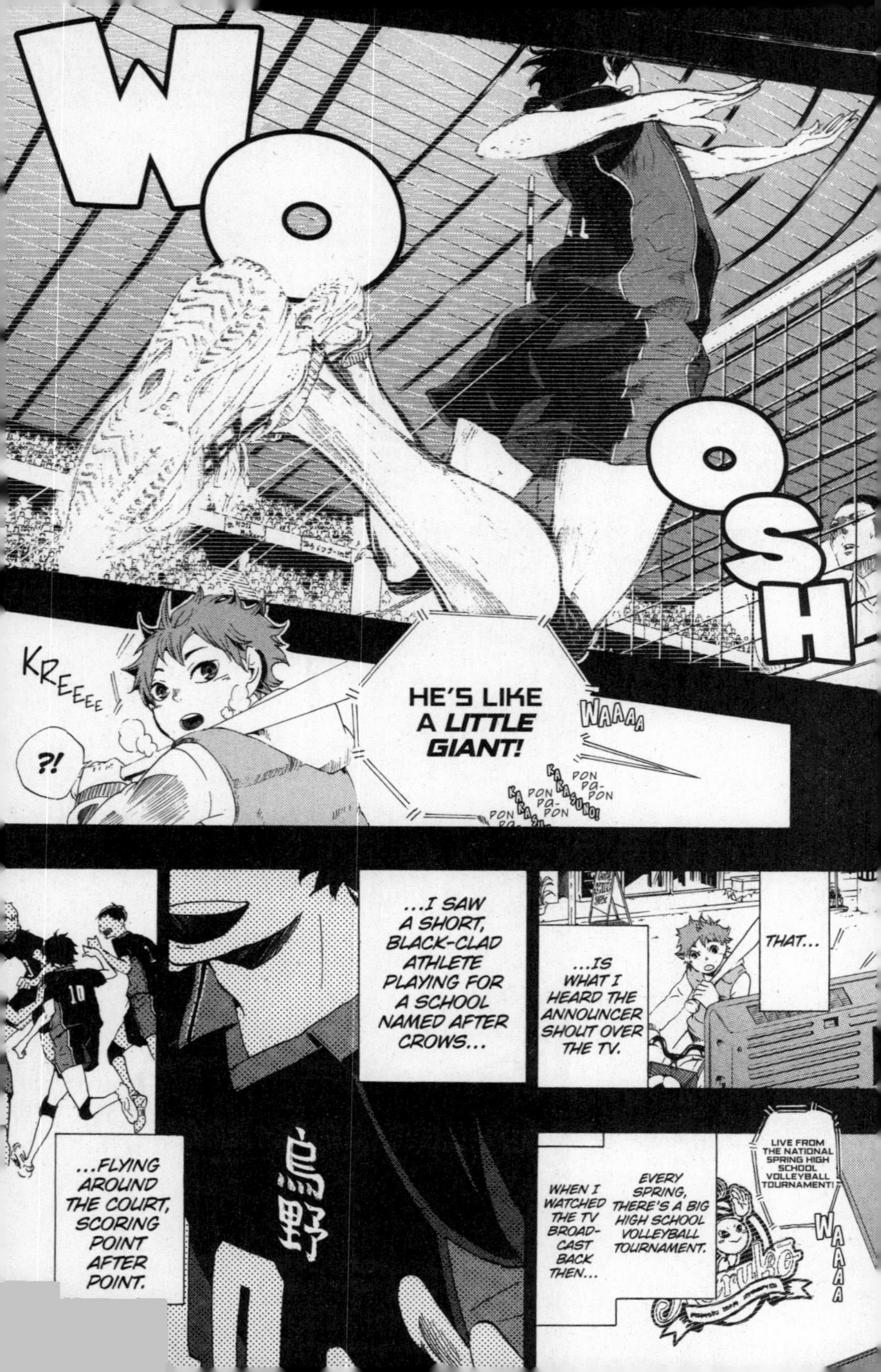
WOOOSH
HE'S LIKE A LITTLE GIANT!
WAAAA
PON PA-PON
KARASUNO!
PON PA-PON
KARASU-
PON PA-
KREEEEE
?!
THAT...
...IS WHAT I HEARD THE ANNOUNCER SHOUT OVER THE TV.
LIVE FROM THE NATIONAL SPRING HIGH SCHOOL VOLLEYBALL TOURNAMENT!
WAAAAA
EVERY SPRING, THERE'S A BIG HIGH SCHOOL VOLLEYBALL TOURNAMENT.
WHEN I WATCHED THE TV BROADCAST BACK THEN...
...I SAW A SHORT, BLACK-CLAD ATHLETE PLAYING FOR A SCHOOL NAMED AFTER CROWS...
烏野
...FLYING AROUND THE COURT, SCORING POINT AFTER POINT.

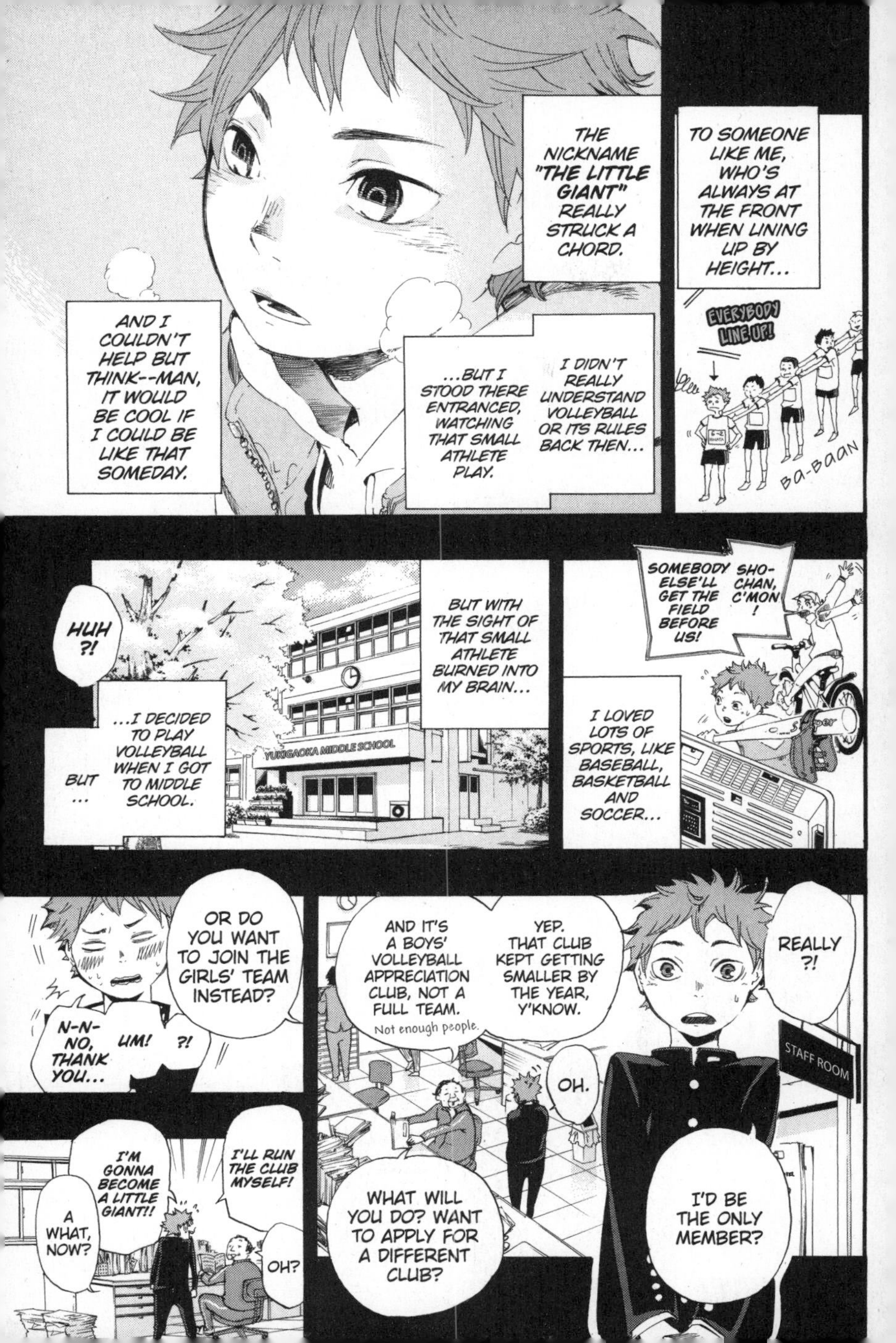
TO SOMEONE LIKE ME, WHO'S ALWAYS AT THE FRONT WHEN LINING UP BY HEIGHT...
EVERYBODY LINE UP!
BA-BAAN
THE NICKNAME "THE LITTLE GIANT" REALLY STRUCK A CHORD.
I DIDN'T REALLY UNDERSTAND VOLLEYBALL OR ITS RULES BACK THEN...
...BUT I STOOD THERE ENTRANCED, WATCHING THAT SMALL ATHLETE PLAY.
AND I COULDN'T HELP BUT THINK--MAN, IT WOULD BE COOL IF I COULD BE LIKE THAT SOMEDAY.
SHO-CHAN, C'MON!
SOMEBODY ELSE'LL GET THE FIELD BEFORE US!
I LOVED LOTS OF SPORTS, LIKE BASEBALL, BASKETBALL AND SOCCER...
BUT WITH THE SIGHT OF THAT SMALL ATHLETE BURNED INTO MY BRAIN...
YUKIGAOKA MIDDLE SCHOOL
...I DECIDED TO PLAY VOLLEYBALL WHEN I GOT TO MIDDLE SCHOOL.
BUT ...
HUH ?!
REALLY ?!
YEP. THAT CLUB KEPT GETTING SMALLER BY THE YEAR, Y'KNOW.
AND IT'S A BOYS' VOLLEYBALL APPRECIATION CLUB, NOT A FULL TEAM.
Not enough people.
OH.
STAFF ROOM
I'D BE THE ONLY MEMBER?
WHAT WILL YOU DO? WANT TO APPLY FOR A DIFFERENT CLUB?
OR DO YOU WANT TO JOIN THE GIRLS' TEAM INSTEAD?
?!
UM!
N-N-NO, THANK YOU...
I'LL RUN THE CLUB MYSELF!
I'M GONNA BECOME A LITTLE GIANT!!
OH?
A WHAT, NOW?

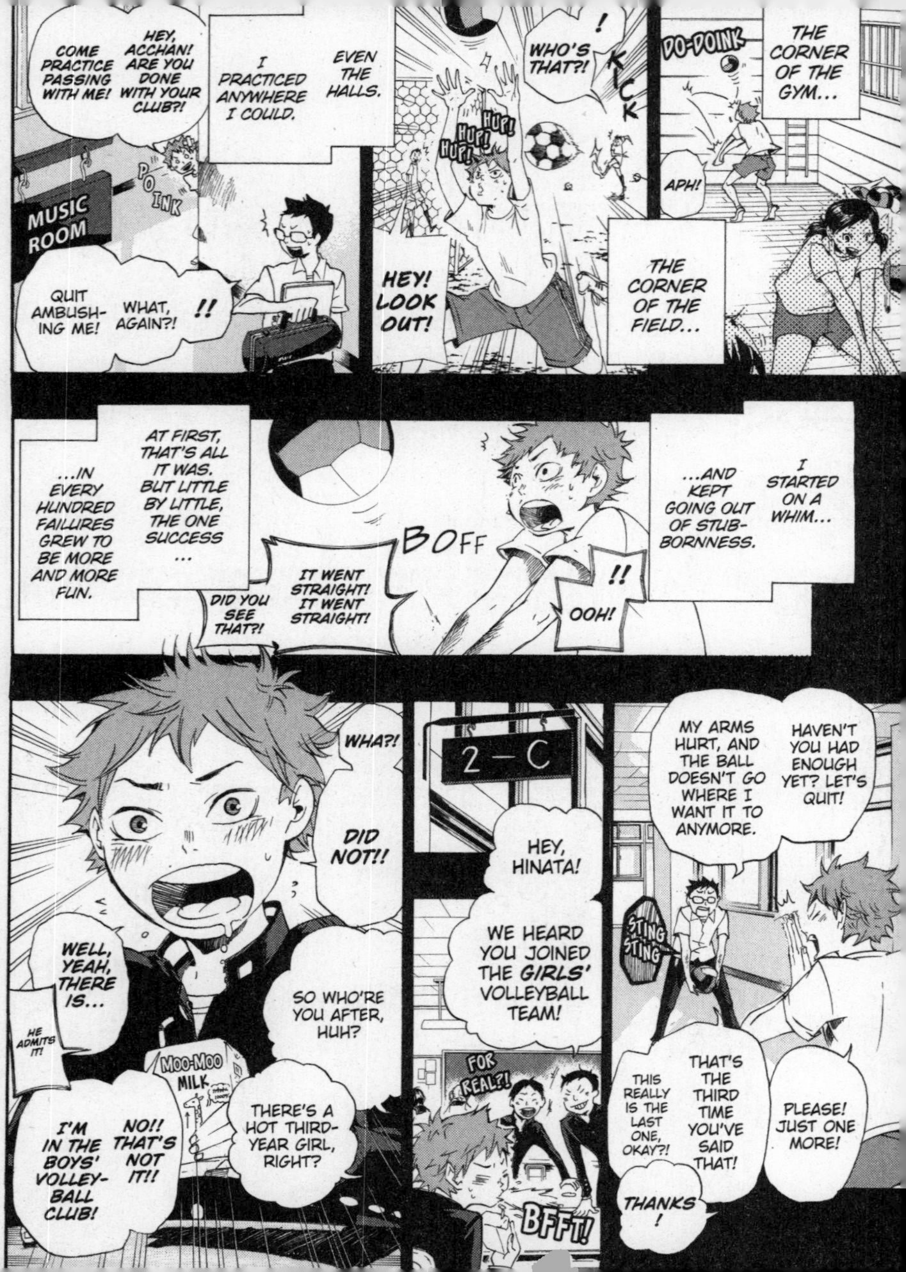
THE CORNER OF THE GYM...
DO-DOINK
APH!
!
WHO'S THAT?!
KICK
HUP! HUP! HUP!
HEY! LOOK OUT!
THE CORNER OF THE FIELD...
EVEN THE HALLS.
I PRACTICED ANYWHERE I COULD.
HEY, ACCHAN! ARE YOU DONE WITH YOUR CLUB?!
COME PRACTICE PASSING WITH ME!
POINK
MUSIC ROOM
!!
WHAT, AGAIN?!
QUIT AMBUSHING ME!
I STARTED ON A WHIM...
...AND KEPT GOING OUT OF STUBBORNNESS.
!!
OOH!
BOFF
IT WENT STRAIGHT! IT WENT STRAIGHT!
DID YOU SEE THAT?!
AT FIRST, THAT'S ALL IT WAS. BUT LITTLE BY LITTLE, THE ONE SUCCESS...
...IN EVERY HUNDRED FAILURES GREW TO BE MORE AND MORE FUN.
HAVEN'T YOU HAD ENOUGH YET? LET'S QUIT!
MY ARMS HURT, AND THE BALL DOESN'T GO WHERE I WANT IT TO ANYMORE.
STING STING
PLEASE! JUST ONE MORE!
THAT'S THE THIRD TIME YOU'VE SAID THAT!
THIS REALLY IS THE LAST ONE, OKAY?!
THANKS!
2-C
HEY, HINATA!
WE HEARD YOU JOINED THE GIRLS' VOLLEYBALL TEAM!
FOR REAL?!
BFFT!
WHA?!
DID NOT!!
SO WHO'RE YOU AFTER, HUH?
THERE'S A HOT THIRD-YEAR GIRL, RIGHT?
WELL, YEAH, THERE IS...
HE ADMITS IT!
NO!! THAT'S NOT IT!!
I'M IN THE BOYS' VOLLEYBALL CLUB!
MOO-MOO MILK

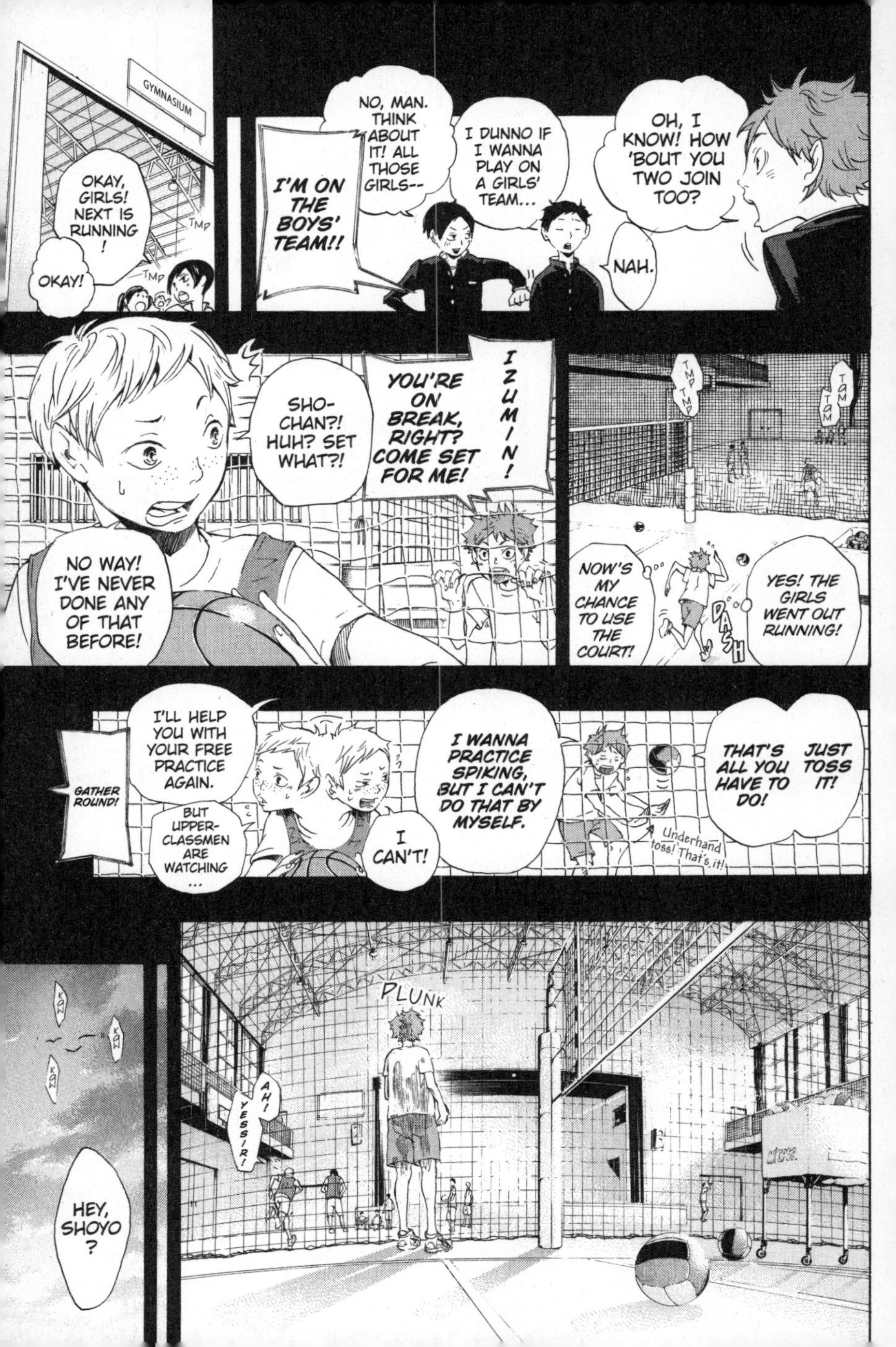
OH, I KNOW! HOW 'BOUT YOU TWO JOIN TOO?
NAH.
I DUNNO IF I WANNA PLAY ON A GIRLS' TEAM...
NO, MAN. THINK ABOUT IT! ALL THOSE GIRLS--
I'M ON THE BOYS' TEAM!!
GYMNASIUM
OKAY, GIRLS! NEXT IS RUNNING!
TMP
TMP
OKAY!
TMP TMP TMP
TAM TAM TAM
YES! THE GIRLS WENT OUT RUNNING!
NOW'S MY CHANCE TO USE THE COURT!
DASH
IZUMIN!
YOU'RE ON BREAK, RIGHT? COME SET FOR ME!
SHO-CHAN?! HUH? SET WHAT?!
NO WAY! I'VE NEVER DONE ANY OF THAT BEFORE!
JUST TOSS IT!
THAT'S ALL YOU HAVE TO DO!
Underhand toss! That's it!
I WANNA PRACTICE SPIKING, BUT I CAN'T DO THAT BY MYSELF.
I CAN'T!
I'LL HELP YOU WITH YOUR FREE PRACTICE AGAIN.
BUT UPPERCLASSMEN ARE WATCHING...
GATHER ROUND!
PLUNK
AH! YESSIR!
KAW
KAW
KAW
HEY, SHOYO?

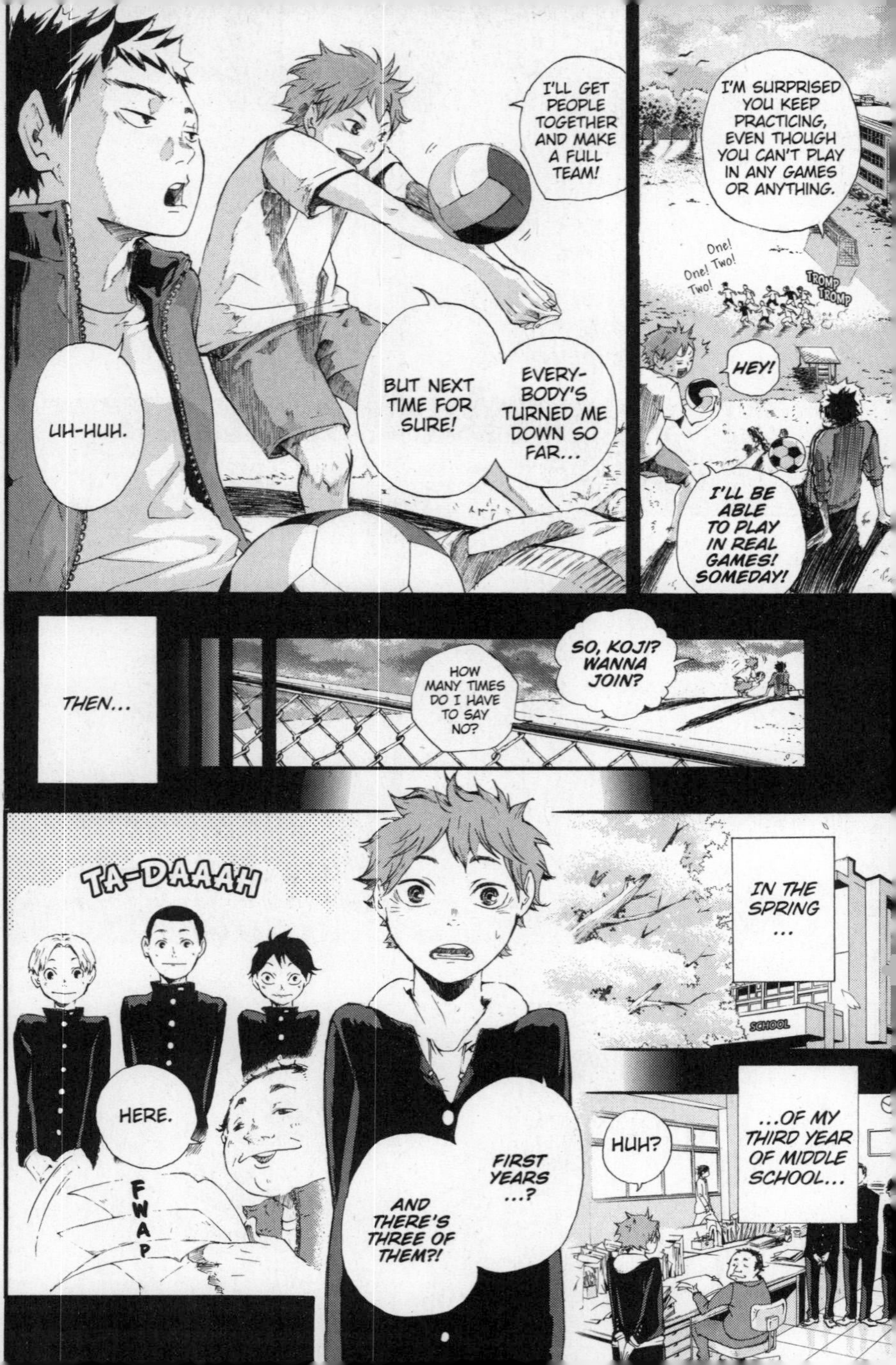
I'M SURPRISED YOU KEEP PRACTICING, EVEN THOUGH YOU CAN'T PLAY IN ANY GAMES OR ANYTHING.
One! Two! One! Two!
TROMP TROMP
HEY!
I'LL BE ABLE TO PLAY IN REAL GAMES! SOMEDAY!
I'LL GET PEOPLE TOGETHER AND MAKE A FULL TEAM!
EVERY-BODY'S TURNED ME DOWN SO FAR...
BUT NEXT TIME FOR SURE!
UH-HUH.
SO, KOJI? WANNA JOIN?
HOW MANY TIMES DO I HAVE TO SAY NO?
THEN...
IN THE SPRING...
SCHOOL
...OF MY THIRD YEAR OF MIDDLE SCHOOL...
HUH?
TA-DAAAH
FIRST YEARS...?
AND THERE'S THREE OF THEM?!
HERE.
FWAP

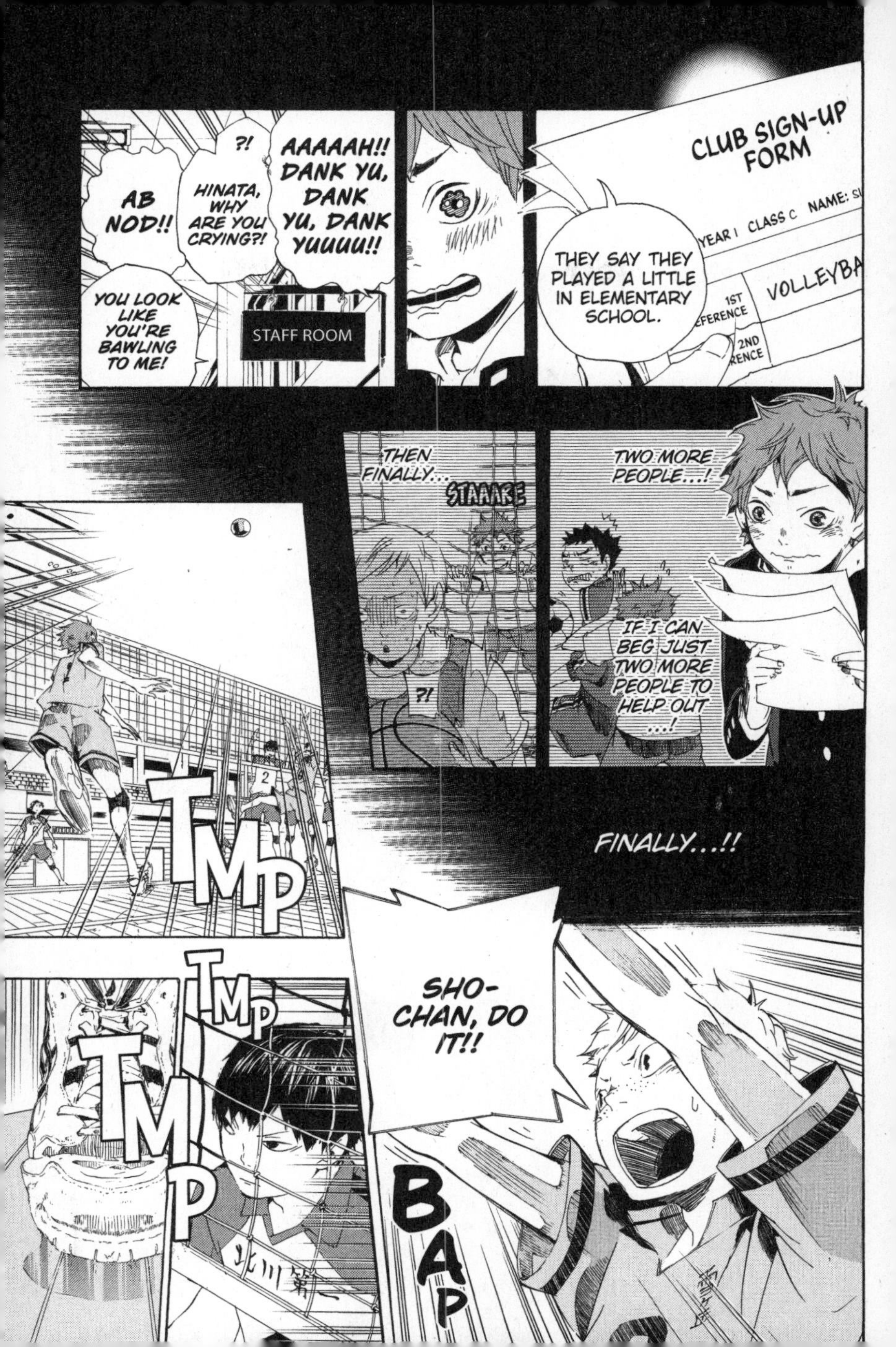
CLUB SIGN-UP FORM
YEAR 1 CLASS C NAME:
1ST PREFERENCE
VOLLEYBA
2ND
THEY SAY THEY PLAYED A LITTLE IN ELEMENTARY SCHOOL.
AAAAAH!! DANK YU, DANK YU, DANK YUUUU!!
?!
HINATA, WHY ARE YOU CRYING?!
AB NOD!!
YOU LOOK LIKE YOU'RE BAWLING TO ME!
STAFF ROOM
TWO MORE PEOPLE...!
IF I CAN BEG JUST TWO MORE PEOPLE TO HELP OUT...!
THEN FINALLY...
STAAARE
?!
FINALLY...!!
TMP
SHO-CHAN, DO IT!!
BAP
TMP
TMP

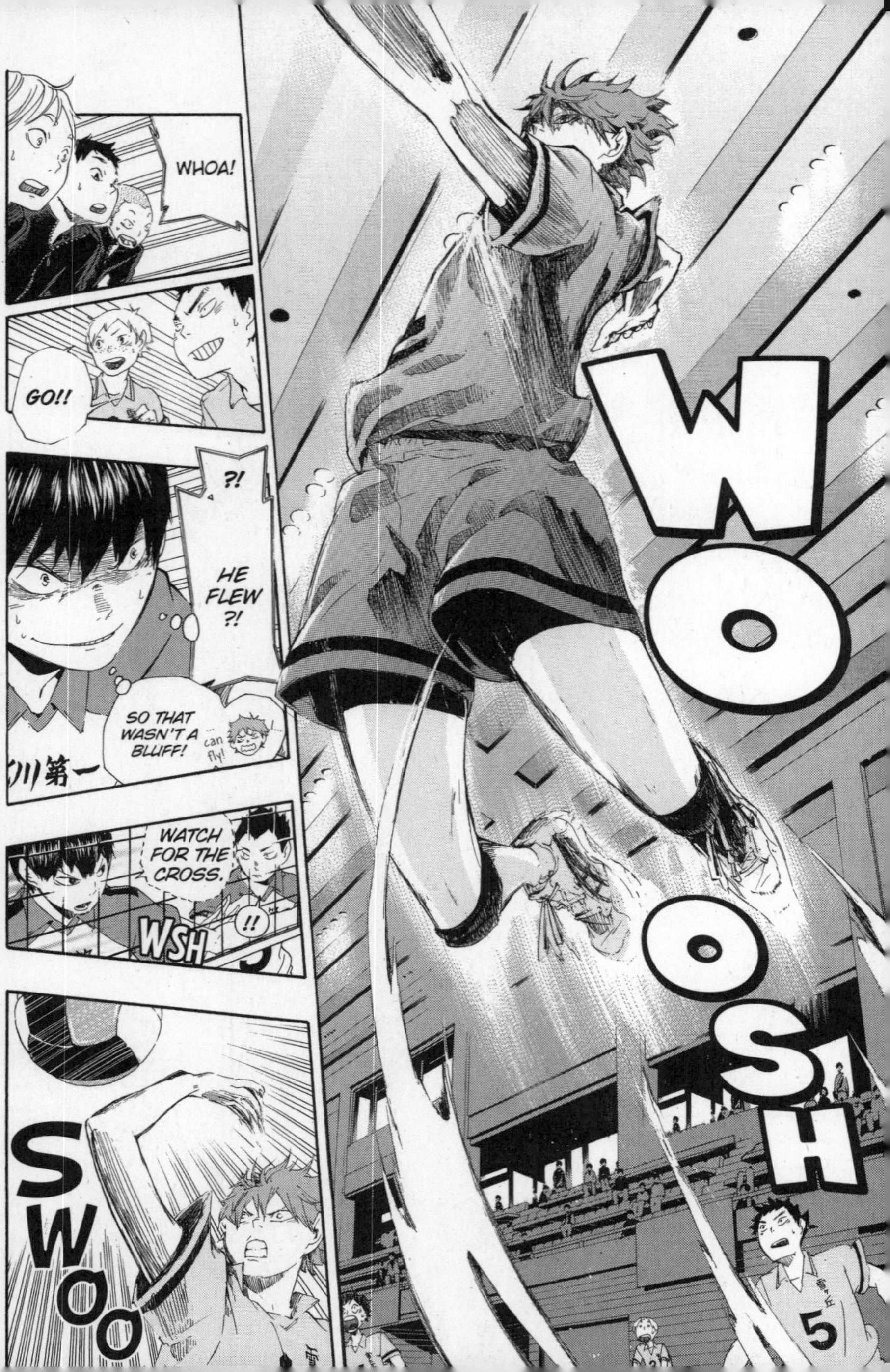
WHOOSH
WHOA!
GO!!
?!
HE FLEW ?!
SO THAT WASN'T A BLUFF!
... can fly!
川第一
WATCH FOR THE CROSS.
!!
WSH
SWOOO

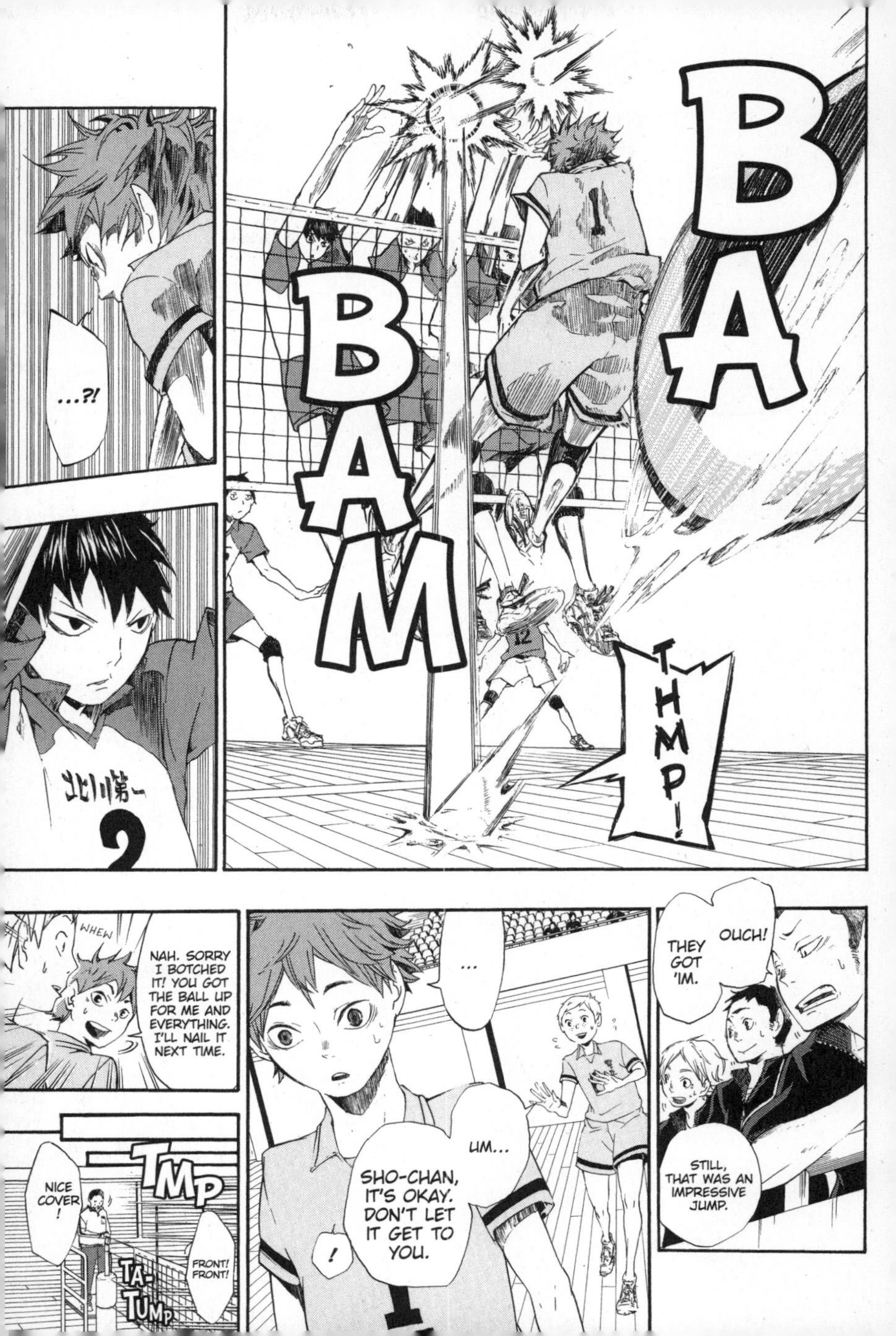
BA
BAM
THMP!
...?!
OUCH!
THEY GOT 'IM.
STILL, THAT WAS AN IMPRESSIVE JUMP.
...
UM...
SHO-CHAN, IT'S OKAY. DON'T LET IT GET TO YOU.
!
WHEW
NAH. SORRY I BOTCHED IT! YOU GOT THE BALL UP FOR ME AND EVERYTHING. I'LL NAIL IT NEXT TIME.
TMP
NICE COVER!
FRONT! FRONT!
TA-TUMP

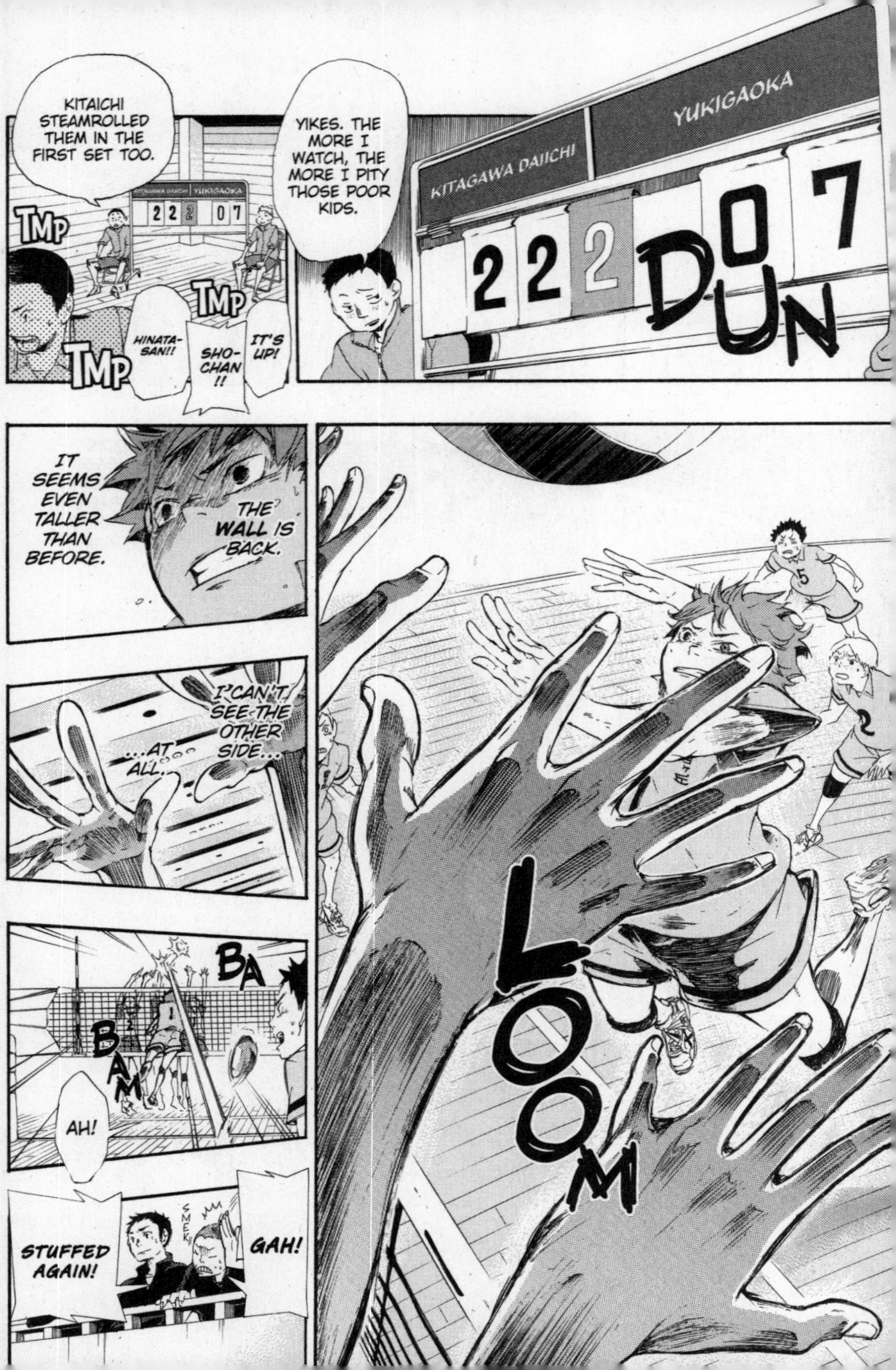

YUKIGAOKA
KITAGAWA DAIICHI
22 2 07
DUN
YIKES. THE MORE I WATCH, THE MORE I PITY THOSE POOR KIDS.
KITAICHI STEAMROLLED THEM IN THE FIRST SET TOO.
KITAGAWA DAIICHI YUKIGAOKA
TMP
TMP
TMP
IT'S UP!
SHO-CHAN!!
HINATA-SAN!!
LOOOM
THE WALL IS BACK.
IT SEEMS EVEN TALLER THAN BEFORE.
I CAN'T SEE THE OTHER SIDE...
...AT ALL...
BA
BAM
AH!
GAH!
SMEK
STUFFED AGAIN!

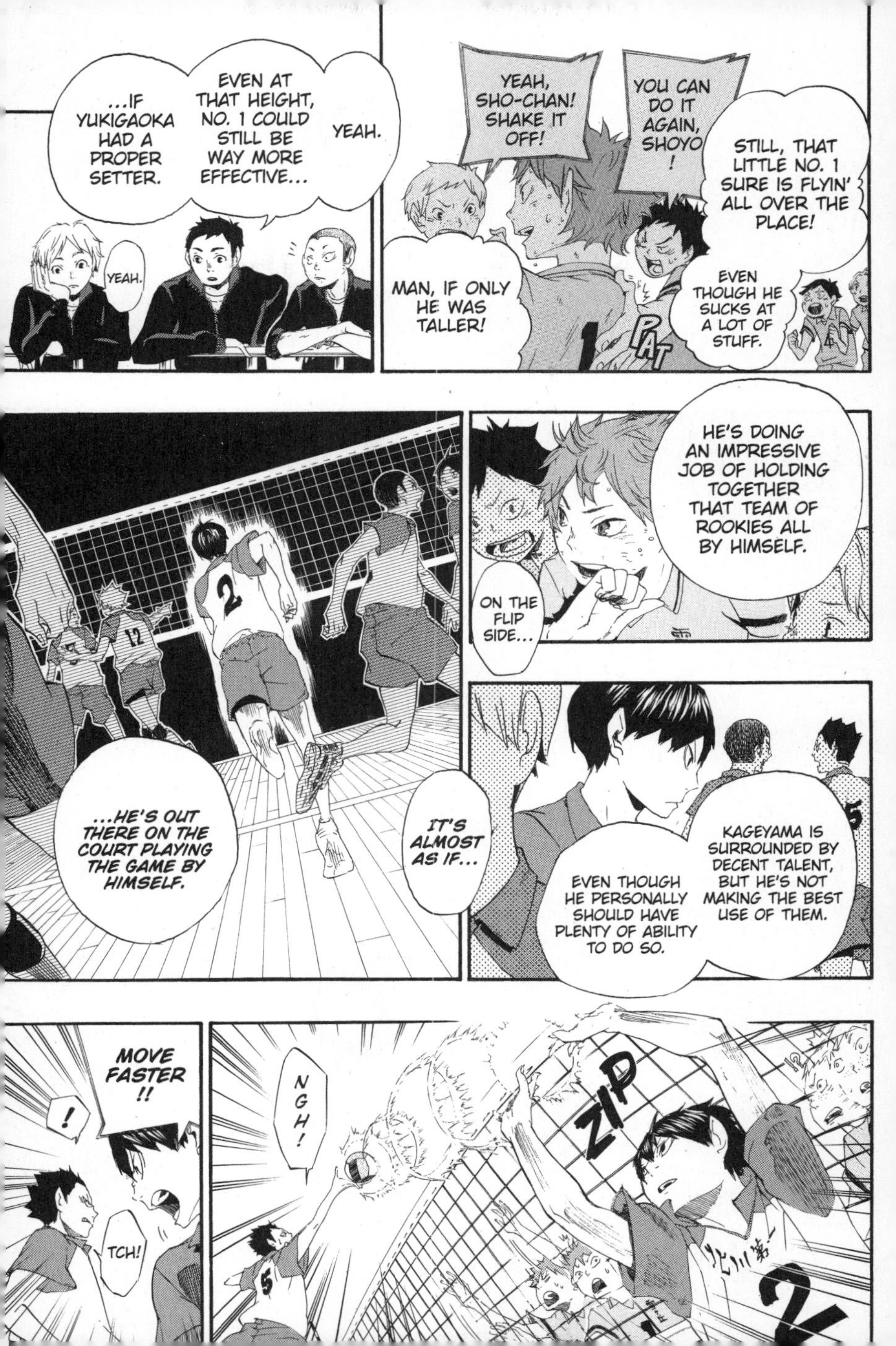

YOU CAN DO IT AGAIN, SHOYO!
YEAH, SHO-CHAN! SHAKE IT OFF!
STILL, THAT LITTLE NO. 1 SURE IS FLYIN' ALL OVER THE PLACE!
EVEN THOUGH HE SUCKS AT A LOT OF STUFF.
PAT
MAN, IF ONLY HE WAS TALLER!
YEAH.
EVEN AT THAT HEIGHT, NO. 1 COULD STILL BE WAY MORE EFFECTIVE...
...IF YUKIGAOKA HAD A PROPER SETTER.
YEAH.
HE'S DOING AN IMPRESSIVE JOB OF HOLDING TOGETHER THAT TEAM OF ROOKIES ALL BY HIMSELF.
ON THE FLIP SIDE...
KAGEYAMA IS SURROUNDED BY DECENT TALENT, BUT HE'S NOT MAKING THE BEST USE OF THEM.
EVEN THOUGH HE PERSONALLY SHOULD HAVE PLENTY OF ABILITY TO DO SO.
IT'S ALMOST AS IF...
...HE'S OUT THERE ON THE COURT PLAYING THE GAME BY HIMSELF.
ZIP
NGH!
MOVE FASTER!!
!
TCH!

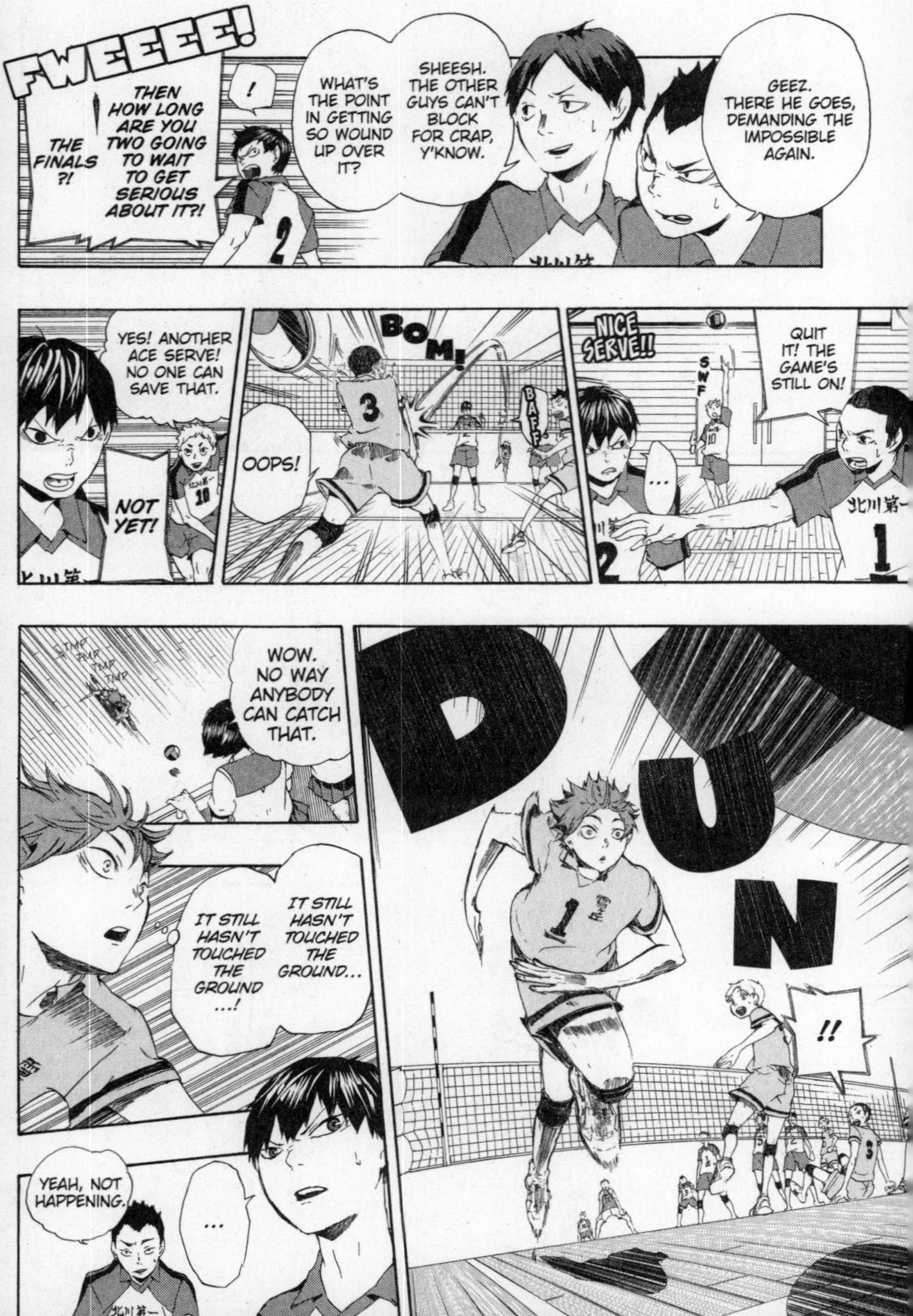
GEEZ. THERE HE GOES, DEMANDING THE IMPOSSIBLE AGAIN.
SHEESH. THE OTHER GUYS CAN'T BLOCK FOR CRAP, Y'KNOW.
WHAT'S THE POINT IN GETTING SO WOUND UP OVER IT?
!
THEN HOW LONG ARE YOU TWO GOING TO WAIT TO GET SERIOUS ABOUT IT?!
THE FINALS ?!
FWEEEE!
QUIT IT! THE GAME'S STILL ON!
NICE SERVE!!
SWF
...
BOM!
BAFF
OOPS!
YES! ANOTHER ACE SERVE! NO ONE CAN SAVE THAT.
NOT YET!
DUN
!!
WOW. NO WAY ANYBODY CAN CATCH THAT.
TMP TMP TMP TMP
IT STILL HASN'T TOUCHED THE GROUND...
IT STILL HASN'T TOUCHED THE GROUND ...!
...
YEAH, NOT HAPPENING.

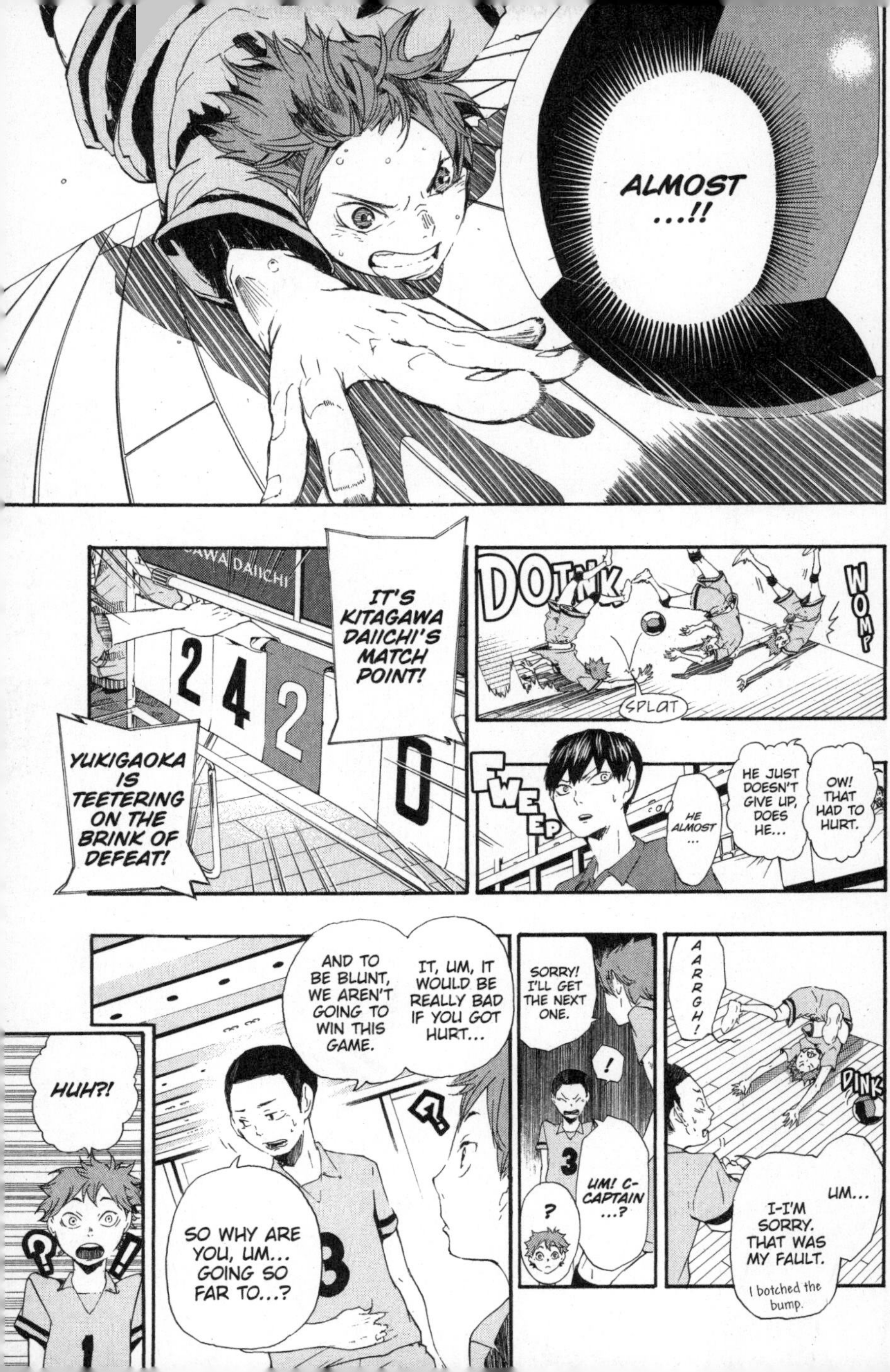
ALMOST ...!!
WOMP
DOINK
SPLAT
OW! THAT HAD TO HURT.
HE JUST DOESN'T GIVE UP, DOES HE...
HE ALMOST...
FWEEP
IT'S KITAGAWA DAIICHI'S MATCH POINT!
YUKIGAOKA IS TEETERING ON THE BRINK OF DEFEAT!
AARRGH!
DINK
UM...
I-I'M SORRY. THAT WAS MY FAULT.
I botched the bump.
SORRY! I'LL GET THE NEXT ONE.
!
UM! C-CAPTAIN...?
?
IT, UM, IT WOULD BE REALLY BAD IF YOU GOT HURT...
AND TO BE BLUNT, WE AREN'T GOING TO WIN THIS GAME.
?
SO WHY ARE YOU, UM... GOING SO FAR TO...?
HUH?!
?!

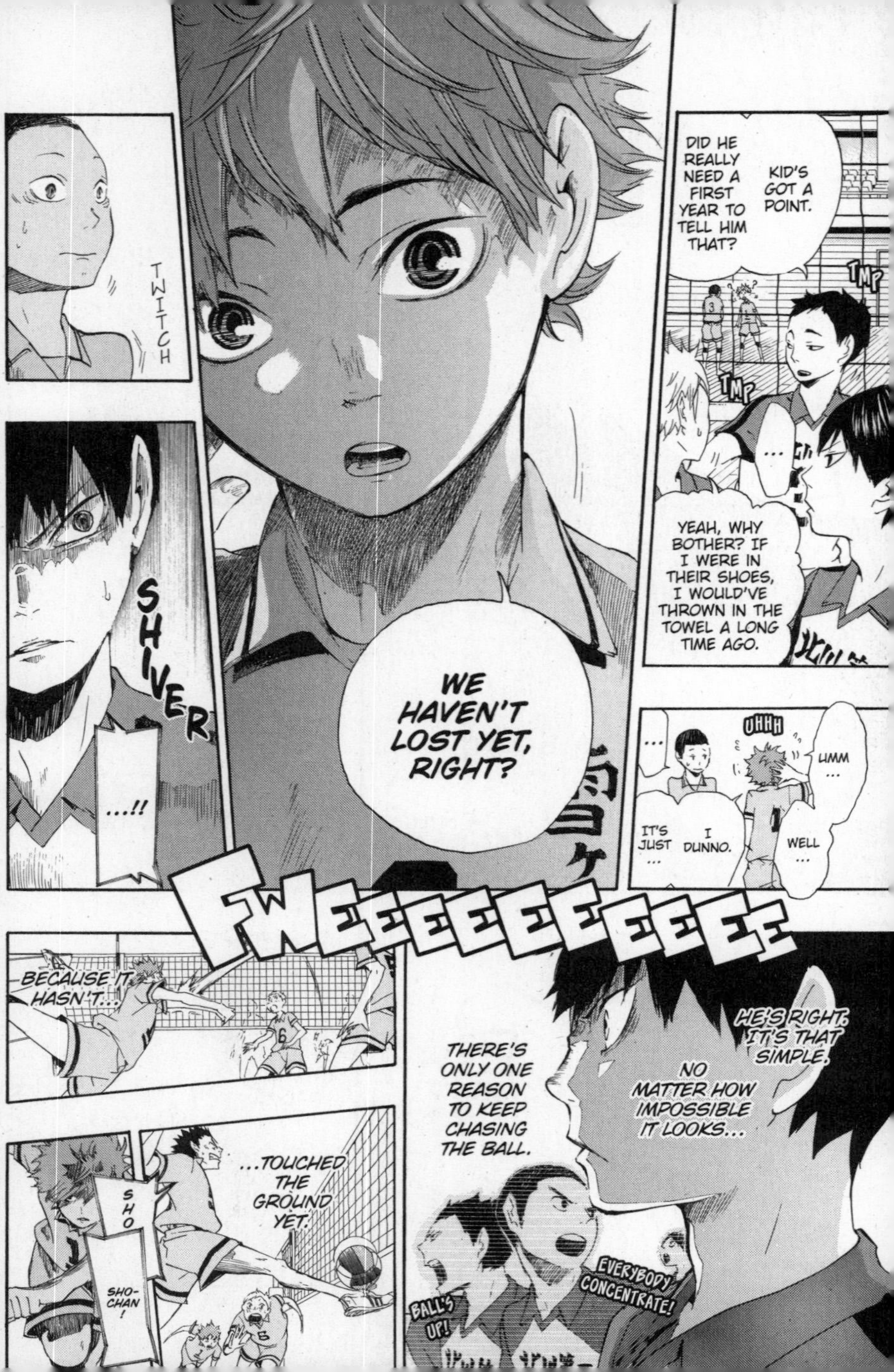
KID'S GOT A POINT.
DID HE REALLY NEED A FIRST YEAR TO TELL HIM THAT?
TMP
TMP
...
YEAH, WHY BOTHER? IF I WERE IN THEIR SHOES, I WOULD'VE THROWN IN THE TOWEL A LONG TIME AGO.
UMM ...
UHHH
WELL ...
...
I DUNNO.
IT'S JUST ...
WE HAVEN'T LOST YET, RIGHT?
TWITCH
SHIVER
...!!
FWEEEEEEEEEEE
HE'S RIGHT. IT'S THAT SIMPLE.
NO MATTER HOW IMPOSSIBLE IT LOOKS...
THERE'S ONLY ONE REASON TO KEEP CHASING THE BALL.
EVERYBODY CONCENTRATE!
BALL'S UP!
BECAUSE IT HASN'T...
...TOUCHED THE GROUND YET.
SHO
SHO-CHAN!

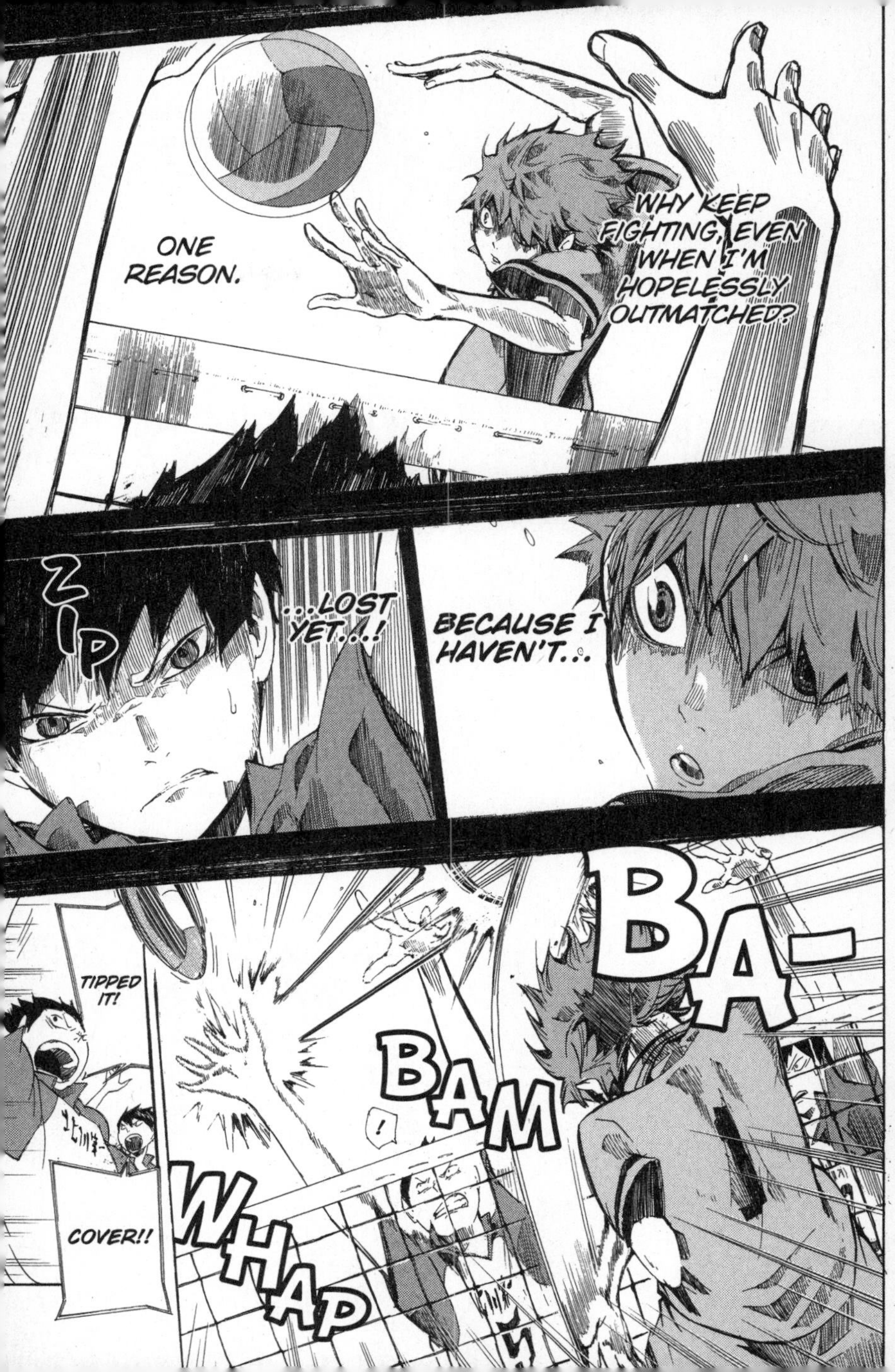
WHY KEEP FIGHTING, EVEN WHEN I'M HOPELESSLY OUTMATCHED?
ONE REASON.
BECAUSE I HAVEN'T...
...LOST YET...!
ZIP
BA-
BAM
TIPPED IT!
!
WHAP
COVER!!

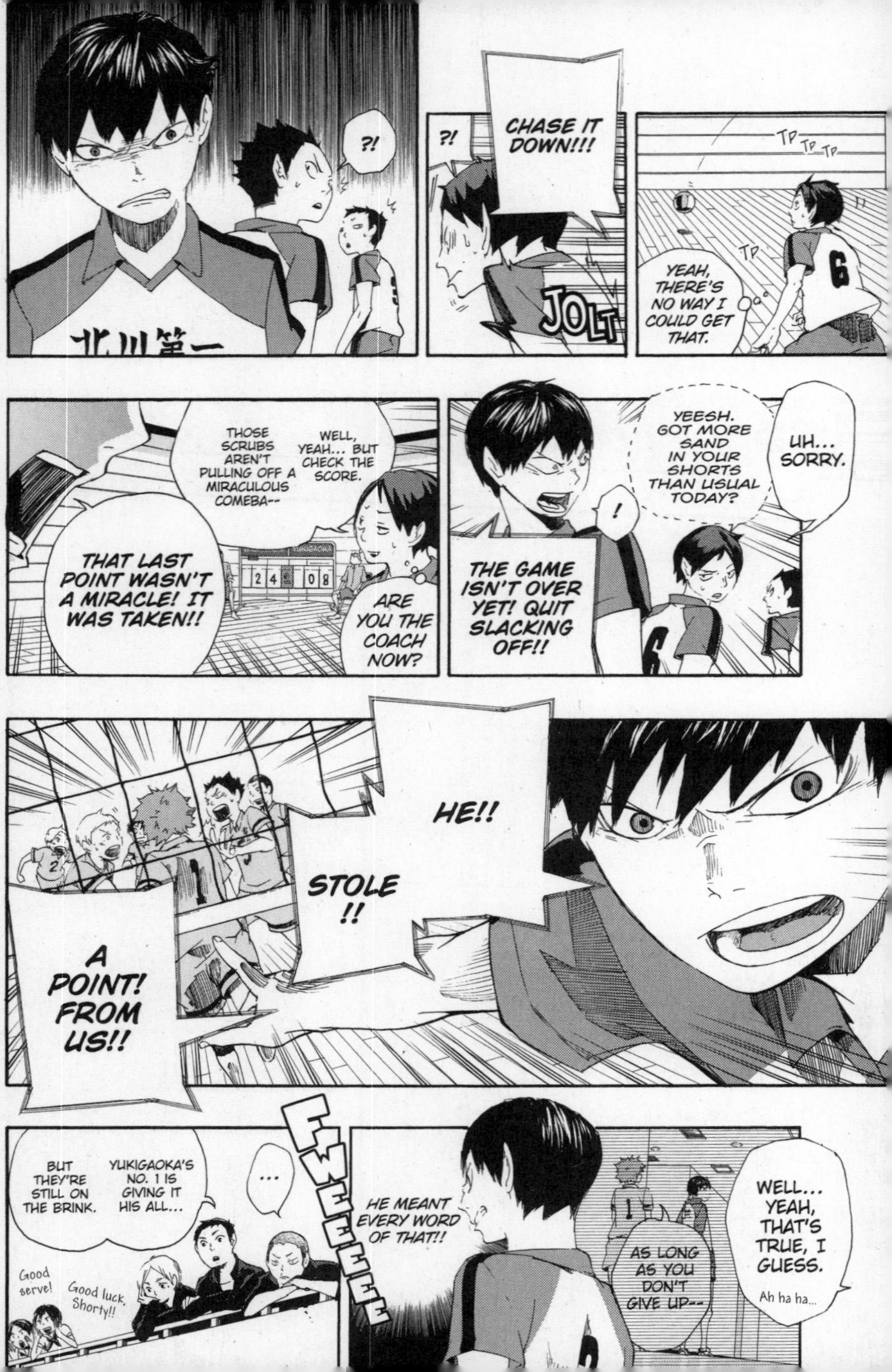

Tp Tp Tp
Tp
YEAH, THERE'S NO WAY I COULD GET THAT.
CHASE IT DOWN!!!
?!
JOLT
?!
北川第一
UH... SORRY.
YEESH. GOT MORE SAND IN YOUR SHORTS THAN USUAL TODAY?
!
THE GAME ISN'T OVER YET! QUIT SLACKING OFF!!
ARE YOU THE COACH NOW?
WELL, YEAH... BUT CHECK THE SCORE.
THOSE SCRUBS AREN'T PULLING OFF A MIRACULOUS COMEBA--
THAT LAST POINT WASN'T A MIRACLE! IT WAS TAKEN!!
24 08
HE!!
STOLE!!
A POINT! FROM US!!
WELL... YEAH, THAT'S TRUE, I GUESS.
Ah ha ha...
AS LONG AS YOU DON'T GIVE UP--
HE MEANT EVERY WORD OF THAT!!
FWEEEEE
...
YUKIGAOKA'S NO. 1 IS GIVING IT HIS ALL...
BUT THEY'RE STILL ON THE BRINK.
Good luck, Shorty!!
Good serve!

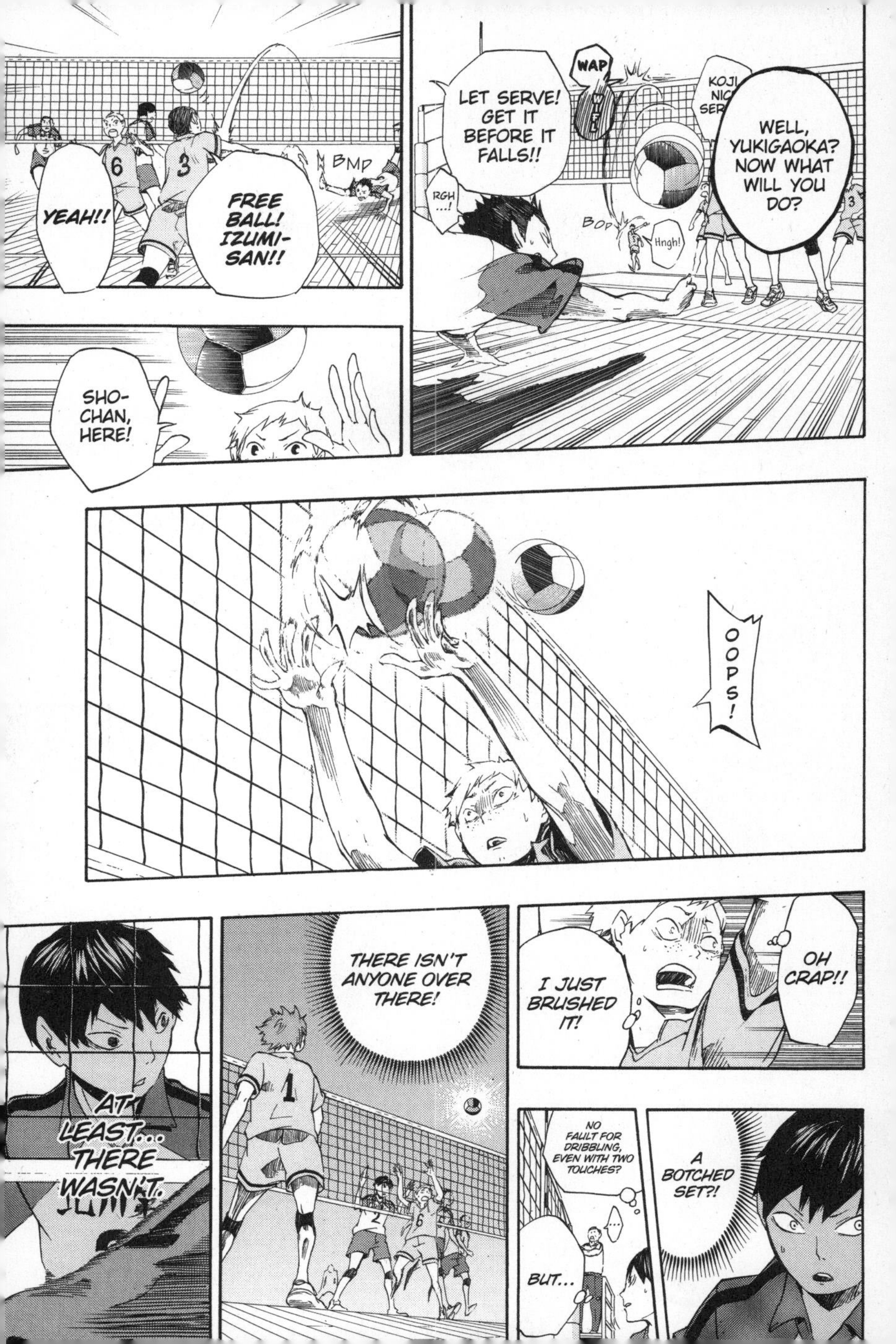
WELL, YUKIGAOKA? NOW WHAT WILL YOU DO?
WAP
LET SERVE! GET IT BEFORE IT FALLS!!
RGH ...!
Hngh!
BOP
FREE BALL! IZUMI-SAN!!
BMP
YEAH!!
SHO-CHAN, HERE!
OOPS!
OH CRAP!!
I JUST BRUSHED IT!
A BOTCHED SET?!
NO FAULT FOR DRIBBLING, EVEN WITH TWO TOUCHES?
...
BUT...
THERE ISN'T ANYONE OVER THERE!
AT LEAST... THERE WASN'T.

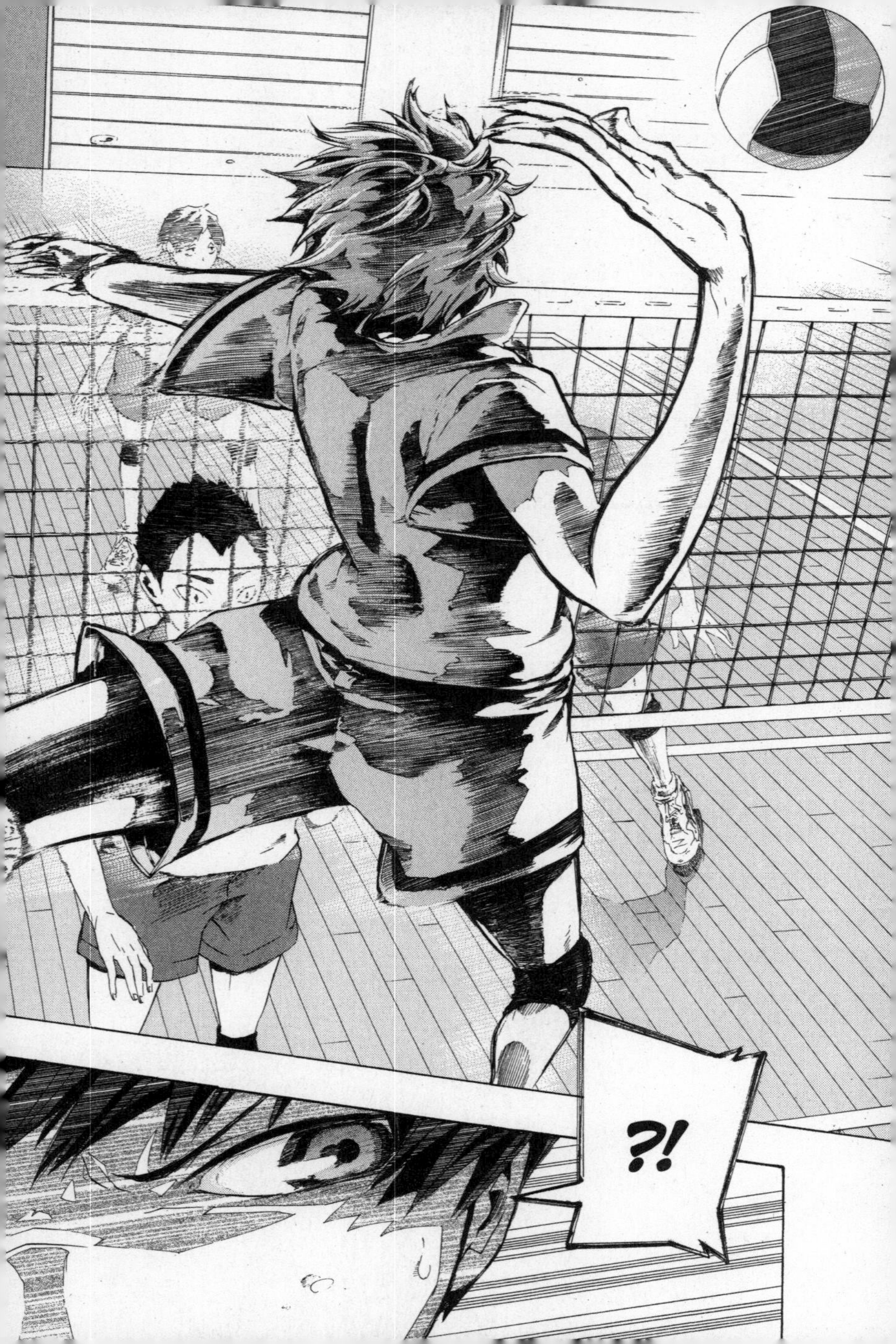
?!

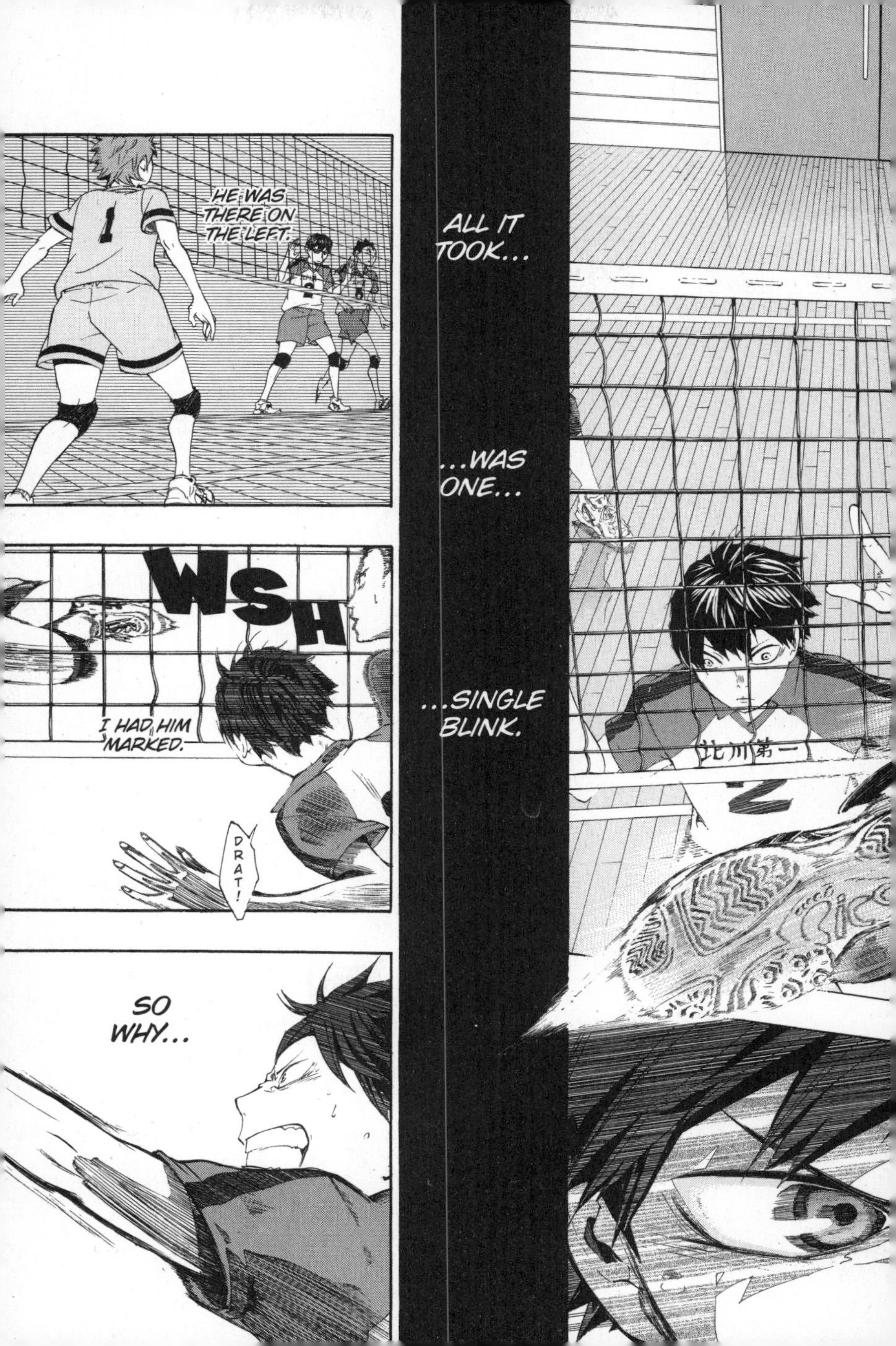
北川第一
ALL IT TOOK...
...WAS ONE...
...SINGLE BLINK.
HE WAS THERE ON THE LEFT.
WSH
I HAD HIM MARKED.
DRAT!
SO WHY...

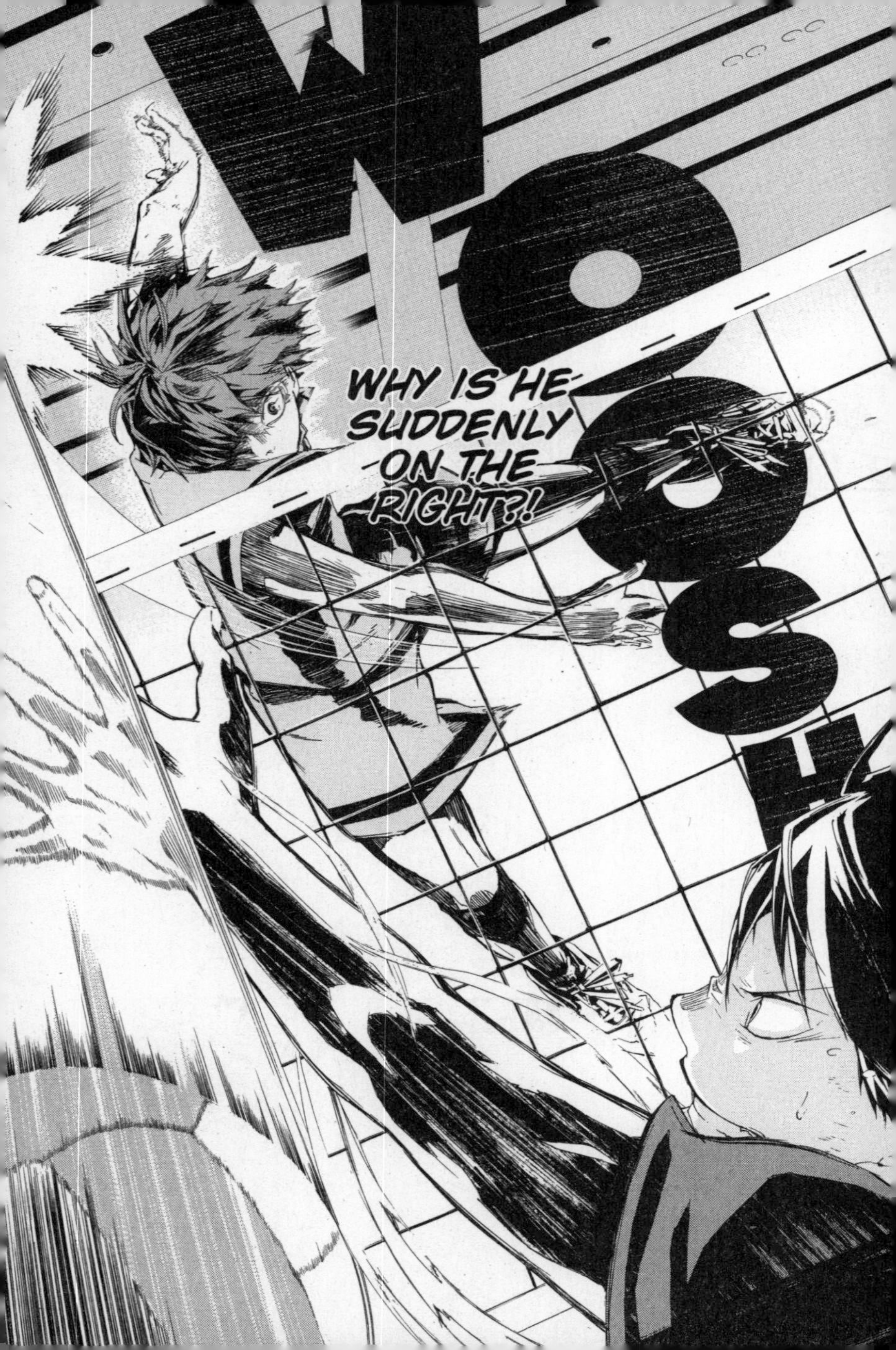
WOOSH
WHY IS HE SUDDENLY ON THE RIGHT?!

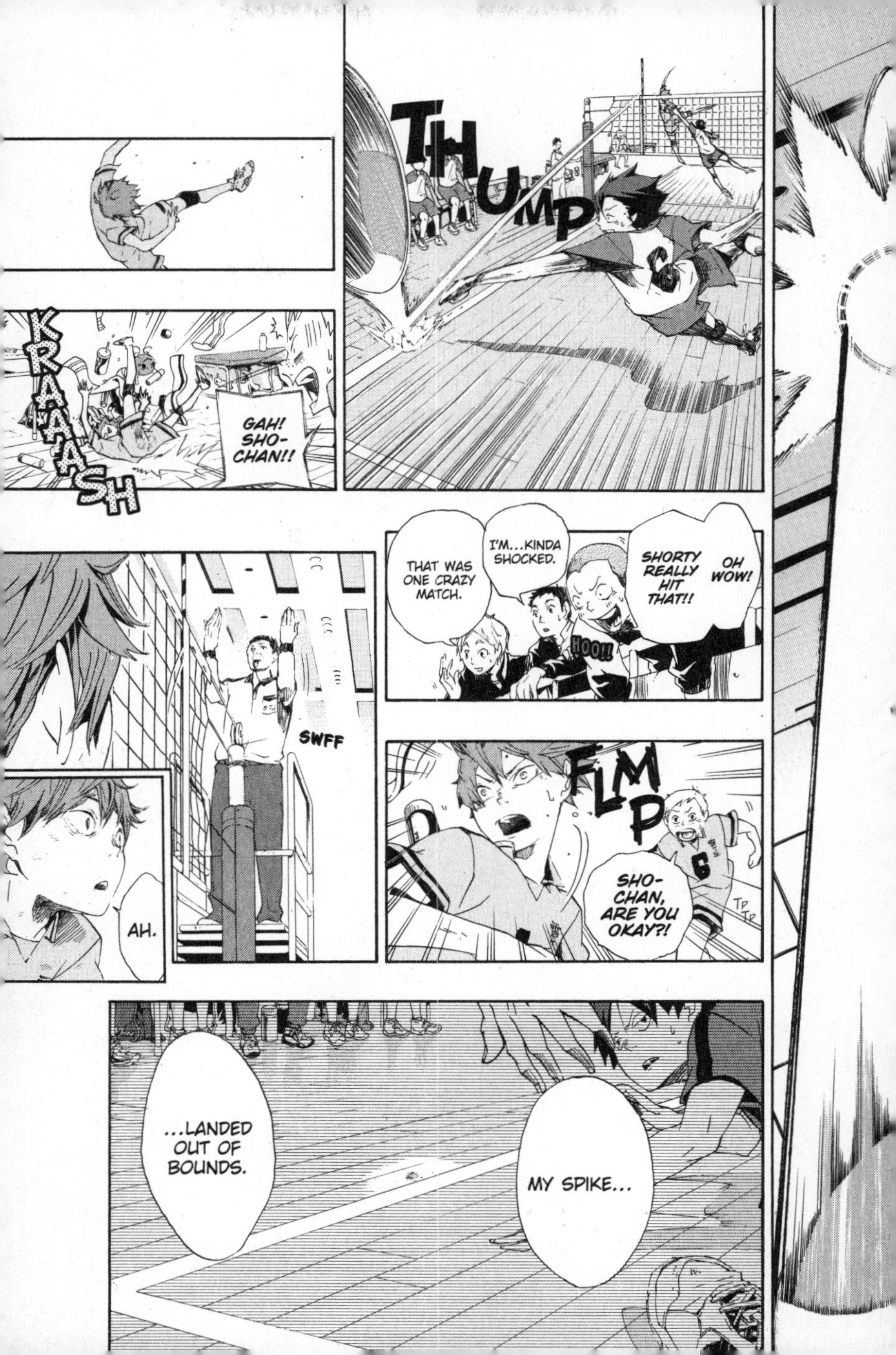

THUMP
KRAAAASH
GAH! SHO-CHAN!!
OH WOW!
SHORTY REALLY HIT THAT!!
HOO!!
I'M...KINDA SHOCKED.
THAT WAS ONE CRAZY MATCH.
FLMP
SHO-CHAN, ARE YOU OKAY?!
TP TP
SWFF
AH.
MY SPIKE...
...LANDED OUT OF BOUNDS.

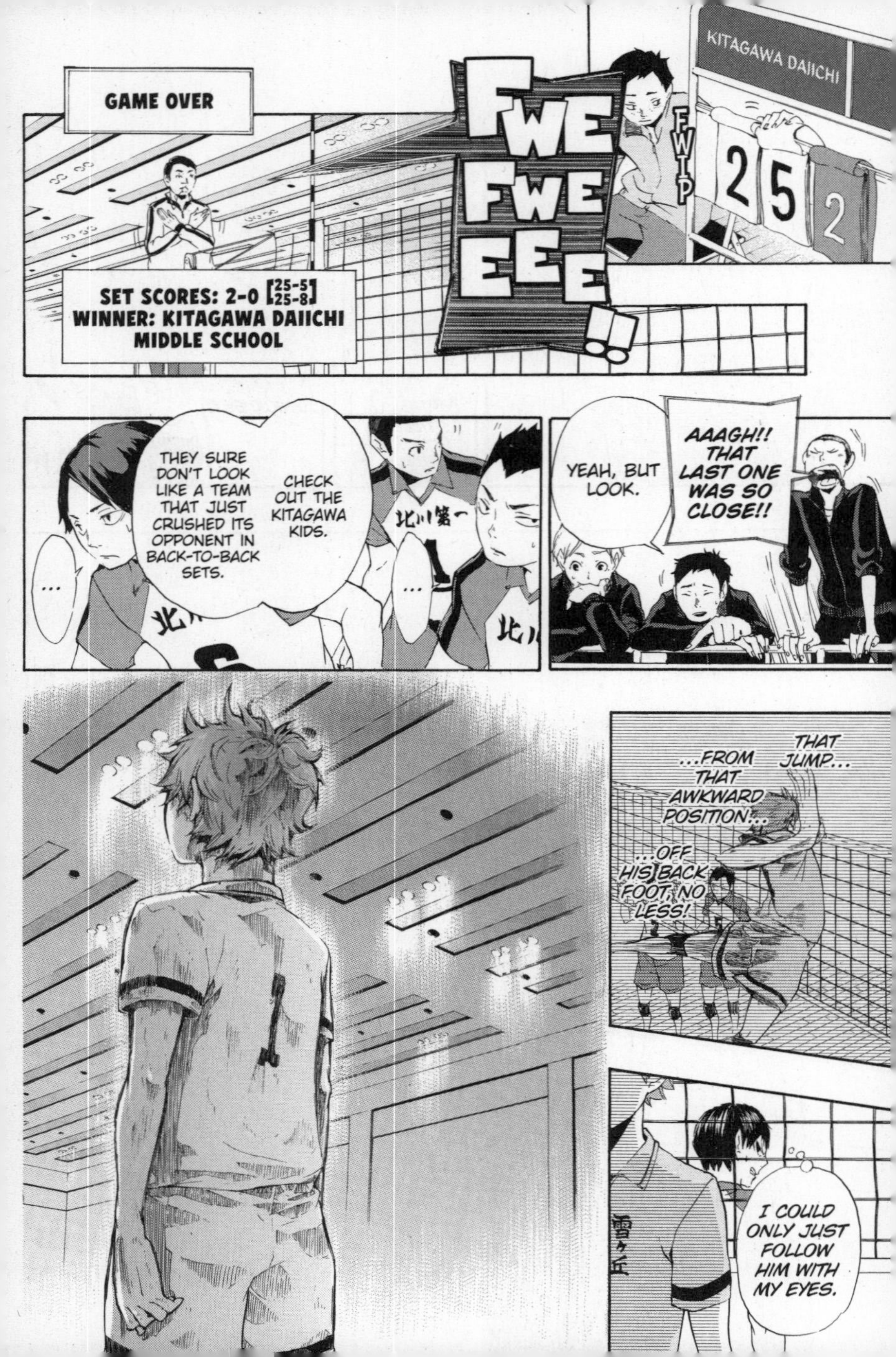
KITAGAWA DAIICHI
FWIP
FWE FWE EEE!!
GAME OVER
SET SCORES: 2-0 [25-5 25-8]
WINNER: KITAGAWA DAIICHI MIDDLE SCHOOL
AAAGH!! THAT LAST ONE WAS SO CLOSE!!
YEAH, BUT LOOK.
CHECK OUT THE KITAGAWA KIDS.
...
THEY SURE DON'T LOOK LIKE A TEAM THAT JUST CRUSHED ITS OPPONENT IN BACK-TO-BACK SETS.
...
THAT JUMP...
...FROM THAT AWKWARD POSITION...
...OFF HIS BACK FOOT, NO LESS!
I COULD ONLY JUST FOLLOW HIM WITH MY EYES.

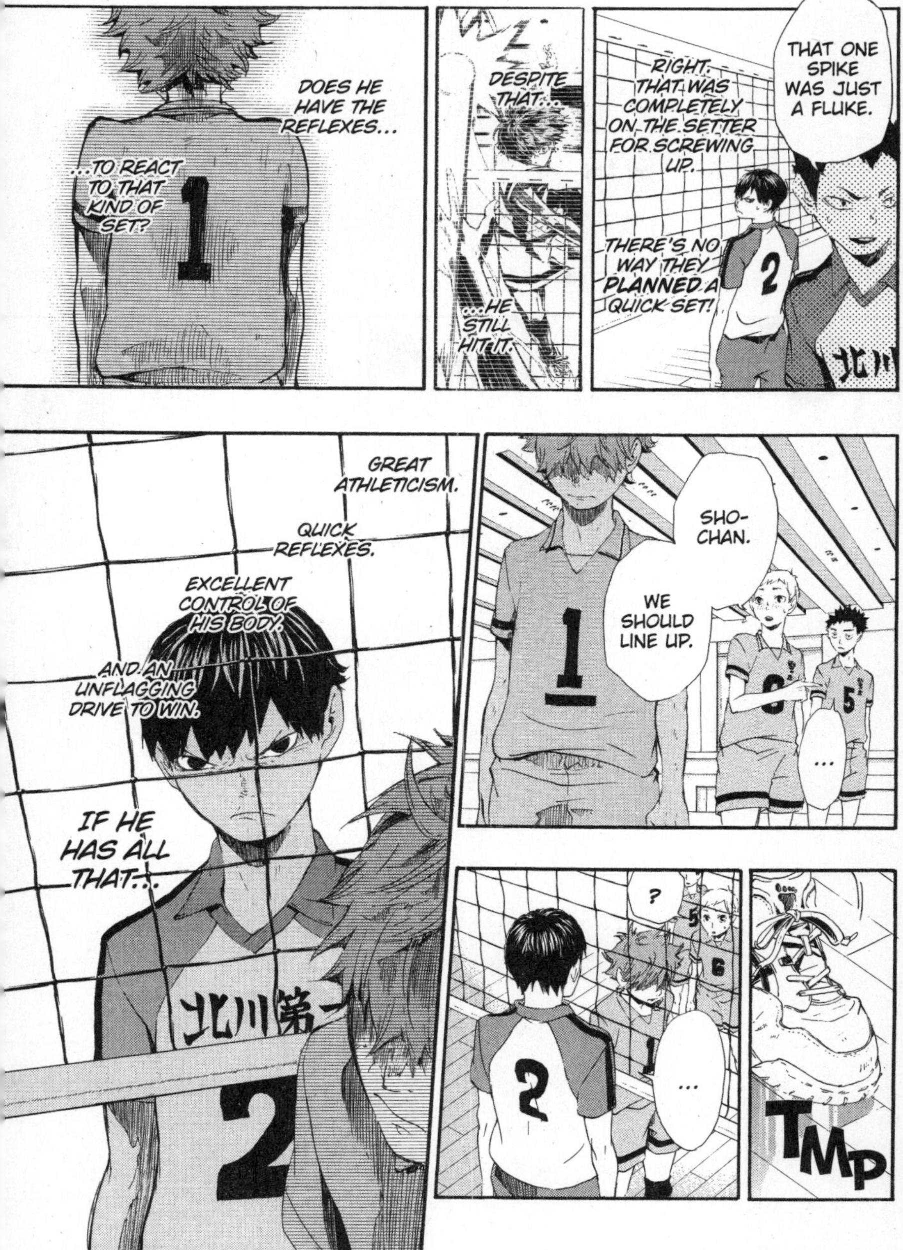
THAT ONE SPIKE WAS JUST A FLUKE.
RIGHT. THAT WAS COMPLETELY ON THE SETTER FOR SCREWING UP.
THERE'S NO WAY THEY PLANNED A QUICK SET!
DESPITE THAT...
...HE STILL HIT IT.
DOES HE HAVE THE REFLEXES...
...TO REACT TO THAT KIND OF SET?
SHO-CHAN.
WE SHOULD LINE UP.
...
TMP
?
...
GREAT ATHLETICISM.
QUICK REFLEXES.
EXCELLENT CONTROL OF HIS BODY.
AND AN UNFLAGGING DRIVE TO WIN.
IF HE HAS ALL THAT...

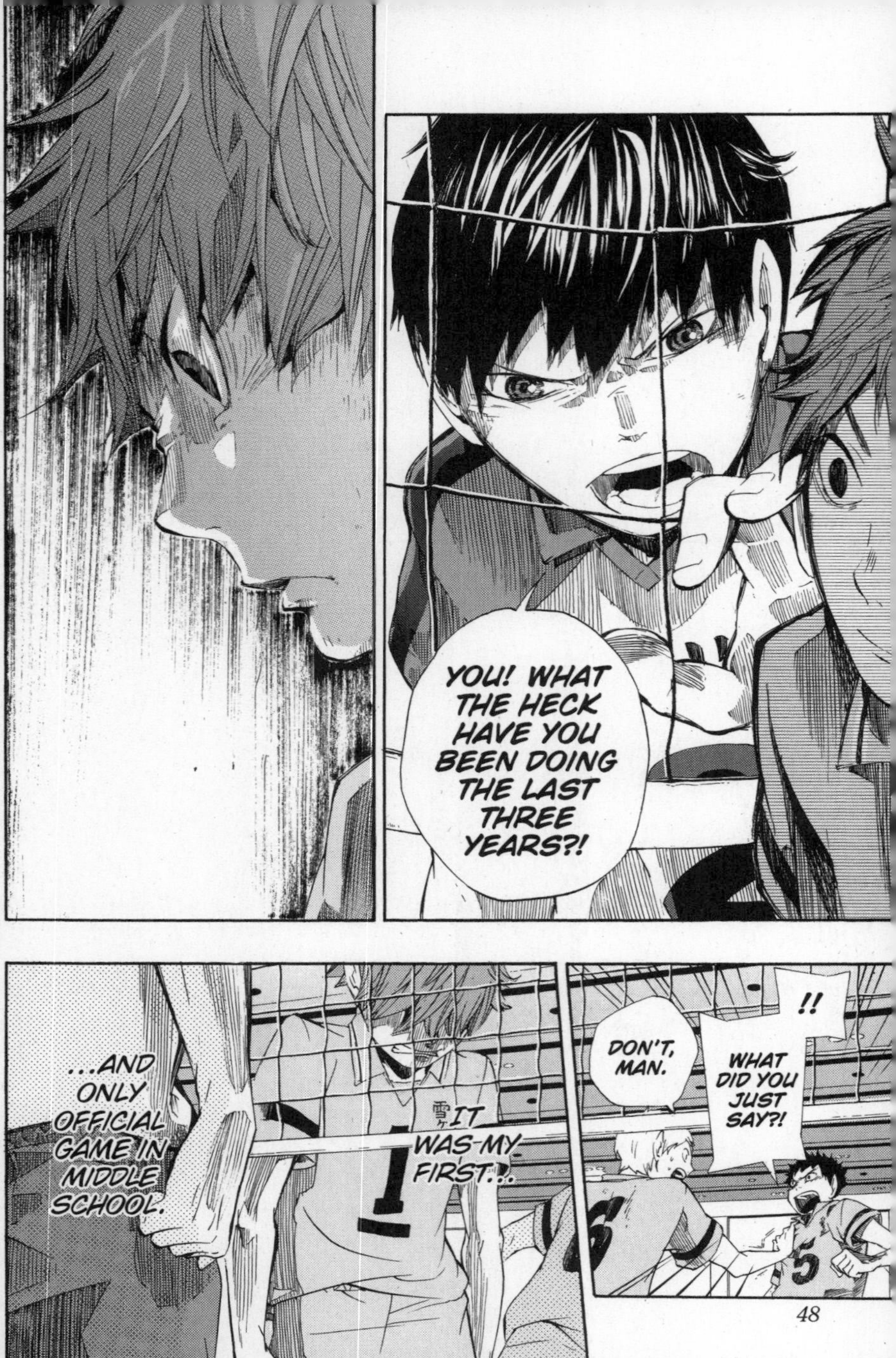
YOU! WHAT THE HECK HAVE YOU BEEN DOING THE LAST THREE YEARS?!
!!
WHAT DID YOU JUST SAY?!
DON'T, MAN.
IT WAS MY FIRST...
...AND ONLY OFFICIAL GAME IN MIDDLE SCHOOL.

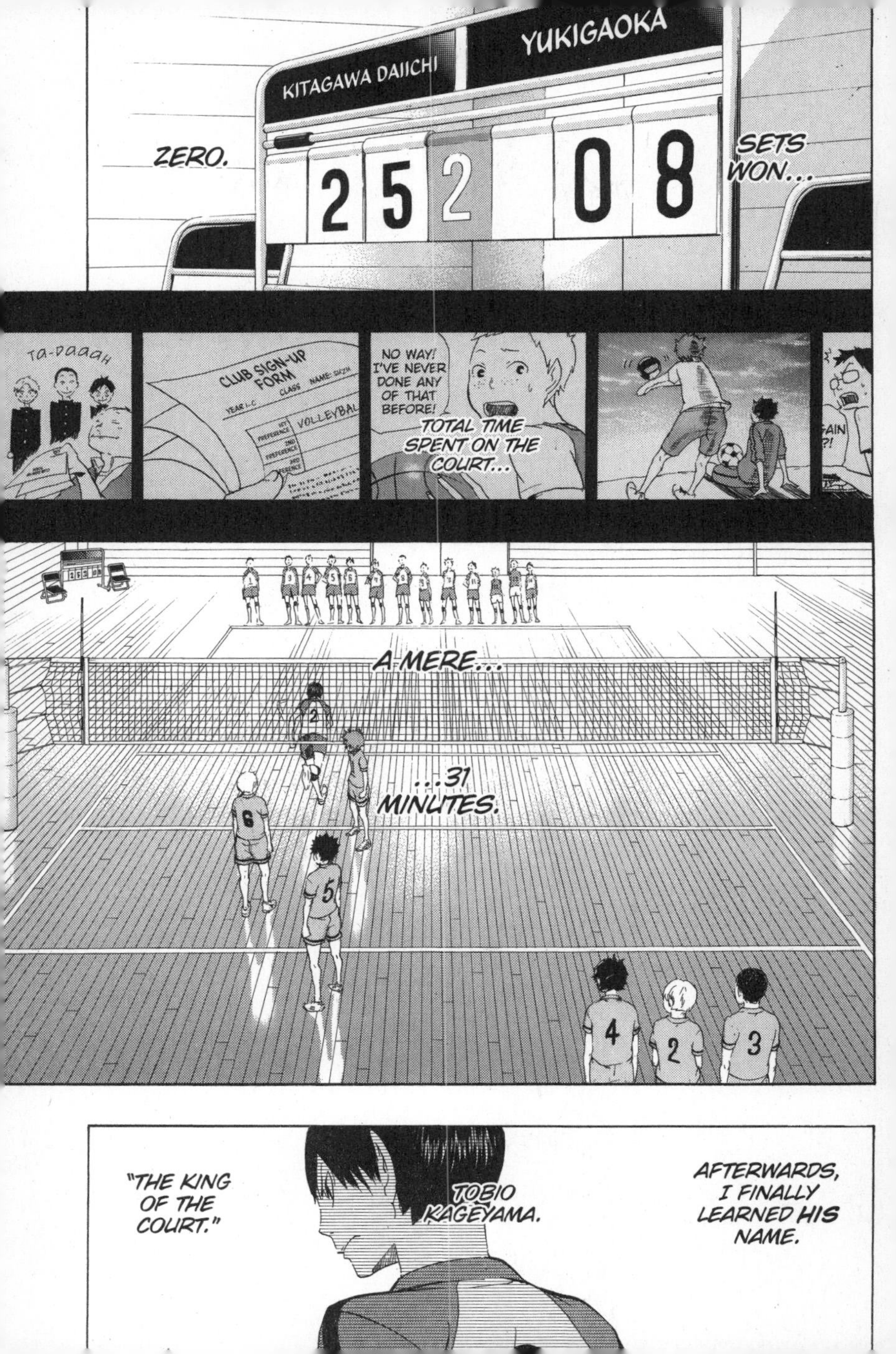
SETS WON...
KITAGAWA DAIICHI
YUKIGAOKA
25 2 0 8
ZERO.
NO WAY! I'VE NEVER DONE ANY OF THAT BEFORE!
TOTAL TIME SPENT ON THE COURT...
CLUB SIGN-UP FORM
TA-DAAAH
A MERE...
...31 MINUTES.
AFTERWARDS, I FINALLY LEARNED HIS NAME.
TOBIO KAGEYAMA.
"THE KING OF THE COURT."

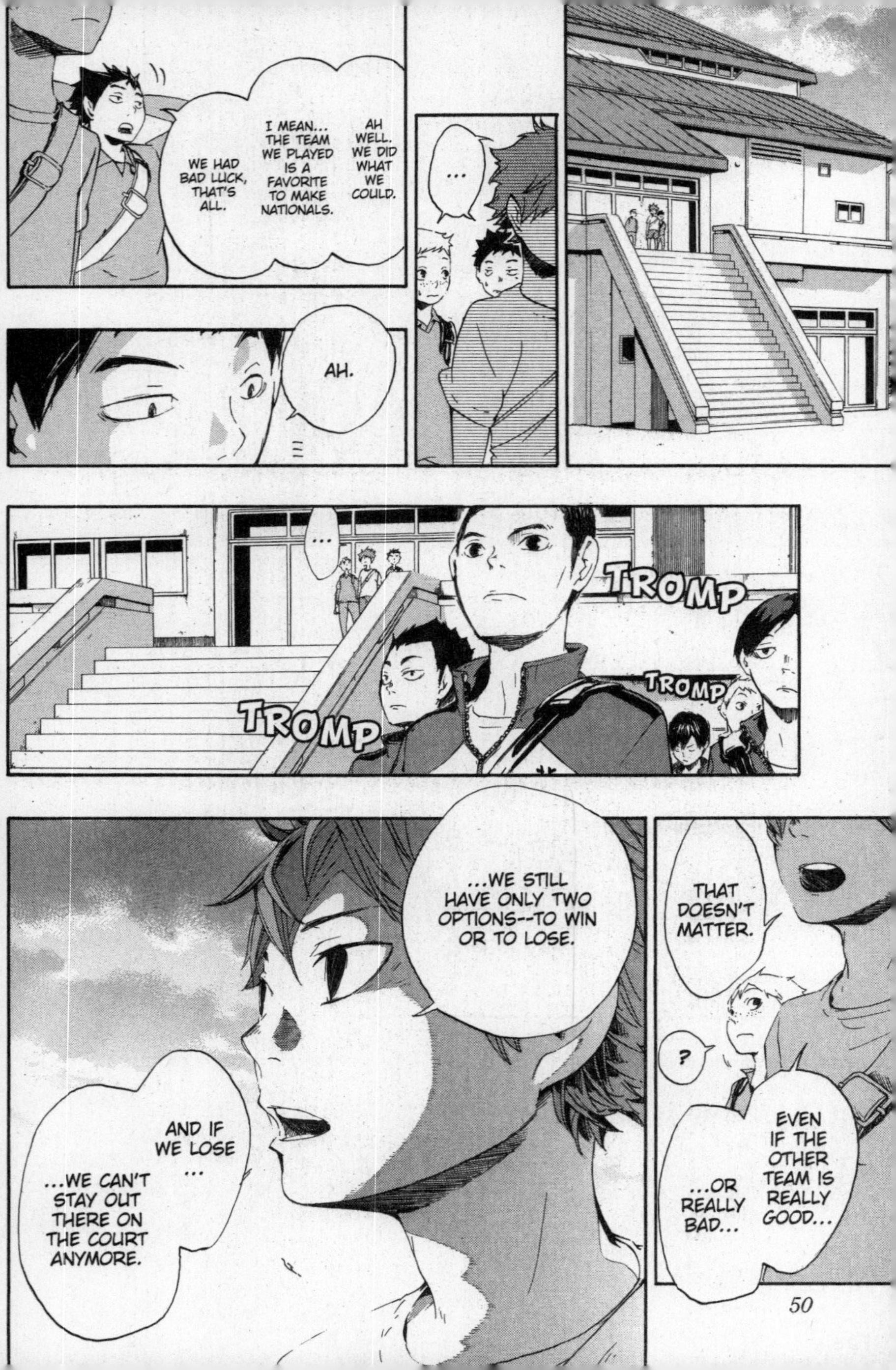
...
AH WELL. WE DID WHAT WE COULD.
I MEAN... THE TEAM WE PLAYED IS A FAVORITE TO MAKE NATIONALS.
WE HAD BAD LUCK, THAT'S ALL.
AH.
TROMP
TROMP
...
TROMP
THAT DOESN'T MATTER.
?
EVEN IF THE OTHER TEAM IS REALLY GOOD...
...OR REALLY BAD...
...WE STILL HAVE ONLY TWO OPTIONS--TO WIN OR TO LOSE.
AND IF WE LOSE ...
...WE CAN'T STAY OUT THERE ON THE COURT ANYMORE.

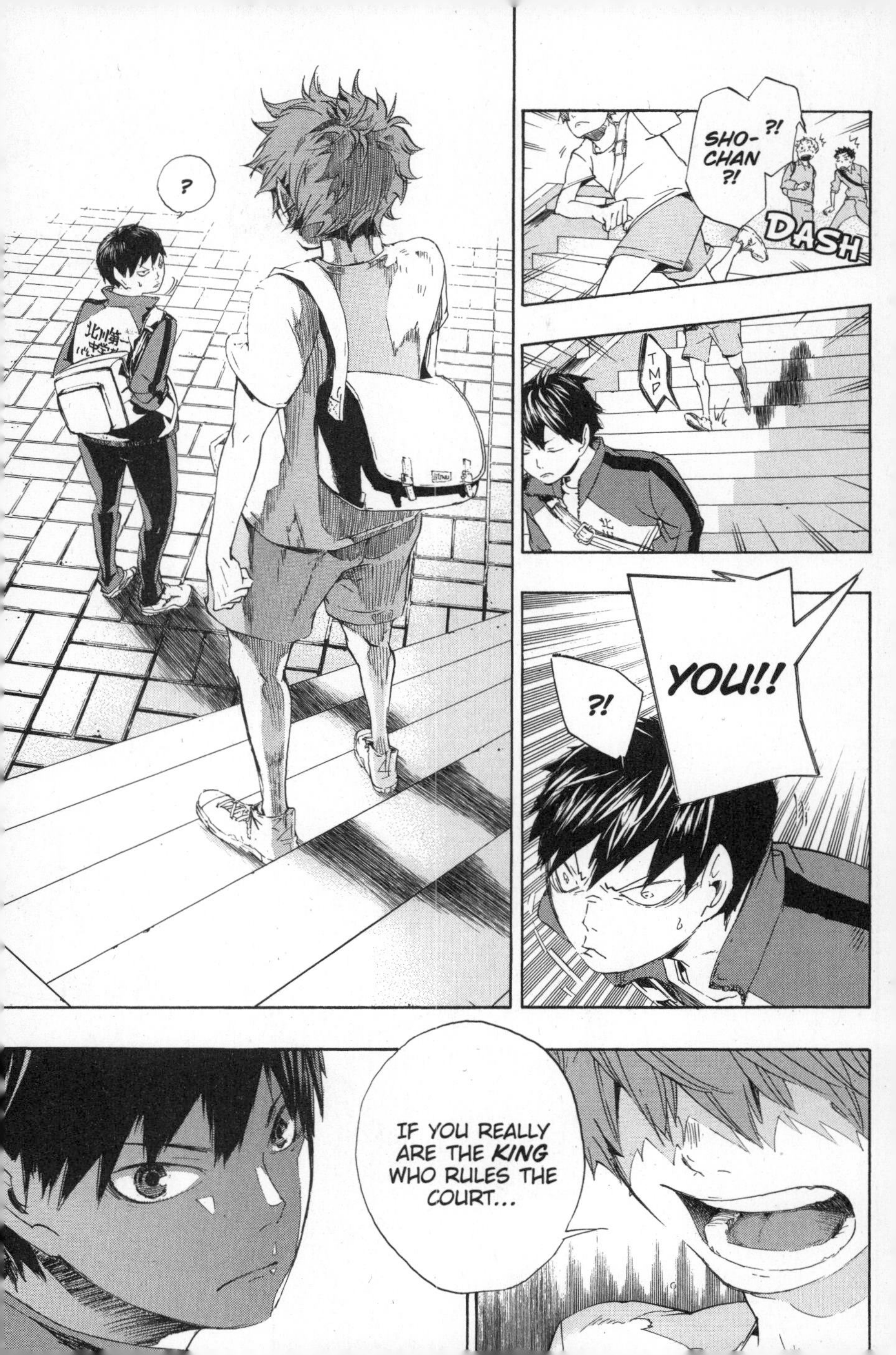
SHO-CHAN ?!
?!
DASH
TMP
YOU!!
?!
?
IF YOU REALLY ARE THE ***KING*** WHO RULES THE COURT...

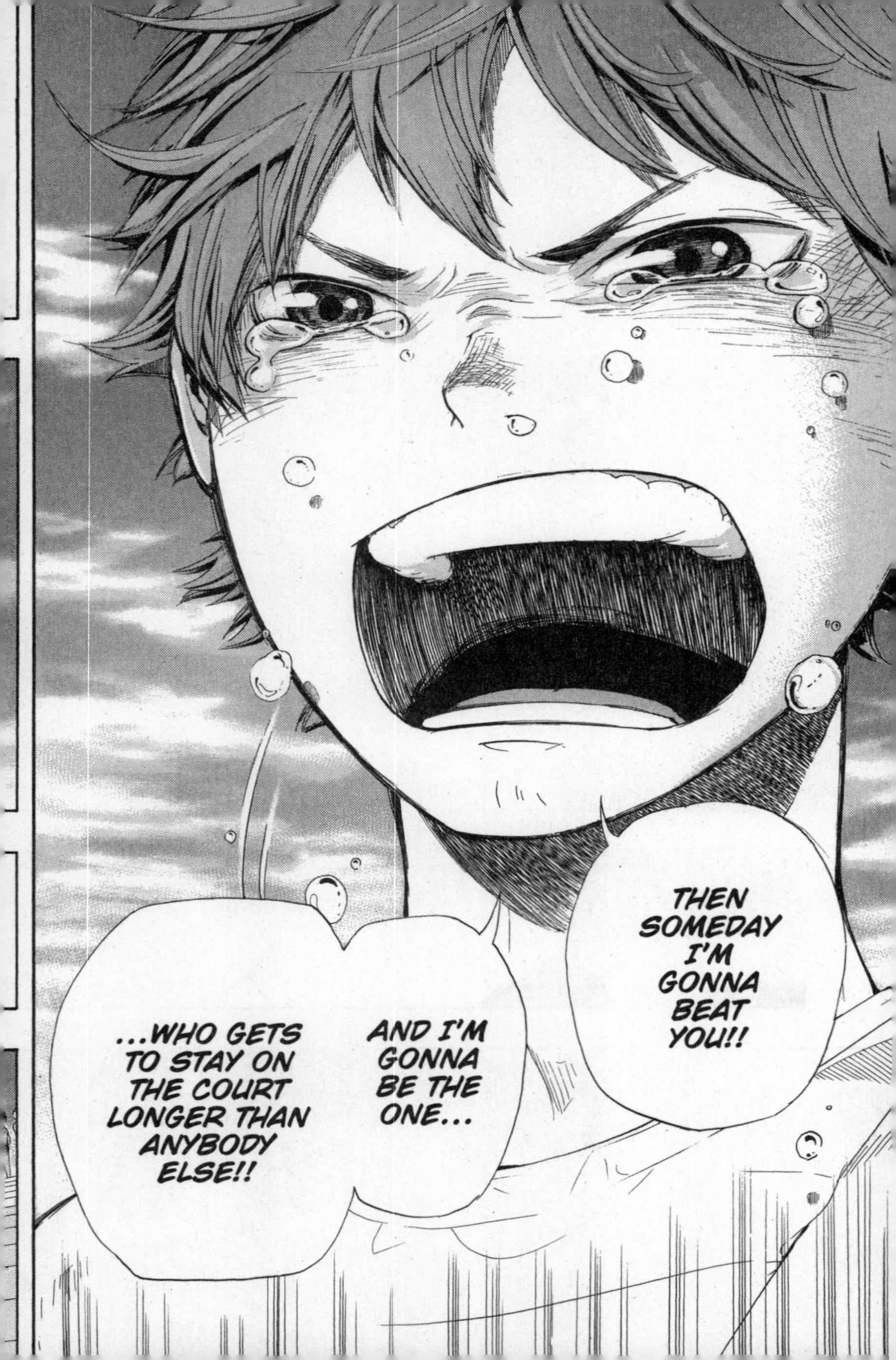
THEN SOMEDAY I'M GONNA BEAT YOU!!
AND I'M GONNA BE THE ONE...
...WHO GETS TO STAY ON THE COURT LONGER THAN ANYBODY ELSE!!

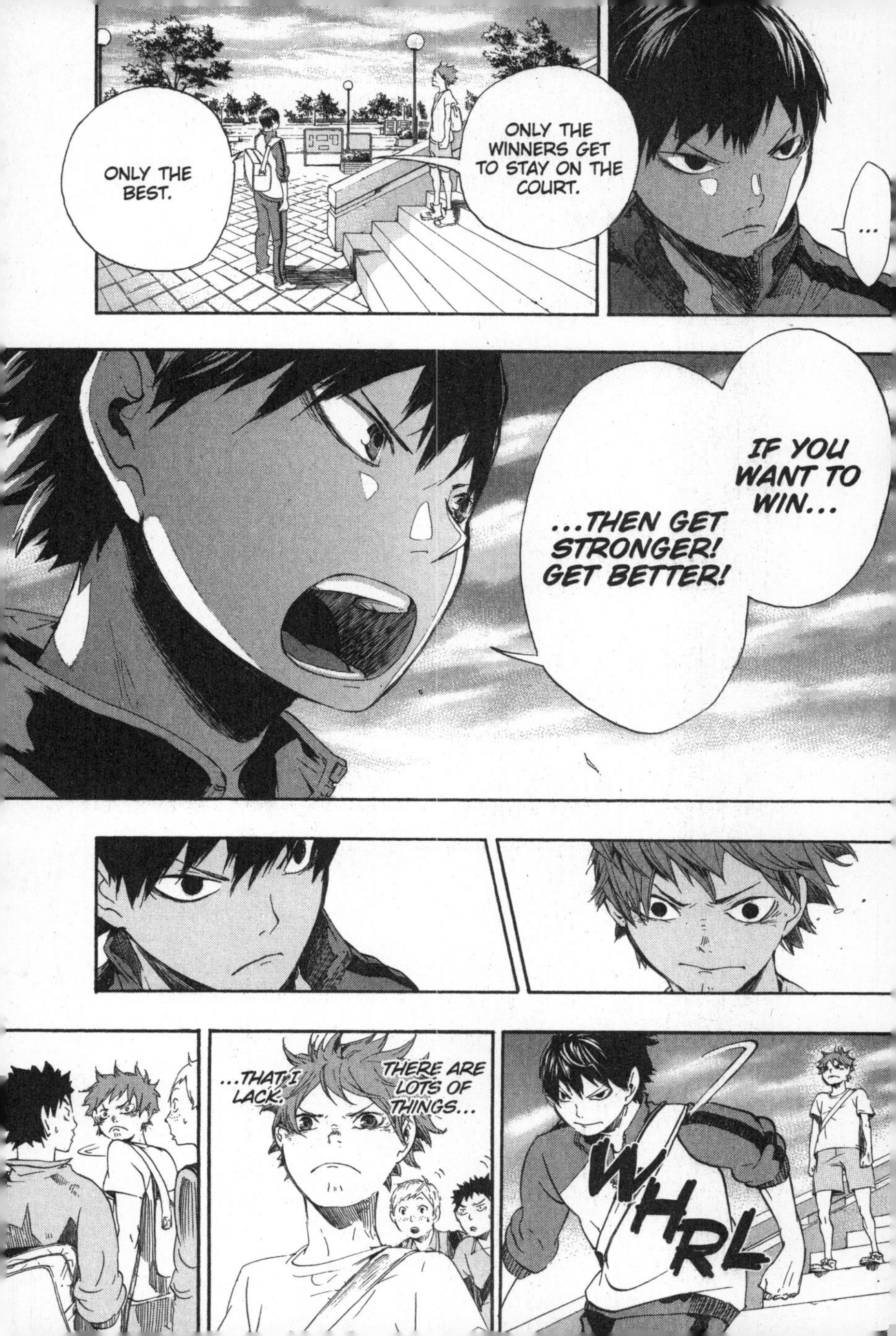
...
ONLY THE WINNERS GET TO STAY ON THE COURT.
ONLY THE BEST.
IF YOU WANT TO WIN...
...THEN GET STRONGER! GET BETTER!
WHRL
THERE ARE LOTS OF THINGS...
...THAT I LACK.

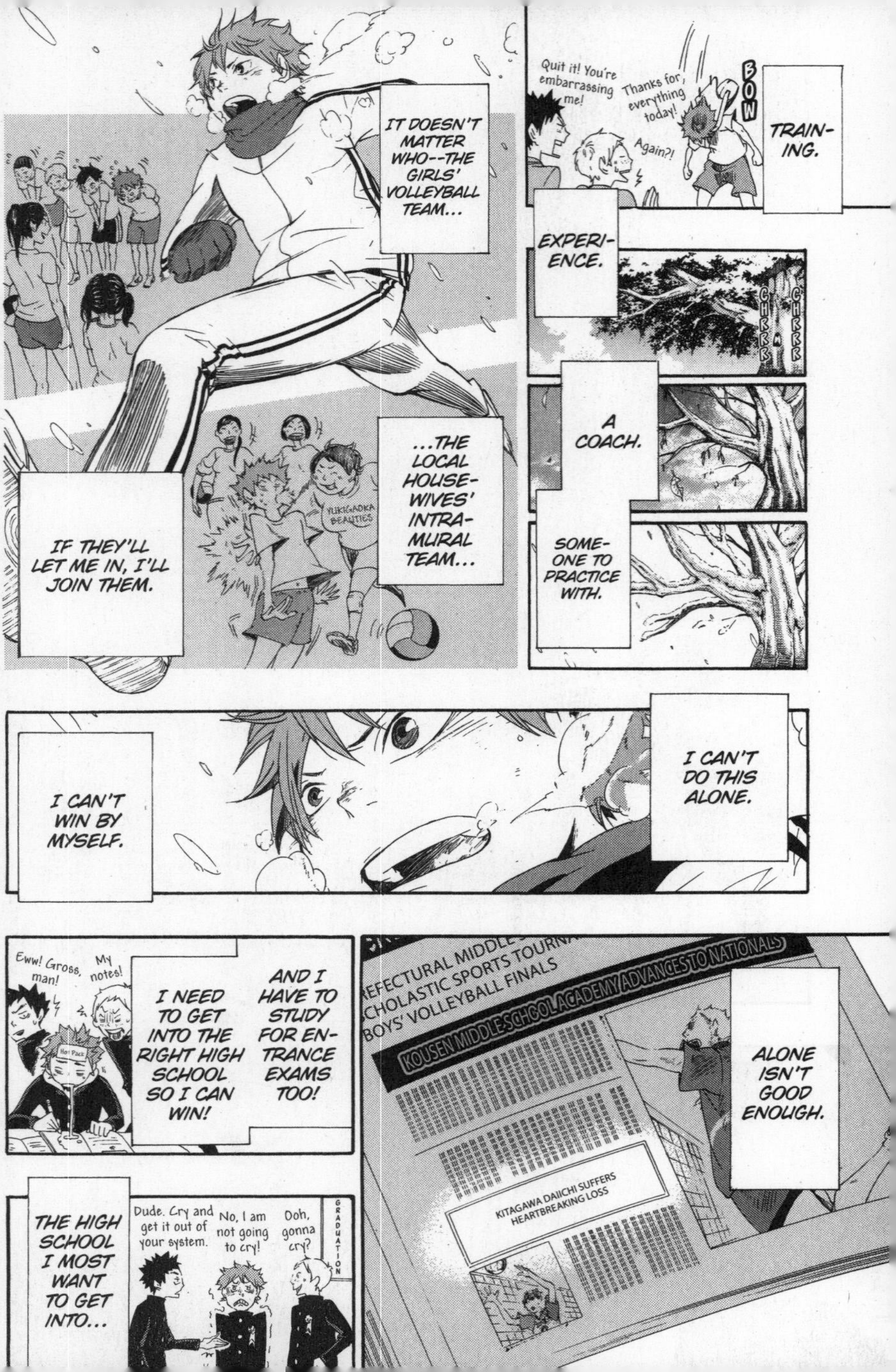
TRAIN-ING.
BOW
Thanks for everything today!
Again?!
Quit it! You're embarrassing me!
EXPERI-ENCE.
CHRRR
CHRRR
A COACH.
SOME-ONE TO PRACTICE WITH.
IT DOESN'T MATTER WHO--THE GIRLS' VOLLEYBALL TEAM...
...THE LOCAL HOUSE-WIVES' INTRA-MURAL TEAM...
YUKIGAOKA BEAUTIES
IF THEY'LL LET ME IN, I'LL JOIN THEM.
I CAN'T DO THIS ALONE.
I CAN'T WIN BY MYSELF.
BOYS' VOLLEYBALL FINALS
KOUSEN MIDDLE SCHOOL ACADEMY ADVANCES TO NATIONALS
KITAGAWA DAIICHI SUFFERS HEARTBREAKING LOSS
ALONE ISN'T GOOD ENOUGH.
AND I HAVE TO STUDY FOR EN-TRANCE EXAMS TOO!
I NEED TO GET INTO THE RIGHT HIGH SCHOOL SO I CAN WIN!
My notes!
Eww! Gross, man!
Hot Pack
GRADUATION
Ooh, gonna cry?
No, I am not going to cry!
Dude. Cry and get it out of your system.
THE HIGH SCHOOL I MOST WANT TO GET INTO...

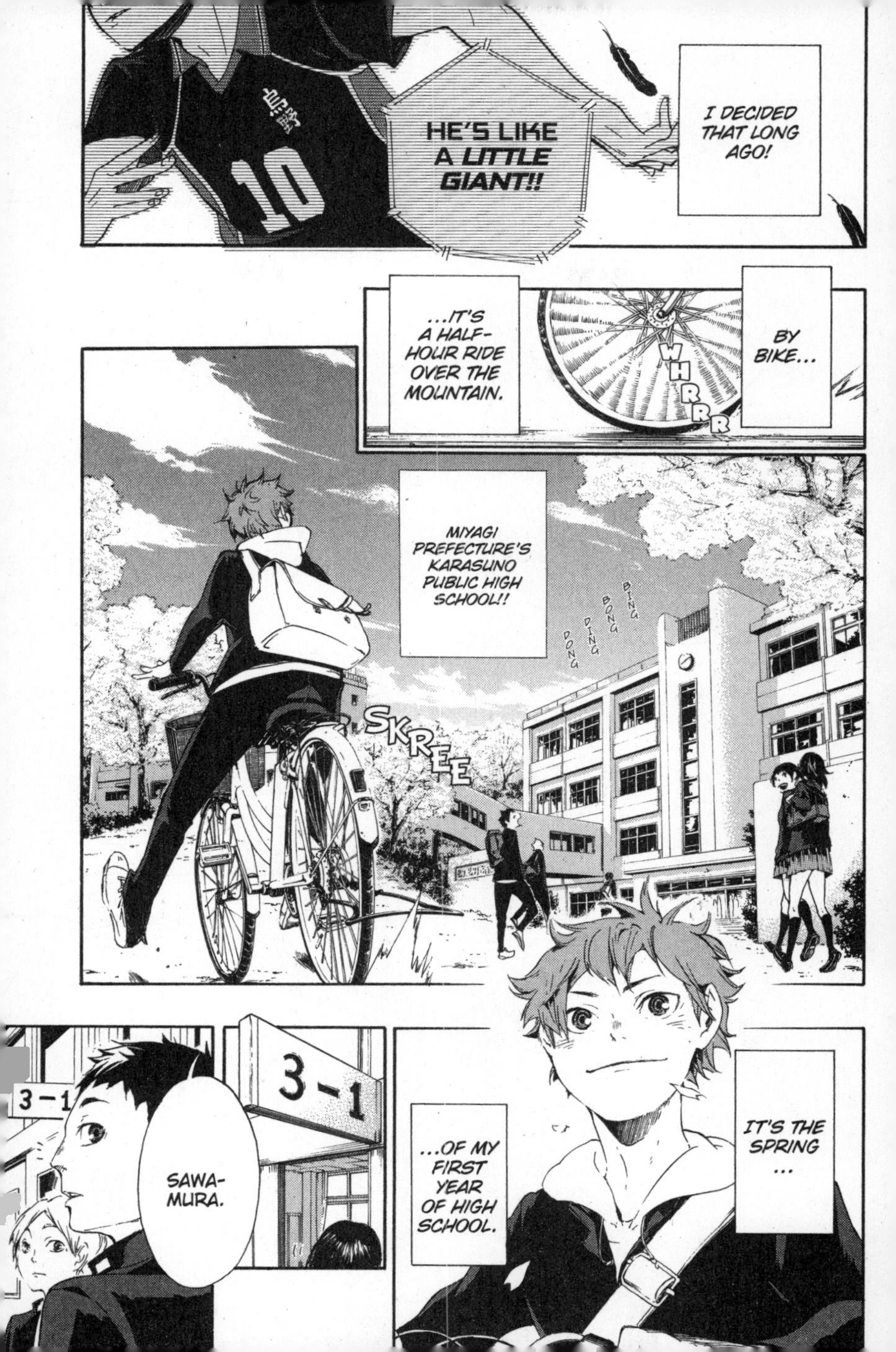
I DECIDED THAT LONG AGO!
HE'S LIKE A *LITTLE GIANT!!*
BY BIKE...
WHRRR
...IT'S A HALF-HOUR RIDE OVER THE MOUNTAIN.
MIYAGI PREFECTURE'S KARASUNO PUBLIC HIGH SCHOOL!!
BING
BONG
DING
DONG
SKREEE
IT'S THE SPRING ...
...OF MY FIRST YEAR OF HIGH SCHOOL.
3-1
SAWA-MURA.
3-1

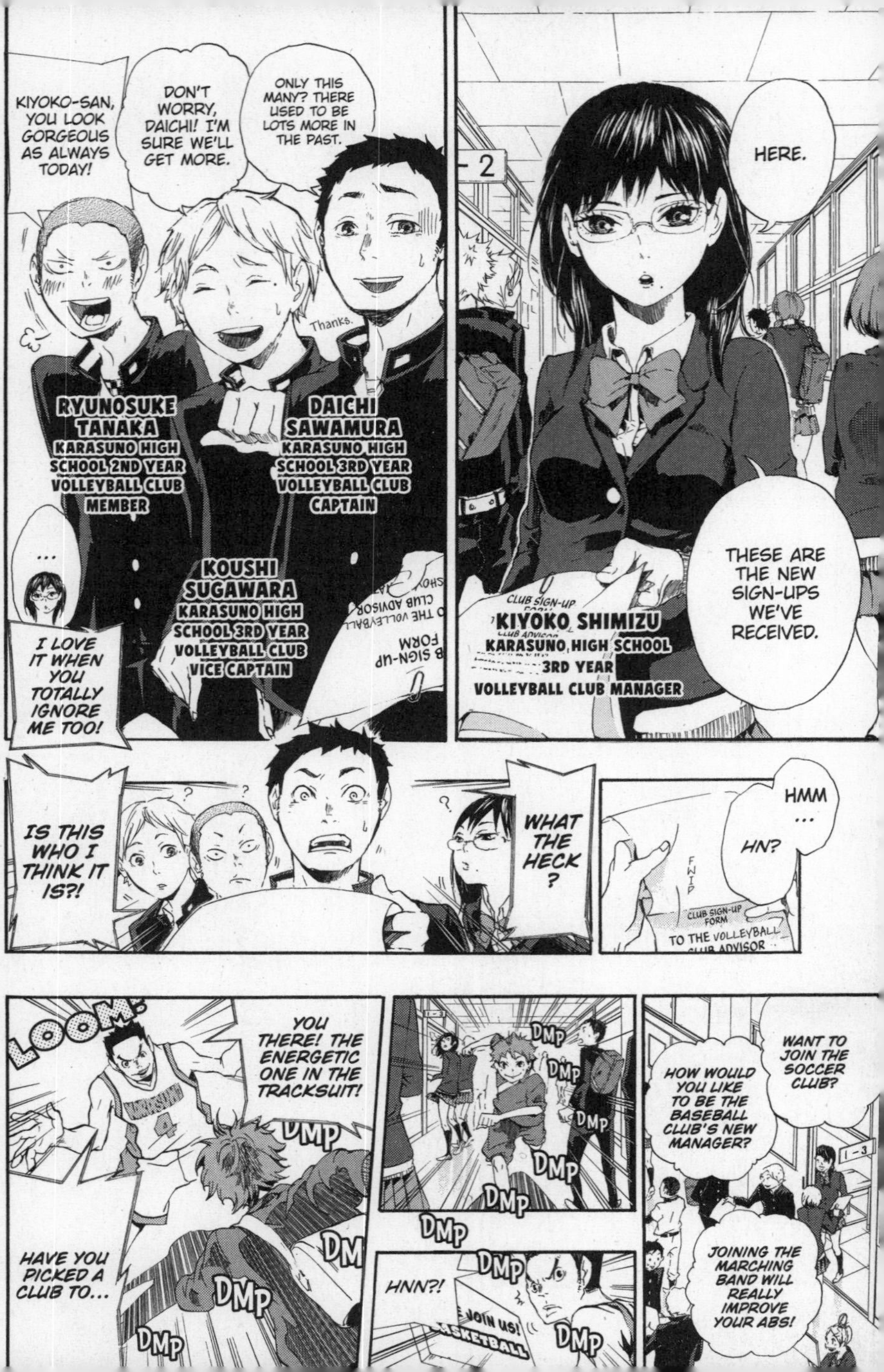
HERE.
THESE ARE THE NEW SIGN-UPS WE'VE RECEIVED.
CLUB SIGN-UP FORM
KIYOKO SHIMIZU KARASUNO HIGH SCHOOL 3RD YEAR VOLLEYBALL CLUB MANAGER
ONLY THIS MANY? THERE USED TO BE LOTS MORE IN THE PAST.
DAICHI SAWAMURA KARASUNO HIGH SCHOOL 3RD YEAR VOLLEYBALL CLUB CAPTAIN
DON'T WORRY, DAICHI! I'M SURE WE'LL GET MORE.
Thanks.
KOUSHI SUGAWARA KARASUNO HIGH SCHOOL 3RD YEAR VOLLEYBALL CLUB VICE CAPTAIN
KIYOKO-SAN, YOU LOOK GORGEOUS AS ALWAYS TODAY!
RYUNOSUKE TANAKA KARASUNO HIGH SCHOOL 2ND YEAR VOLLEYBALL CLUB MEMBER
...
I LOVE IT WHEN YOU TOTALLY IGNORE ME TOO!
HMM ...
HN?
FWIP
CLUB SIGN-UP FORM
TO THE VOLLEYBALL CLUB ADVISOR
WHAT THE HECK?
IS THIS WHO I THINK IT IS?!
WANT TO JOIN THE SOCCER CLUB?
HOW WOULD YOU LIKE TO BE THE BASEBALL CLUB'S NEW MANAGER?
JOINING THE MARCHING BAND WILL REALLY IMPROVE YOUR ABS!
DMP DMP DMP DMP DMP DMP
HNN?!
JOIN US!
DMP
LOOM!
YOU THERE! THE ENERGETIC ONE IN THE TRACKSUIT!
DMP
HAVE YOU PICKED A CLUB TO...
DMP DMP DMP

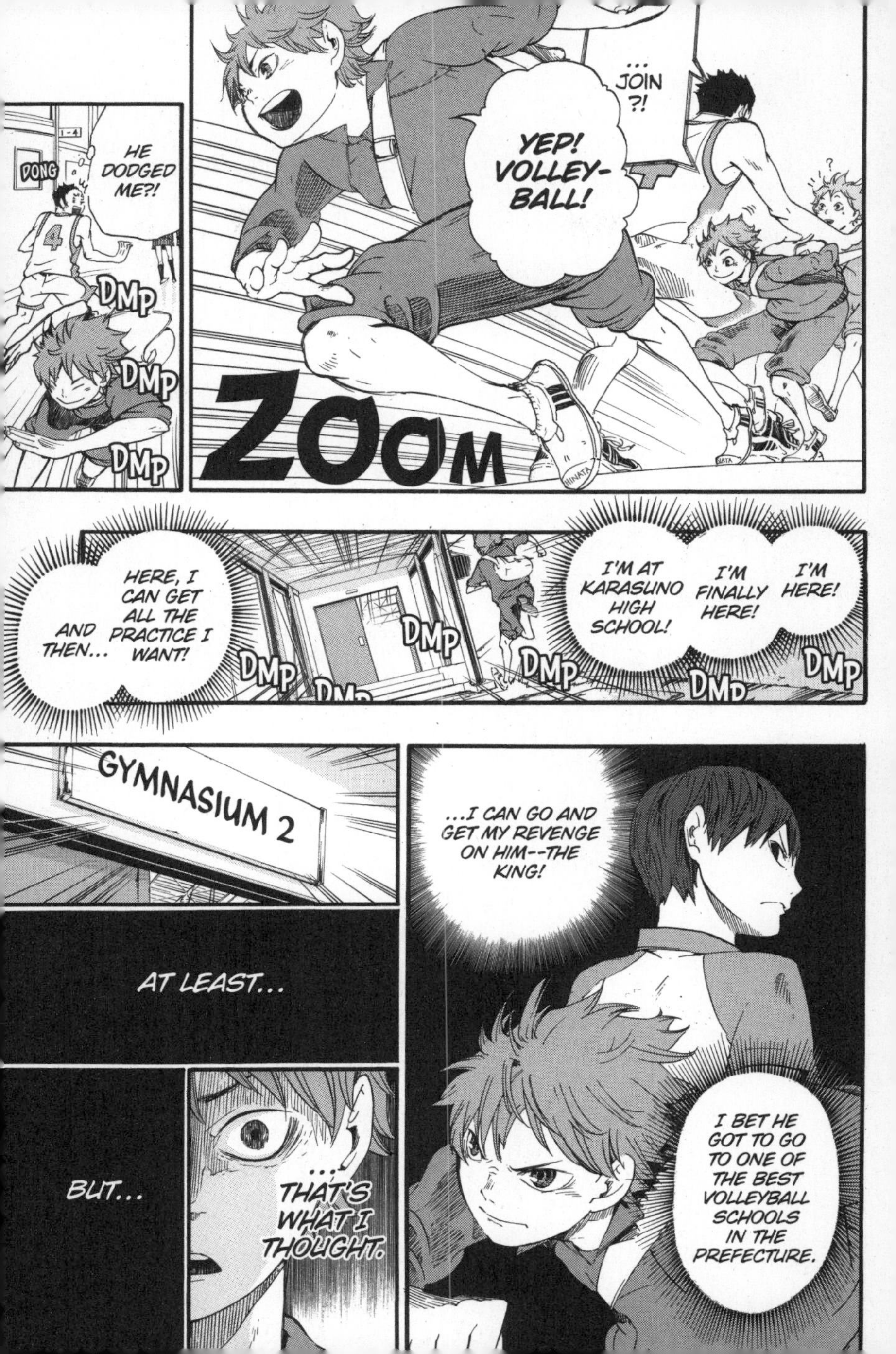
...JOIN?!
YEP! VOLLEY-BALL!
ZOOM
DONG
HE DODGED ME?!
DMP
DMP
DMP
I'M HERE!
I'M FINALLY HERE!
I'M AT KARASUNO HIGH SCHOOL!
HERE, I CAN GET ALL THE PRACTICE I WANT!
AND THEN...
DMP
DMP
DMP
DMP
...I CAN GO AND GET MY REVENGE ON HIM--THE KING!
I BET HE GOT TO GO TO ONE OF THE BEST VOLLEYBALL SCHOOLS IN THE PREFECTURE.
GYMNASIUM 2
AT LEAST...
BUT...
...THAT'S WHAT I THOUGHT.

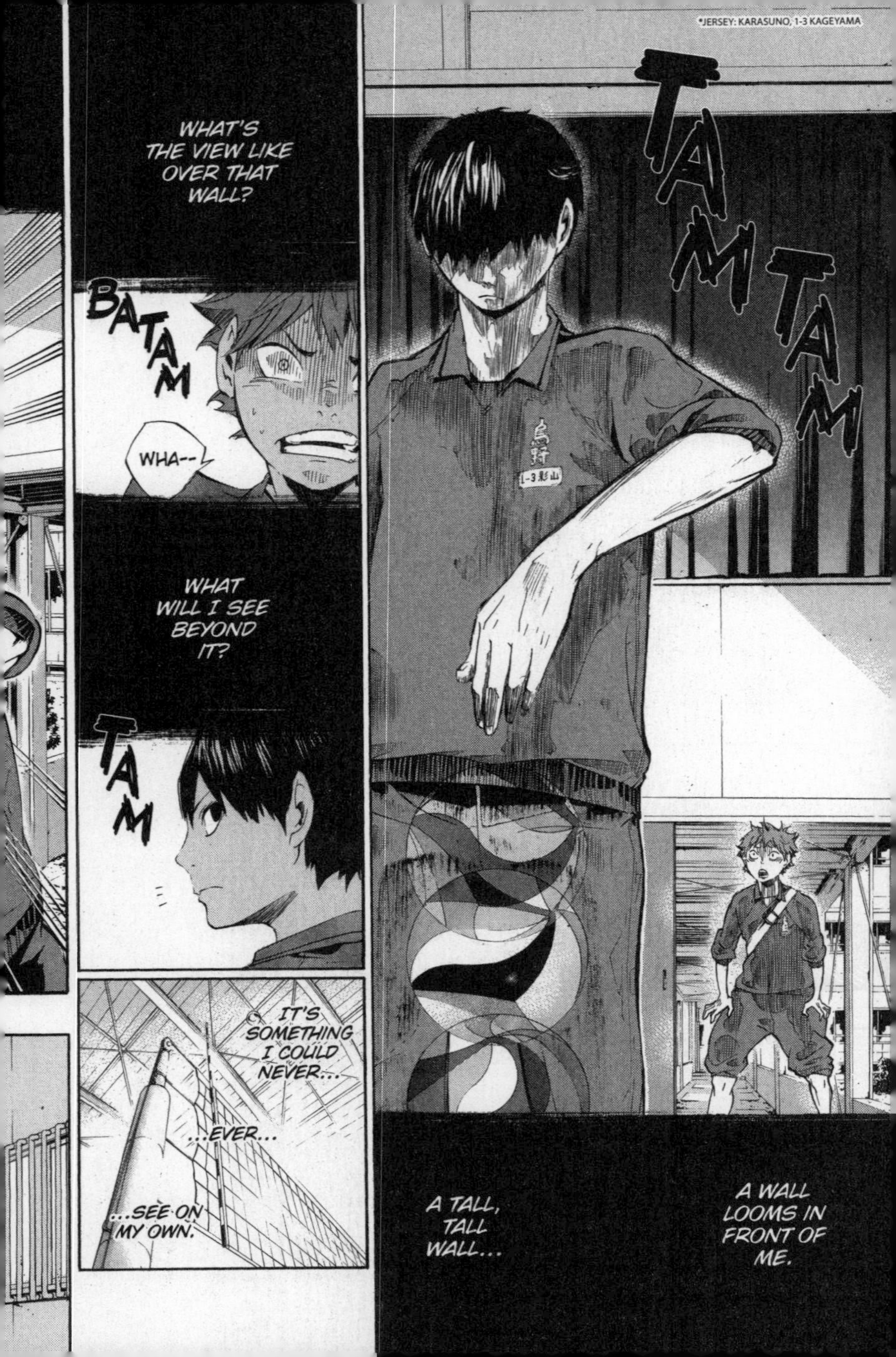
*JERSEY: KARASUNO, 1-3 KAGEYAMA
TAM TAM TAM
A WALL LOOMS IN FRONT OF ME.
A TALL, TALL WALL...
WHAT'S THE VIEW LIKE OVER THAT WALL?
BATAM
WHA--
WHAT WILL I SEE BEYOND IT?
TAM
IT'S SOMETHING I COULD NEVER...
...EVER...
...SEE ON MY OWN.

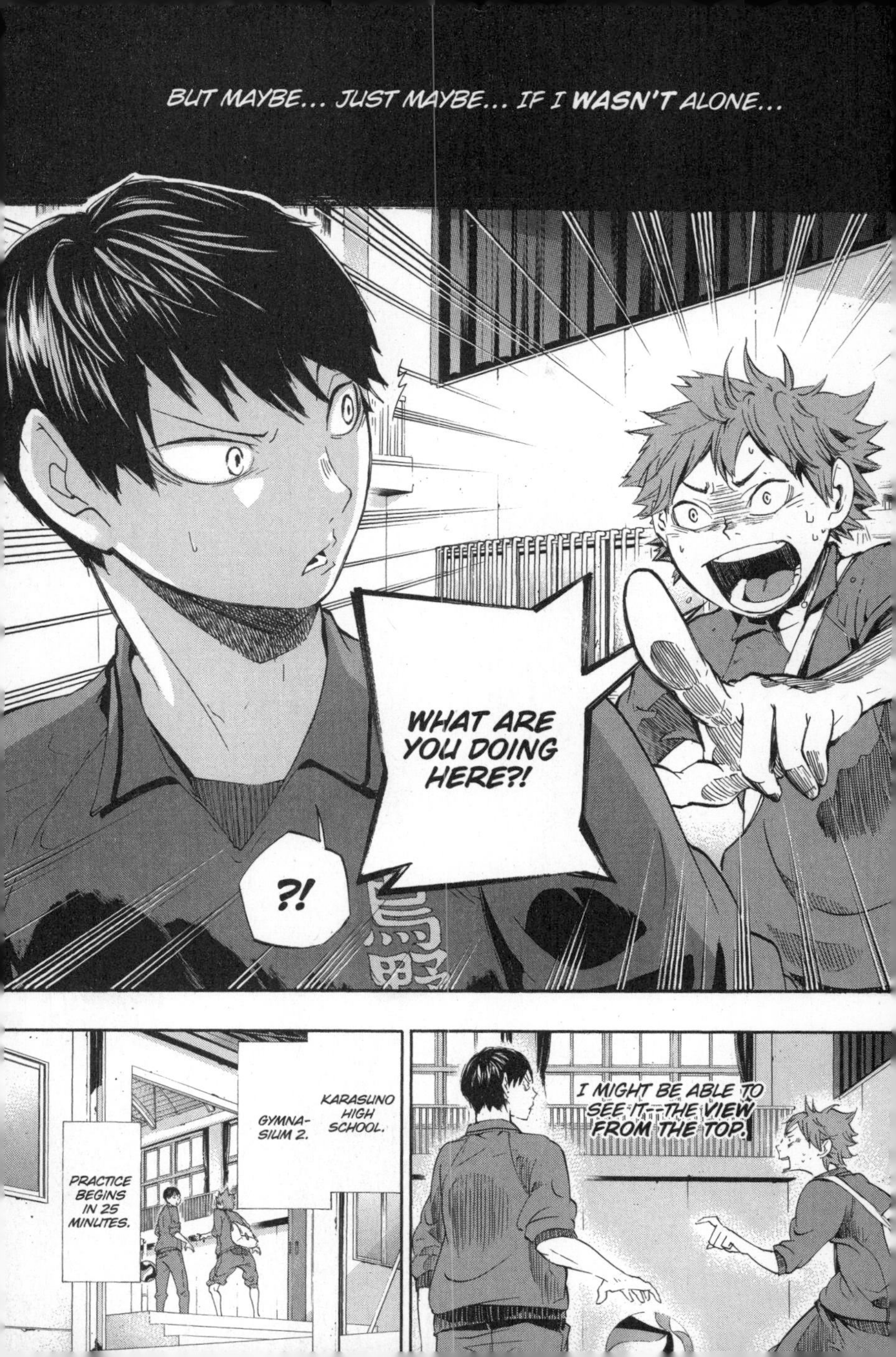
BUT MAYBE... JUST MAYBE... IF I WASN'T ALONE...
WHAT ARE YOU DOING HERE?!
?!
I MIGHT BE ABLE TO SEE IT--THE VIEW FROM THE TOP.
KARASUNO HIGH SCHOOL.
GYMNASIUM 2.
PRACTICE BEGINS IN 25 MINUTES.

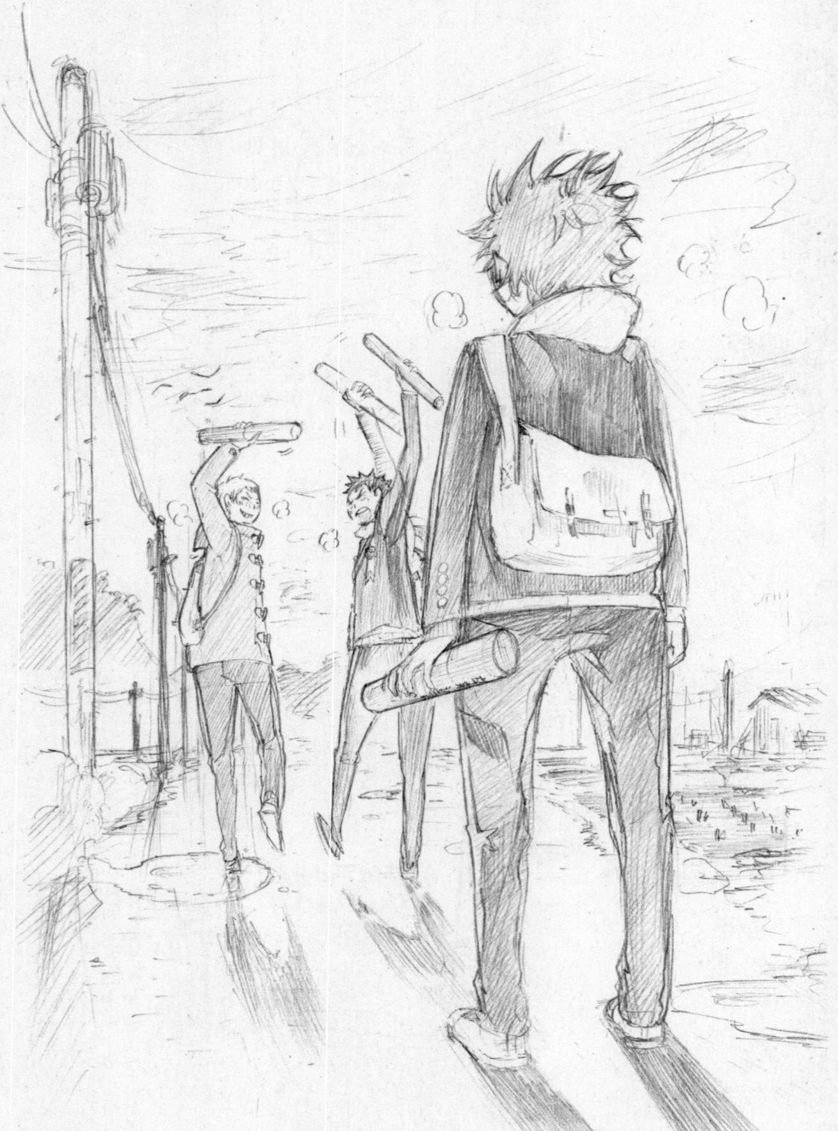

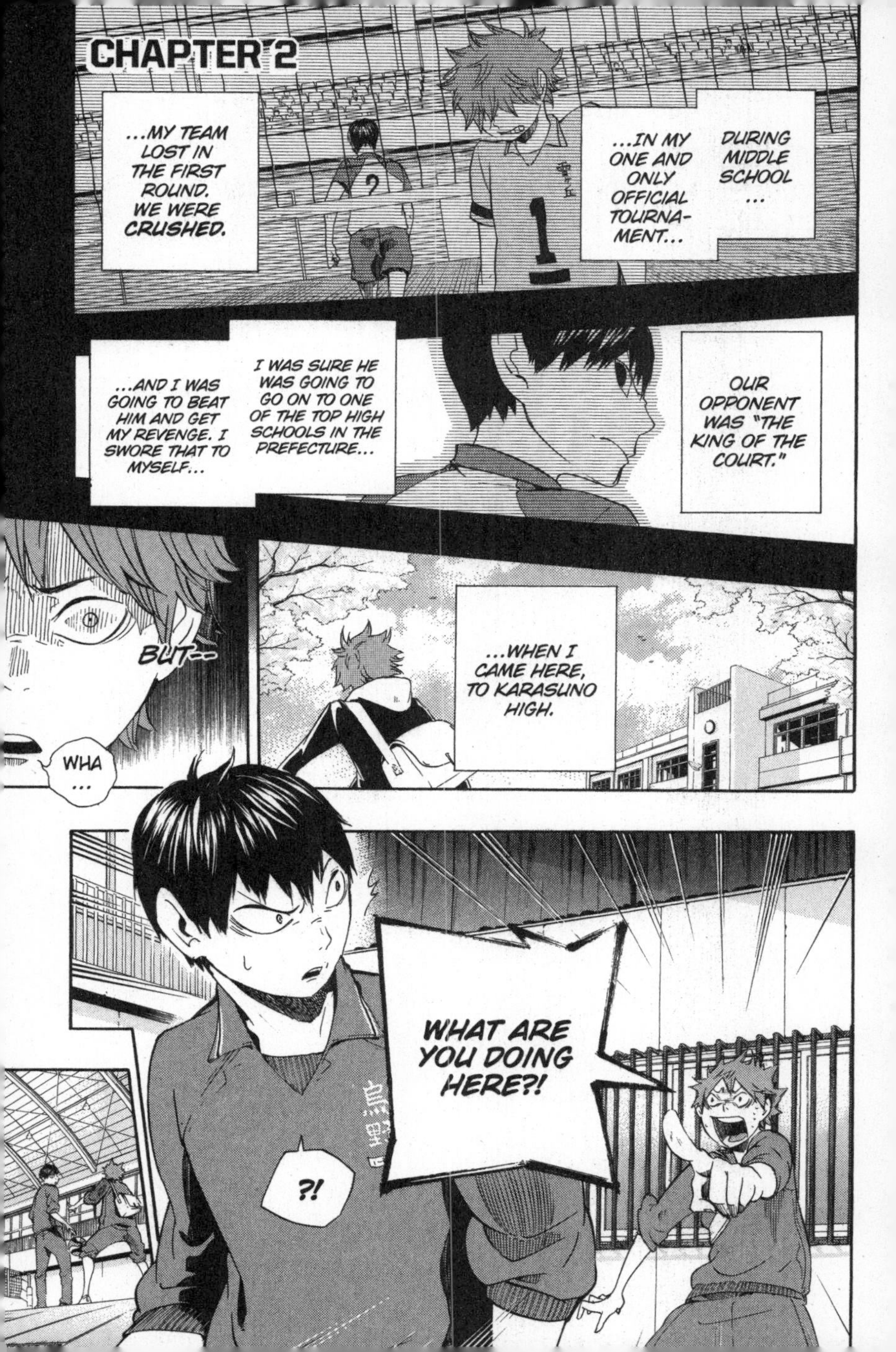
CHAPTER 2
DURING MIDDLE SCHOOL ...
...IN MY ONE AND ONLY OFFICIAL TOURNAMENT...
...MY TEAM LOST IN THE FIRST ROUND. WE WERE CRUSHED.
OUR OPPONENT WAS "THE KING OF THE COURT."
I WAS SURE HE WAS GOING TO GO ON TO ONE OF THE TOP HIGH SCHOOLS IN THE PREFECTURE...
...AND I WAS GOING TO BEAT HIM AND GET MY REVENGE. I SWORE THAT TO MYSELF...
...WHEN I CAME HERE, TO KARASUNO HIGH.
BUT--
WHA ...
WHAT ARE YOU DOING HERE?!
?!

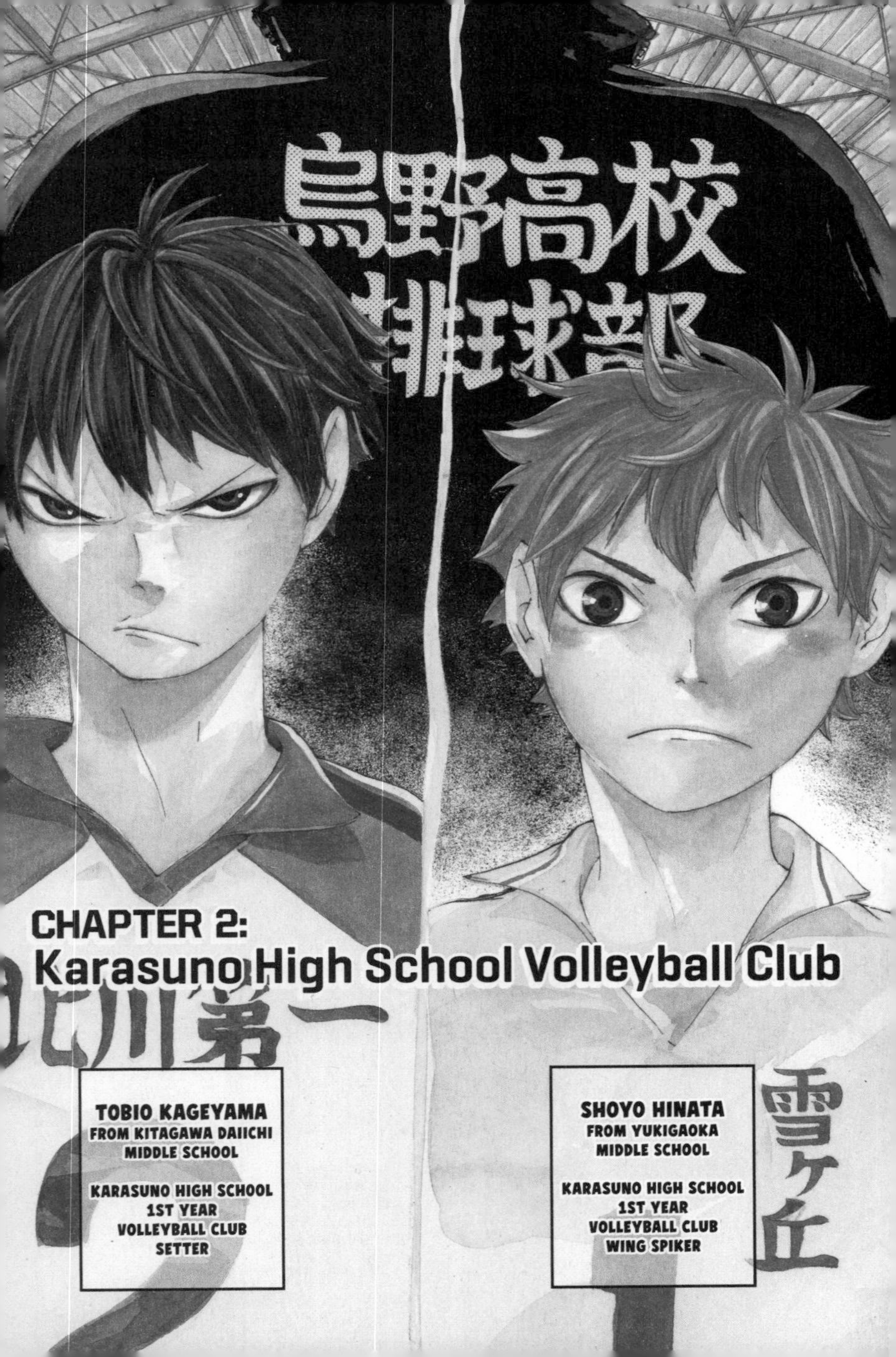
烏野高校
排球部
CHAPTER 2:
Karasuno High School Volleyball Club
雪ケ丘
SHOYO HINATA
FROM YUKIGAOKA
MIDDLE SCHOOL
KARASUNO HIGH SCHOOL
1ST YEAR
VOLLEYBALL CLUB
WING SPIKER
北川第一
TOBIO KAGEYAMA
FROM KITAGAWA DAIICHI
MIDDLE SCHOOL
KARASUNO HIGH SCHOOL
1ST YEAR
VOLLEYBALL CLUB
SETTER

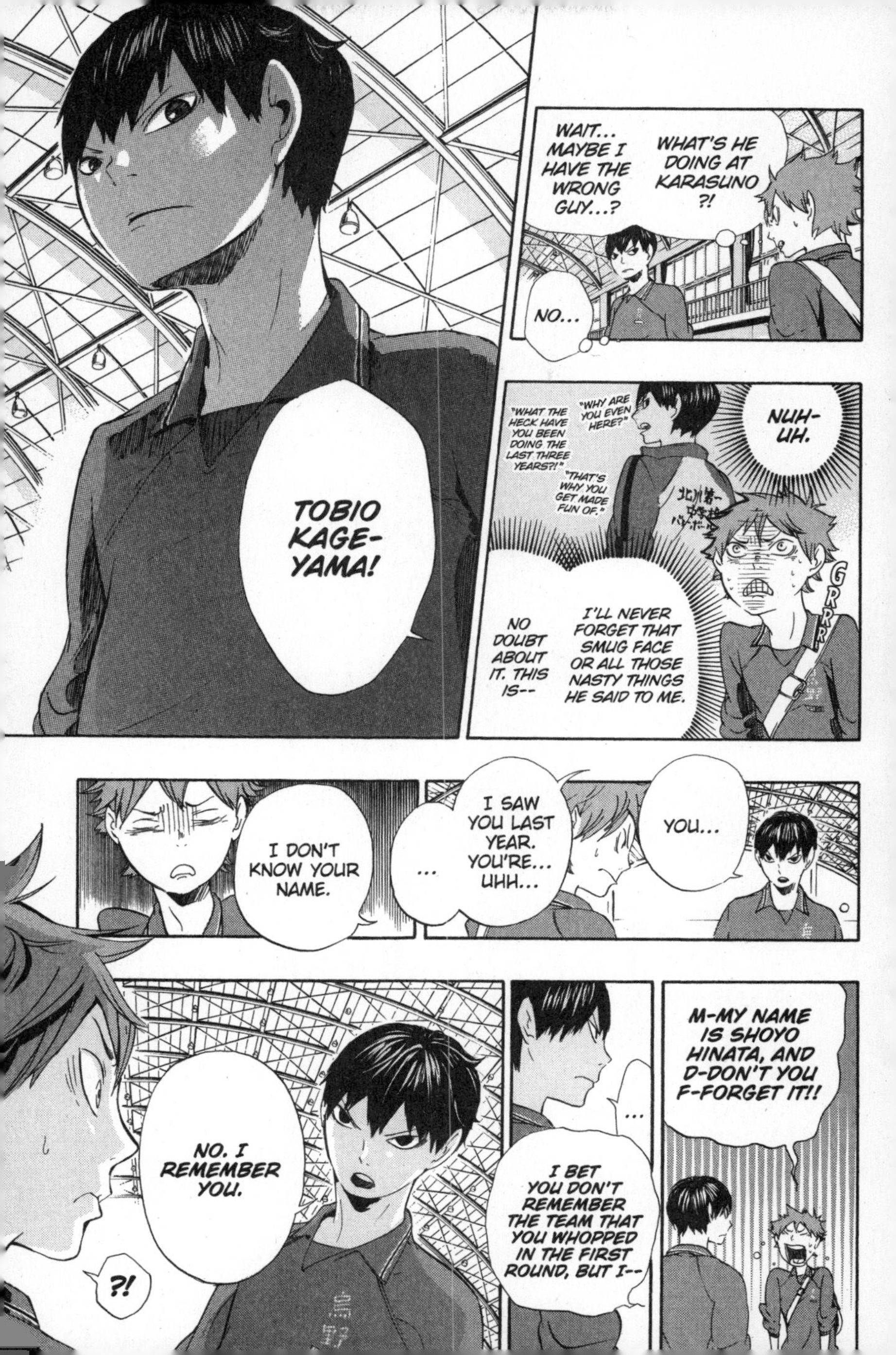
WHAT'S HE DOING AT KARASUNO?!
WAIT... MAYBE I HAVE THE WRONG GUY...?
NO...
NUH-UH.
"WHY ARE YOU EVEN HERE?"
"WHAT THE HECK HAVE YOU BEEN DOING THE LAST THREE YEARS?!"
"THAT'S WHY YOU GET MADE FUN OF."
GRRR
I'LL NEVER FORGET THAT SMUG FACE OR ALL THOSE NASTY THINGS HE SAID TO ME.
NO DOUBT ABOUT IT. THIS IS--
TOBIO KAGE-YAMA!
YOU...
I SAW YOU LAST YEAR. YOU'RE... UHH...
...
I DON'T KNOW YOUR NAME.
M-MY NAME IS SHOYO HINATA, AND D-DON'T YOU F-FORGET IT!!
...
I BET YOU DON'T REMEMBER THE TEAM THAT YOU WHOPPED IN THE FIRST ROUND, BUT I--
NO. I REMEMBER YOU.
?!

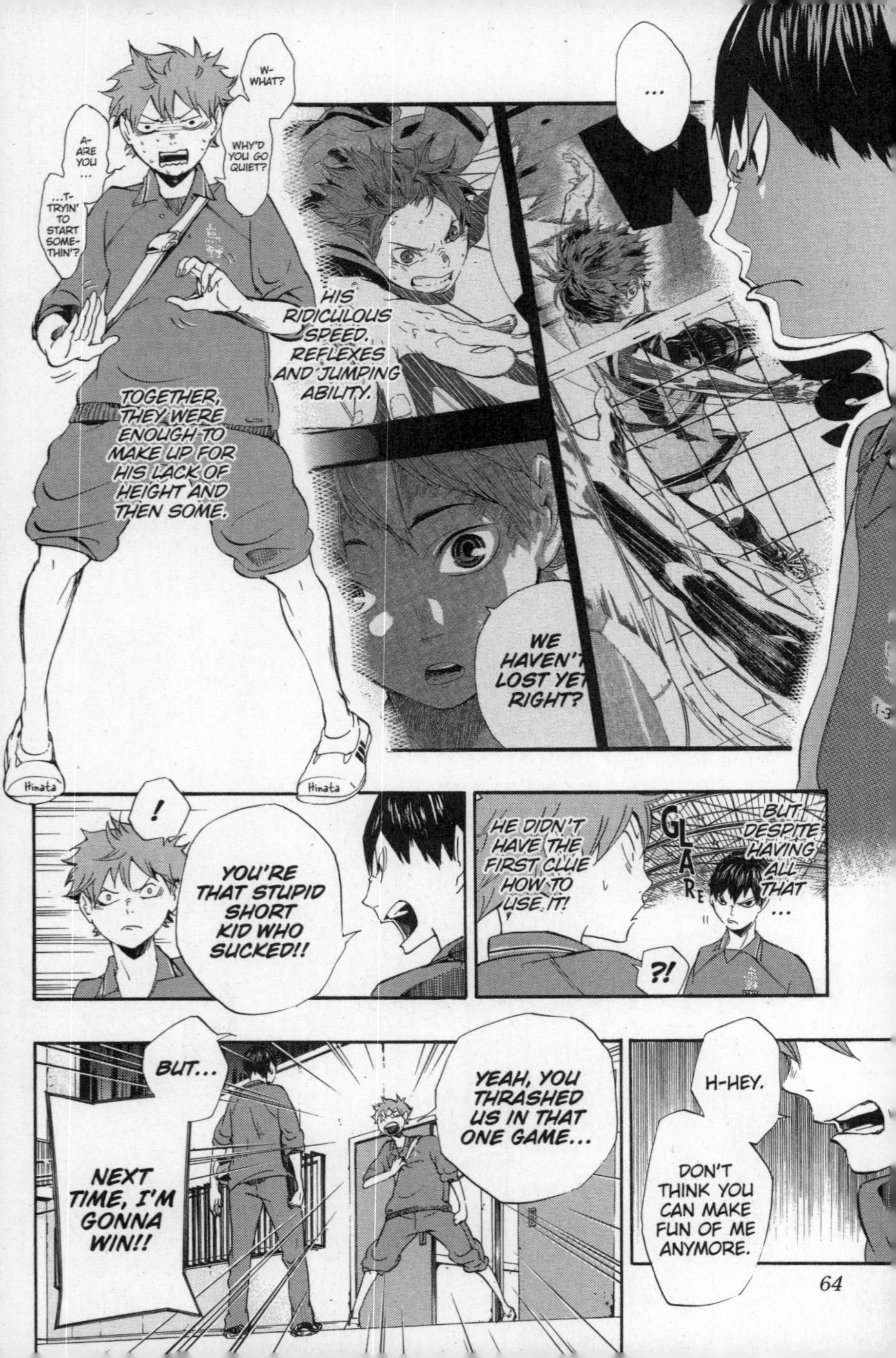

...
HIS RIDICULOUS SPEED, REFLEXES AND JUMPING ABILITY.
WE HAVEN'T LOST YET, RIGHT?
W-WHAT?
WHY'D YOU GO QUIET?
A-ARE YOU...
...T-TRYIN' TO START SOME-THIN'?
TOGETHER, THEY WERE ENOUGH TO MAKE UP FOR HIS LACK OF HEIGHT AND THEN SOME.
Hinata
Hinata
BUT DESPITE HAVING ALL THAT...
GLARE
HE DIDN'T HAVE THE FIRST CLUE HOW TO USE IT!
?!
!
YOU'RE THAT STUPID SHORT KID WHO SUCKED!!
H-HEY.
DON'T THINK YOU CAN MAKE FUN OF ME ANYMORE.
YEAH, YOU THRASHED US IN THAT ONE GAME...
BUT...
NEXT TIME, I'M GONNA WIN!!

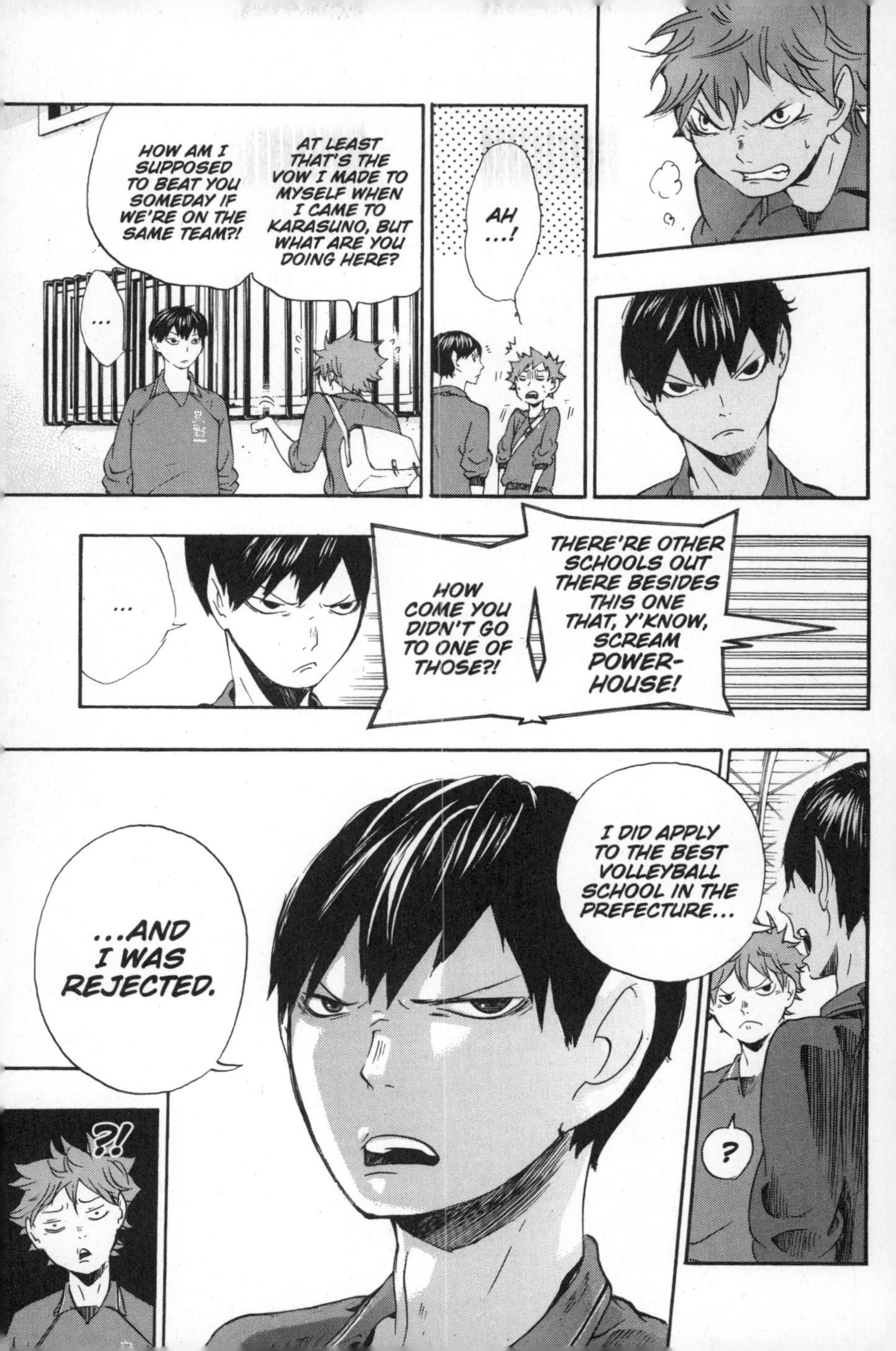
AH ...!
AT LEAST THAT'S THE VOW I MADE TO MYSELF WHEN I CAME TO KARASUNO, BUT WHAT ARE YOU DOING HERE?
HOW AM I SUPPOSED TO BEAT YOU SOMEDAY IF WE'RE ON THE SAME TEAM?!
...
THERE'RE OTHER SCHOOLS OUT THERE BESIDES THIS ONE THAT, Y'KNOW, SCREAM POWER-HOUSE!
HOW COME YOU DIDN'T GO TO ONE OF THOSE?!
...
I DID APPLY TO THE BEST VOLLEYBALL SCHOOL IN THE PREFECTURE...
?
...AND I WAS REJECTED.
?!

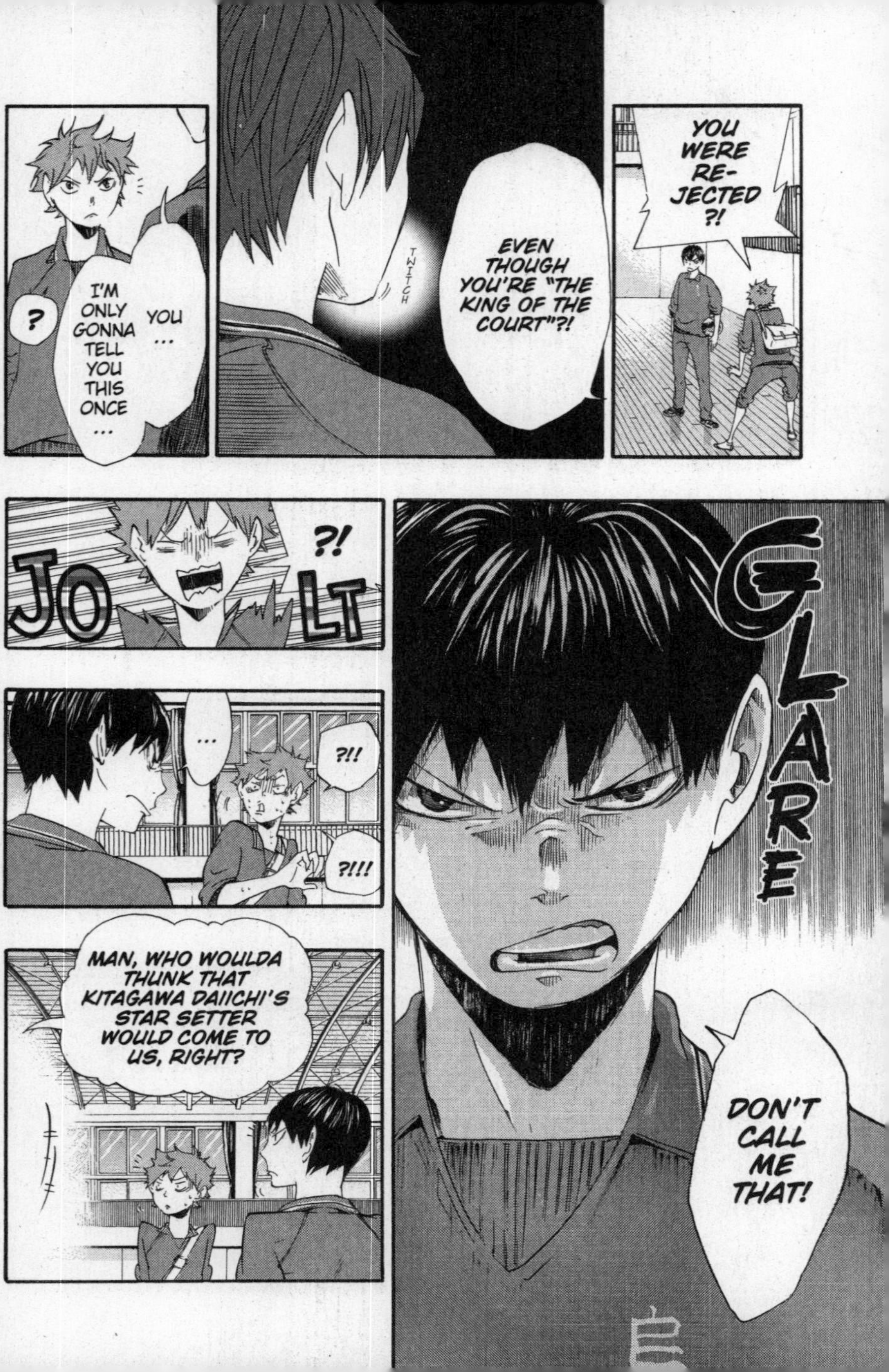
YOU WERE RE-JECTED ?!
EVEN THOUGH YOU'RE "THE KING OF THE COURT"?!
TWITCH
YOU ...
I'M ONLY GONNA TELL YOU THIS ONCE ...
?
GLARE
DON'T CALL ME THAT!
?!
JOLT
...
?!!
?!!!
MAN, WHO WOULDA THUNK THAT KITAGAWA DAIICHI'S STAR SETTER WOULD COME TO US, RIGHT?

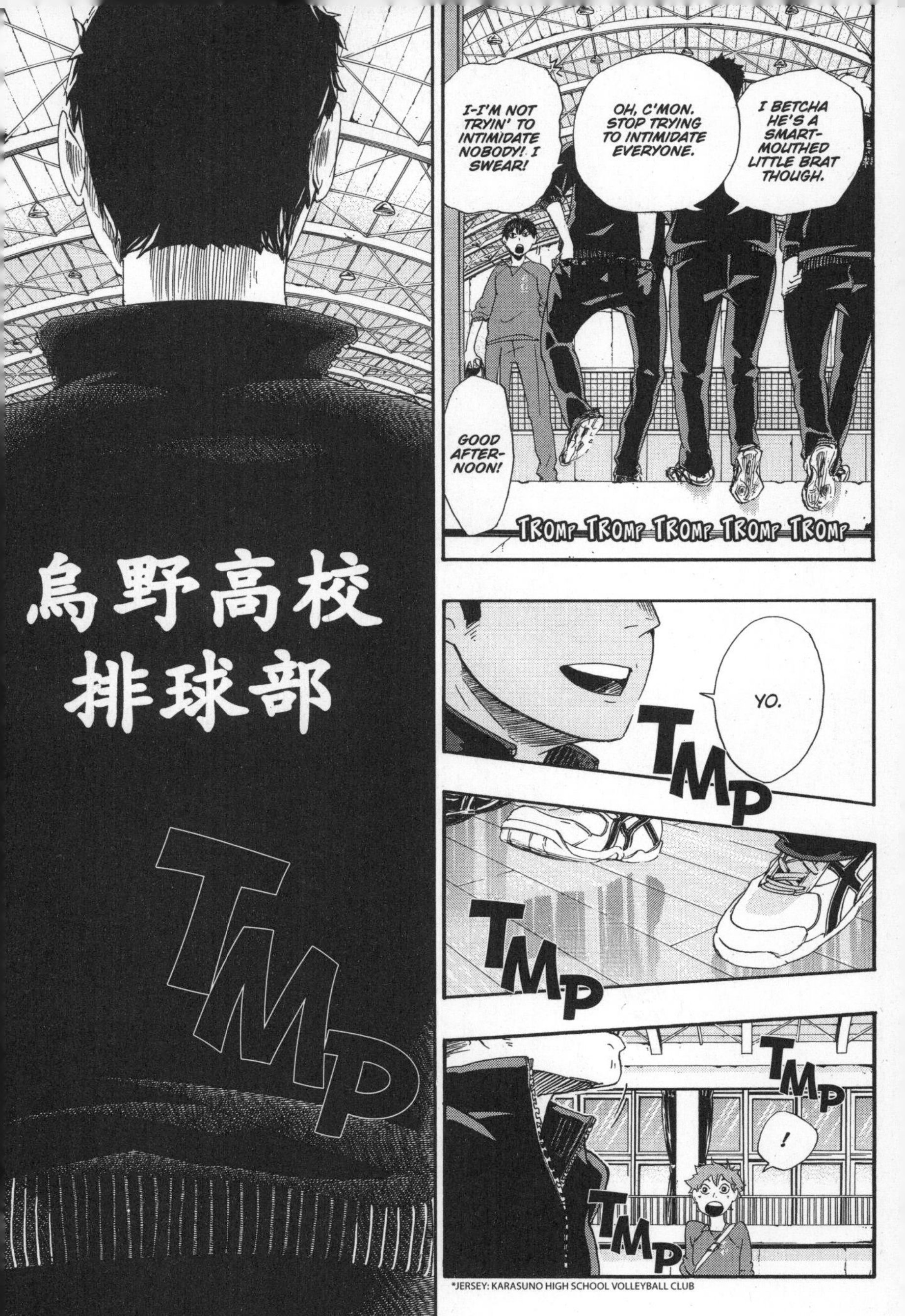
I BETCHA HE'S A SMART-MOUTHED LITTLE BRAT THOUGH.
OH, C'MON. STOP TRYING TO INTIMIDATE EVERYONE.
I-I'M NOT TRYIN' TO INTIMIDATE NOBODY!! I SWEAR!
GOOD AFTER-NOON!
TROMP TROMP TROMP TROMP TROMP
YO.
TMP
TMP
TMP
!
TMP
鳥野高校
排球部
TMP

*JERSEY: KARASUNO HIGH SCHOOL VOLLEYBALL CLUB

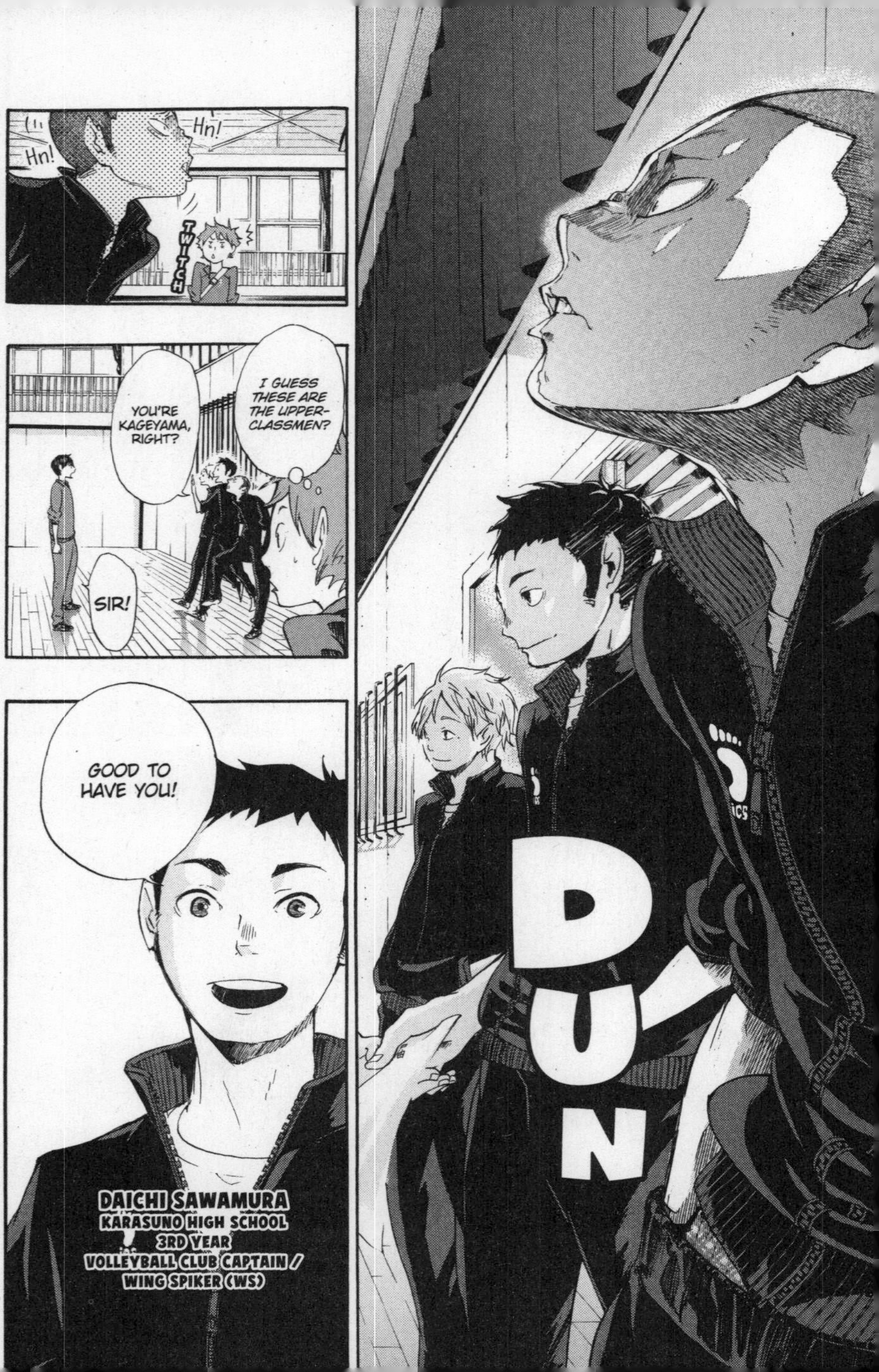
DUN
Hn!
Hn!
TWITCH
I GUESS THESE ARE THE UPPER-CLASSMEN?
YOU'RE KAGEYAMA, RIGHT?
SIR!
GOOD TO HAVE YOU!
DAICHI SAWAMURA
KARASUNO HIGH SCHOOL
3RD YEAR
VOLLEYBALL CLUB CAPTAIN / WING SPIKER (WS)

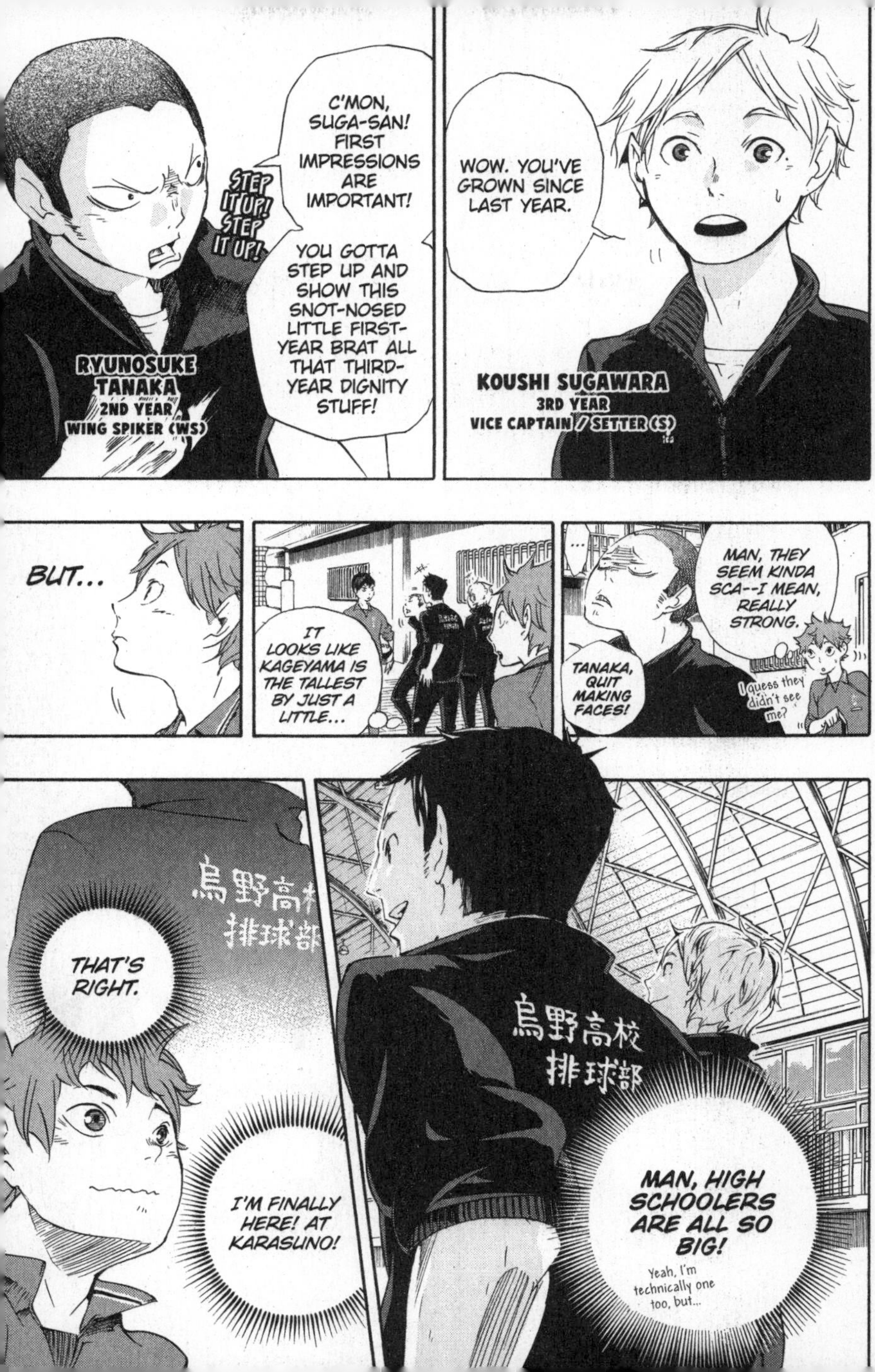
WOW. YOU'VE GROWN SINCE LAST YEAR.
KOUSHI SUGAWARA
3RD YEAR
VICE CAPTAIN / SETTER (S)
C'MON, SUGA-SAN! FIRST IMPRESSIONS ARE IMPORTANT!
YOU GOTTA STEP UP AND SHOW THIS SNOT-NOSED LITTLE FIRST-YEAR BRAT ALL THAT THIRD-YEAR DIGNITY STUFF!
STEP IT UP! STEP IT UP!
RYUNOSUKE TANAKA
2ND YEAR
WING SPIKER (WS)
...
MAN, THEY SEEM KINDA SCA--I MEAN, REALLY STRONG.
TANAKA, QUIT MAKING FACES!
I guess they didn't see me?
IT LOOKS LIKE KAGEYAMA IS THE TALLEST BY JUST A LITTLE...
BUT...
烏野高校
排球部
MAN, HIGH SCHOOLERS ARE ALL SO BIG!
Yeah, I'm technically one too, but...
烏野高校
排球部
I'M FINALLY HERE! AT KARASUNO!
THAT'S RIGHT.

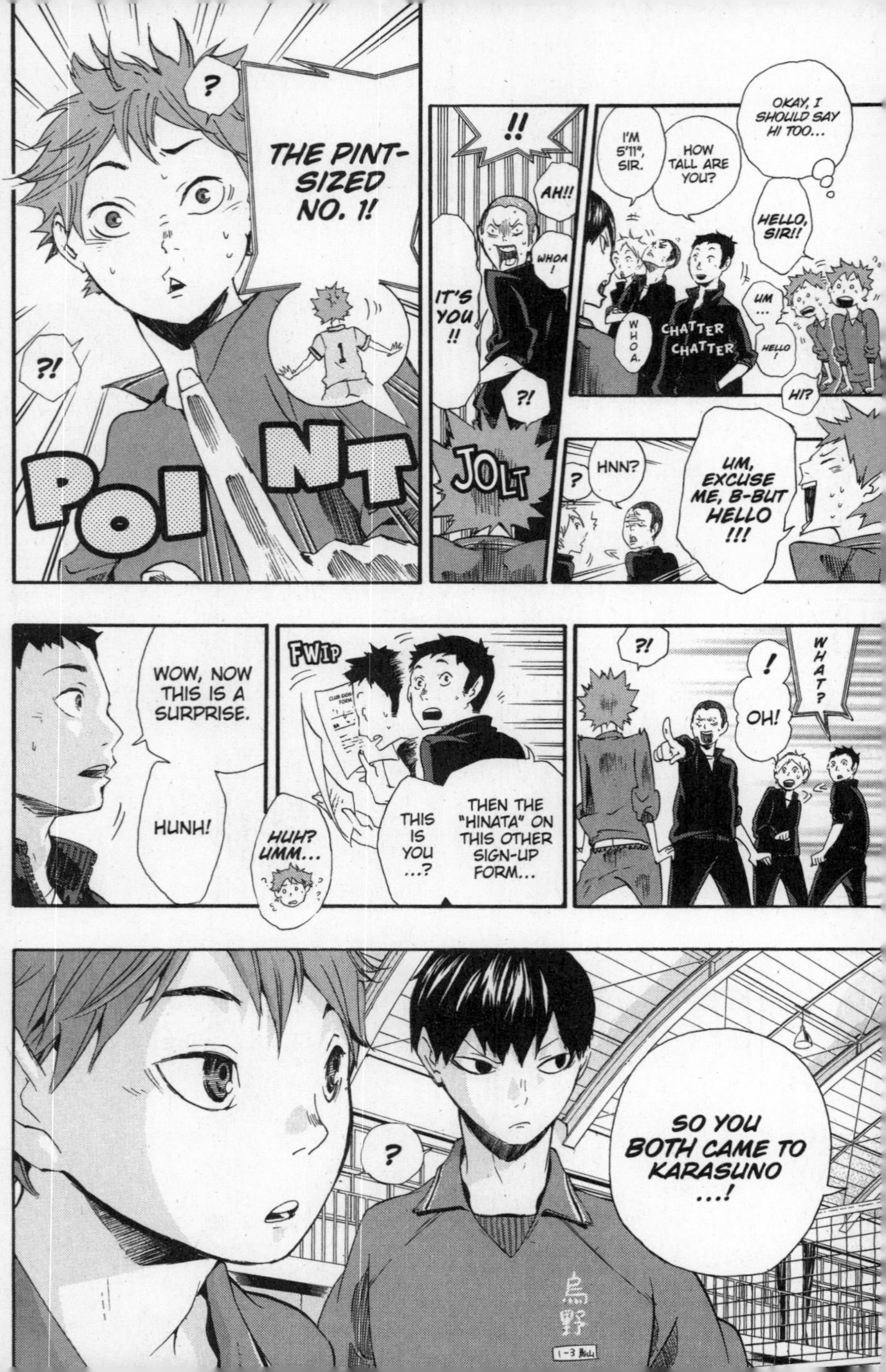
OKAY, I SHOULD SAY HI TOO...
HELLO, SIR!!
HOW TALL ARE YOU?
I'M 5'11", SIR.
UM ... HELLO!
HI?
CHATTER CHATTER
WHOA.
UM, EXCUSE ME, B-BUT HELLO!!!
HNN?
?
!!
AH!!
WHOA!
IT'S YOU!!
?!
JOLT
?
THE PINT-SIZED NO. 1!
?!
POINT
WHAT?
?!
!
OH!
FWIP
THEN THE "HINATA" ON THIS OTHER SIGN-UP FORM...
THIS IS YOU ...?
HUH? UMM...
WOW, NOW THIS IS A SURPRISE.
HUNH!
SO YOU BOTH CAME TO KARASUNO ...!
?
烏野

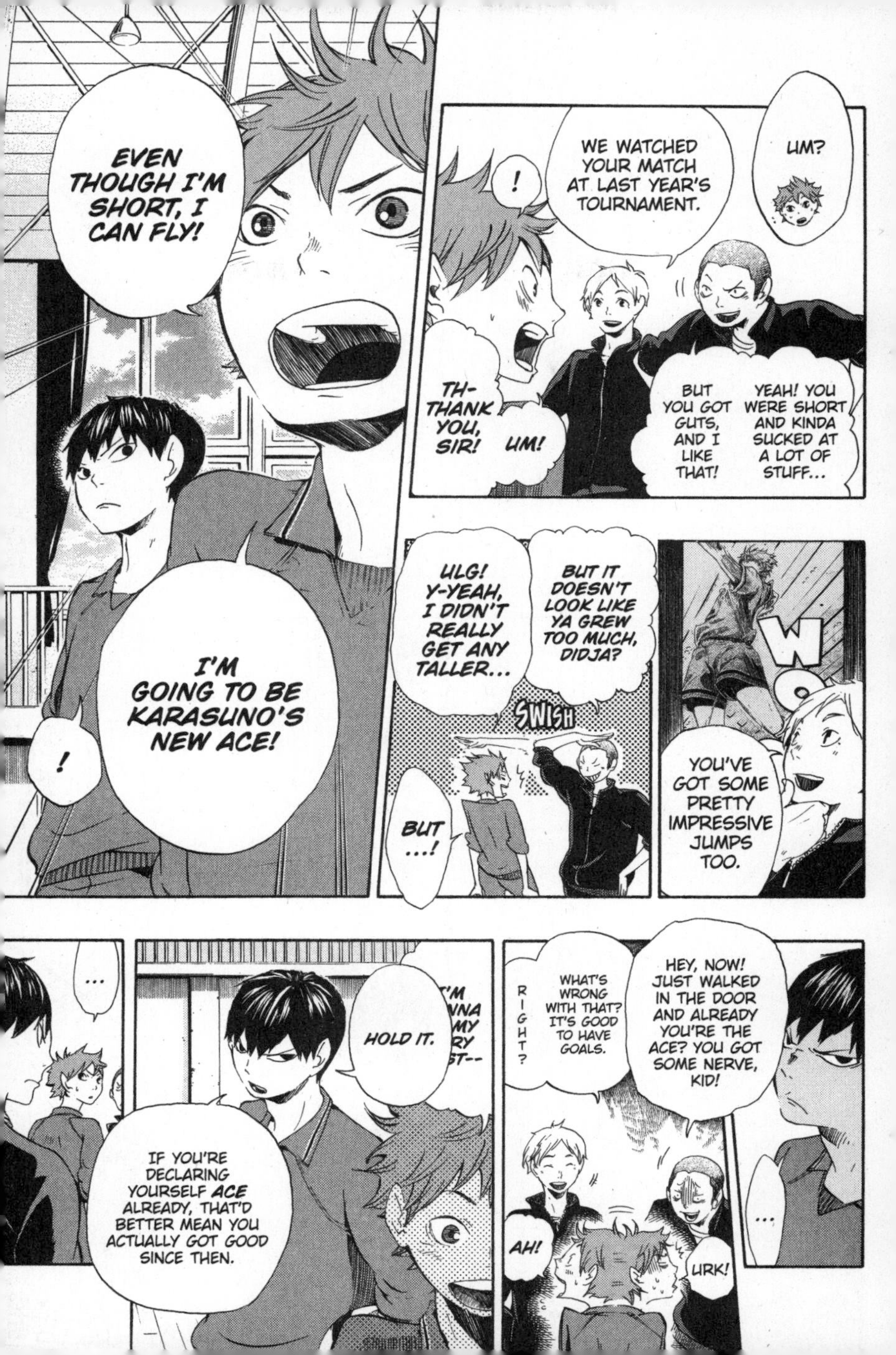
UM?
WE WATCHED YOUR MATCH AT LAST YEAR'S TOURNAMENT.
!
YEAH! YOU WERE SHORT AND KINDA SUCKED AT A LOT OF STUFF...
BUT YOU GOT GUTS, AND I LIKE THAT!
UM!
TH-THANK YOU, SIR!
YOU'VE GOT SOME PRETTY IMPRESSIVE JUMPS TOO.
BUT IT DOESN'T LOOK LIKE YA GREW TOO MUCH, DIDJA?
ULG! Y-YEAH, I DIDN'T REALLY GET ANY TALLER...
SWISH
BUT ...!
EVEN THOUGH I'M SHORT, I CAN FLY!
I'M GOING TO BE KARASUNO'S NEW ACE!
!
...
HEY, NOW! JUST WALKED IN THE DOOR AND ALREADY YOU'RE THE ACE? YOU GOT SOME NERVE, KID!
WHAT'S WRONG WITH THAT? IT'S GOOD TO HAVE GOALS.
RIGHT?
URK!
AH!
HOLD IT.
IF YOU'RE DECLARING YOURSELF ACE ALREADY, THAT'D BETTER MEAN YOU ACTUALLY GOT GOOD SINCE THEN.
...

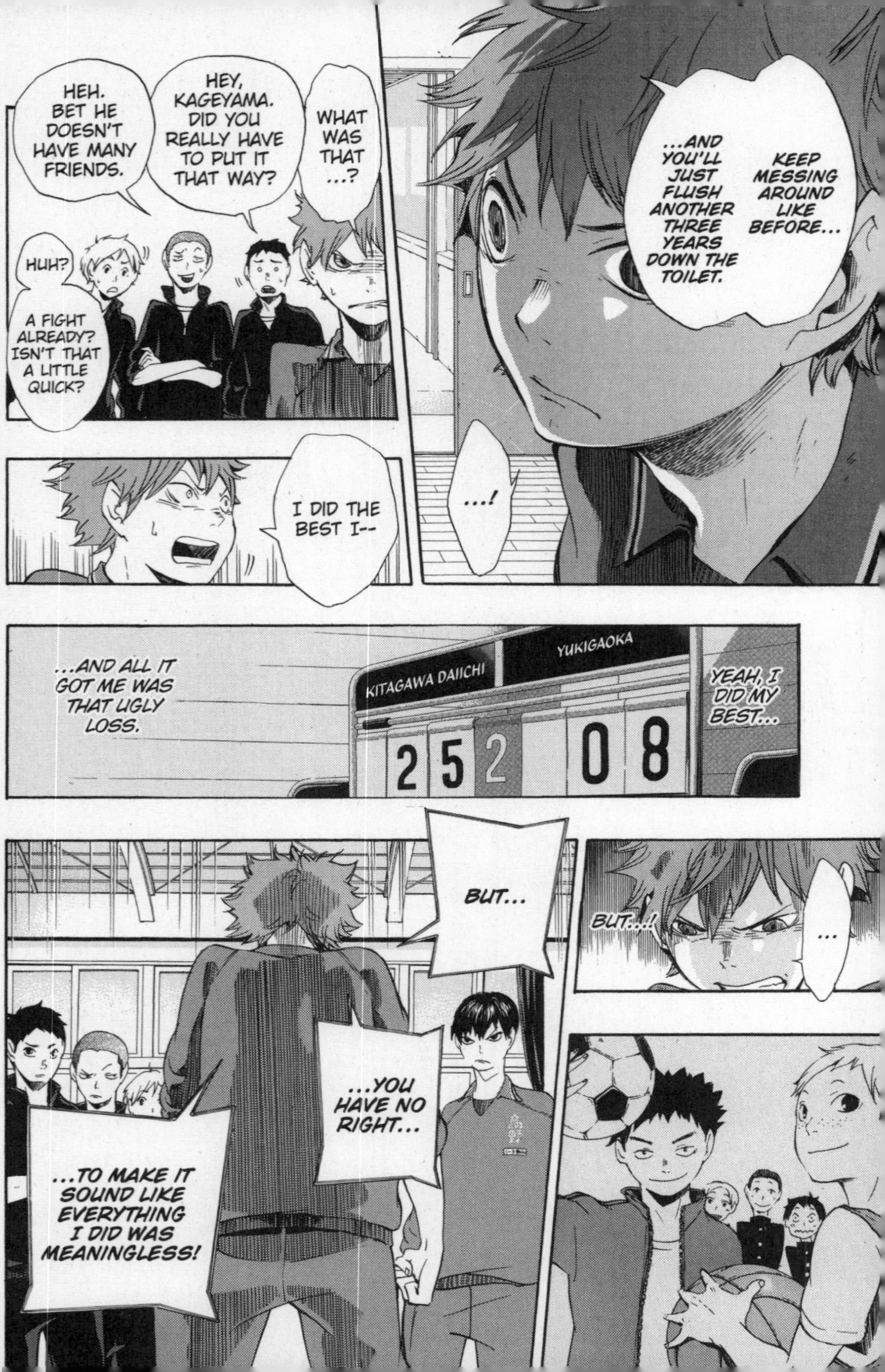
KEEP MESSING AROUND LIKE BEFORE...
...AND YOU'LL JUST FLUSH ANOTHER THREE YEARS DOWN THE TOILET.
...!
WHAT WAS THAT ...?
HEY, KAGEYAMA. DID YOU REALLY HAVE TO PUT IT THAT WAY?
HEH. BET HE DOESN'T HAVE MANY FRIENDS.
HUH?
A FIGHT ALREADY? ISN'T THAT A LITTLE QUICK?
I DID THE BEST I--
YEAH, I DID MY BEST...
YUKIGAOKA
KITAGAWA DAIICHI
25 2 08
...AND ALL IT GOT ME WAS THAT UGLY LOSS.
...
BUT...!
BUT...
...YOU HAVE NO RIGHT...
...TO MAKE IT SOUND LIKE EVERYTHING I DID WAS MEANINGLESS!

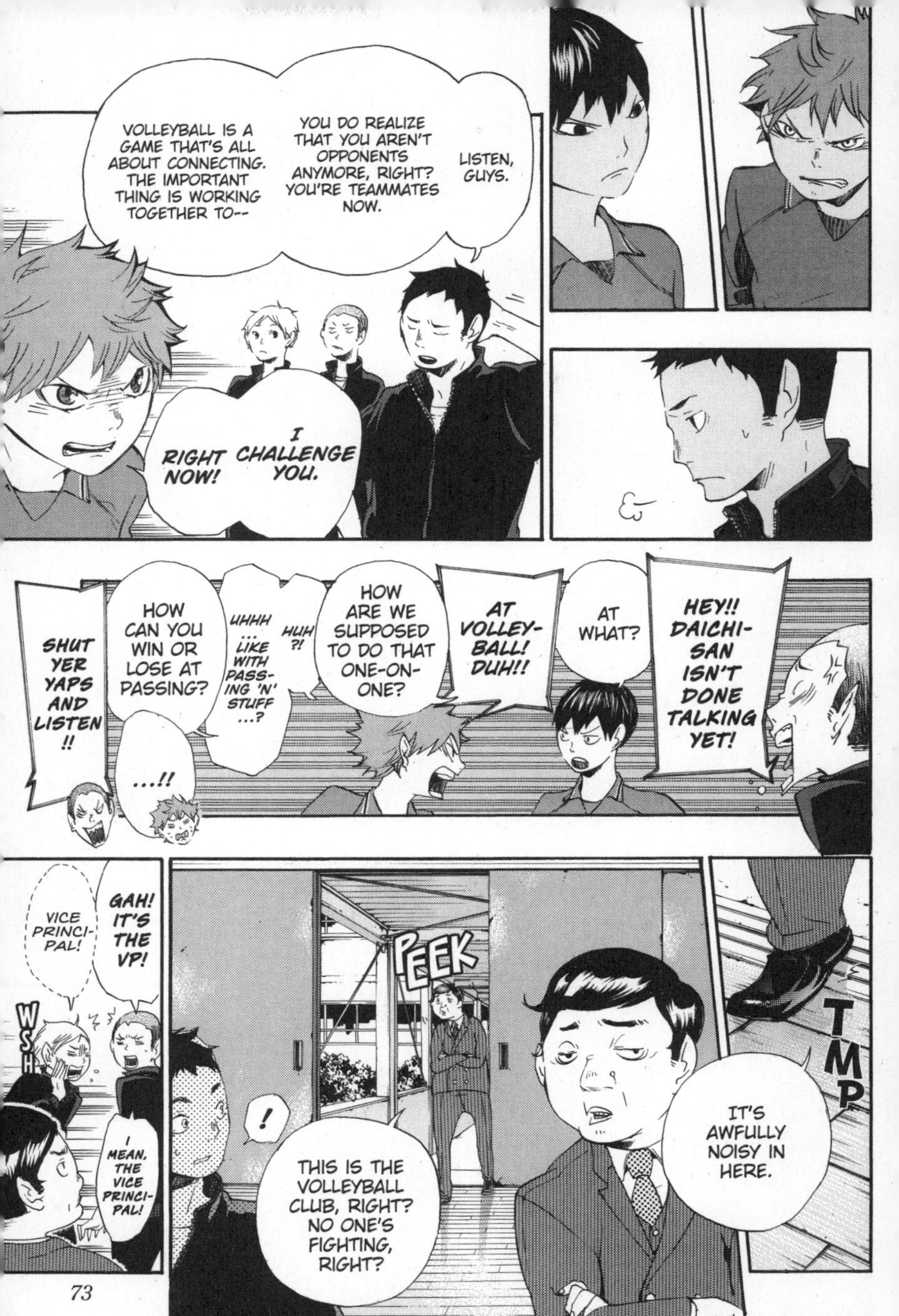

LISTEN, GUYS.
YOU DO REALIZE THAT YOU AREN'T OPPONENTS ANYMORE, RIGHT? YOU'RE TEAMMATES NOW.
VOLLEYBALL IS A GAME THAT'S ALL ABOUT CONNECTING. THE IMPORTANT THING IS WORKING TOGETHER TO--
I CHALLENGE YOU.
RIGHT NOW!
HEY!! DAICHI-SAN ISN'T DONE TALKING YET!
AT WHAT?
AT VOLLEY-BALL! DUH!!
HOW ARE WE SUPPOSED TO DO THAT ONE-ON-ONE?
HUH ?!
UHHH ... LIKE WITH PASS-ING 'N' STUFF ...?
HOW CAN YOU WIN OR LOSE AT PASSING?
...!!
SHUT YER YAPS AND LISTEN !!
TMP
IT'S AWFULLY NOISY IN HERE.
PEEK
!
THIS IS THE VOLLEYBALL CLUB, RIGHT? NO ONE'S FIGHTING, RIGHT?
GAH! IT'S THE VP!
VICE PRINCI-PAL!
WSH
I MEAN, THE VICE PRINCI-PAL!

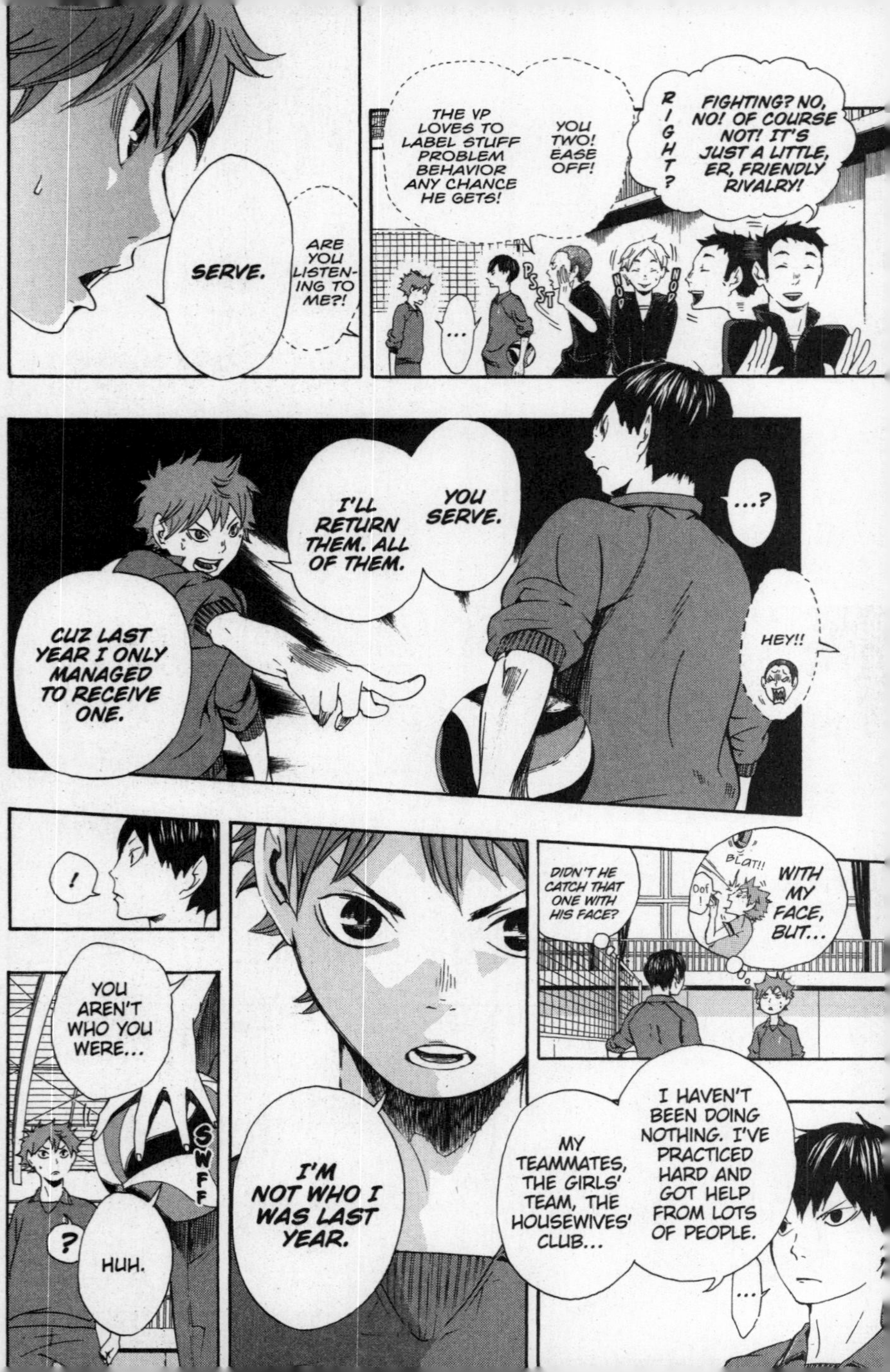
FIGHTING? NO, NO! OF COURSE NOT! IT'S JUST A LITTLE, ER, FRIENDLY RIVALRY!
RIGHT?
YOU TWO! EASE OFF!
THE VP LOVES TO LABEL STUFF PROBLEM BEHAVIOR ANY CHANCE HE GETS!
NOD NOD
PSST
...
ARE YOU LISTENING TO ME?!
SERVE.
...?
HEY!!
YOU SERVE.
I'LL RETURN THEM. ALL OF THEM.
CUZ LAST YEAR I ONLY MANAGED TO RECEIVE ONE.
WITH MY FACE, BUT...
BLAT!!
Oof!
DIDN'T HE CATCH THAT ONE WITH HIS FACE?
I HAVEN'T BEEN DOING NOTHING. I'VE PRACTICED HARD AND GOT HELP FROM LOTS OF PEOPLE.
MY TEAMMATES, THE GIRLS' TEAM, THE HOUSEWIVES' CLUB...
...
I'M NOT WHO I WAS LAST YEAR.
!
YOU AREN'T WHO YOU WERE...
SWFF
?
HUH.

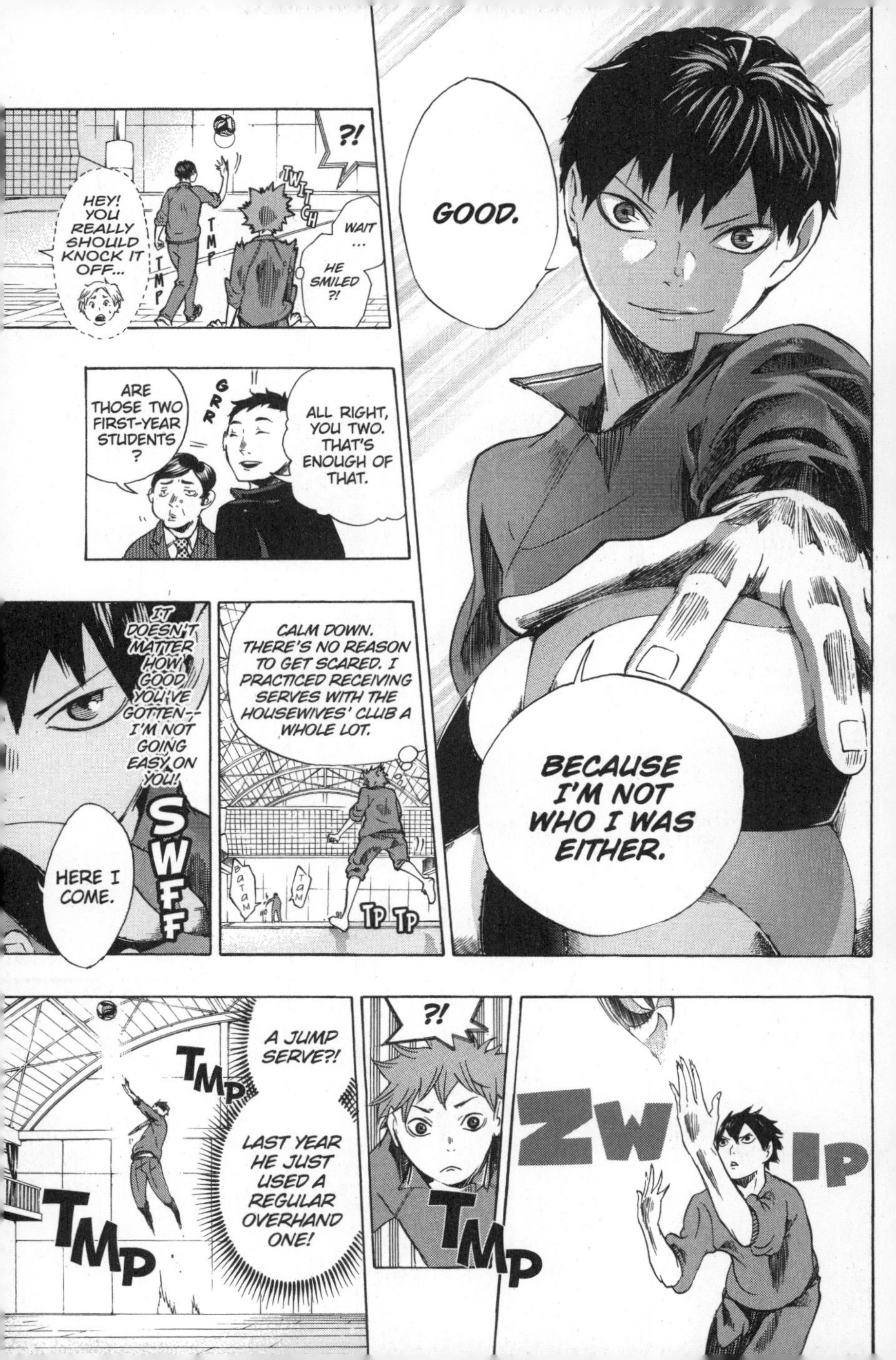
GOOD.
BECAUSE I'M NOT WHO I WAS EITHER.
?!
TWITCH
WAIT ... HE SMILED ?!
TMP TMP
HEY! YOU REALLY SHOULD KNOCK IT OFF...
ALL RIGHT, YOU TWO. THAT'S ENOUGH OF THAT.
GRR
ARE THOSE TWO FIRST-YEAR STUDENTS ?
CALM DOWN. THERE'S NO REASON TO GET SCARED. I PRACTICED RECEIVING SERVES WITH THE HOUSEWIVES' CLUB A WHOLE LOT.
TP TP
IT DOESN'T MATTER HOW GOOD YOU'VE GOTTEN--I'M NOT GOING EASY ON YOU!!
SWFF
HERE I COME.
ZWIP
?!
TMP
A JUMP SERVE?!
TMP
LAST YEAR HE JUST USED A REGULAR OVERHAND ONE!
TMP

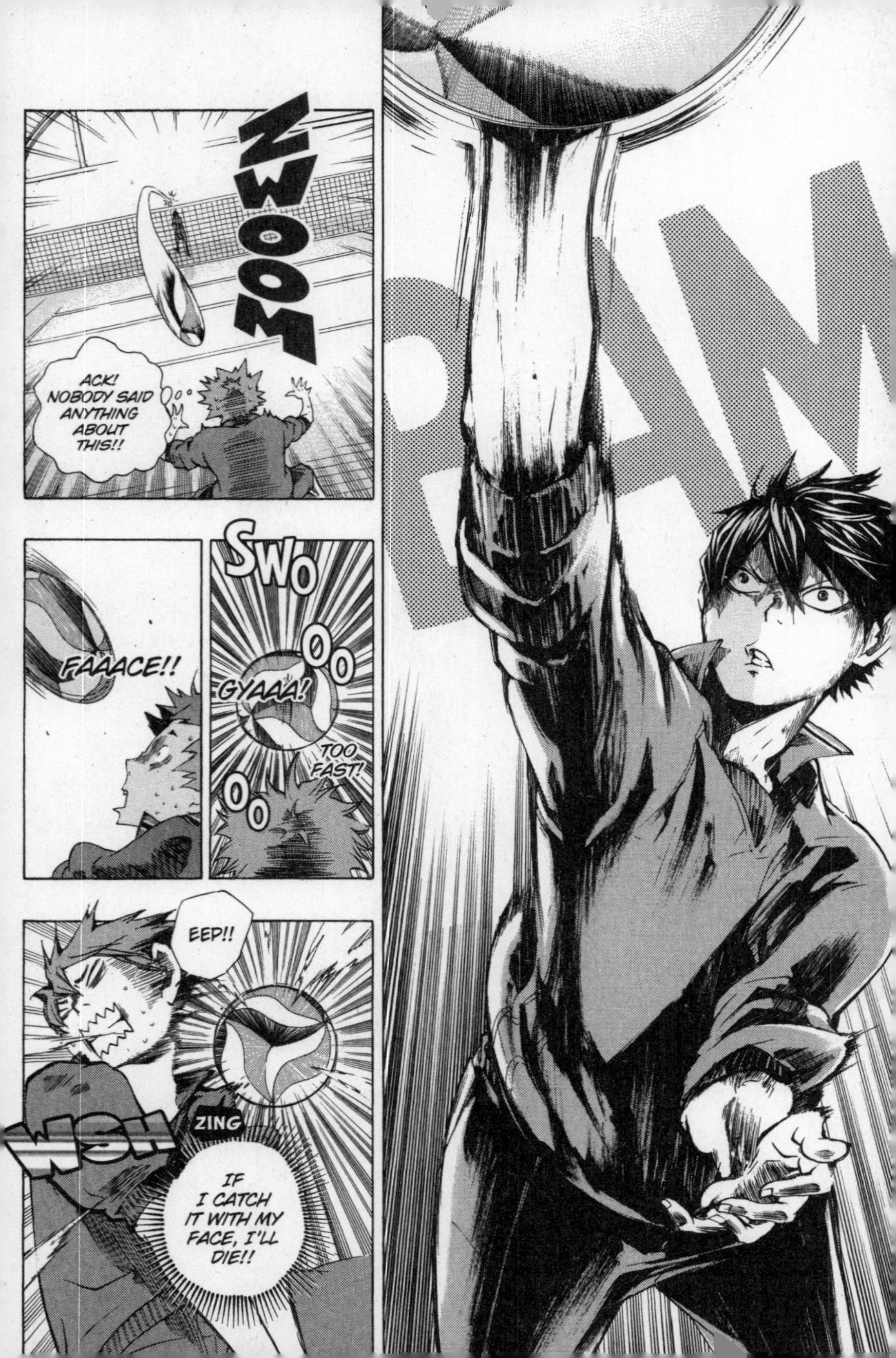
ZWOOM
ACK! NOBODY SAID ANYTHING ABOUT THIS!!
SWO
GYAAA!
TOO FAST!
FAAACE!!
EEP!!
ZING
IF I CATCH IT WITH MY FACE, I'LL DIE!!

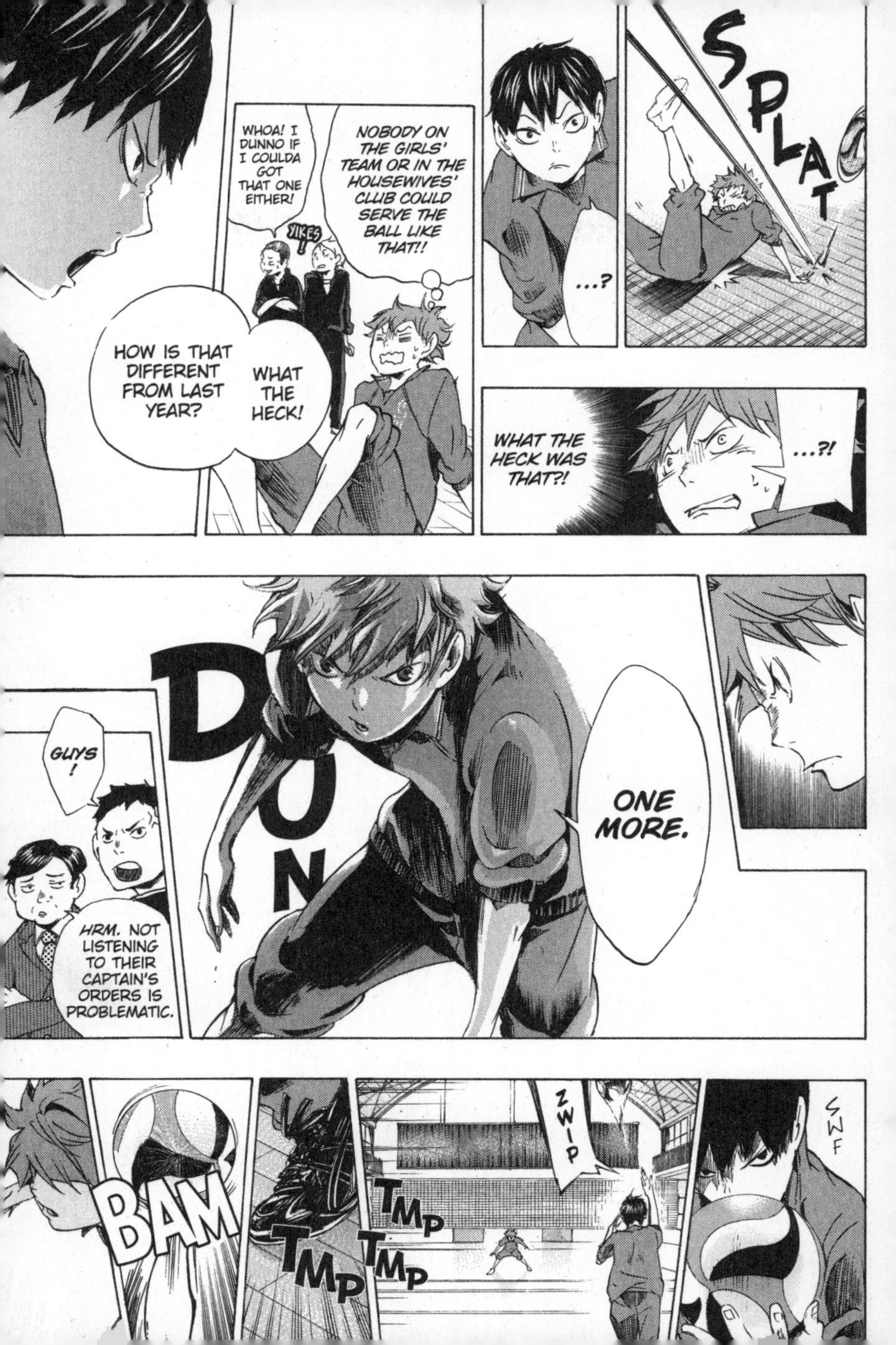

SPLAT
...?
...?!
WHAT THE HECK WAS THAT?!
NOBODY ON THE GIRLS' TEAM OR IN THE HOUSEWIVES' CLUB COULD SERVE THE BALL LIKE THAT!!
WHOA! I DUNNO IF I COULDA GOT THAT ONE EITHER!
YIKES
WHAT THE HECK!
HOW IS THAT DIFFERENT FROM LAST YEAR?
DUN
ONE MORE.
GUYS!
HRM. NOT LISTENING TO THEIR CAPTAIN'S ORDERS IS PROBLEMATIC.
SWF
ZWIP
TMP
TMP
TMP
TMP
BAM

GLURF!!

GABAP

BLAT

GET RIGHT IN FRONT OF THE BALL AND--

!

HE REACTED TO THAT QUICKLY!

ZNG

...IS RATE, DECIDE WISER ALLOW E OTHER RT CLUB USE THIS ...IASIUM

BLAH BLAH

AS CAP YOU MA BE A LIT TOO LENIE ON THEM, WHAT I AM SAYIN

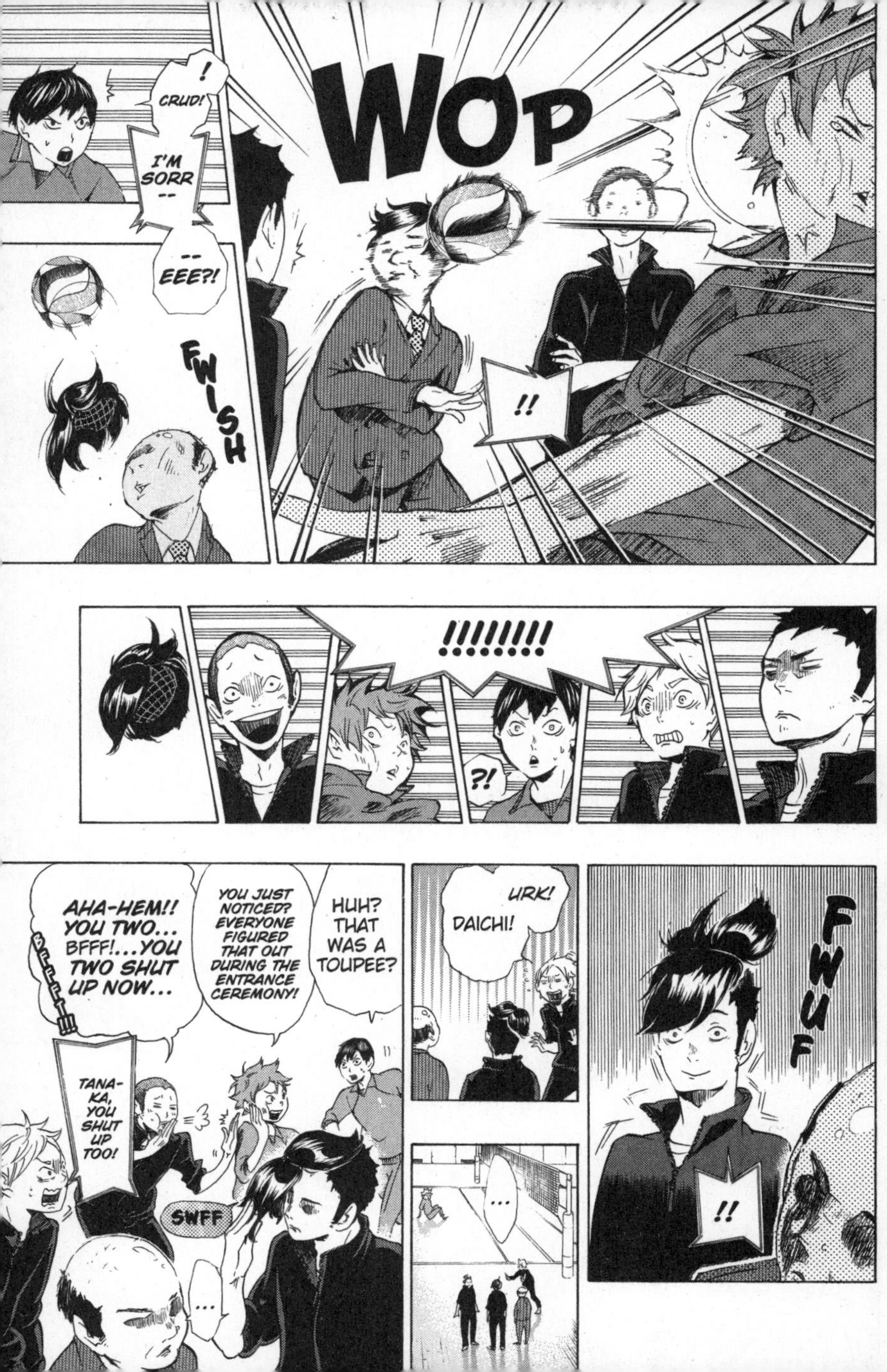
WOP
!!
!
CRUD!
I'M SORR --
-- EEE?!
FWISH
!!!!!!!!
?!
FWUF
!!
URK!
DAICHI!
...
HUH? THAT WAS A TOUPEE?
YOU JUST NOTICED? EVERYONE FIGURED THAT OUT DURING THE ENTRANCE CEREMONY!
AHA-HEM!! YOU TWO... BFFF!...YOU TWO SHUT UP NOW...
TANAKA, YOU SHUT UP TOO!
SWFF
...

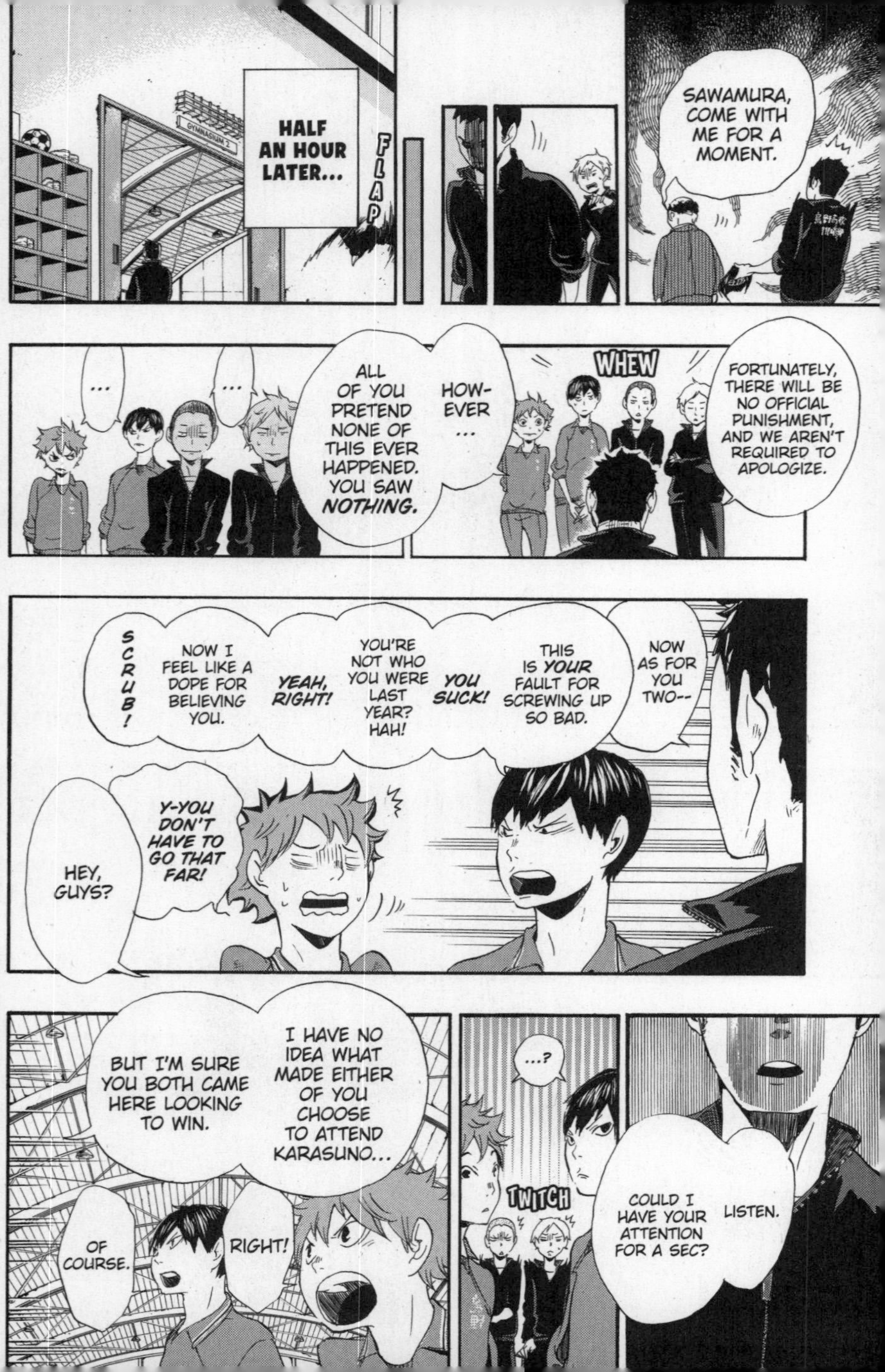
SAWAMURA, COME WITH ME FOR A MOMENT.
FLAP
HALF AN HOUR LATER...
GYMNASIUM 2
FORTUNATELY, THERE WILL BE NO OFFICIAL PUNISHMENT, AND WE AREN'T REQUIRED TO APOLOGIZE.
WHEW
HOW-EVER ...
ALL OF YOU PRETEND NONE OF THIS EVER HAPPENED. YOU SAW *NOTHING.*
...
...
NOW AS FOR YOU TWO--
THIS IS *YOUR* FAULT FOR SCREWING UP SO BAD.
YOU SUCK!
YOU'RE NOT WHO YOU WERE LAST YEAR? HAH!
YEAH, RIGHT!
NOW I FEEL LIKE A DOPE FOR BELIEVING YOU.
SCRUB!
Y-YOU DON'T HAVE TO GO THAT FAR!
HEY, GUYS?
LISTEN.
COULD I HAVE YOUR ATTENTION FOR A SEC?
...?
TWITCH
I HAVE NO IDEA WHAT MADE EITHER OF YOU CHOOSE TO ATTEND KARASUNO...
BUT I'M SURE YOU BOTH CAME HERE LOOKING TO WIN.
RIGHT!
OF COURSE.

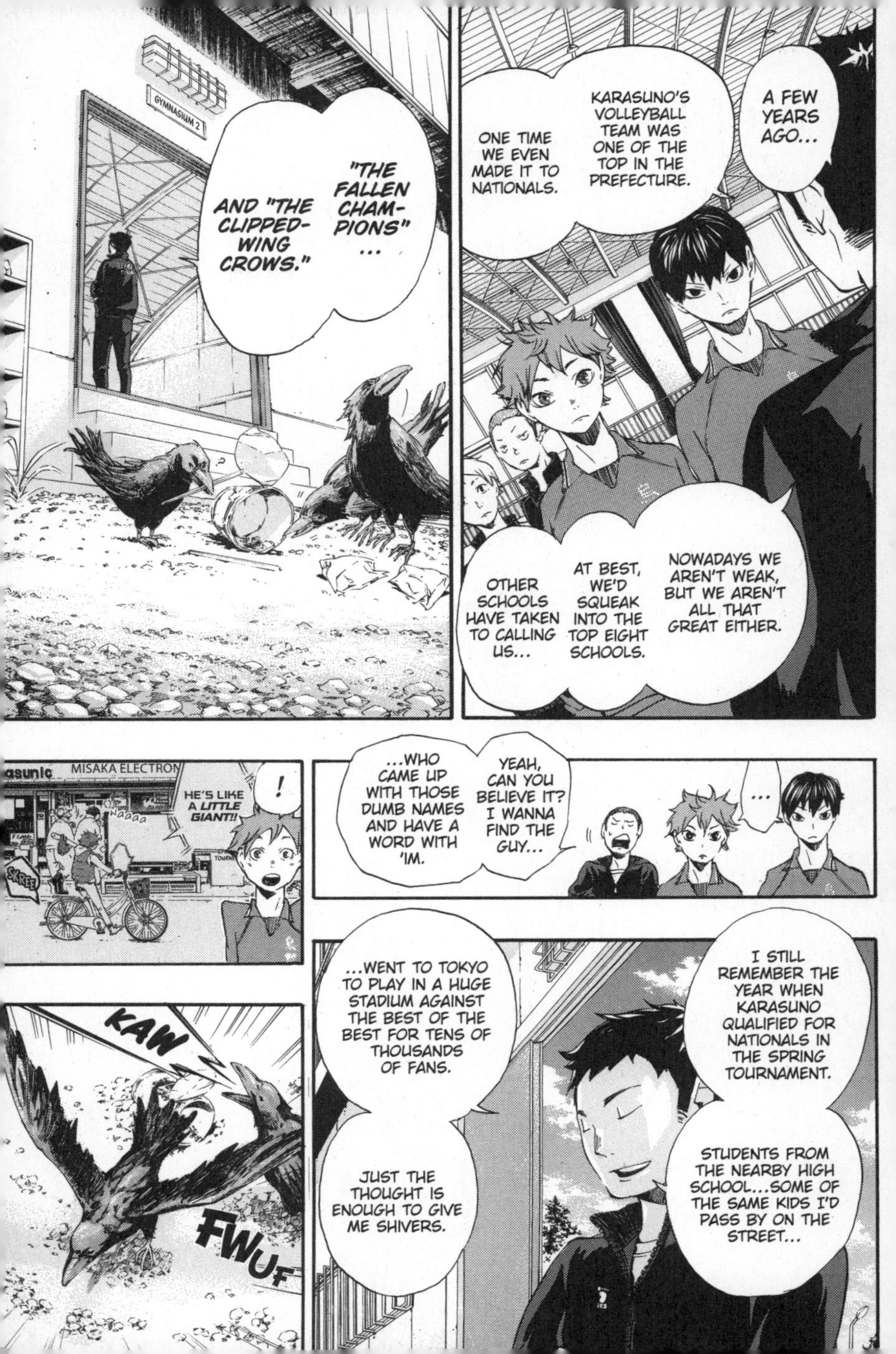
A FEW YEARS AGO...
KARASUNO'S VOLLEYBALL TEAM WAS ONE OF THE TOP IN THE PREFECTURE.
ONE TIME WE EVEN MADE IT TO NATIONALS.
NOWADAYS WE AREN'T WEAK, BUT WE AREN'T ALL THAT GREAT EITHER.
AT BEST, WE'D SQUEAK INTO THE TOP EIGHT SCHOOLS.
OTHER SCHOOLS HAVE TAKEN TO CALLING US...
GYMNASIUM 2
"THE FALLEN CHAMPIONS"...
AND "THE CLIPPED-WING CROWS."
...
YEAH, CAN YOU BELIEVE IT? I WANNA FIND THE GUY...
...WHO CAME UP WITH THOSE DUMB NAMES AND HAVE A WORD WITH 'IM.
!
MISAKA ELECTRON
HE'S LIKE A *LITTLE GIANT!!*
WAAAA
SKREE
I STILL REMEMBER THE YEAR WHEN KARASUNO QUALIFIED FOR NATIONALS IN THE SPRING TOURNAMENT.
STUDENTS FROM THE NEARBY HIGH SCHOOL...SOME OF THE SAME KIDS I'D PASS BY ON THE STREET...
...WENT TO TOKYO TO PLAY IN A HUGE STADIUM AGAINST THE BEST OF THE BEST FOR TENS OF THOUSANDS OF FANS.
JUST THE THOUGHT IS ENOUGH TO GIVE ME SHIVERS.
KAW
FWUF

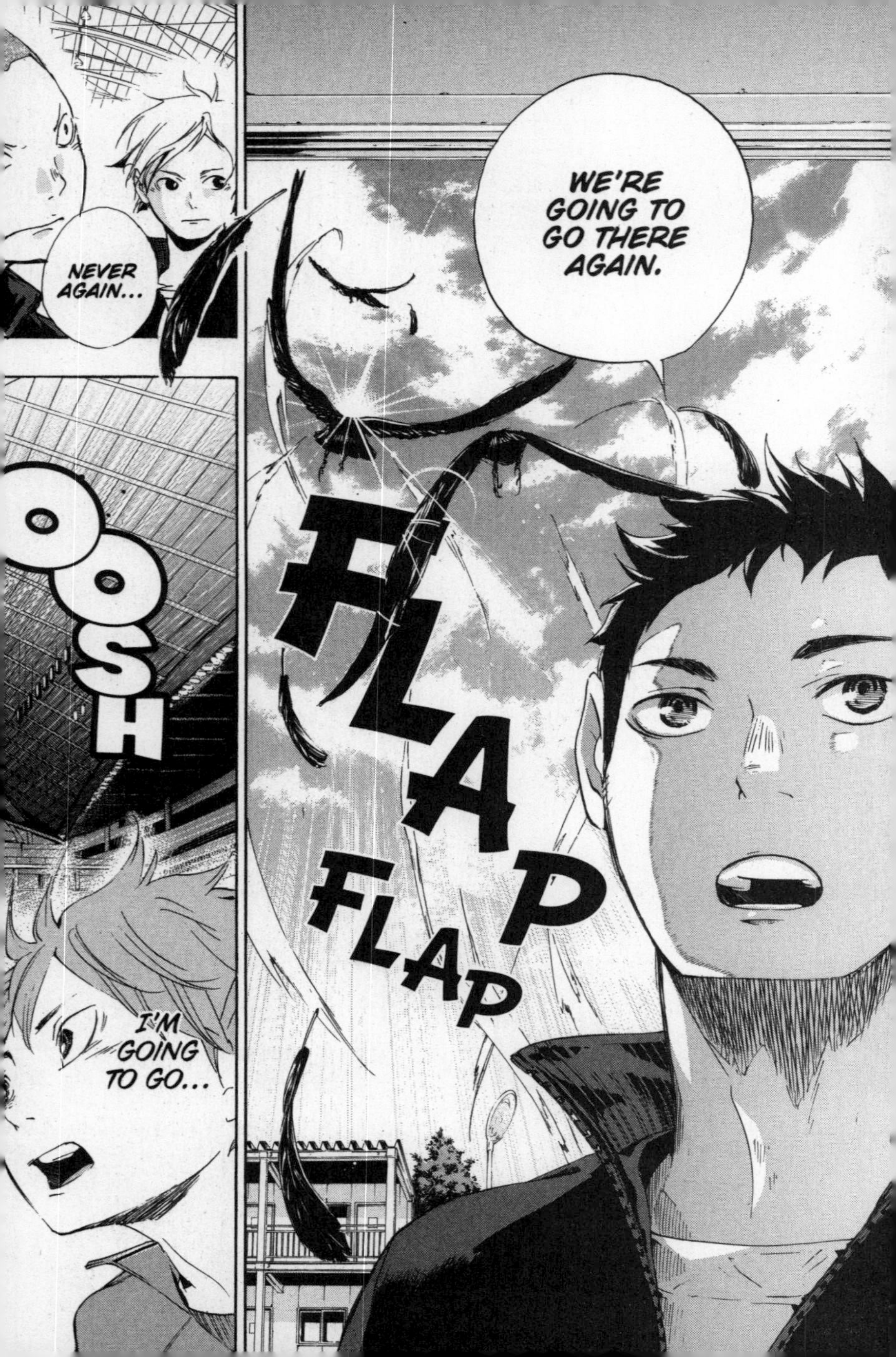
WE'RE GOING TO GO THERE AGAIN.
FLAP
FLAP
NEVER AGAIN...
OOOSH
I'M GOING TO GO...

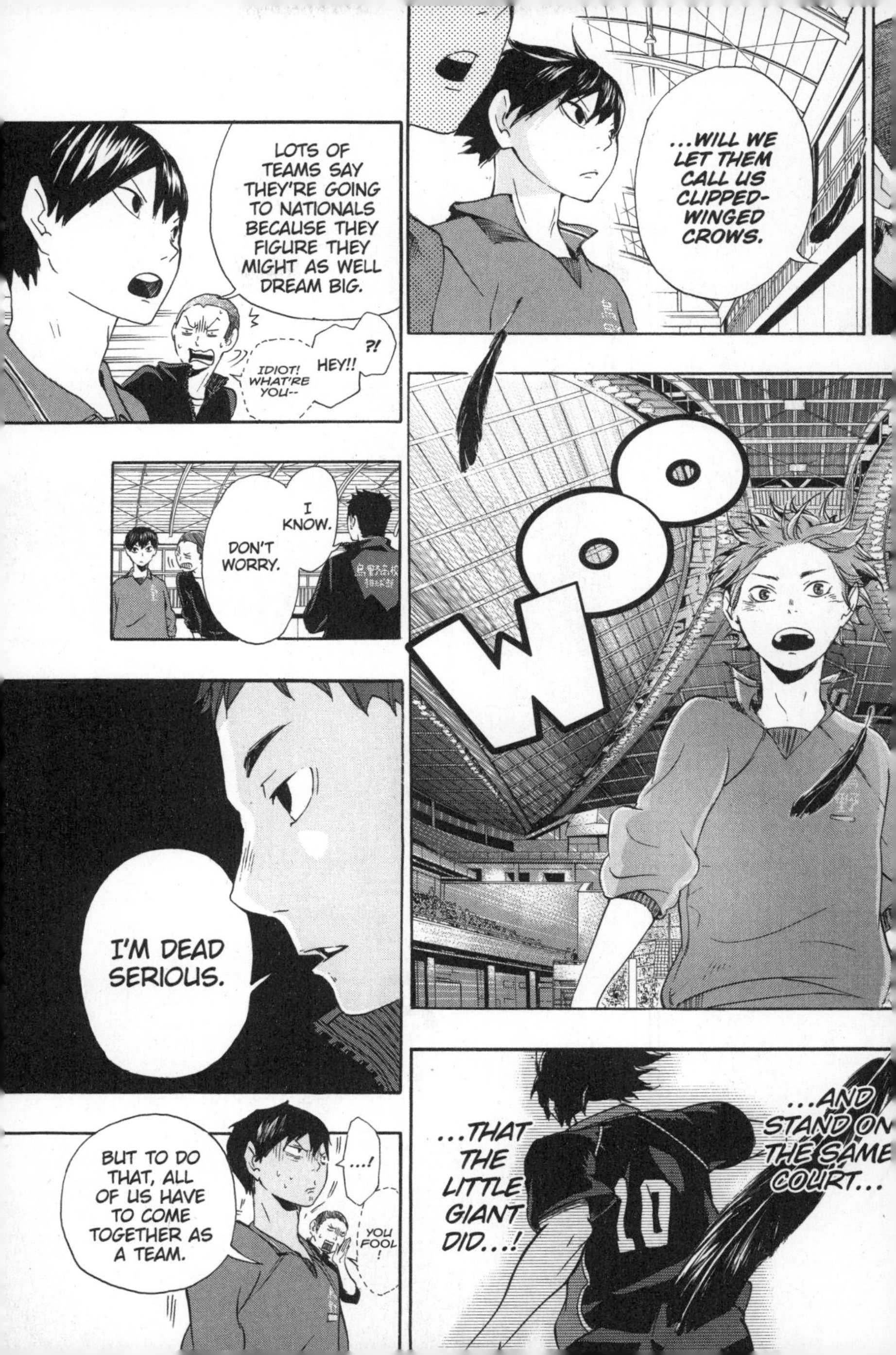
...WILL WE LET THEM CALL US CLIPPED-WINGED CROWS.
WOO
...AND STAND ON THE SAME COURT...
...THAT THE LITTLE GIANT DID...!
LOTS OF TEAMS SAY THEY'RE GOING TO NATIONALS BECAUSE THEY FIGURE THEY MIGHT AS WELL DREAM BIG.
?!
HEY!!
IDIOT! WHAT'RE YOU--
I KNOW.
DON'T WORRY.
I'M DEAD SERIOUS.
...!
BUT TO DO THAT, ALL OF US HAVE TO COME TOGETHER AS A TEAM.
YOU FOOL!

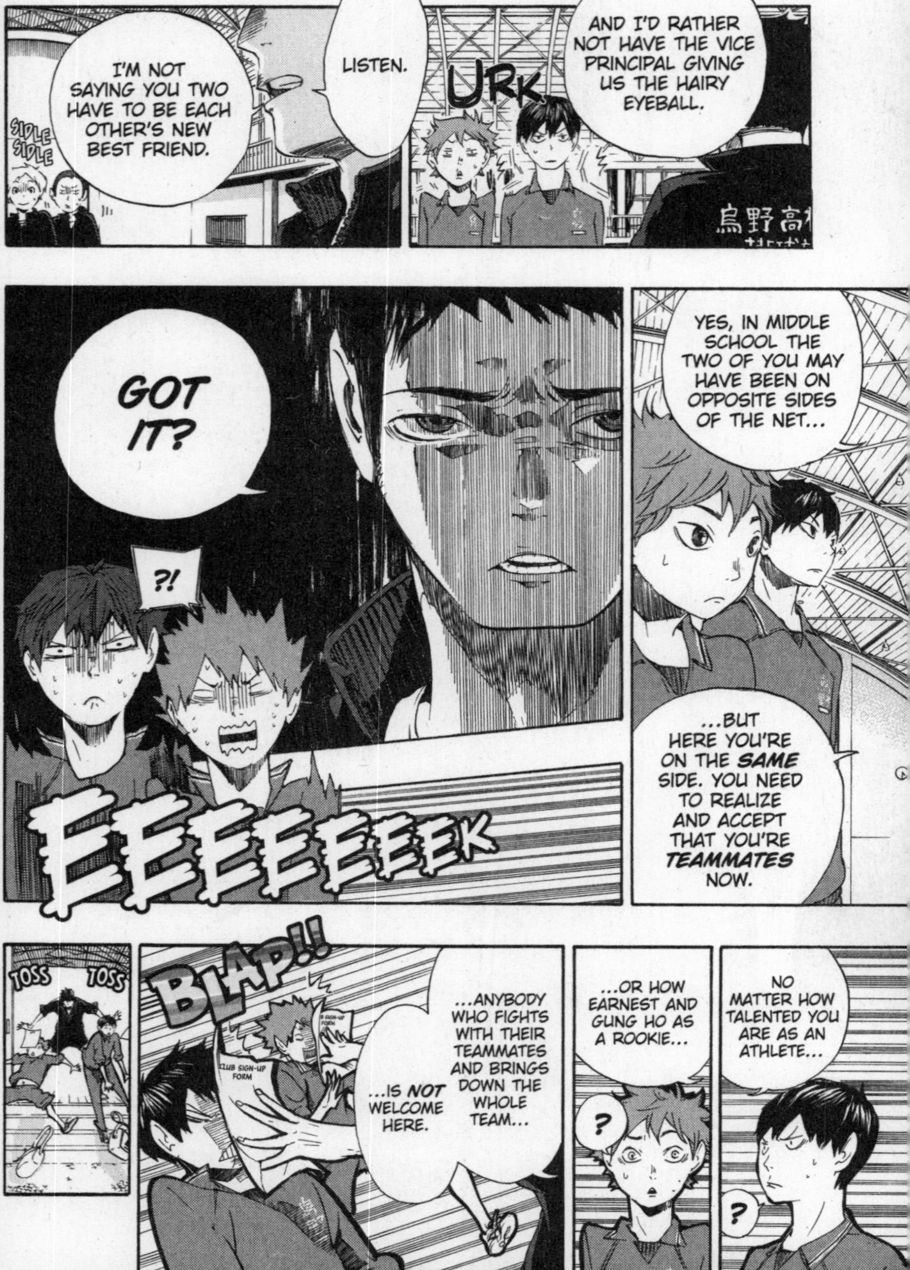
AND I'D RATHER NOT HAVE THE VICE PRINCIPAL GIVING US THE HAIRY EYEBALL.
URK
LISTEN.
I'M NOT SAYING YOU TWO HAVE TO BE EACH OTHER'S NEW BEST FRIEND.
SIDLE SIDLE
YES, IN MIDDLE SCHOOL THE TWO OF YOU MAY HAVE BEEN ON OPPOSITE SIDES OF THE NET...
...BUT HERE YOU'RE ON THE ***SAME*** SIDE. YOU NEED TO REALIZE AND ACCEPT THAT YOU'RE ***TEAMMATES*** NOW.
GOT IT?
?!
EEEEEEEK
NO MATTER HOW TALENTED YOU ARE AS AN ATHLETE...
?
...OR HOW EARNEST AND GUNG HO AS A ROOKIE...
?
...ANYBODY WHO FIGHTS WITH THEIR TEAMMATES AND BRINGS DOWN THE WHOLE TEAM...
...IS ***NOT*** WELCOME HERE.
BLAP!!
CLUB SIGN-UP FORM
TOSS
TOSS

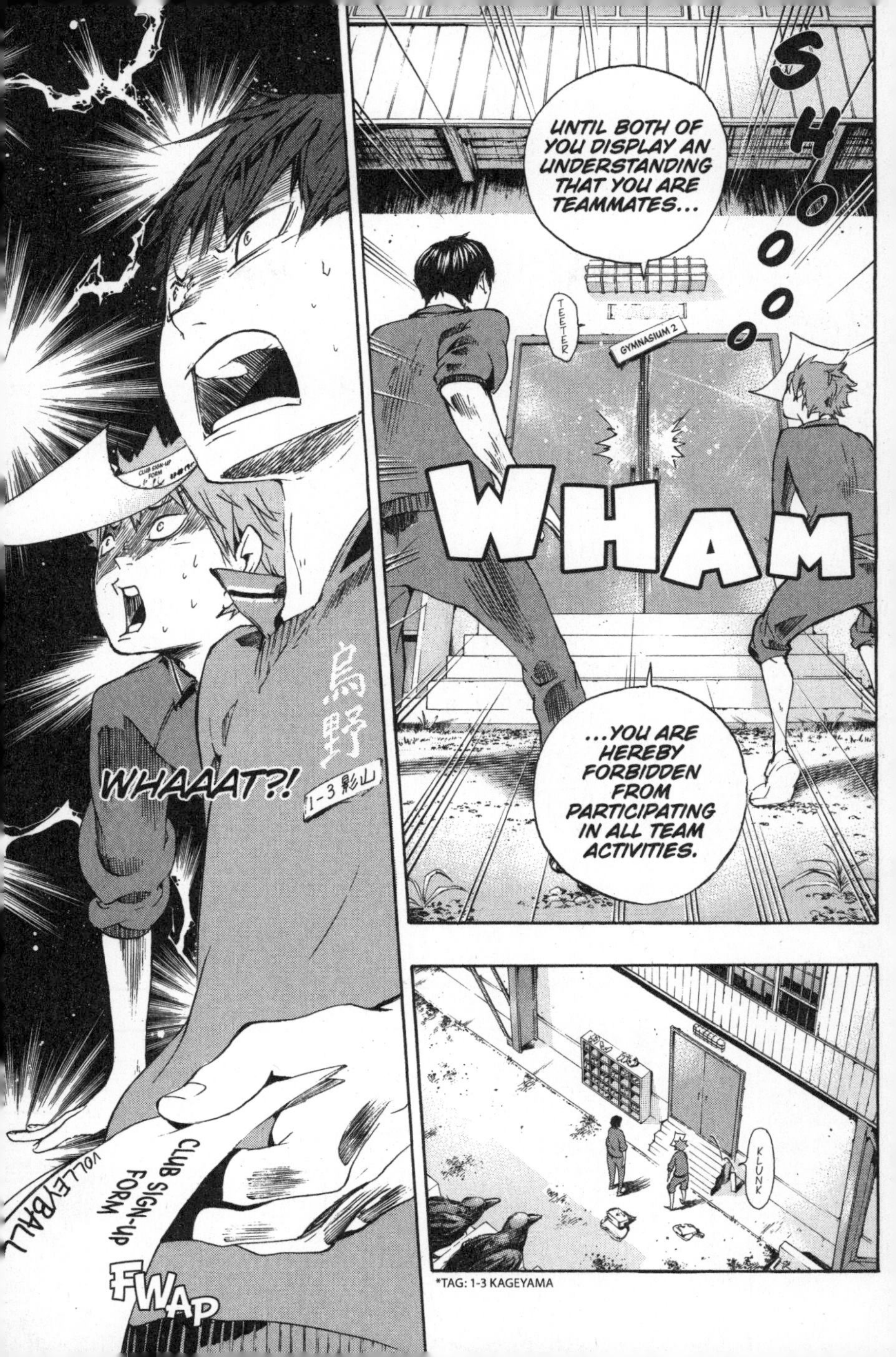
SHOOOOOO
UNTIL BOTH OF YOU DISPLAY AN UNDERSTANDING THAT YOU ARE TEAMMATES...
TEETER
GYMNASIUM 2
WHAM
...YOU ARE HEREBY FORBIDDEN FROM PARTICIPATING IN ALL TEAM ACTIVITIES.
KLUNK
CLUB SIGN-UP FORM
WHAAAT?!
烏野
1-3 影山
VOLLEYBALL CLUB SIGN-UP FORM
FWAP

*TAG: 1-3 KAGEYAMA

SHOYO HINATA

KARASUNO HIGH SCHOOL
CLASS 1-1

POSITION:
WING SPIKER (TEMP)

HEIGHT: 5'4"
WEIGHT: 114 LBS.
(AS OF APRIL, 1ST YEAR
OF HIGH SCHOOL)

BIRTHDAY: JUNE 21

FAVORITE FOOD:
EGGS OVER RICE

CURRENT WORRY:
NOT BEING ABLE TO
PALM A VOLLEYBALL.

ABILITY PARAMETERS
(5-POINT SCALE)

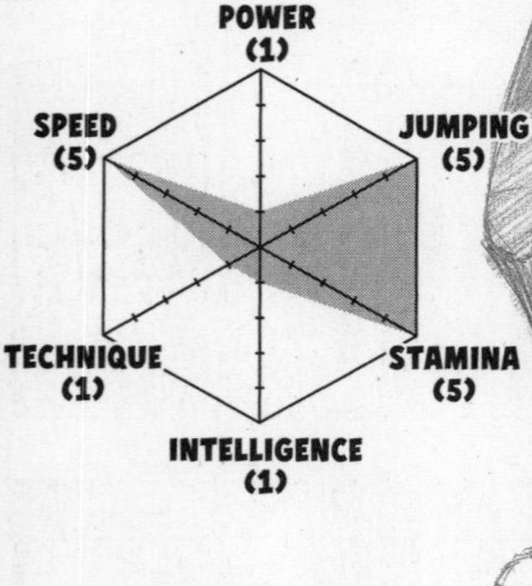
POWER
(1)
JUMPING
(5)
STAMINA
(5)
INTELLIGENCE
(1)
TECHNIQUE
(1)
SPEED
(5)

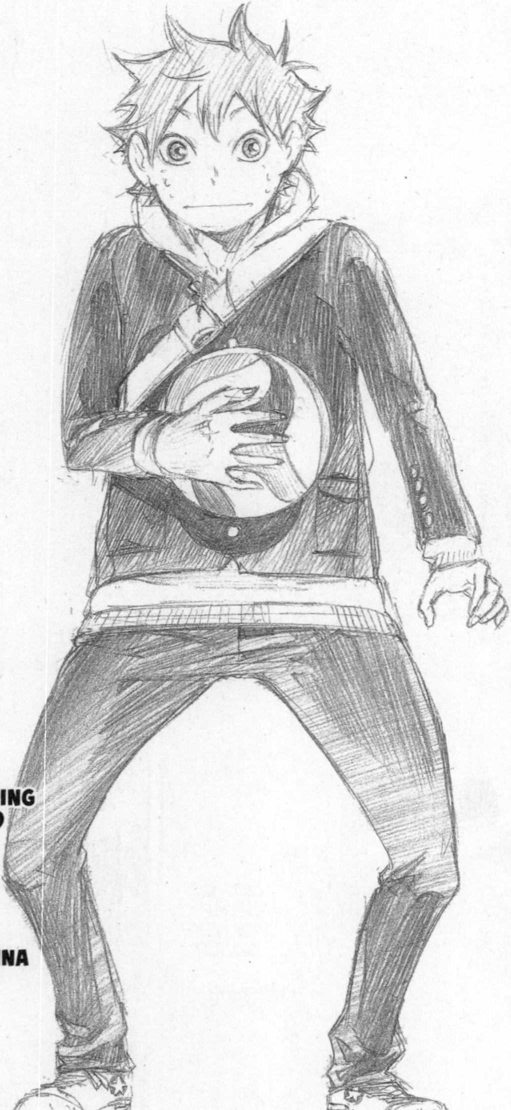

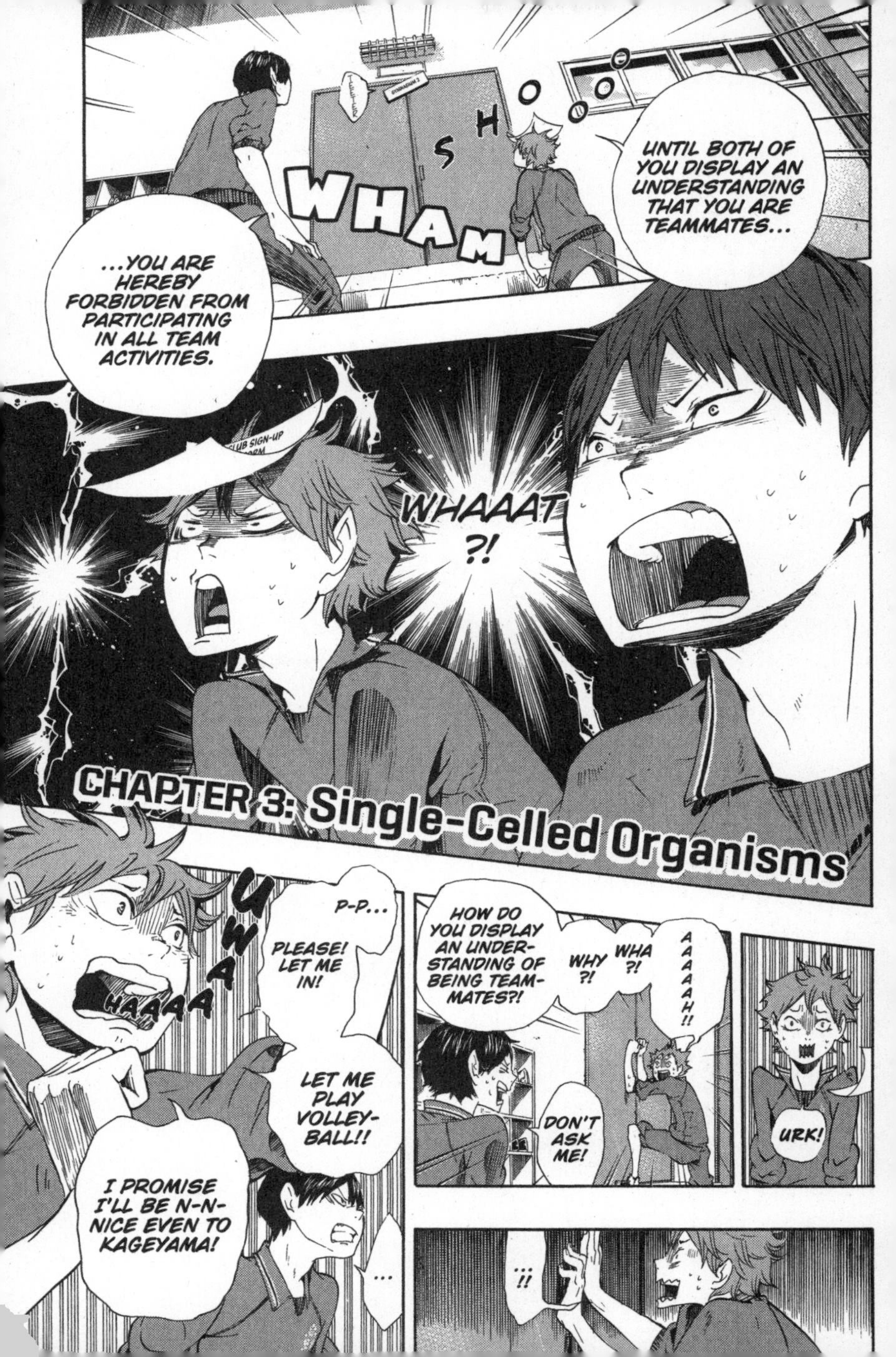
UNTIL BOTH OF YOU DISPLAY AN UNDERSTANDING THAT YOU ARE TEAMMATES...
SHOOOO
TEETER
WHAM
...YOU ARE HEREBY FORBIDDEN FROM PARTICIPATING IN ALL TEAM ACTIVITIES.
WHAAAT?!
CHAPTER 3: Single-Celled Organisms
URK!
AAAAAAH!!
WHA?!
WHY?!
HOW DO YOU DISPLAY AN UNDERSTANDING OF BEING TEAMMATES?!
DON'T ASK ME!
...!!
P-P...
PLEASE! LET ME IN!
UWAHAAAA
LET ME PLAY VOLLEYBALL!!
I PROMISE I'LL BE N-N-NICE EVEN TO KAGEYAMA!
...

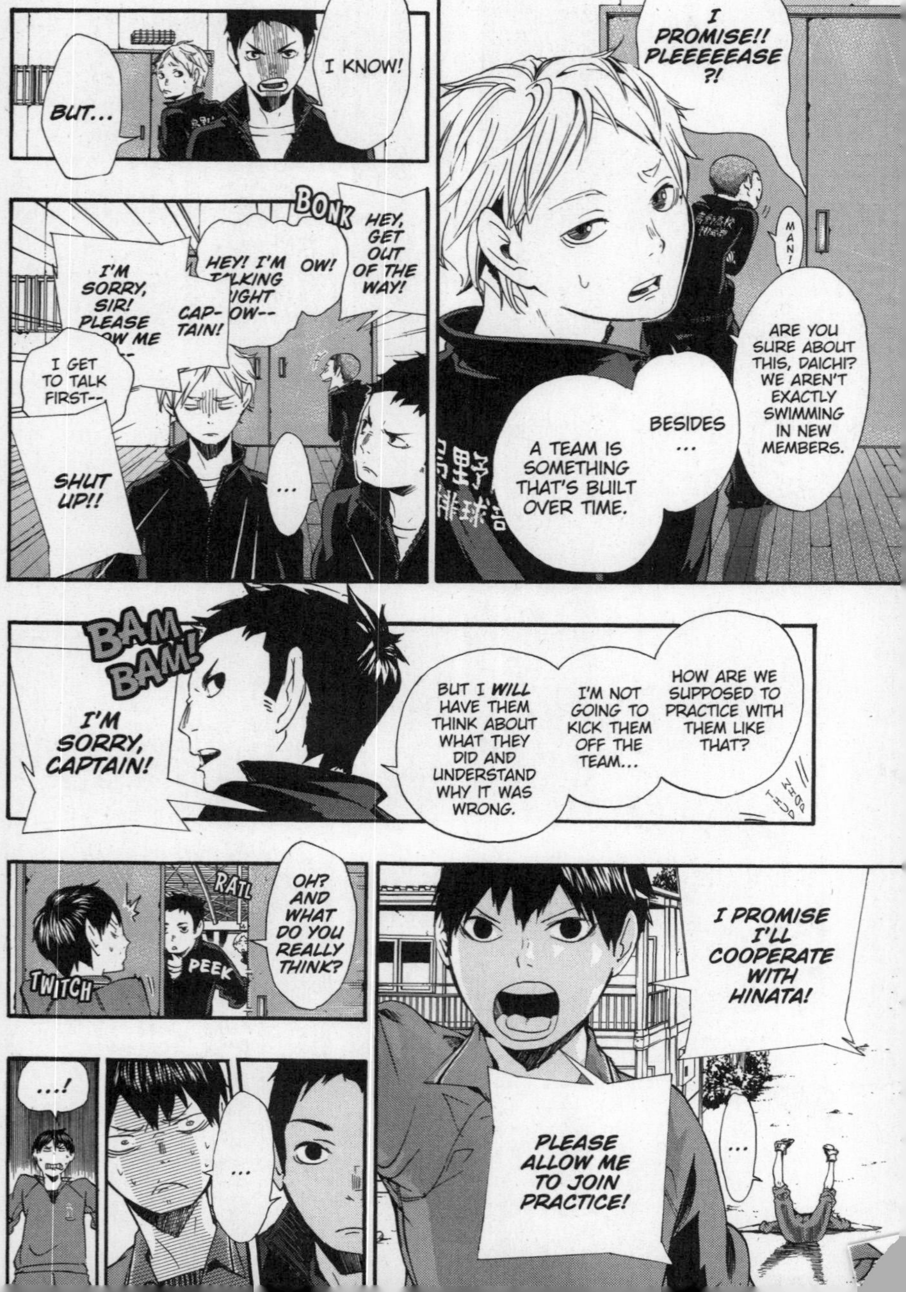
I PROMISE!! PLEEEEEASE ?!
MAN!
ARE YOU SURE ABOUT THIS, DAICHI? WE AREN'T EXACTLY SWIMMING IN NEW MEMBERS.
BESIDES ...
A TEAM IS SOMETHING THAT'S BUILT OVER TIME.
I KNOW!
BUT...
BONK
HEY, GET OUT OF THE WAY!
OW!
HEY! I'M TALKING RIGHT NOW--
CAP- TAIN!
I'M SORRY, SIR! PLEASE ALLOW ME
I GET TO TALK FIRST--
...
SHUT UP!!
HOW ARE WE SUPPOSED TO PRACTICE WITH THEM LIKE THAT?
I'M NOT GOING TO KICK THEM OFF THE TEAM...
BUT I WILL HAVE THEM THINK ABOUT WHAT THEY DID AND UNDERSTAND WHY IT WAS WRONG.
BAM BAM!
I'M SORRY, CAPTAIN!
I PROMISE I'LL COOPERATE WITH HINATA!
PLEASE ALLOW ME TO JOIN PRACTICE!
...
OH? AND WHAT DO YOU REALLY THINK?
RATL
PEEK
TWITCH
...
...!

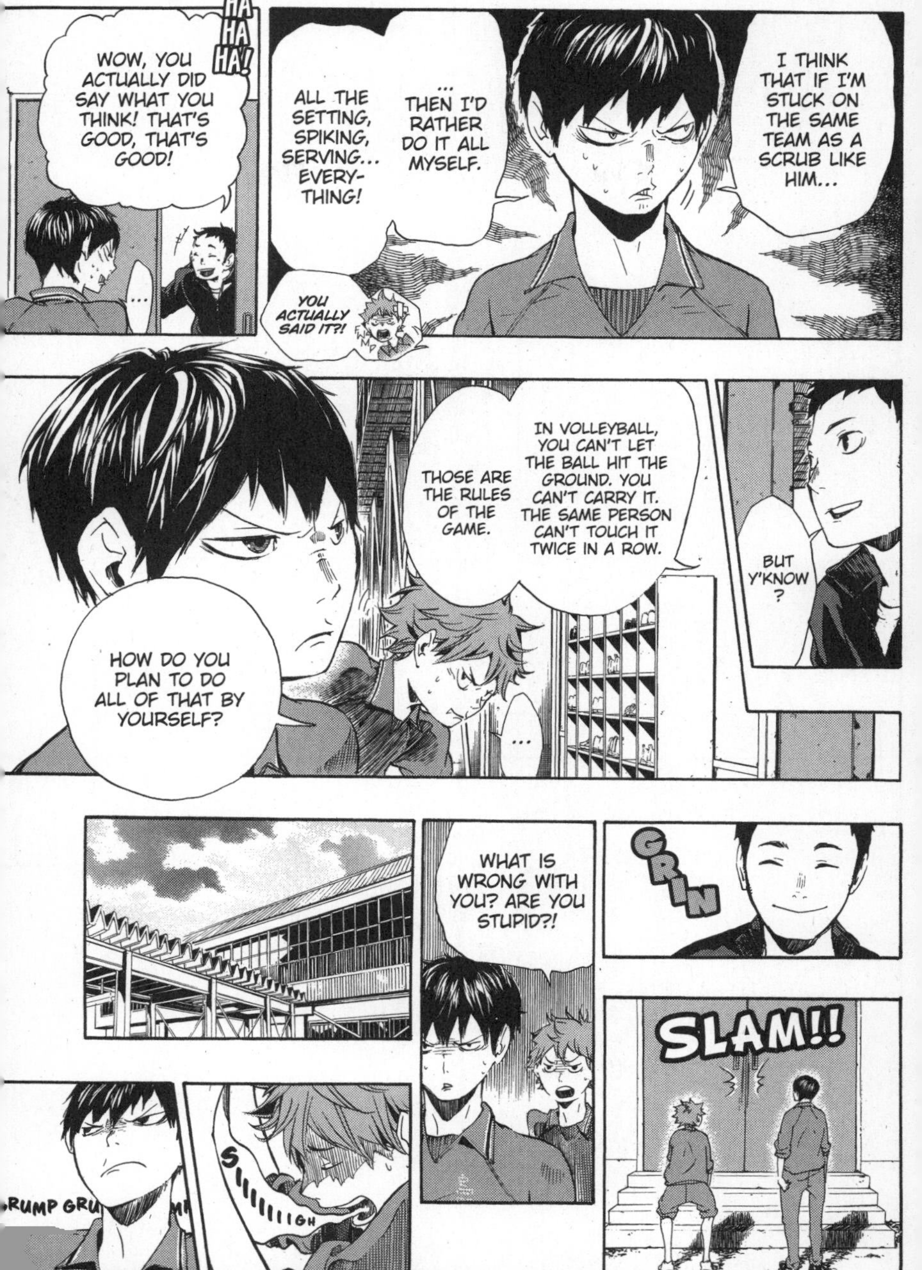

I THINK THAT IF I'M STUCK ON THE SAME TEAM AS A SCRUB LIKE HIM...
... THEN I'D RATHER DO IT ALL MYSELF.
ALL THE SETTING, SPIKING, SERVING... EVERYTHING!
YOU ACTUALLY SAID IT?!
HA HA HA!
WOW, YOU ACTUALLY DID SAY WHAT YOU THINK! THAT'S GOOD, THAT'S GOOD!
...
BUT Y'KNOW?
IN VOLLEYBALL, YOU CAN'T LET THE BALL HIT THE GROUND. YOU CAN'T CARRY IT. THE SAME PERSON CAN'T TOUCH IT TWICE IN A ROW.
THOSE ARE THE RULES OF THE GAME.
HOW DO YOU PLAN TO DO ALL OF THAT BY YOURSELF?
...
GRIN
SLAM!!
WHAT IS WRONG WITH YOU? ARE YOU STUPID?!
SIIIIIIIGH
RUMP GRU

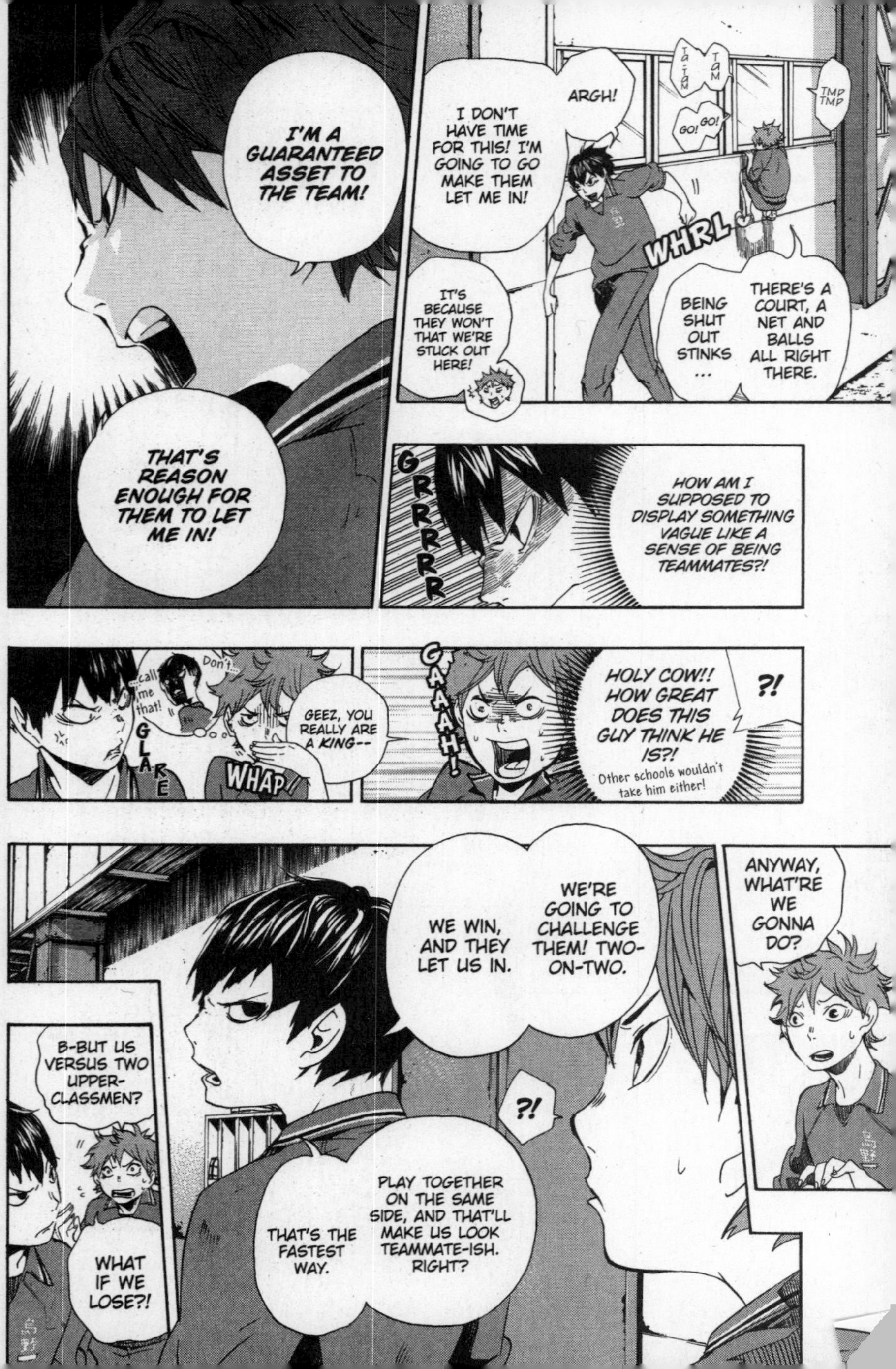

TMP TMP
TAM
Ta-tam
GO! GO!
ARGH!
I DON'T HAVE TIME FOR THIS! I'M GOING TO GO MAKE THEM LET ME IN!
WHRL
THERE'S A COURT, A NET AND BALLS ALL RIGHT THERE.
BEING SHUT OUT STINKS...
IT'S BECAUSE THEY WON'T THAT WE'RE STUCK OUT HERE!
HOW AM I SUPPOSED TO DISPLAY SOMETHING VAGUE LIKE A SENSE OF BEING TEAMMATES?!
GRRRRR
I'M A GUARANTEED ASSET TO THE TEAM!
THAT'S REASON ENOUGH FOR THEM TO LET ME IN!
?!
HOLY COW!! HOW GREAT DOES THIS GUY THINK HE IS?!
Other schools wouldn't take him either!
GAAAH!
GEEZ, YOU REALLY ARE A KING--
WHAP
Don't...
...call me that!
GLARE
ANYWAY, WHAT'RE WE GONNA DO?
WE'RE GOING TO CHALLENGE THEM! TWO-ON-TWO.
WE WIN, AND THEY LET US IN.
?!
PLAY TOGETHER ON THE SAME SIDE, AND THAT'LL MAKE US LOOK TEAMMATE-ISH. RIGHT?
THAT'S THE FASTEST WAY.
B-BUT US VERSUS TWO UPPERCLASSMEN?
WHAT IF WE LOSE?!

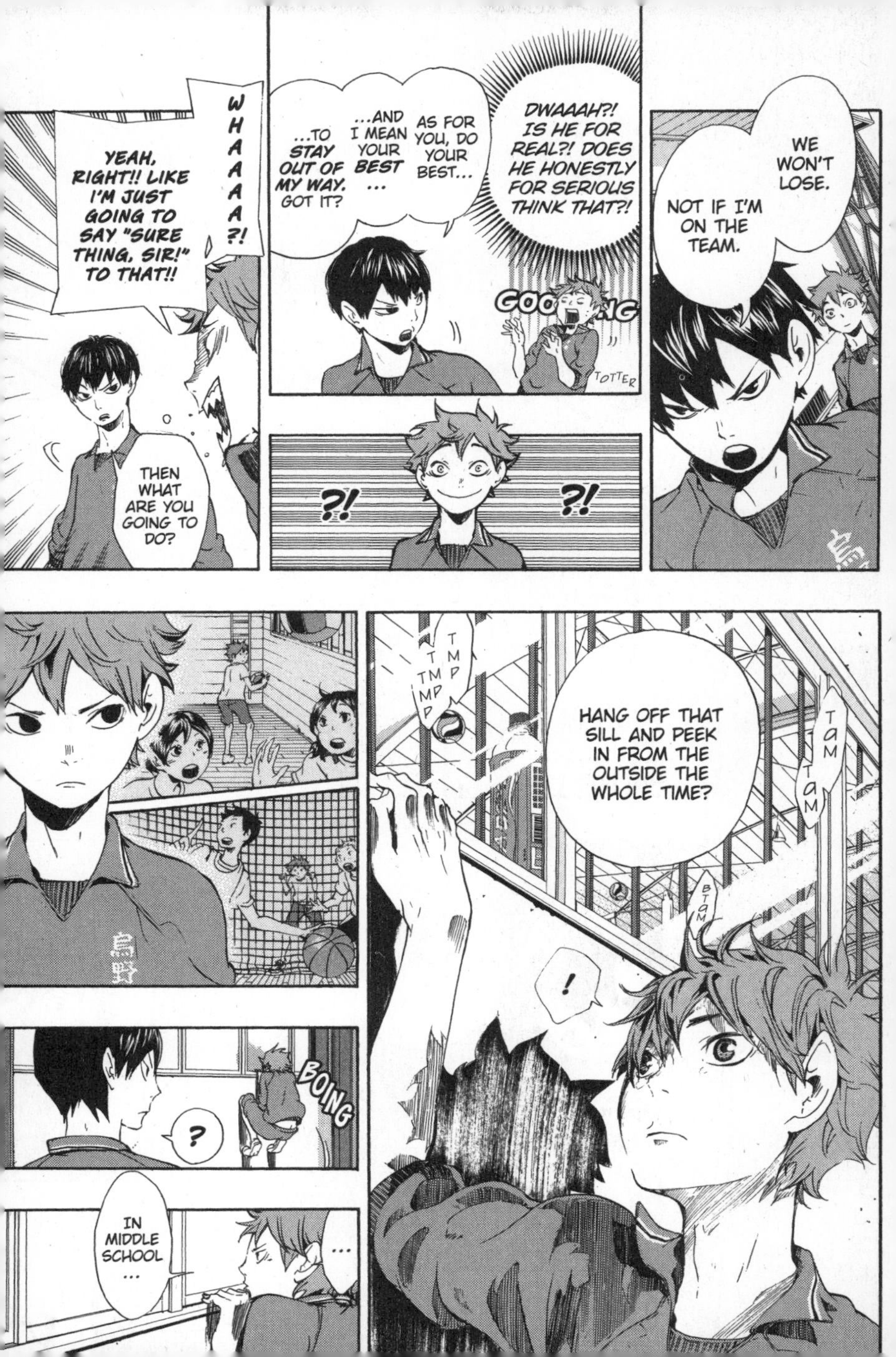
WE WON'T LOSE.
NOT IF I'M ON THE TEAM.
DWAAAH?! IS HE FOR REAL?! DOES HE HONESTLY FOR SERIOUS THINK THAT?!
AS FOR YOU, DO YOUR BEST...
...AND I MEAN YOUR BEST...
...TO STAY OUT OF MY WAY. GOT IT?
TOTTER
?!
?!
WHAAAAA?!
YEAH, RIGHT!! LIKE I'M JUST GOING TO SAY "SURE THING, SIR!" TO THAT!!
THEN WHAT ARE YOU GOING TO DO?
TMP TMP
TMP TMP
HANG OFF THAT SILL AND PEEK IN FROM THE OUTSIDE THE WHOLE TIME?
TAM
TAM
TAM
BTAM
!
BOING
?
IN MIDDLE SCHOOL...
...

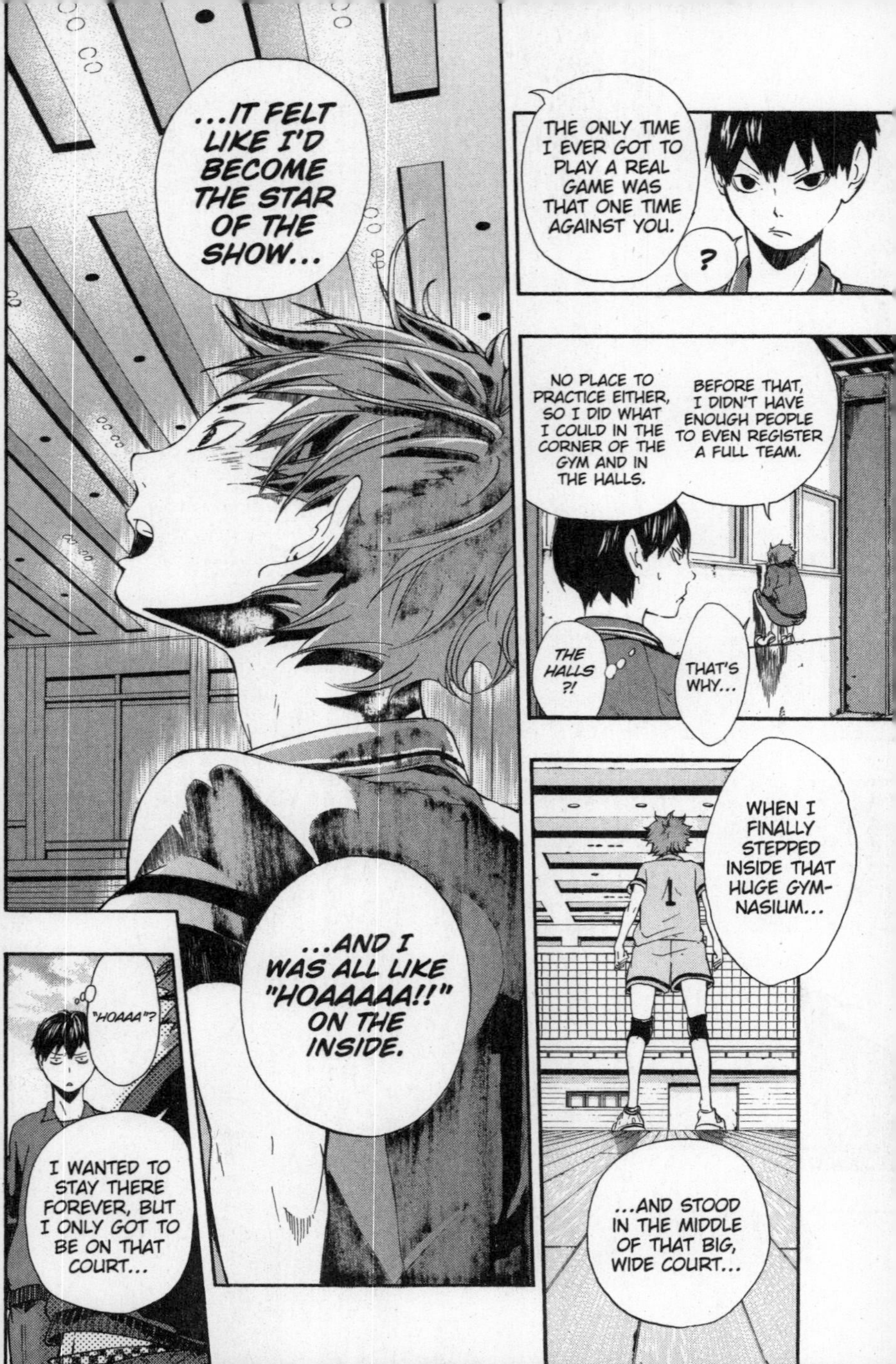
THE ONLY TIME I EVER GOT TO PLAY A REAL GAME WAS THAT ONE TIME AGAINST YOU.
?
BEFORE THAT, I DIDN'T HAVE ENOUGH PEOPLE TO EVEN REGISTER A FULL TEAM.
NO PLACE TO PRACTICE EITHER, SO I DID WHAT I COULD IN THE CORNER OF THE GYM AND IN THE HALLS.
THAT'S WHY...
THE HALLS ?!
WHEN I FINALLY STEPPED INSIDE THAT HUGE GYM-NASIUM...
...AND STOOD IN THE MIDDLE OF THAT BIG, WIDE COURT...
...IT FELT LIKE I'D BECOME THE STAR OF THE SHOW...
...AND I WAS ALL LIKE "HOAAAAA!!" ON THE INSIDE.
"HOAAA"?
I WANTED TO STAY THERE FOREVER, BUT I ONLY GOT TO BE ON THAT COURT...

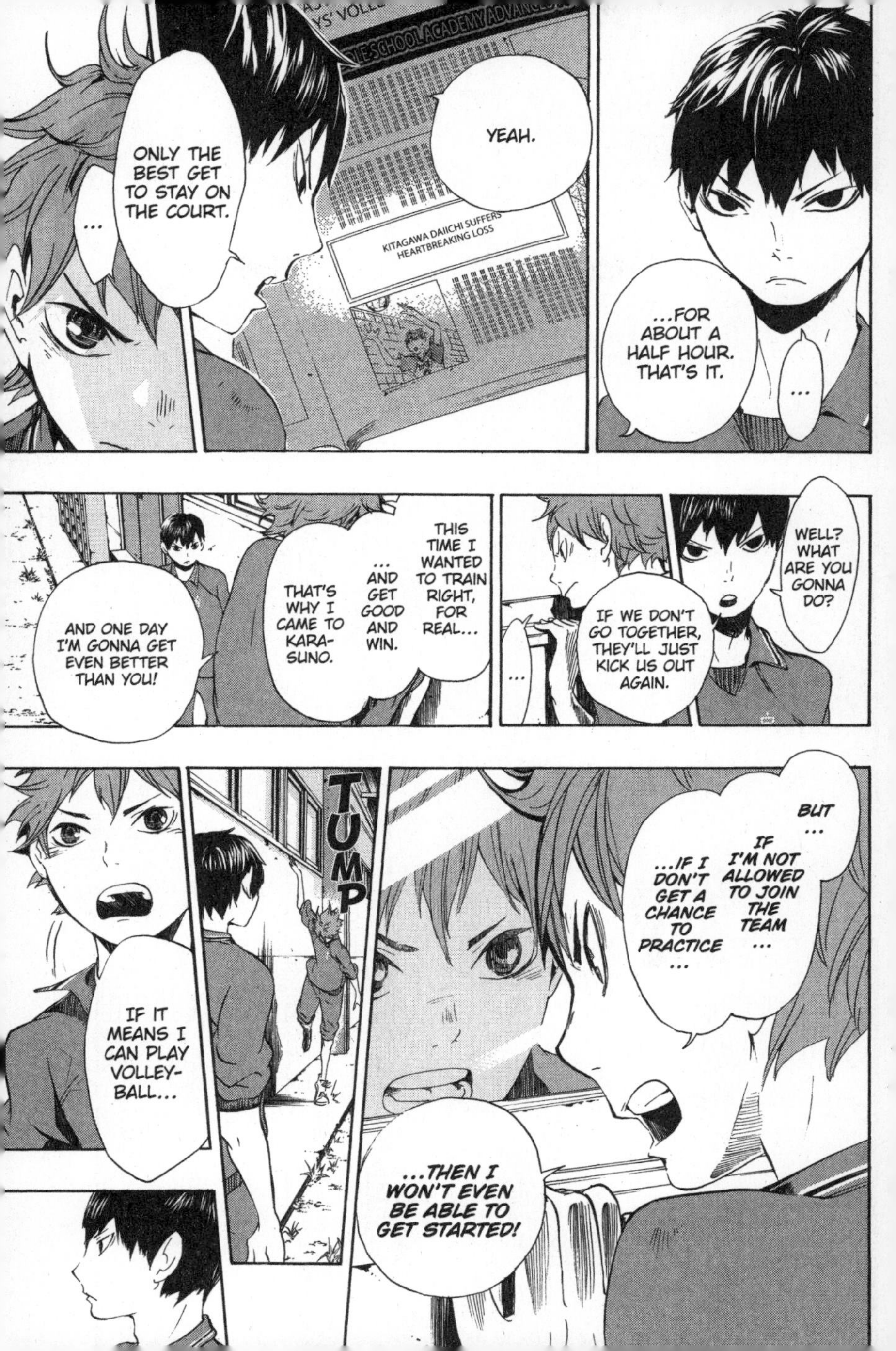
...FOR ABOUT A HALF HOUR. THAT'S IT.
...
YEAH.
KITAGAWA DAIICHI SUFFERS HEARTBREAKING LOSS
ONLY THE BEST GET TO STAY ON THE COURT.
...
WELL? WHAT ARE YOU GONNA DO?
IF WE DON'T GO TOGETHER, THEY'LL JUST KICK US OUT AGAIN.
...
THIS TIME I WANTED TO TRAIN RIGHT, FOR REAL...
...AND GET GOOD AND WIN.
THAT'S WHY I CAME TO KARA-SUNO.
AND ONE DAY I'M GONNA GET EVEN BETTER THAN YOU!
BUT...
IF I'M NOT ALLOWED TO JOIN THE TEAM...
...IF I DON'T GET A CHANCE TO PRACTICE...
...THEN I WON'T EVEN BE ABLE TO GET STARTED!
TUMP
IF IT MEANS I CAN PLAY VOLLEY-BALL...

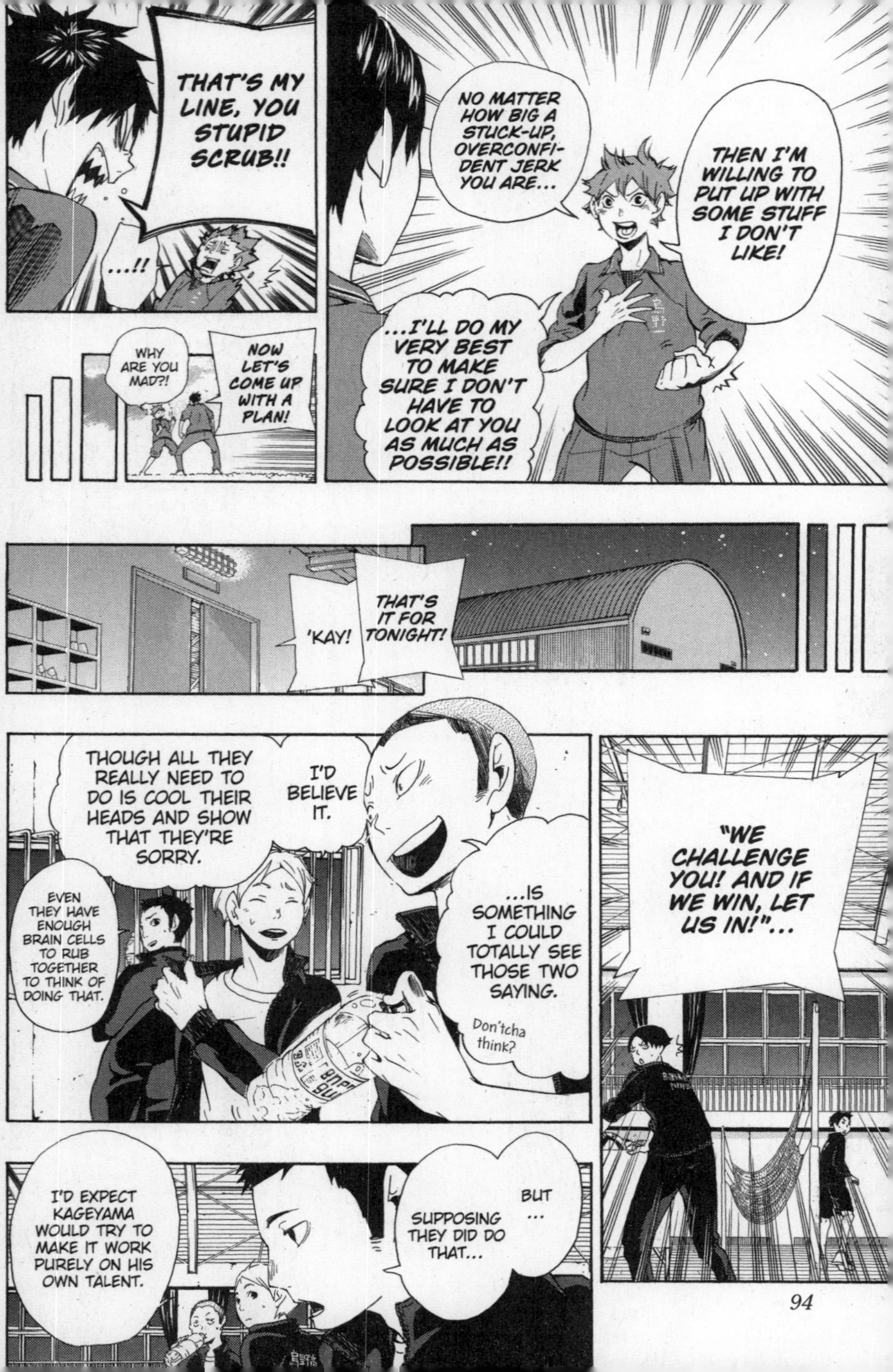
NO MATTER HOW BIG A STUCK-UP, OVERCONFIDENT JERK YOU ARE...
THEN I'M WILLING TO PUT UP WITH SOME STUFF I DON'T LIKE!
...I'LL DO MY VERY BEST TO MAKE SURE I DON'T HAVE TO LOOK AT YOU AS MUCH AS POSSIBLE!!
THAT'S MY LINE, YOU STUPID SCRUB!!
...!!
NOW LET'S COME UP WITH A PLAN!
WHY ARE YOU MAD?!
THAT'S IT FOR TONIGHT!
'KAY!
"WE CHALLENGE YOU! AND IF WE WIN, LET US IN!"...
...IS SOMETHING I COULD TOTALLY SEE THOSE TWO SAYING.
Don'tcha think?
I'D BELIEVE IT.
THOUGH ALL THEY REALLY NEED TO DO IS COOL THEIR HEADS AND SHOW THAT THEY'RE SORRY.
EVEN THEY HAVE ENOUGH BRAIN CELLS TO RUB TOGETHER TO THINK OF DOING THAT.
BUT...
SUPPOSING THEY DID DO THAT...
I'D EXPECT KAGEYAMA WOULD TRY TO MAKE IT WORK PURELY ON HIS OWN TALENT.

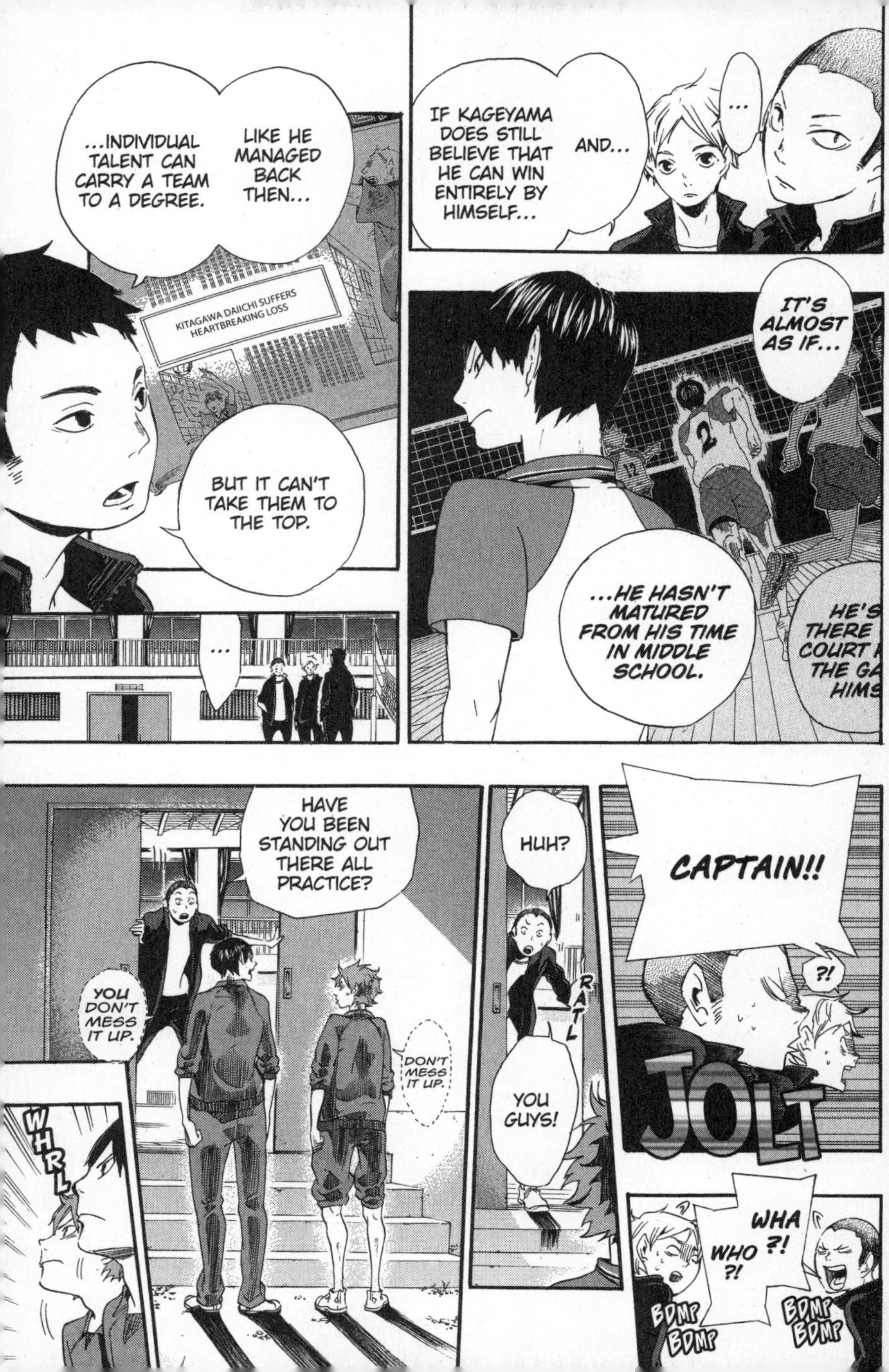
...
AND...
IF KAGEYAMA DOES STILL BELIEVE THAT HE CAN WIN ENTIRELY BY HIMSELF...
IT'S ALMOST AS IF...
...HE HASN'T MATURED FROM HIS TIME IN MIDDLE SCHOOL.
HE'S THERE COURT THE GA HIMS
LIKE HE MANAGED BACK THEN...
...INDIVIDUAL TALENT CAN CARRY A TEAM TO A DEGREE.
KITAGAWA DAIICHI SUFFERS HEARTBREAKING LOSS
BUT IT CAN'T TAKE THEM TO THE TOP.
...
CAPTAIN!!
?!
JOLT
WHA ?!
WHO ?!
BDMP BDMP
BDMP BDMP
HUH?
RATL
YOU GUYS!
HAVE YOU BEEN STANDING OUT THERE ALL PRACTICE?
DON'T MESS IT UP.
YOU DON'T MESS IT UP.
WHRL

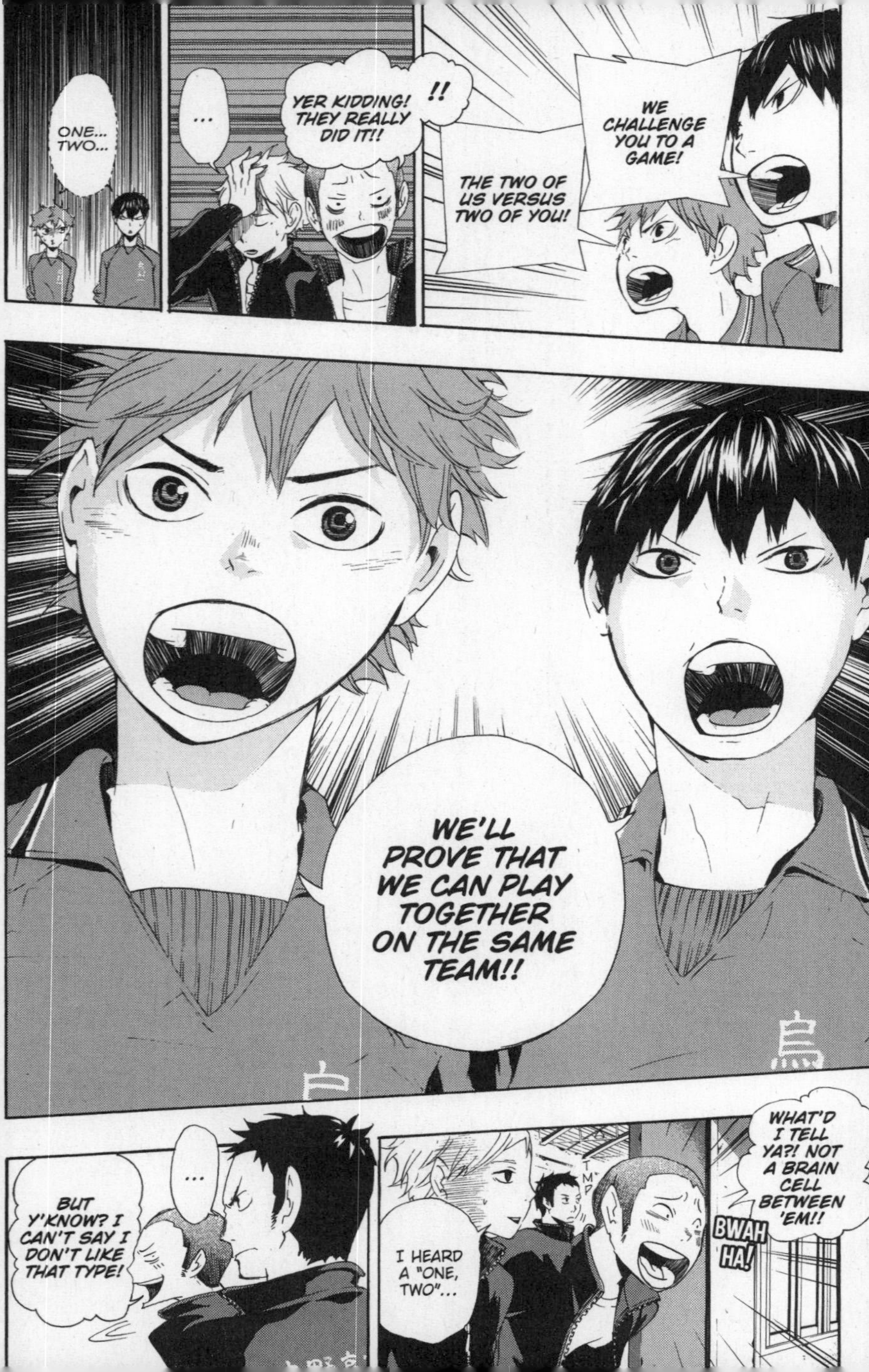

WE CHALLENGE YOU TO A GAME!
THE TWO OF US VERSUS TWO OF YOU!
!!
YER KIDDING! THEY REALLY DID IT!!
...
ONE... TWO...
WE'LL PROVE THAT WE CAN PLAY TOGETHER ON THE SAME TEAM!!
WHAT'D I TELL YA?! NOT A BRAIN CELL BETWEEN 'EM!!
BWAH HA!
TMP
I HEARD A "ONE, TWO"...
...
BUT Y'KNOW? I CAN'T SAY I DON'T LIKE THAT TYPE!

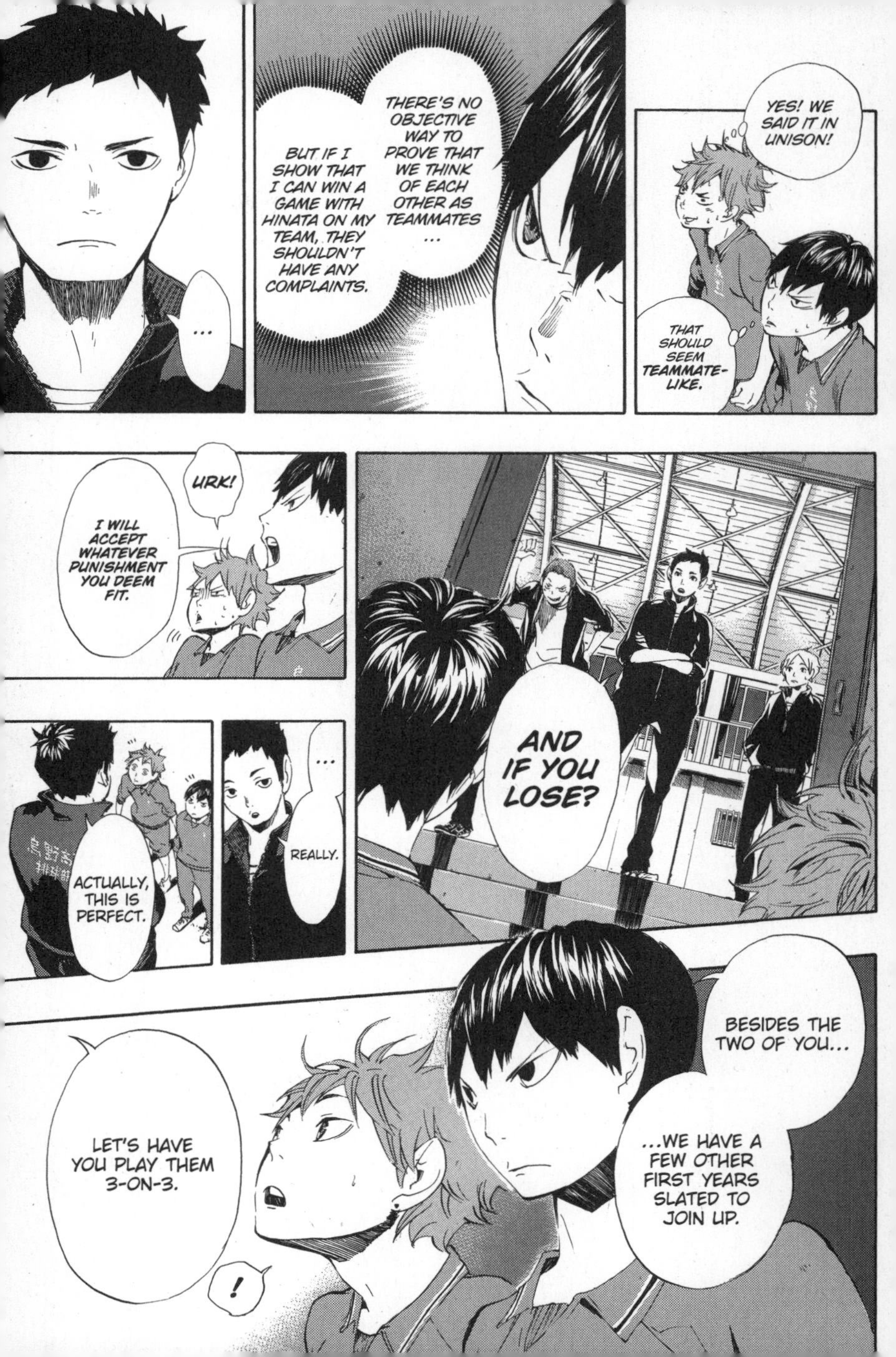
YES! WE SAID IT IN UNISON!
THAT SHOULD SEEM TEAMMATE-LIKE.
THERE'S NO OBJECTIVE WAY TO PROVE THAT WE THINK OF EACH OTHER AS TEAMMATES...
BUT IF I SHOW THAT I CAN WIN A GAME WITH HINATA ON MY TEAM, THEY SHOULDN'T HAVE ANY COMPLAINTS.
...
AND IF YOU LOSE?
I WILL ACCEPT WHATEVER PUNISHMENT YOU DEEM FIT.
URK!
...
REALLY.
ACTUALLY, THIS IS PERFECT.
BESIDES THE TWO OF YOU...
...WE HAVE A FEW OTHER FIRST YEARS SLATED TO JOIN UP.
LET'S HAVE YOU PLAY THEM 3-ON-3.
!

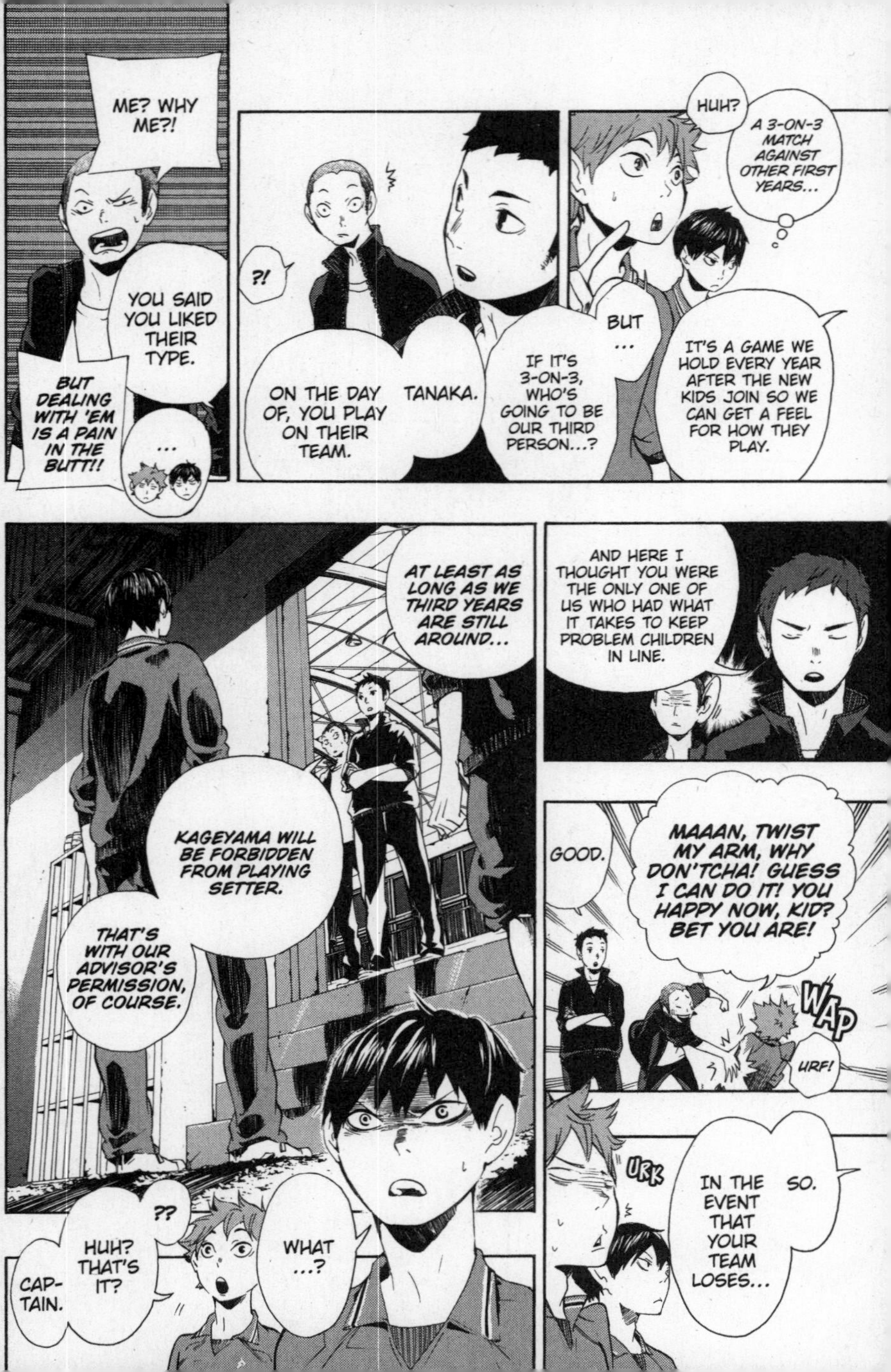
HUH?
A 3-ON-3 MATCH AGAINST OTHER FIRST YEARS...
IT'S A GAME WE HOLD EVERY YEAR AFTER THE NEW KIDS JOIN SO WE CAN GET A FEEL FOR HOW THEY PLAY.
BUT ...
IF IT'S 3-ON-3, WHO'S GOING TO BE OUR THIRD PERSON...?
TANAKA.
ON THE DAY OF, YOU PLAY ON THEIR TEAM.
?!
ME? WHY ME?!
YOU SAID YOU LIKED THEIR TYPE.
BUT DEALING WITH 'EM IS A PAIN IN THE BUTT!!
...
AND HERE I THOUGHT YOU WERE THE ONLY ONE OF US WHO HAD WHAT IT TAKES TO KEEP PROBLEM CHILDREN IN LINE.
MAAAN, TWIST MY ARM, WHY DON'TCHA! GUESS I CAN DO IT! YOU HAPPY NOW, KID? BET YOU ARE!
GOOD.
WAP
URF!
SO.
IN THE EVENT THAT YOUR TEAM LOSES...
URK
AT LEAST AS LONG AS WE THIRD YEARS ARE STILL AROUND...
KAGEYAMA WILL BE FORBIDDEN FROM PLAYING SETTER.
THAT'S WITH OUR ADVISOR'S PERMISSION, OF COURSE.
WHAT ...?
??
HUH? THAT'S IT?
CAP-TAIN.

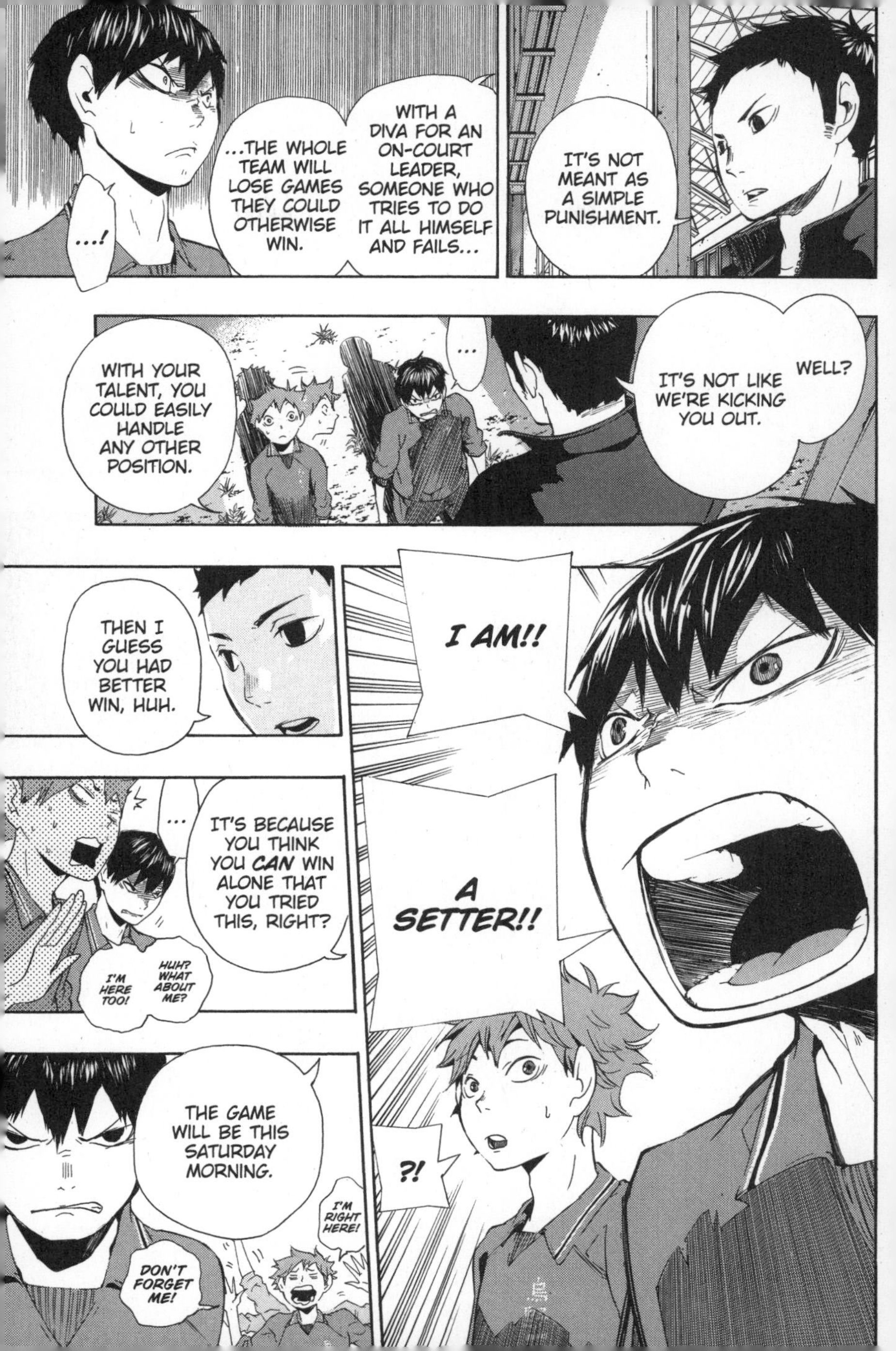
IT'S NOT MEANT AS A SIMPLE PUNISHMENT.
WITH A DIVA FOR AN ON-COURT LEADER, SOMEONE WHO TRIES TO DO IT ALL HIMSELF AND FAILS...
...THE WHOLE TEAM WILL LOSE GAMES THEY COULD OTHERWISE WIN.
...!
WELL?
IT'S NOT LIKE WE'RE KICKING YOU OUT.
...
WITH YOUR TALENT, YOU COULD EASILY HANDLE ANY OTHER POSITION.
I AM!!
A SETTER!!
?!
THEN I GUESS YOU HAD BETTER WIN, HUH.
...
IT'S BECAUSE YOU THINK YOU CAN WIN ALONE THAT YOU TRIED THIS, RIGHT?
HUH? WHAT ABOUT ME?
I'M HERE TOO!
THE GAME WILL BE THIS SATURDAY MORNING.
I'M RIGHT HERE!
DON'T FORGET ME!

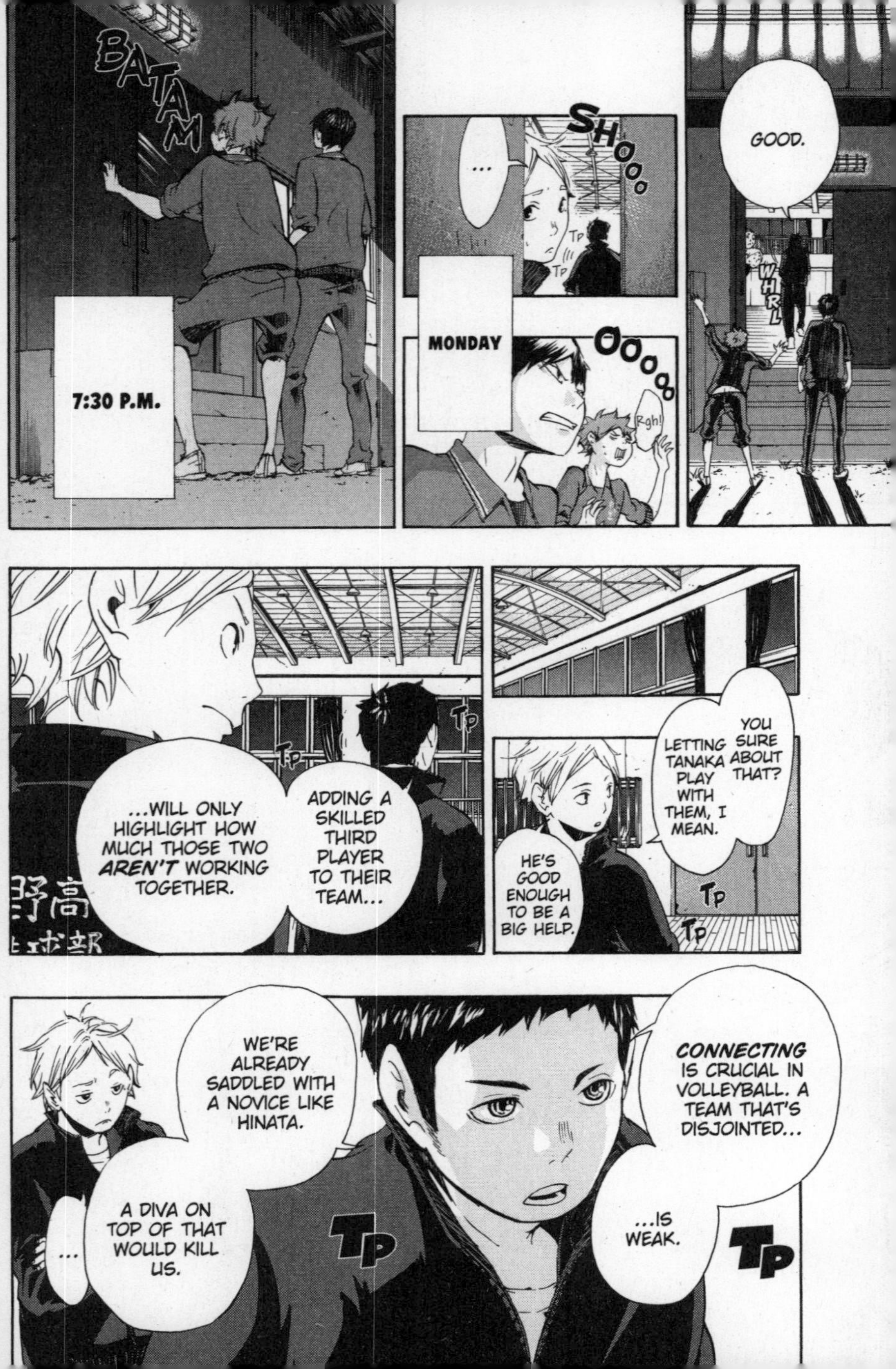

GOOD.
WHRL
...
SHOOOO
Tp
Tp
MONDAY
OOOO
Rgh!
BATAM
7:30 P.M.
YOU SURE ABOUT THAT?
LETTING TANAKA PLAY WITH THEM, I MEAN.
HE'S GOOD ENOUGH TO BE A BIG HELP.
Tp
Tp
ADDING A SKILLED THIRD PLAYER TO THEIR TEAM...
...WILL ONLY HIGHLIGHT HOW MUCH THOSE TWO *AREN'T* WORKING TOGETHER.
Tp
Tp
CONNECTING IS CRUCIAL IN VOLLEYBALL. A TEAM THAT'S DISJOINTED...
...IS WEAK.
TP
WE'RE ALREADY SADDLED WITH A NOVICE LIKE HINATA.
A DIVA ON TOP OF THAT WOULD KILL US.
...
TP

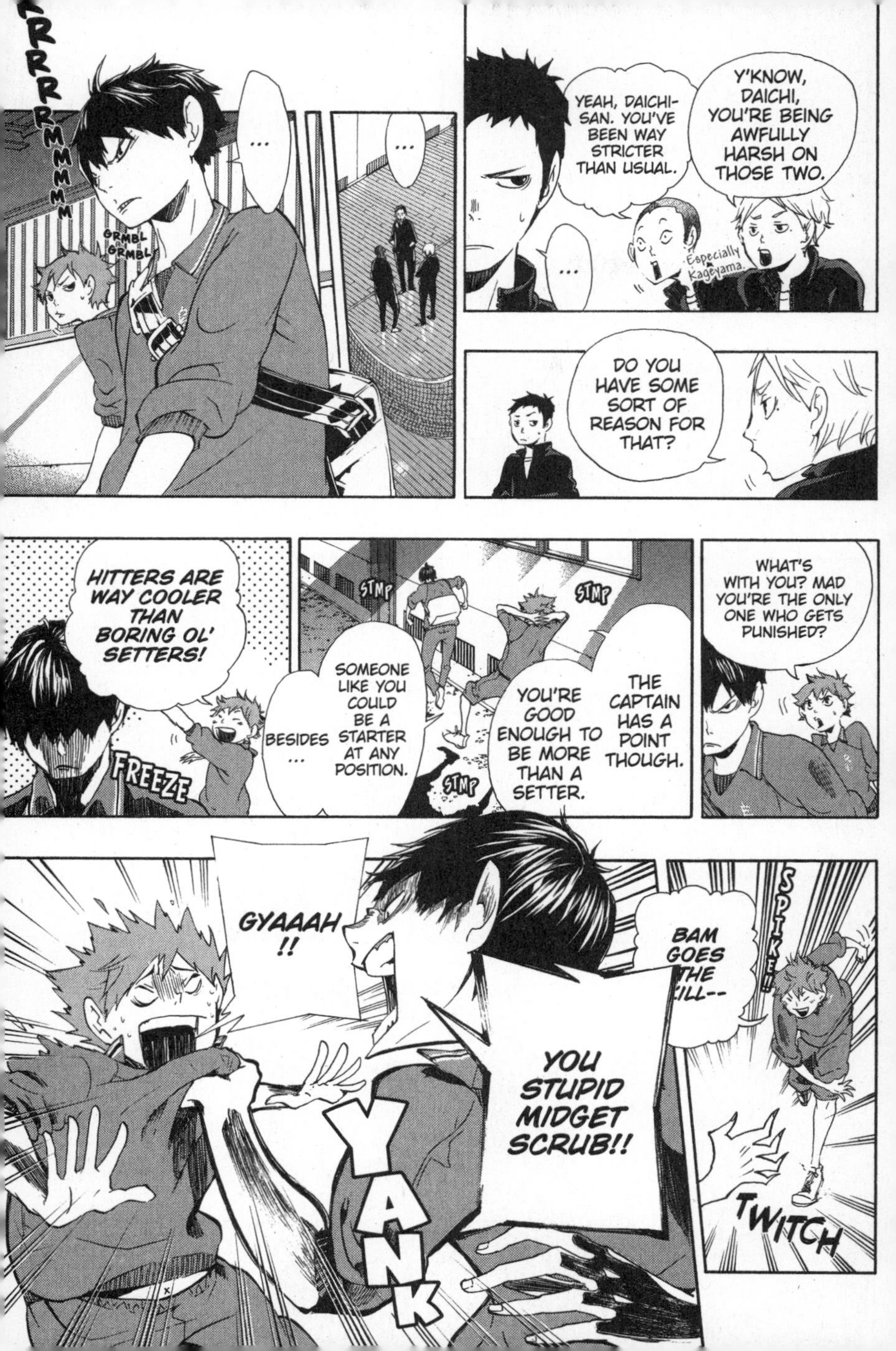
Y'KNOW, DAICHI, YOU'RE BEING AWFULLY HARSH ON THOSE TWO.
YEAH, DAICHI-SAN. YOU'VE BEEN WAY STRICTER THAN USUAL.
Especially Kageyama.
...
DO YOU HAVE SOME SORT OF REASON FOR THAT?
...
...
RRRRMMMMM
GRMBL GRMBL
WHAT'S WITH YOU? MAD YOU'RE THE ONLY ONE WHO GETS PUNISHED?
STMP
STMP
THE CAPTAIN HAS A POINT THOUGH.
YOU'RE GOOD ENOUGH TO BE MORE THAN A SETTER.
SOMEONE LIKE YOU COULD BE A STARTER AT ANY POSITION.
BESIDES ...
STMP
HITTERS ARE WAY COOLER THAN BORING OL' SETTERS!
FREEZE
SPIKE!!
BAM GOES THE KILL--
TWITCH
YOU STUPID MIDGET SCRUB!!
GYAAAH!!
YANK

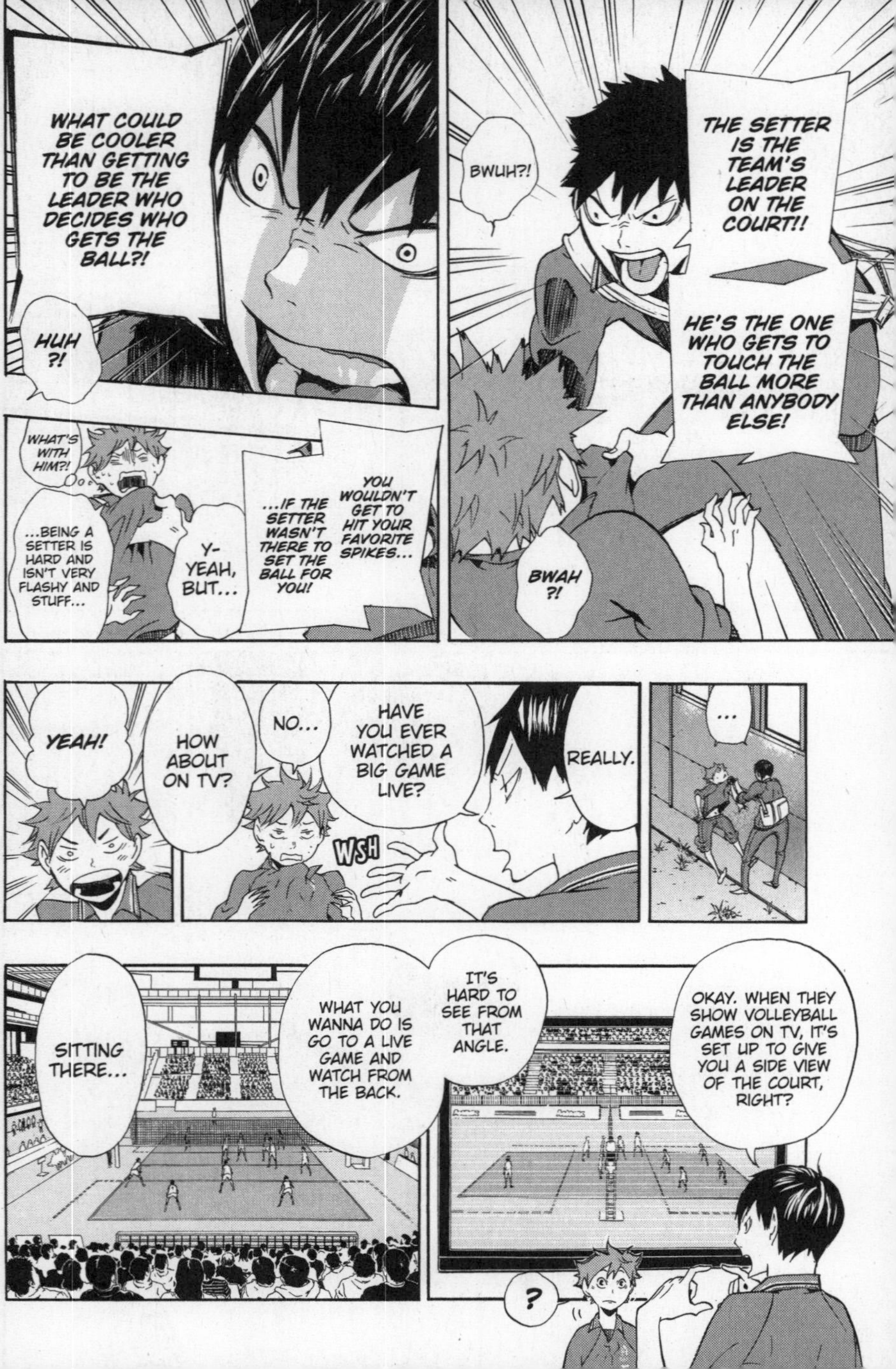
THE SETTER IS THE TEAM'S LEADER ON THE COURT!!
BWUH?!
HE'S THE ONE WHO GETS TO TOUCH THE BALL MORE THAN ANYBODY ELSE!
BWAH?!
WHAT COULD BE COOLER THAN GETTING TO BE THE LEADER WHO DECIDES WHO GETS THE BALL?!
HUH?!
YOU WOULDN'T GET TO HIT YOUR FAVORITE SPIKES...
...IF THE SETTER WASN'T THERE TO SET THE BALL FOR YOU!
Y-YEAH, BUT...
WHAT'S WITH HIM?!
...BEING A SETTER IS HARD AND ISN'T VERY FLASHY AND STUFF...
...
REALLY.
HAVE YOU EVER WATCHED A BIG GAME LIVE?
NO...
WSH
HOW ABOUT ON TV?
YEAH!
OKAY. WHEN THEY SHOW VOLLEYBALL GAMES ON TV, IT'S SET UP TO GIVE YOU A SIDE VIEW OF THE COURT, RIGHT?
IT'S HARD TO SEE FROM THAT ANGLE.
?
WHAT YOU WANNA DO IS GO TO A LIVE GAME AND WATCH FROM THE BACK.
SITTING THERE...

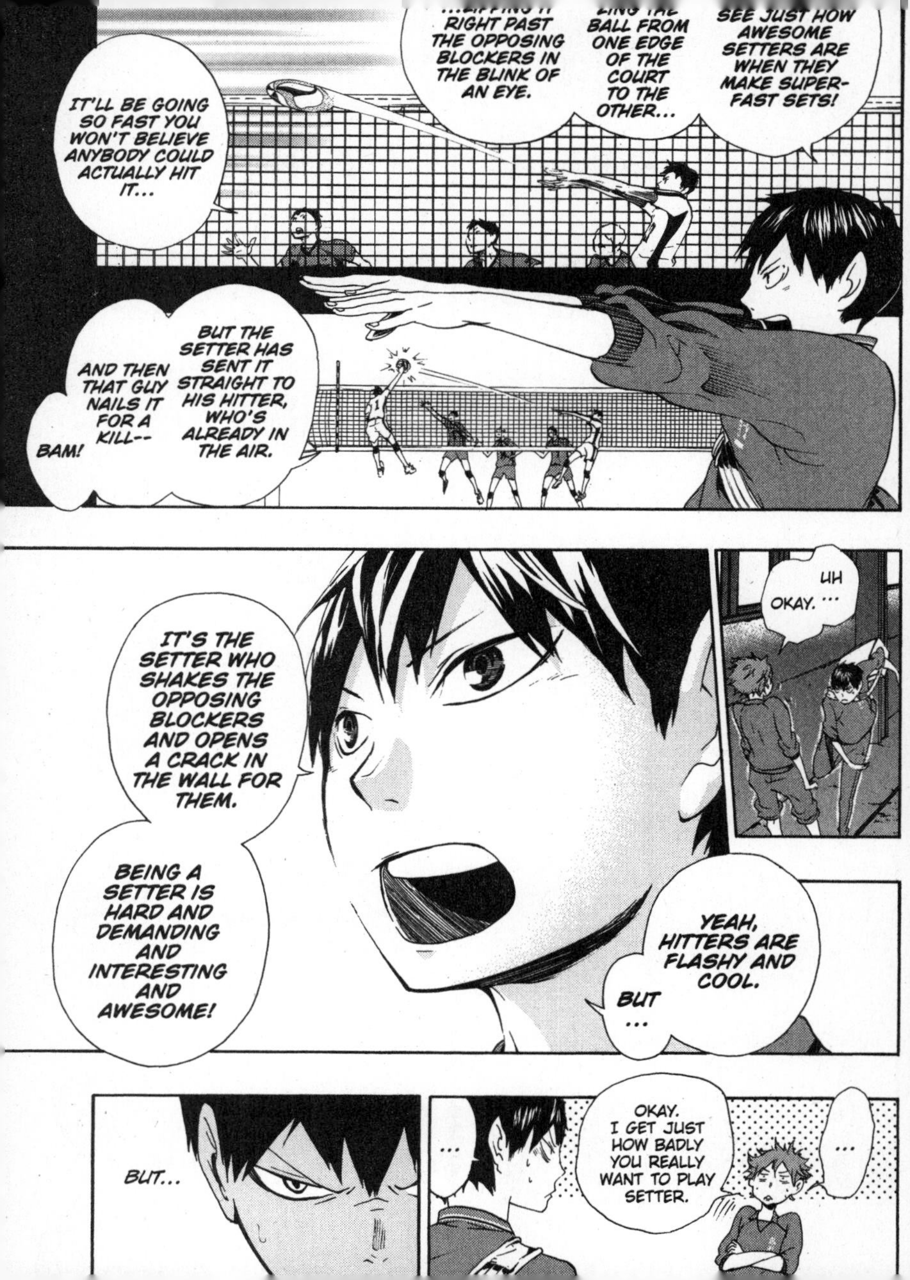
SEE JUST HOW AWESOME SETTERS ARE WHEN THEY MAKE SUPER-FAST SETS!
BALL FROM ONE EDGE OF THE COURT TO THE OTHER...
RIGHT PAST THE OPPOSING BLOCKERS IN THE BLINK OF AN EYE.
IT'LL BE GOING SO FAST YOU WON'T BELIEVE ANYBODY COULD ACTUALLY HIT IT...
BUT THE SETTER HAS SENT IT STRAIGHT TO HIS HITTER, WHO'S ALREADY IN THE AIR.
AND THEN THAT GUY NAILS IT FOR A KILL-- BAM!
UH ... OKAY.
YEAH, HITTERS ARE FLASHY AND COOL.
BUT ...
IT'S THE SETTER WHO SHAKES THE OPPOSING BLOCKERS AND OPENS A CRACK IN THE WALL FOR THEM.
BEING A SETTER IS HARD AND DEMANDING AND INTERESTING AND AWESOME!
...
OKAY. I GET JUST HOW BADLY YOU REALLY WANT TO PLAY SETTER.
...
BUT...

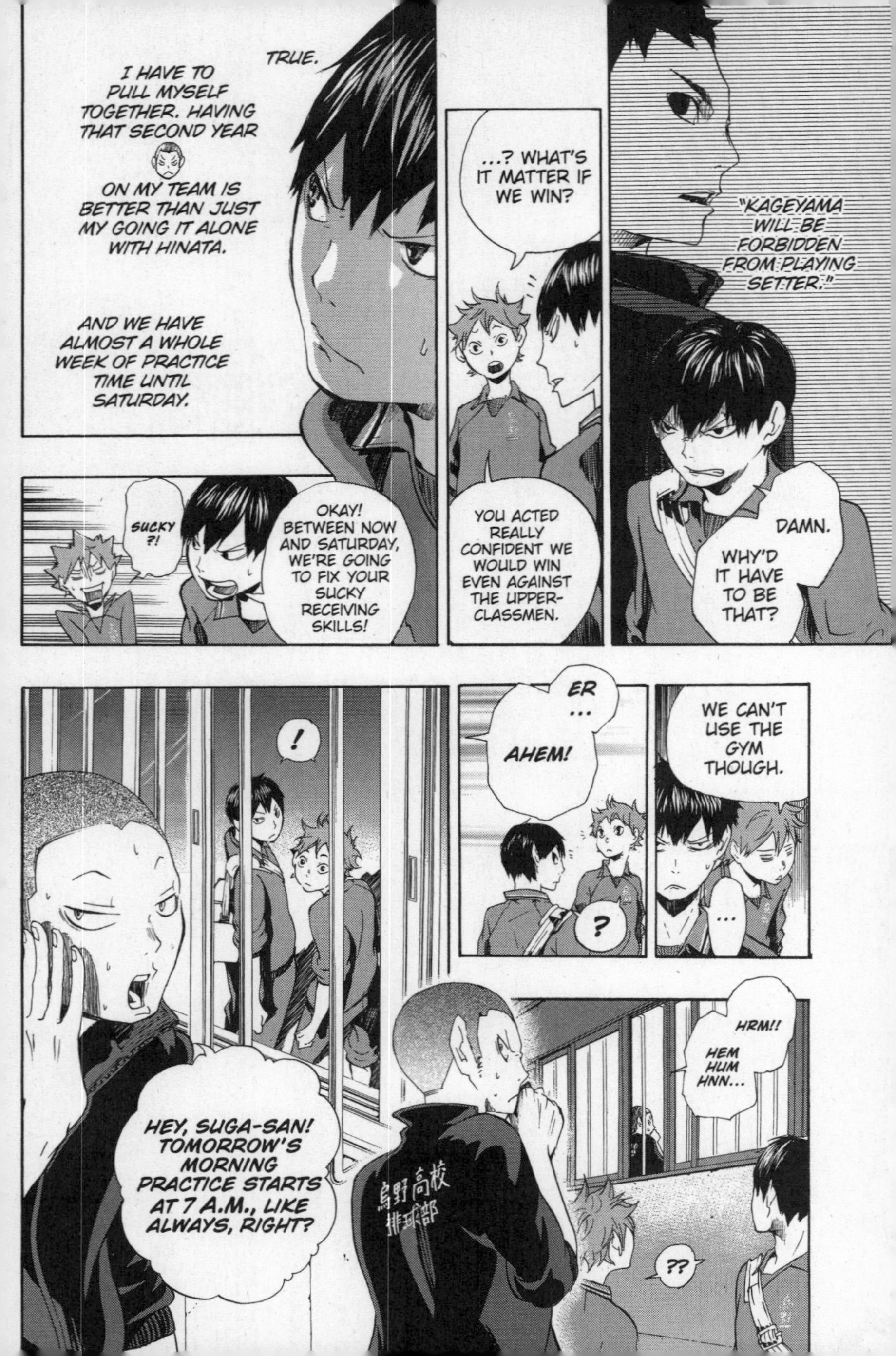
"KAGEYAMA WILL BE FORBIDDEN FROM PLAYING SETTER."
DAMN.
WHY'D IT HAVE TO BE THAT?
...? WHAT'S IT MATTER IF WE WIN?
YOU ACTED REALLY CONFIDENT WE WOULD WIN EVEN AGAINST THE UPPER-CLASSMEN.
TRUE.
I HAVE TO PULL MYSELF TOGETHER. HAVING THAT SECOND YEAR
ON MY TEAM IS BETTER THAN JUST MY GOING IT ALONE WITH HINATA.
AND WE HAVE ALMOST A WHOLE WEEK OF PRACTICE TIME UNTIL SATURDAY.
OKAY! BETWEEN NOW AND SATURDAY, WE'RE GOING TO FIX YOUR SUCKY RECEIVING SKILLS!
SUCKY?!
WE CAN'T USE THE GYM THOUGH.
...
ER...
AHEM!
?
HRM!!
HEM HUM HNN...
??
!
HEY, SUGA-SAN! TOMORROW'S MORNING PRACTICE STARTS AT 7 A.M., LIKE ALWAYS, RIGHT?

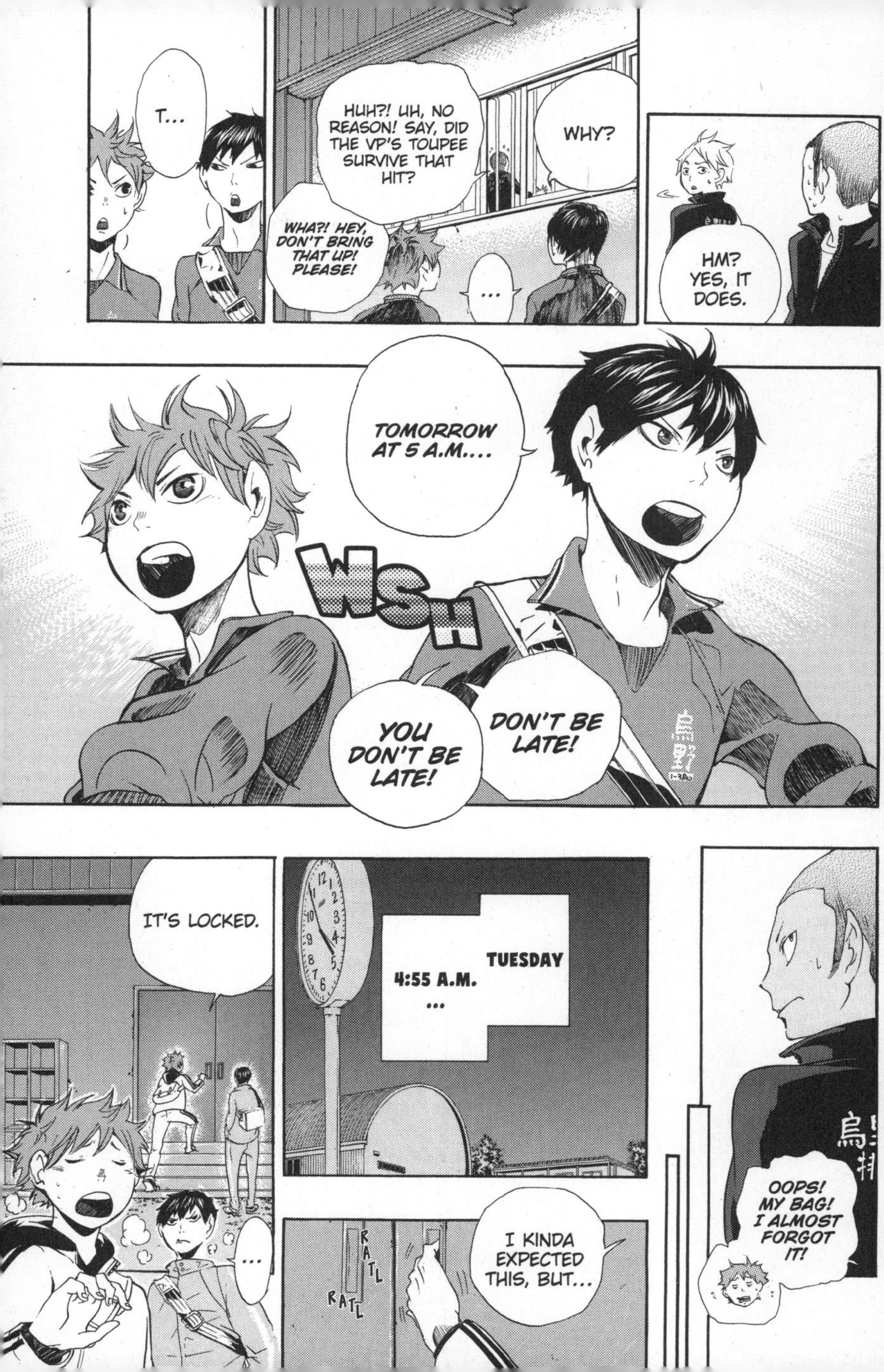
HM? YES, IT DOES.
WHY?
HUH?! UH, NO REASON! SAY, DID THE VP'S TOUPEE SURVIVE THAT HIT?
WHA?! HEY, DON'T BRING THAT UP! PLEASE!
...
T...
TOMORROW AT 5 A.M....
WSH
DON'T BE LATE!
YOU DON'T BE LATE!
OOPS! MY BAG! I ALMOST FORGOT IT!
TUESDAY
4:55 A.M.
...
I KINDA EXPECTED THIS, BUT...
RATL
RATL
IT'S LOCKED.
...

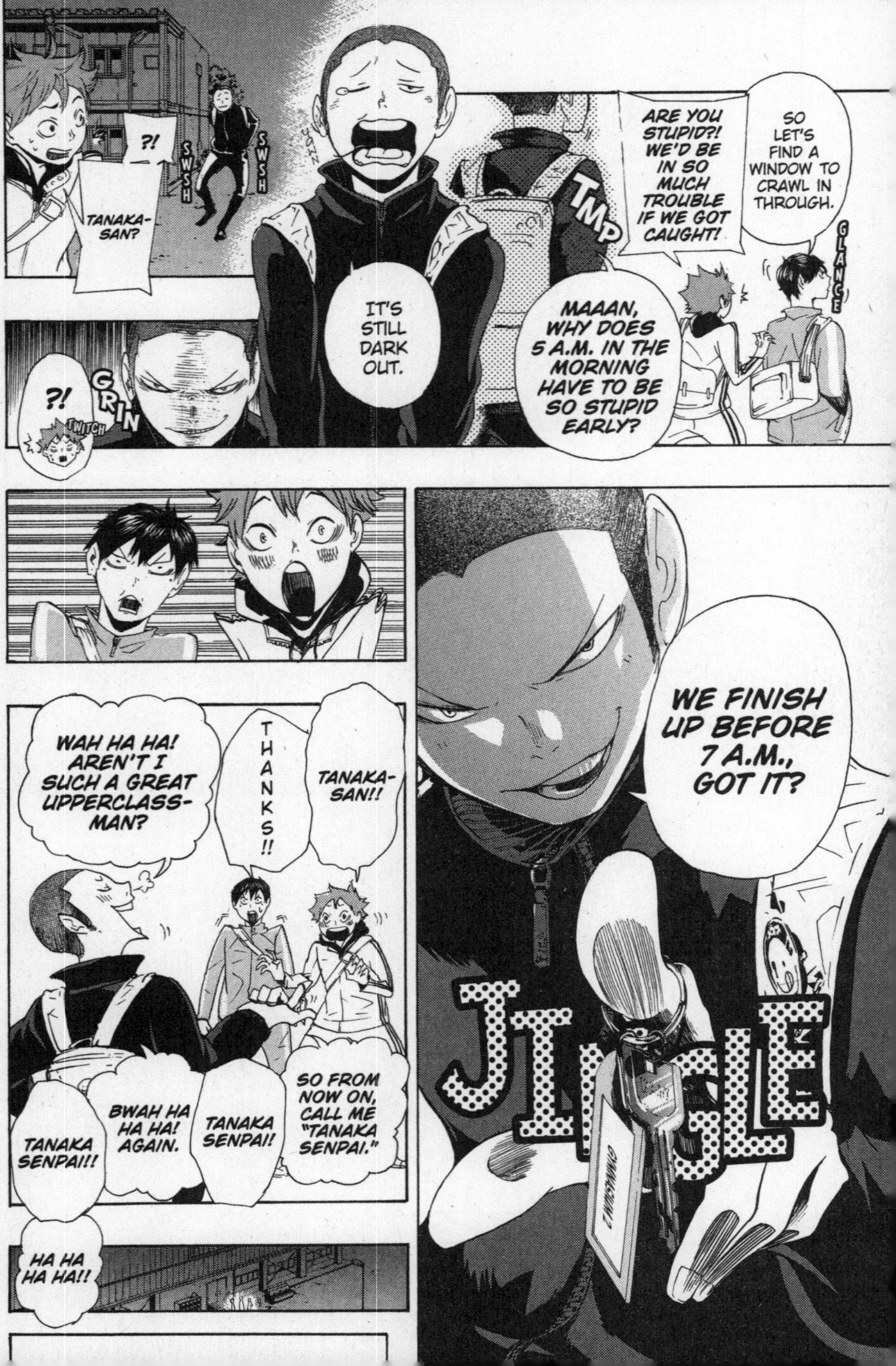
SO LET'S FIND A WINDOW TO CRAWL IN THROUGH.
GLANCE
ARE YOU STUPID?! WE'D BE IN SO MUCH TROUBLE IF WE GOT CAUGHT!
TMP
MAAAN, WHY DOES 5 A.M. IN THE MORNING HAVE TO BE SO STUPID EARLY?
YAWN
IT'S STILL DARK OUT.
SWSH
SWSH
?!
TANAKA-SAN?
GRIN
?!
TWITCH
WE FINISH UP BEFORE 7 A.M., GOT IT?
JINGLE
TANAKA-SAN!!
THANKS!!
WAH HA HA! AREN'T I SUCH A GREAT UPPERCLASSMAN?
SO FROM NOW ON, CALL ME "TANAKA SENPAI."
TANAKA SENPAI!
BWAH HA HA HA! AGAIN.
TANAKA SENPAI!!
HA HA HA HA!!

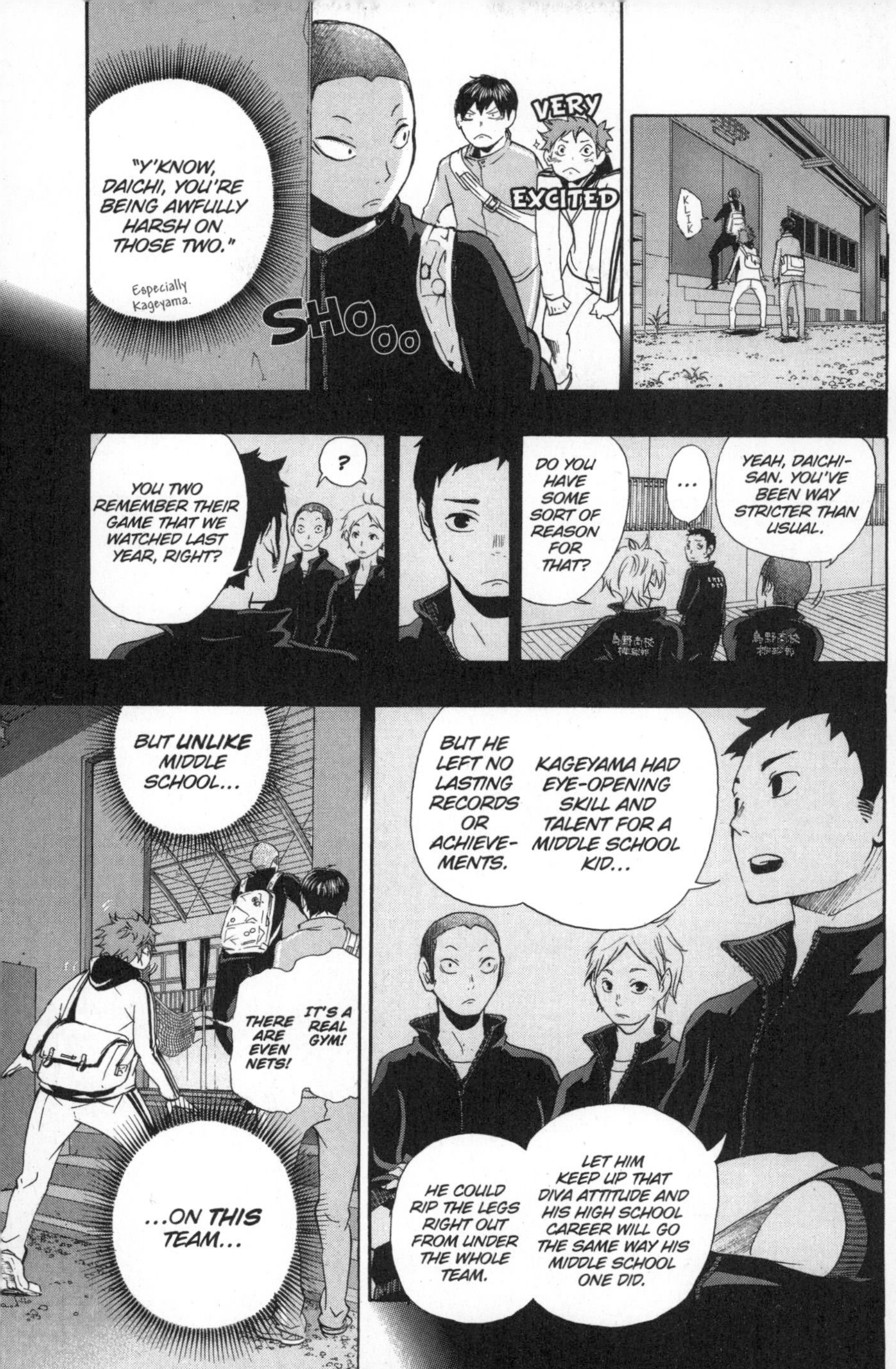
KLIK
VERY EXCITED
"Y'KNOW, DAICHI, YOU'RE BEING AWFULLY HARSH ON THOSE TWO."
Especially Kageyama.
SHOooo
YEAH, DAICHI-SAN. YOU'VE BEEN WAY STRICTER THAN USUAL.
...
DO YOU HAVE SOME SORT OF REASON FOR THAT?
?
YOU TWO REMEMBER THEIR GAME THAT WE WATCHED LAST YEAR, RIGHT?
KAGEYAMA HAD EYE-OPENING SKILL AND TALENT FOR A MIDDLE SCHOOL KID...
BUT HE LEFT NO LASTING RECORDS OR ACHIEVEMENTS.
LET HIM KEEP UP THAT DIVA ATTITUDE AND HIS HIGH SCHOOL CAREER WILL GO THE SAME WAY HIS MIDDLE SCHOOL ONE DID.
HE COULD RIP THE LEGS RIGHT OUT FROM UNDER THE WHOLE TEAM.
BUT UNLIKE MIDDLE SCHOOL...
IT'S A REAL GYM!
THERE ARE EVEN NETS!
...ON THIS TEAM...

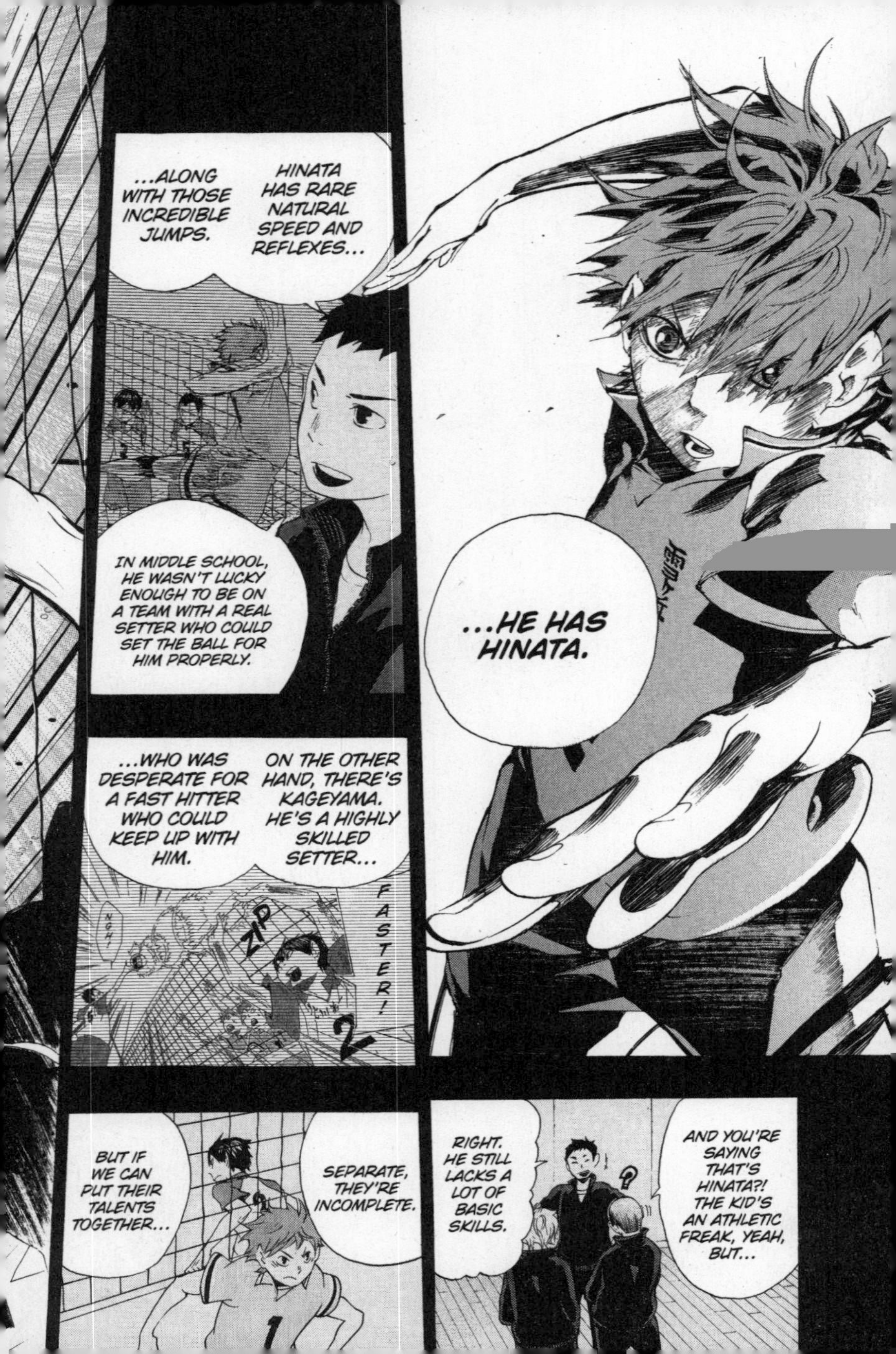
...HE HAS HINATA.
HINATA HAS RARE NATURAL SPEED AND REFLEXES...
...ALONG WITH THOSE INCREDIBLE JUMPS.
IN MIDDLE SCHOOL, HE WASN'T LUCKY ENOUGH TO BE ON A TEAM WITH A REAL SETTER WHO COULD SET THE BALL FOR HIM PROPERLY.
ON THE OTHER HAND, THERE'S KAGEYAMA. HE'S A HIGHLY SKILLED SETTER...
...WHO WAS DESPERATE FOR A FAST HITTER WHO COULD KEEP UP WITH HIM.
FASTER!
ZIP
NGH!
AND YOU'RE SAYING THAT'S HINATA?! THE KID'S AN ATHLETIC FREAK, YEAH, BUT...
RIGHT. HE STILL LACKS A LOT OF BASIC SKILLS.
SEPARATE, THEY'RE INCOMPLETE.
BUT IF WE CAN PUT THEIR TALENTS TOGETHER...

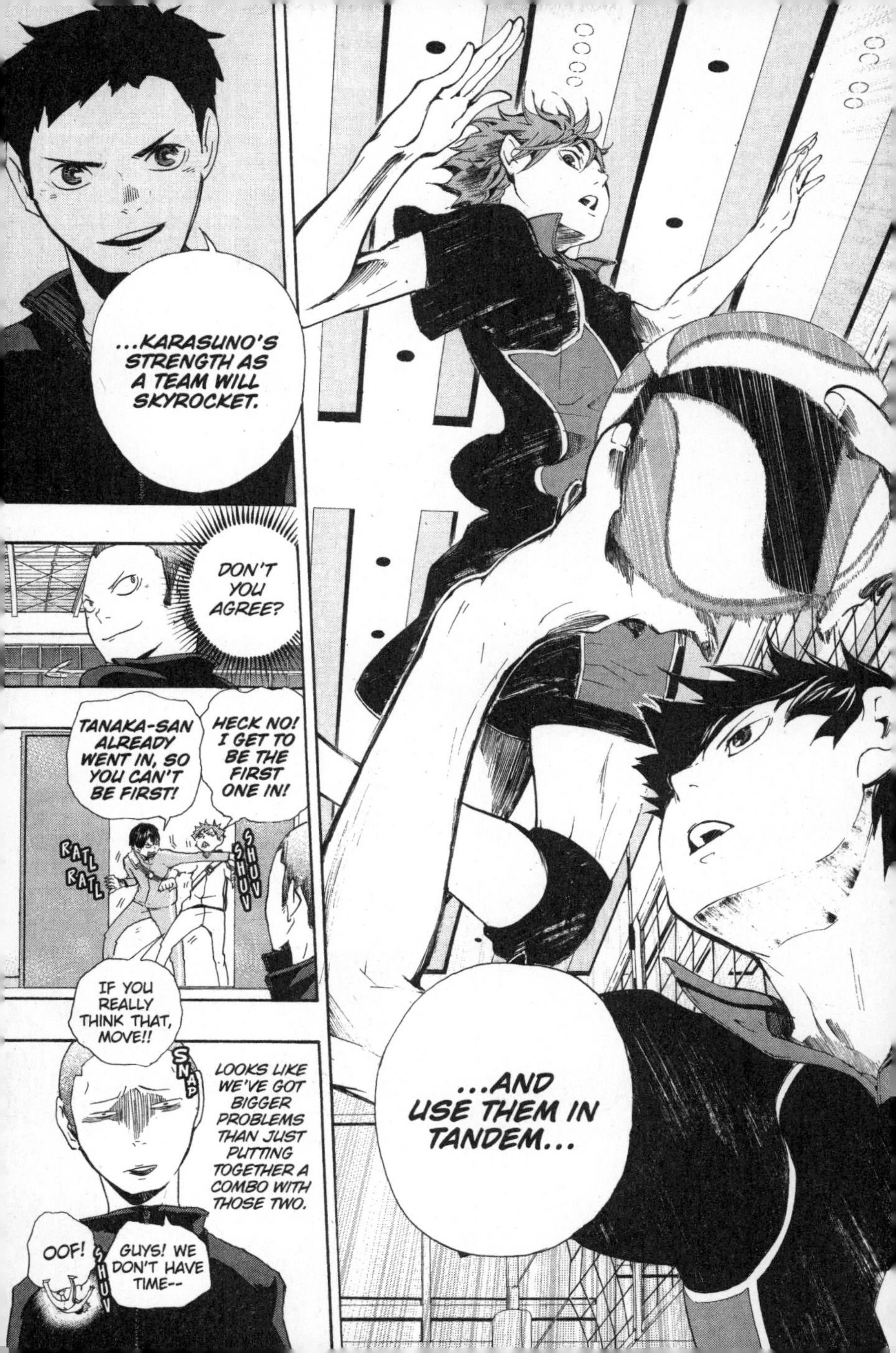
...AND USE THEM IN TANDEM...
...KARASUNO'S STRENGTH AS A TEAM WILL SKYROCKET.
DON'T YOU AGREE?
HECK NO! I GET TO BE THE FIRST ONE IN!
TANAKA-SAN ALREADY WENT IN, SO YOU CAN'T BE FIRST!
SHUV SHUV
RATTL RATTL
IF YOU REALLY THINK THAT, MOVE!!
SNAP
LOOKS LIKE WE'VE GOT BIGGER PROBLEMS THAN JUST PUTTING TOGETHER A COMBO WITH THOSE TWO.
GUYS! WE DON'T HAVE TIME--
SHUV
OOF!

TOBIO KAGEYAMA

KARASUNO HIGH SCHOOL
CLASS 1-3

POSITION: SETTER

HEIGHT: 5’11”
WEIGHT: 146 LBS.
(AS OF APRIL, 1ST YEAR OF HIGH SCHOOL)

BIRTHDAY: DECEMBER 22

FAVORITE FOOD:
PORK CURRY WITH SLOW-COOKED EGGS

CURRENT WORRY:
HE THINKS ANIMALS DON’T LIKE HIM.

ABILITY PARAMETERS
(5-POINT SCALE)

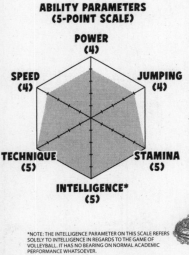

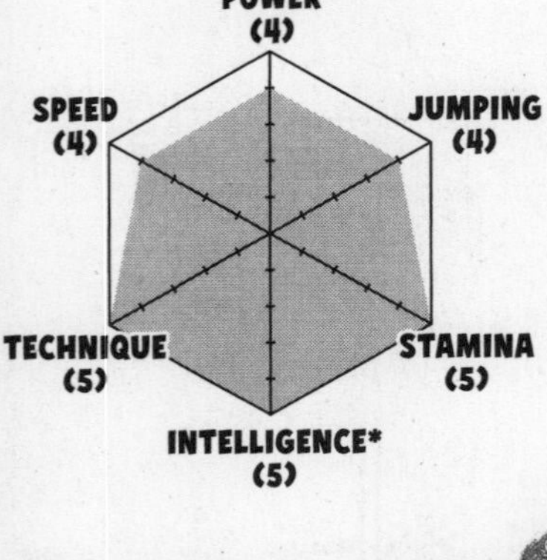
POWER (4)
JUMPING (4)
STAMINA (5)
INTELLIGENCE* (5)
TECHNIQUE (5)
SPEED (4)

*NOTE: THE INTELLIGENCE PARAMETER ON THIS SCALE REFERS SOLELY TO INTELLIGENCE IN REGARDS TO THE GAME OF VOLLEYBALL. IT HAS NO BEARING ON NORMAL ACADEMIC PERFORMANCE WHATSOEVER.

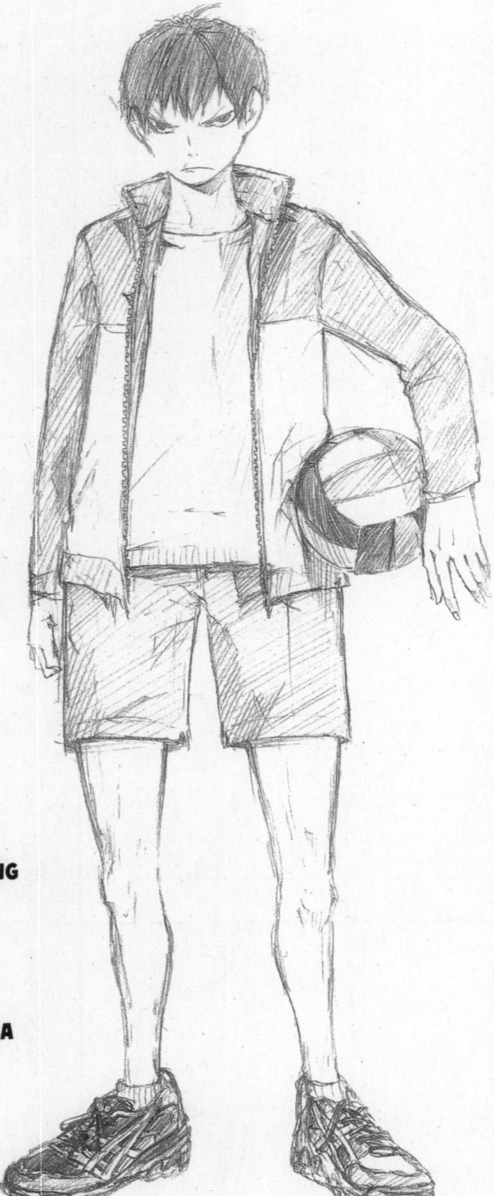

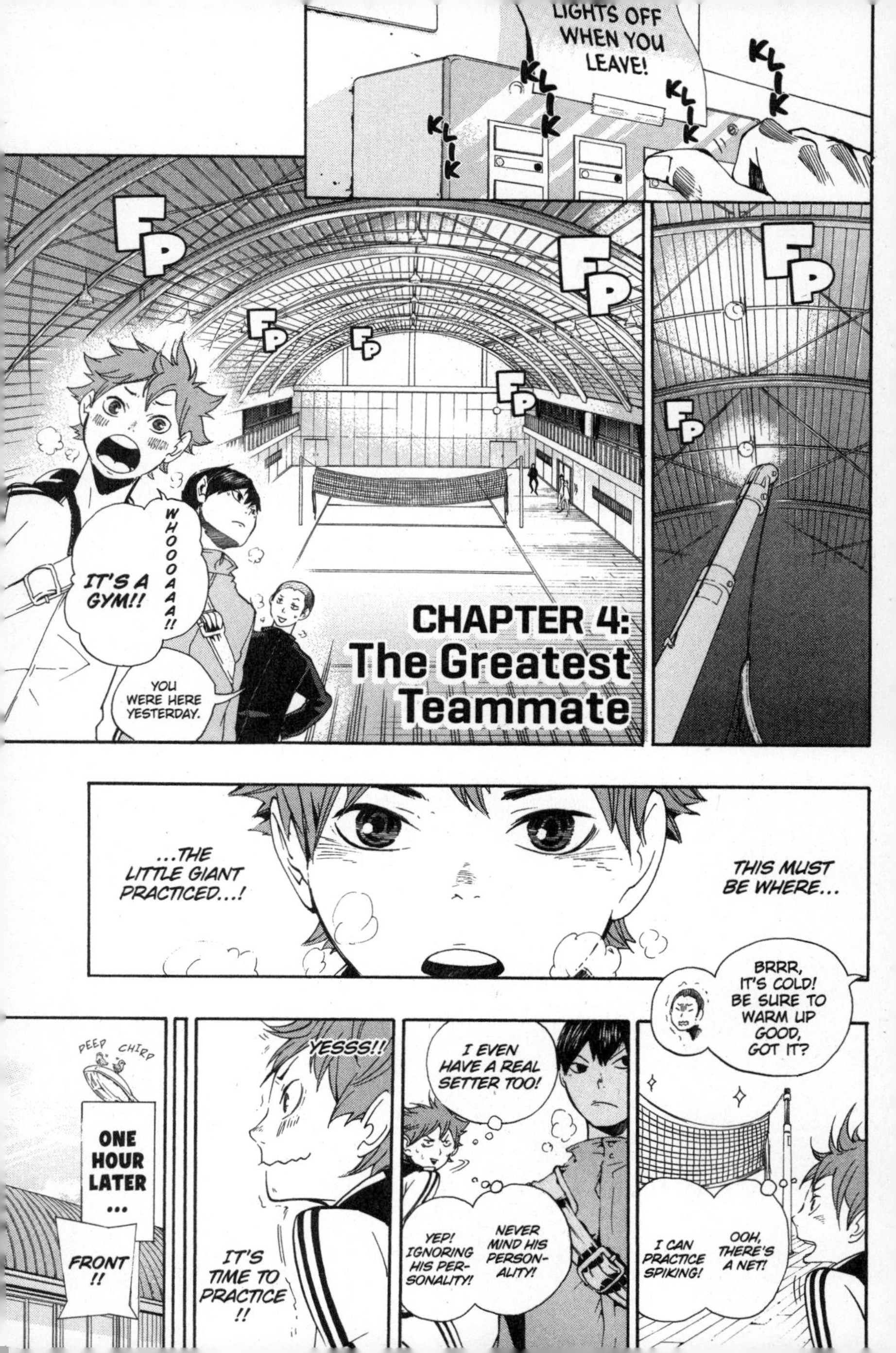
LIGHTS OFF WHEN YOU LEAVE!
KLIK
KLIK
KLIK
KLIK
FP
FP
FP
FP
FP
FP
FP
WHOOOOAAAA!!
IT'S A GYM!!
YOU WERE HERE YESTERDAY.
CHAPTER 4: The Greatest Teammate
THIS MUST BE WHERE...
...THE LITTLE GIANT PRACTICED...!
BRRR, IT'S COLD! BE SURE TO WARM UP GOOD, GOT IT?
OOH, THERE'S A NET!
I CAN PRACTICE SPIKING!
I EVEN HAVE A REAL SETTER TOO!
NEVER MIND HIS PERSONALITY!
YEP! IGNORING HIS PERSONALITY!
YESSS!!
IT'S TIME TO PRACTICE!!
PEEP
CHIRP
ONE HOUR LATER...
FRONT!!

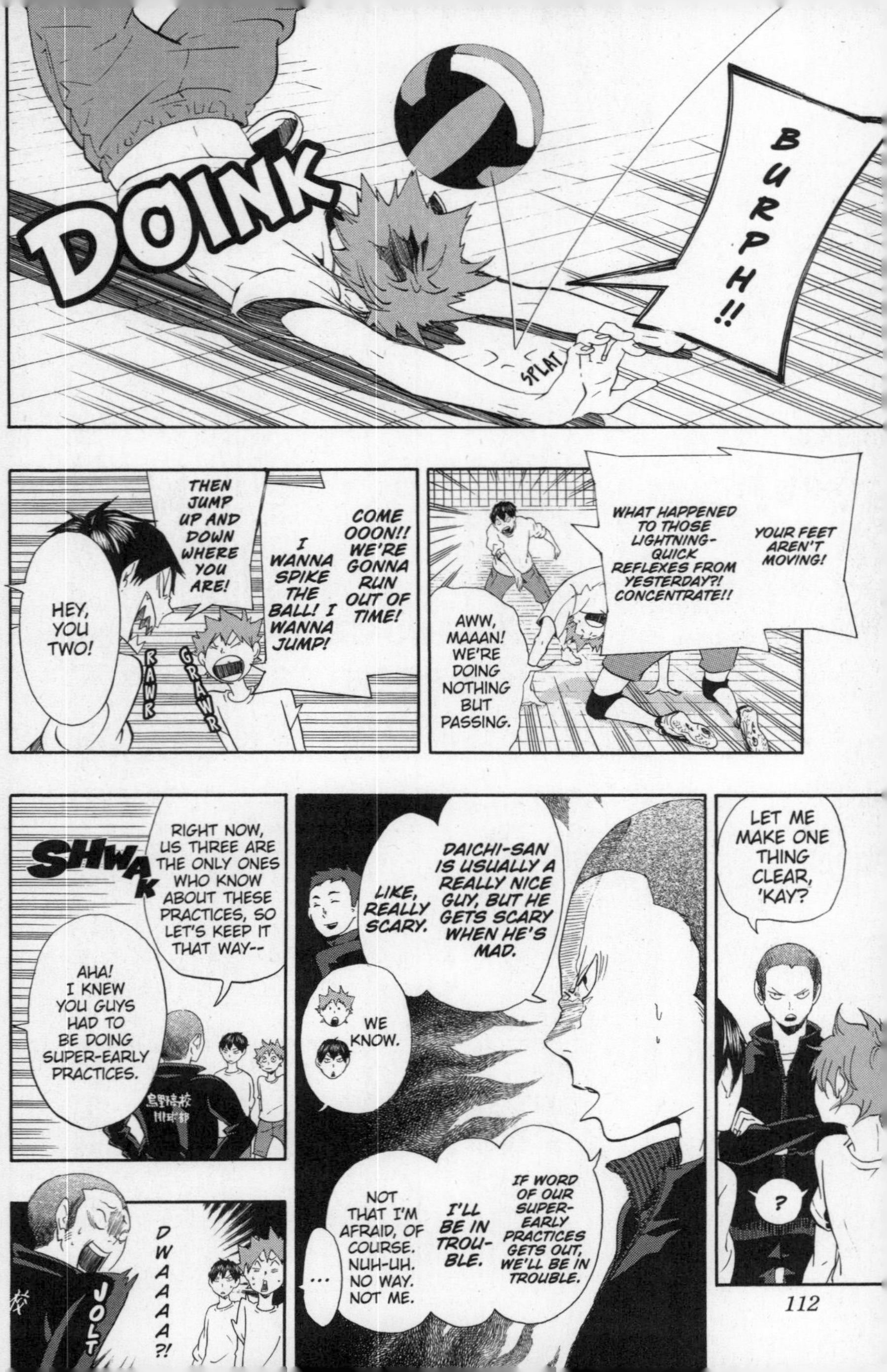

BURPH!!
SPLAT
DOINK
YOUR FEET AREN'T MOVING!
WHAT HAPPENED TO THOSE LIGHTNING-QUICK REFLEXES FROM YESTERDAY?! CONCENTRATE!!
AWW, MAAAN! WE'RE DOING NOTHING BUT PASSING.
COME OOON!! WE'RE GONNA RUN OUT OF TIME!
I WANNA SPIKE THE BALL! I WANNA JUMP!
THEN JUMP UP AND DOWN WHERE YOU ARE!
HEY, YOU TWO!
GRAWR
RAWR
LET ME MAKE ONE THING CLEAR, 'KAY?
?
DAICHI-SAN IS USUALLY A REALLY NICE GUY, BUT HE GETS SCARY WHEN HE'S MAD.
LIKE, REALLY SCARY.
WE KNOW.
IF WORD OF OUR SUPER-EARLY PRACTICES GETS OUT, WE'LL BE IN TROUBLE.
I'LL BE IN TROUBLE.
NOT THAT I'M AFRAID, OF COURSE. NUH-UH. NO WAY. NOT ME.
...
RIGHT NOW, US THREE ARE THE ONLY ONES WHO KNOW ABOUT THESE PRACTICES, SO LET'S KEEP IT THAT WAY--
SHWAK
AHA! I KNEW YOU GUYS HAD TO BE DOING SUPER-EARLY PRACTICES.
DWAAAAA?!
JOLT

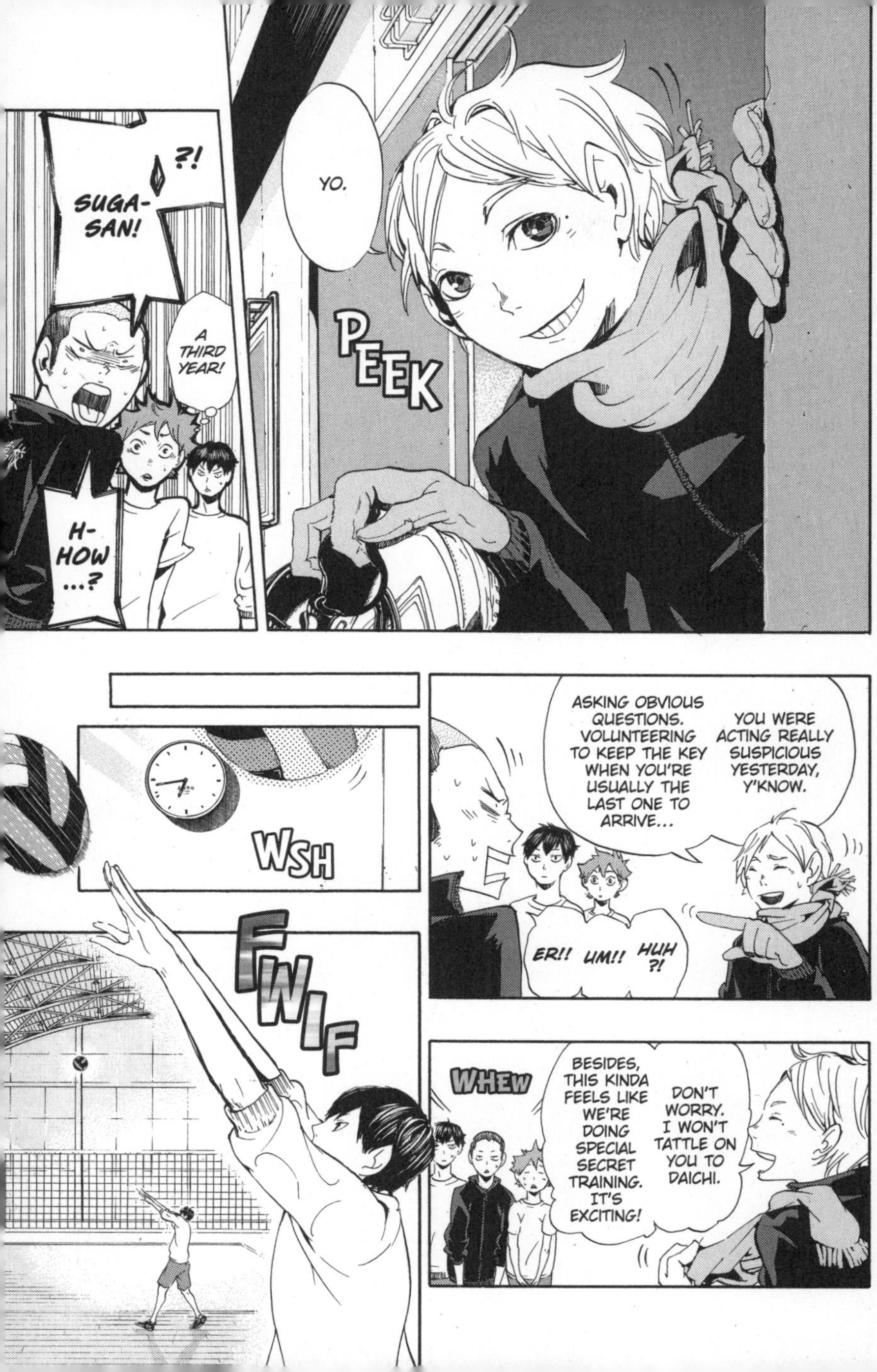
YO.
PEEK
?!
SUGA-SAN!
A THIRD YEAR!
H-HOW...?
YOU WERE ACTING REALLY SUSPICIOUS YESTERDAY, Y'KNOW.
ASKING OBVIOUS QUESTIONS. VOLUNTEERING TO KEEP THE KEY WHEN YOU'RE USUALLY THE LAST ONE TO ARRIVE...
HUH?!
UM!!
ER!!
DON'T WORRY. I WON'T TATTLE ON YOU TO DAICHI.
BESIDES, THIS KINDA FEELS LIKE WE'RE DOING SPECIAL SECRET TRAINING. IT'S EXCITING!
WHEW
WSH
FWIF

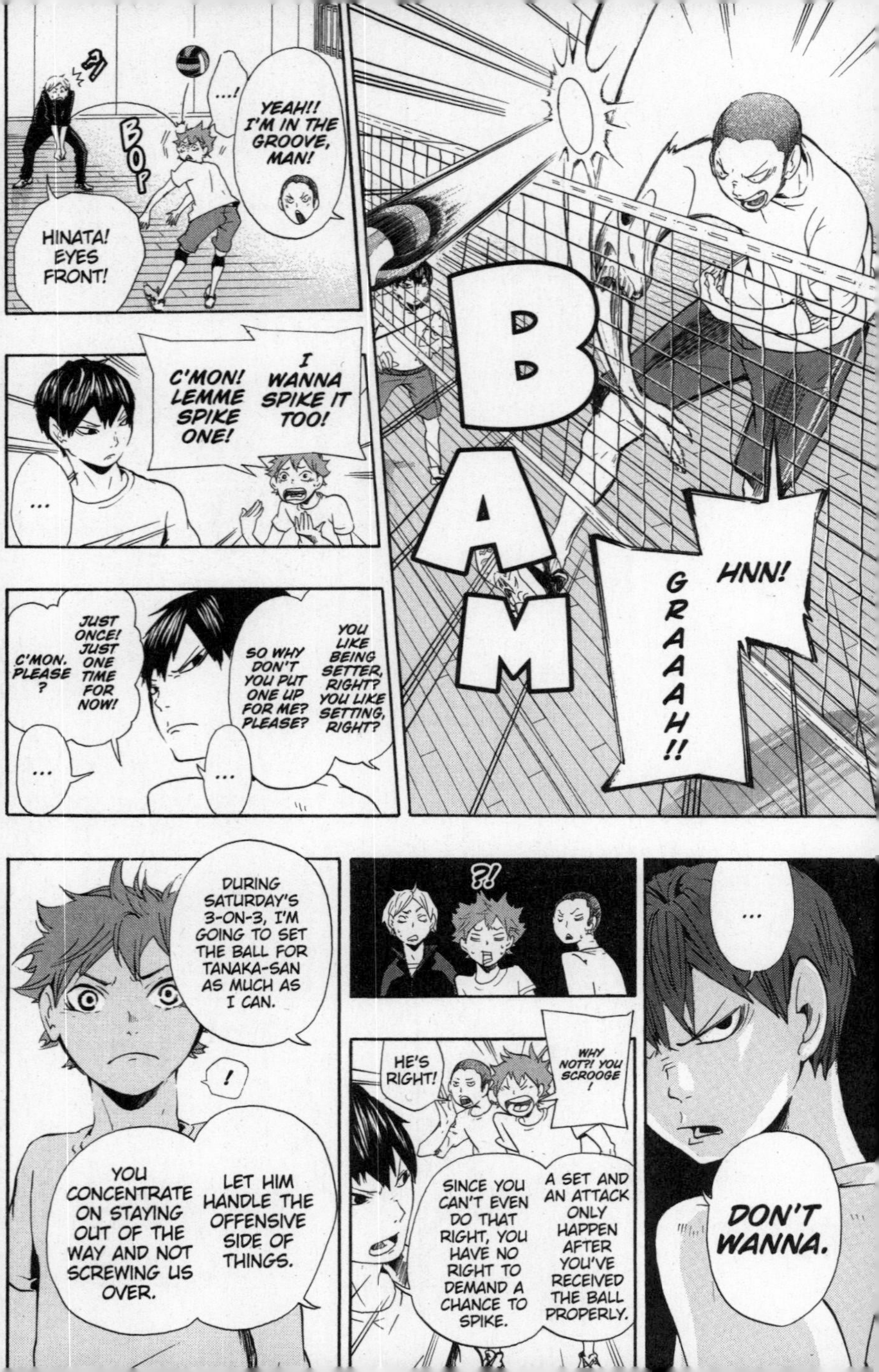
BAM
HNN! GRAAAAH!!
YEAH!! I'M IN THE GROOVE, MAN!
...!
BOP
HINATA! EYES FRONT!
I WANNA SPIKE IT TOO!
C'MON! LEMME SPIKE ONE!
...
YOU LIKE BEING SETTER, RIGHT? YOU LIKE SETTING, RIGHT?
SO WHY DON'T YOU PUT ONE UP FOR ME? PLEASE?
JUST ONCE! JUST ONE TIME FOR NOW!
C'MON. PLEASE?
...
...
...
DON'T WANNA.
?!
WHY NOT?! YOU SCROOGE!
HE'S RIGHT!
A SET AND AN ATTACK ONLY HAPPEN AFTER YOU'VE RECEIVED THE BALL PROPERLY.
SINCE YOU CAN'T EVEN DO THAT RIGHT, YOU HAVE NO RIGHT TO DEMAND A CHANCE TO SPIKE.
DURING SATURDAY'S 3-ON-3, I'M GOING TO SET THE BALL FOR TANAKA-SAN AS MUCH AS I CAN.
!
LET HIM HANDLE THE OFFENSIVE SIDE OF THINGS.
YOU CONCENTRATE ON STAYING OUT OF THE WAY AND NOT SCREWING US OVER.

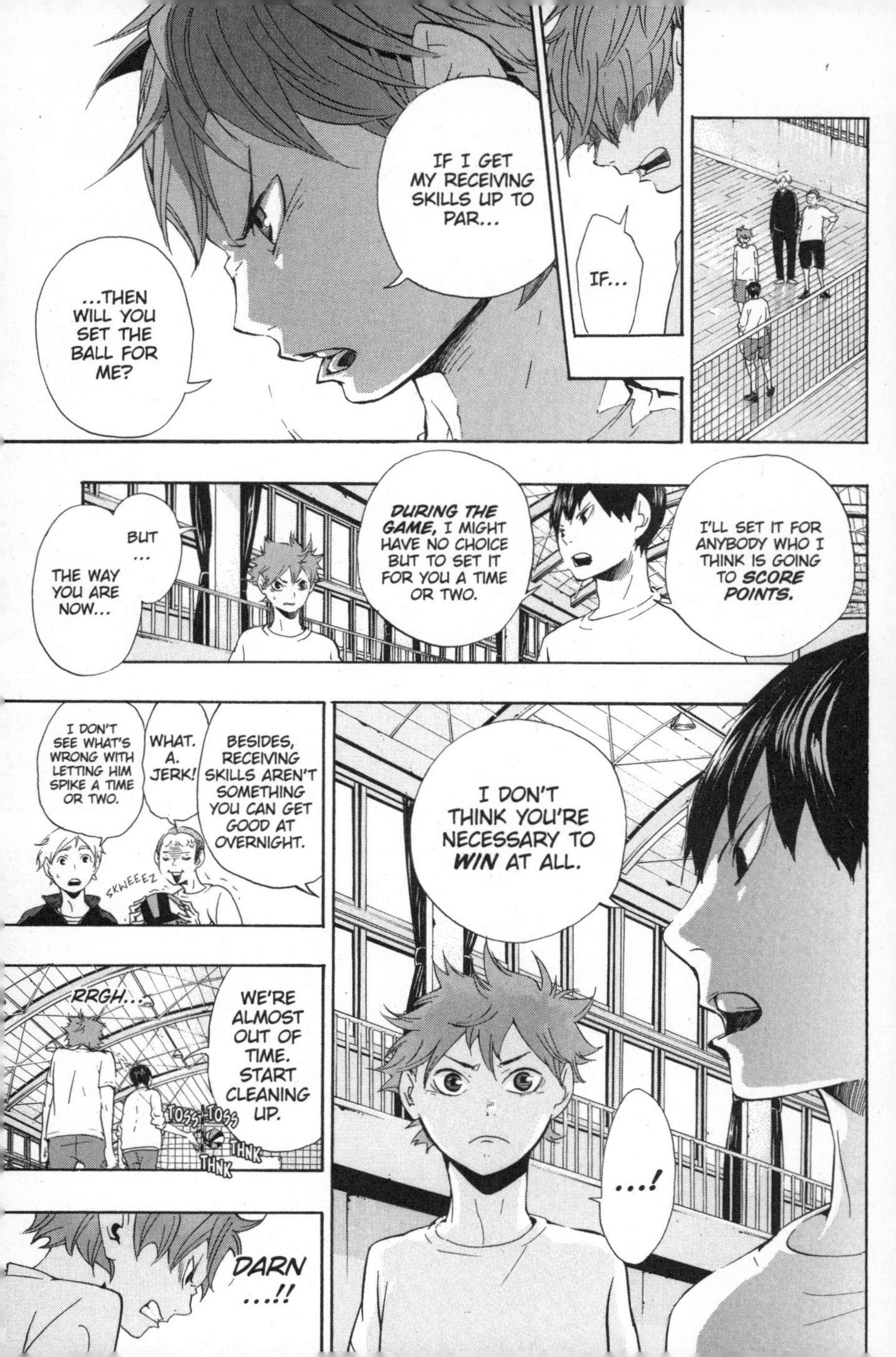
IF...
IF I GET MY RECEIVING SKILLS UP TO PAR...
...THEN WILL YOU SET THE BALL FOR ME?
I'LL SET IT FOR ANYBODY WHO I THINK IS GOING TO SCORE POINTS.
DURING THE GAME, I MIGHT HAVE NO CHOICE BUT TO SET IT FOR YOU A TIME OR TWO.
BUT ... THE WAY YOU ARE NOW...
I DON'T THINK YOU'RE NECESSARY TO WIN AT ALL.
...!
BESIDES, RECEIVING SKILLS AREN'T SOMETHING YOU CAN GET GOOD AT OVERNIGHT.
WHAT. A. JERK!
I DON'T SEE WHAT'S WRONG WITH LETTING HIM SPIKE A TIME OR TWO.
SKWEEEZ
WE'RE ALMOST OUT OF TIME. START CLEANING UP.
RRGH...
TOSS TOSS
THNK
THNK
DARN ...!!

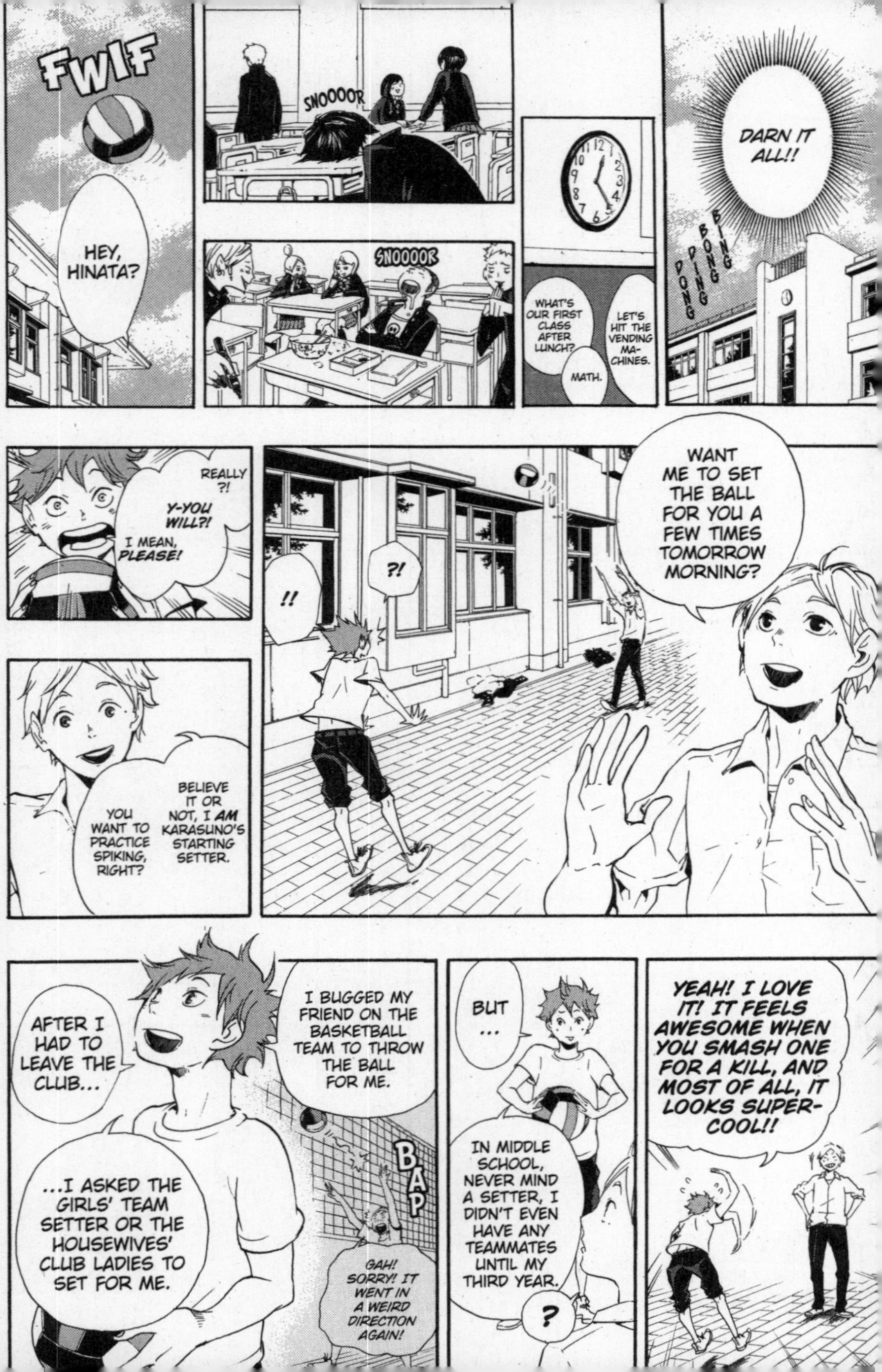
DARN IT ALL!!
DONG DING BONG BING
LET'S HIT THE VENDING MA-CHINES.
WHAT'S OUR FIRST CLASS AFTER LUNCH?
MATH.
SNOOOOR
SNOOOOR
FWIF
HEY, HINATA?
WANT ME TO SET THE BALL FOR YOU A FEW TIMES TOMORROW MORNING?
?!
!!
REALLY?!
Y-YOU WILL?!
I MEAN, PLEASE!
BELIEVE IT OR NOT, I AM KARASUNO'S STARTING SETTER.
YOU WANT TO PRACTICE SPIKING, RIGHT?
YEAH! I LOVE IT! IT FEELS AWESOME WHEN YOU SMASH ONE FOR A KILL, AND MOST OF ALL, IT LOOKS SUPER-COOL!!
BUT...
IN MIDDLE SCHOOL, NEVER MIND A SETTER, I DIDN'T EVEN HAVE ANY TEAMMATES UNTIL MY THIRD YEAR.
?
I BUGGED MY FRIEND ON THE BASKETBALL TEAM TO THROW THE BALL FOR ME.
AFTER I HAD TO LEAVE THE CLUB...
BAP
...I ASKED THE GIRLS' TEAM SETTER OR THE HOUSEWIVES' CLUB LADIES TO SET FOR ME.
GAH! SORRY! IT WENT IN A WEIRD DIRECTION AGAIN!

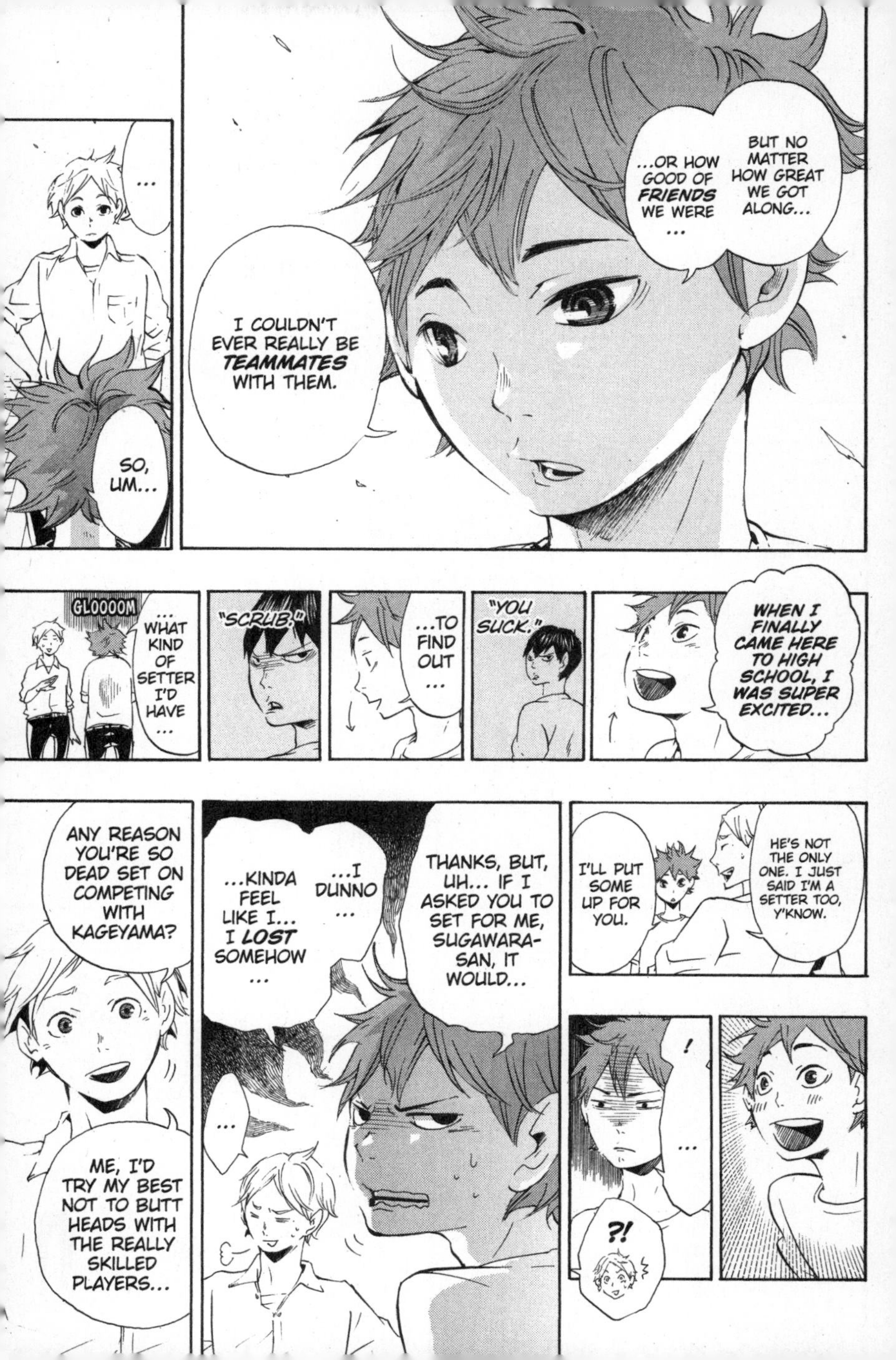
BUT NO MATTER HOW GREAT WE GOT ALONG...
...OR HOW GOOD OF **FRIENDS** WE WERE ...
I COULDN'T EVER REALLY BE **TEAMMATES** WITH THEM.
...
SO, UM...
WHEN I FINALLY CAME HERE TO HIGH SCHOOL, I WAS SUPER EXCITED...
"YOU SUCK."
...TO FIND OUT ...
"SCRUB."
GLOOOOM
... WHAT KIND OF SETTER I'D HAVE ...
HE'S NOT THE ONLY ONE. I JUST SAID I'M A SETTER TOO, Y'KNOW.
I'LL PUT SOME UP FOR YOU.
!
...
?!
THANKS, BUT, UH... IF I ASKED YOU TO SET FOR ME, SUGAWARA-SAN, IT WOULD...
...I DUNNO ...
...KINDA FEEL LIKE I... I **LOST** SOMEHOW ...
...
ANY REASON YOU'RE SO DEAD SET ON COMPETING WITH KAGEYAMA?
ME, I'D TRY MY BEST NOT TO BUTT HEADS WITH THE REALLY SKILLED PLAYERS...

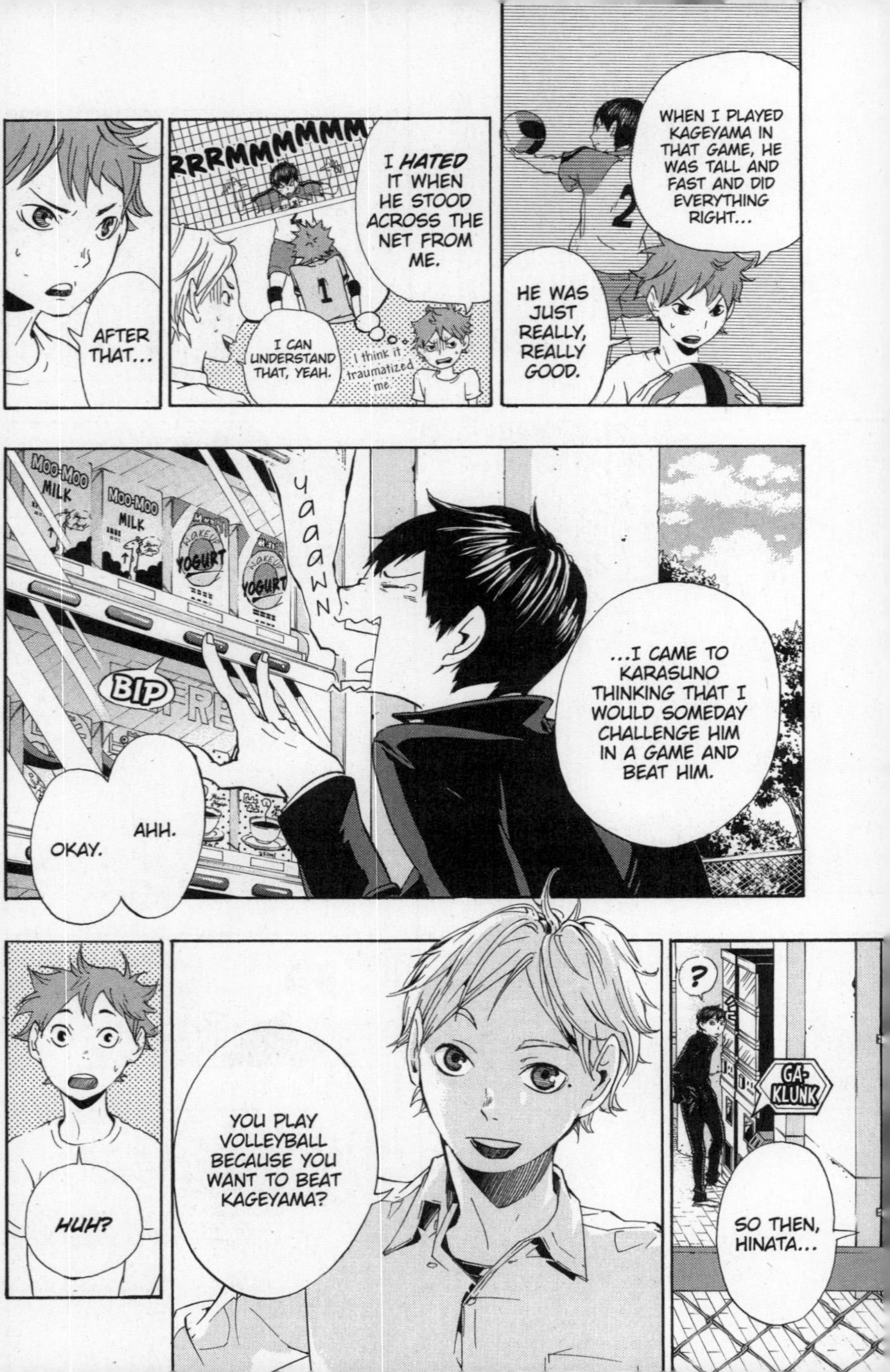
WHEN I PLAYED KAGEYAMA IN THAT GAME, HE WAS TALL AND FAST AND DID EVERYTHING RIGHT...
HE WAS JUST REALLY, REALLY GOOD.
RRRMMMMMMM
I HATED IT WHEN HE STOOD ACROSS THE NET FROM ME.
I think it traumatized me.
I CAN UNDERSTAND THAT, YEAH.
AFTER THAT...
...I CAME TO KARASUNO THINKING THAT I WOULD SOMEDAY CHALLENGE HIM IN A GAME AND BEAT HIM.
yaaawn
MOO-MOO MILK
MOO-MOO MILK
YOGURT
YOGURT
BIP
AHH.
OKAY.
?
GA-KLUNK
SO THEN, HINATA...
YOU PLAY VOLLEYBALL BECAUSE YOU WANT TO BEAT KAGEYAMA?
HUH?

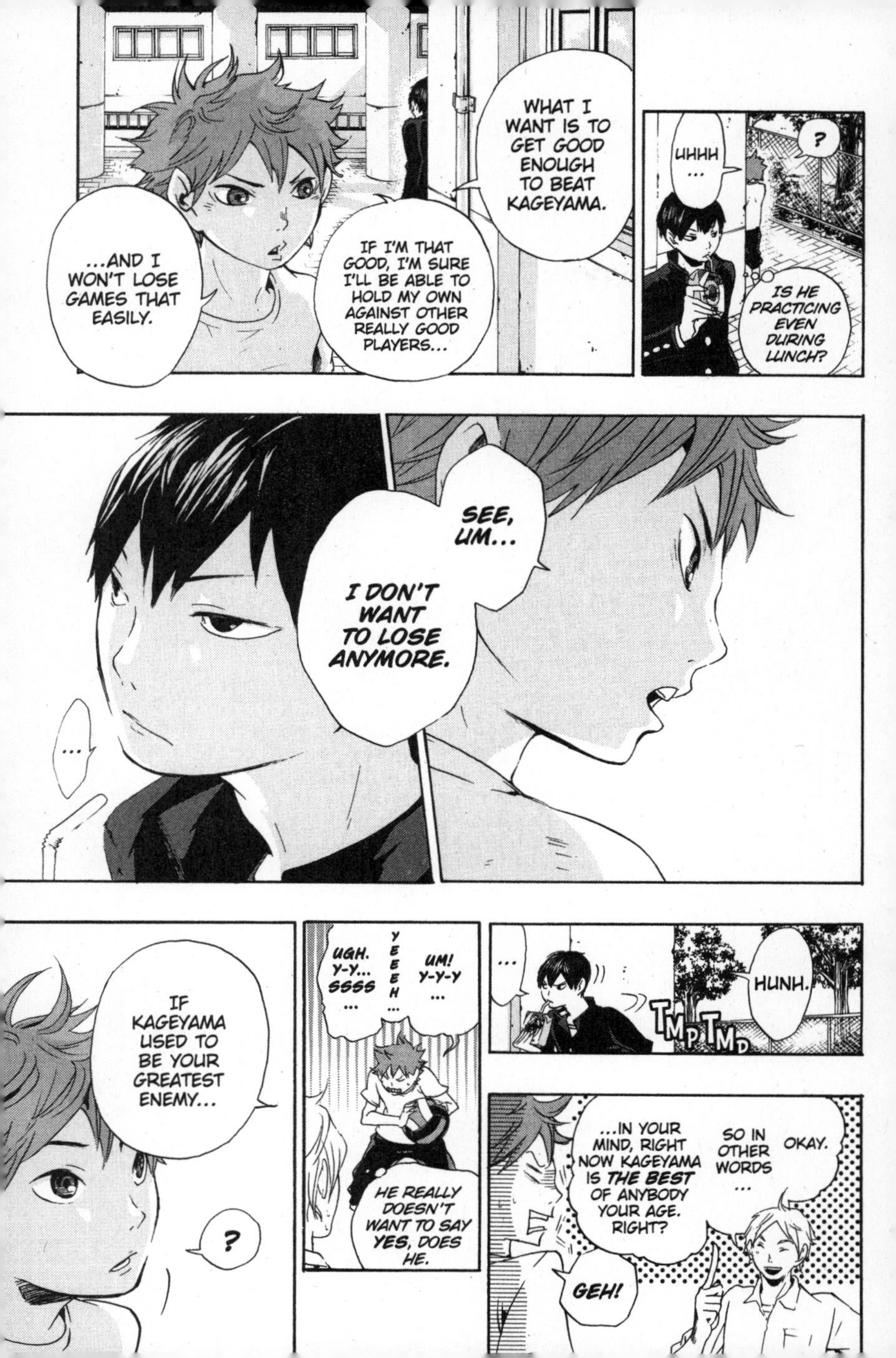
?
UHHH ...
IS HE PRACTICING EVEN DURING LUNCH?
WHAT I WANT IS TO GET GOOD ENOUGH TO BEAT KAGEYAMA.
IF I'M THAT GOOD, I'M SURE I'LL BE ABLE TO HOLD MY OWN AGAINST OTHER REALLY GOOD PLAYERS...
...AND I WON'T LOSE GAMES THAT EASILY.
SEE, UM...
I DON'T WANT TO LOSE ANYMORE.
...
HUNH.
TMP TMP
...
OKAY.
SO IN OTHER WORDS ...
...IN YOUR MIND, RIGHT NOW KAGEYAMA IS THE BEST OF ANYBODY YOUR AGE. RIGHT?
GEH!
UM! Y-Y-Y ...
YEEEH ...
UGH. Y-Y... SSSS ...
HE REALLY DOESN'T WANT TO SAY YES, DOES HE.
IF KAGEYAMA USED TO BE YOUR GREATEST ENEMY...
?

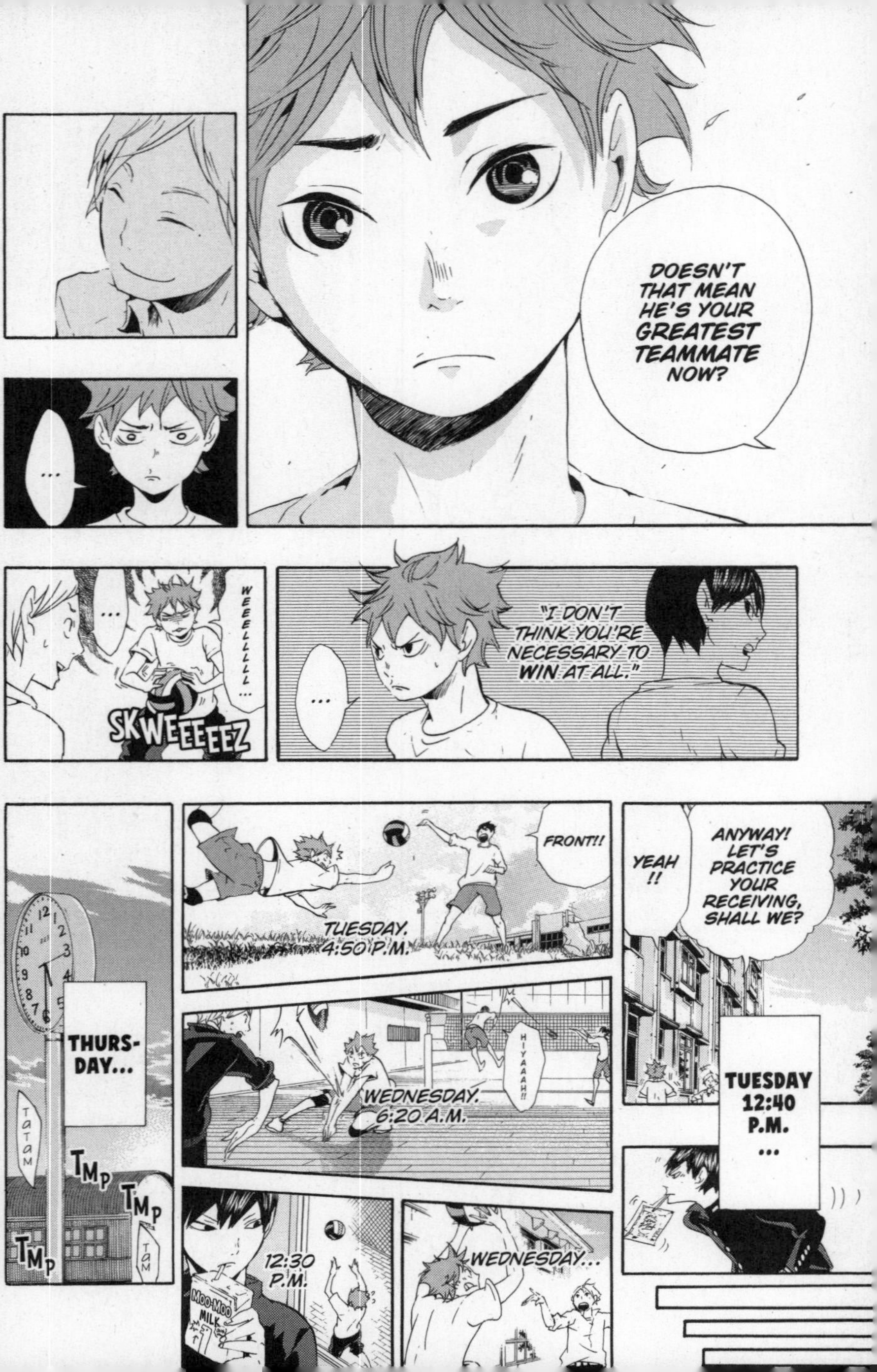
DOESN'T THAT MEAN HE'S YOUR GREATEST TEAMMATE NOW?
...
"I DON'T THINK YOU'RE NECESSARY TO WIN AT ALL."
...
WEEEELLLLLL...
...
SKWEEEEEZ
ANYWAY! LET'S PRACTICE YOUR RECEIVING, SHALL WE?
YEAH!!
TUESDAY 12:40 P.M. ...
FRONT!!
TUESDAY. 4:50 P.M.
HIYAAAH!!
WEDNESDAY. 6:20 A.M.
WEDNESDAY...
12:30 P.M.
MOO-MOO MILK
THURS-DAY...
TATAM
TMP
TMP
TMP
TAM

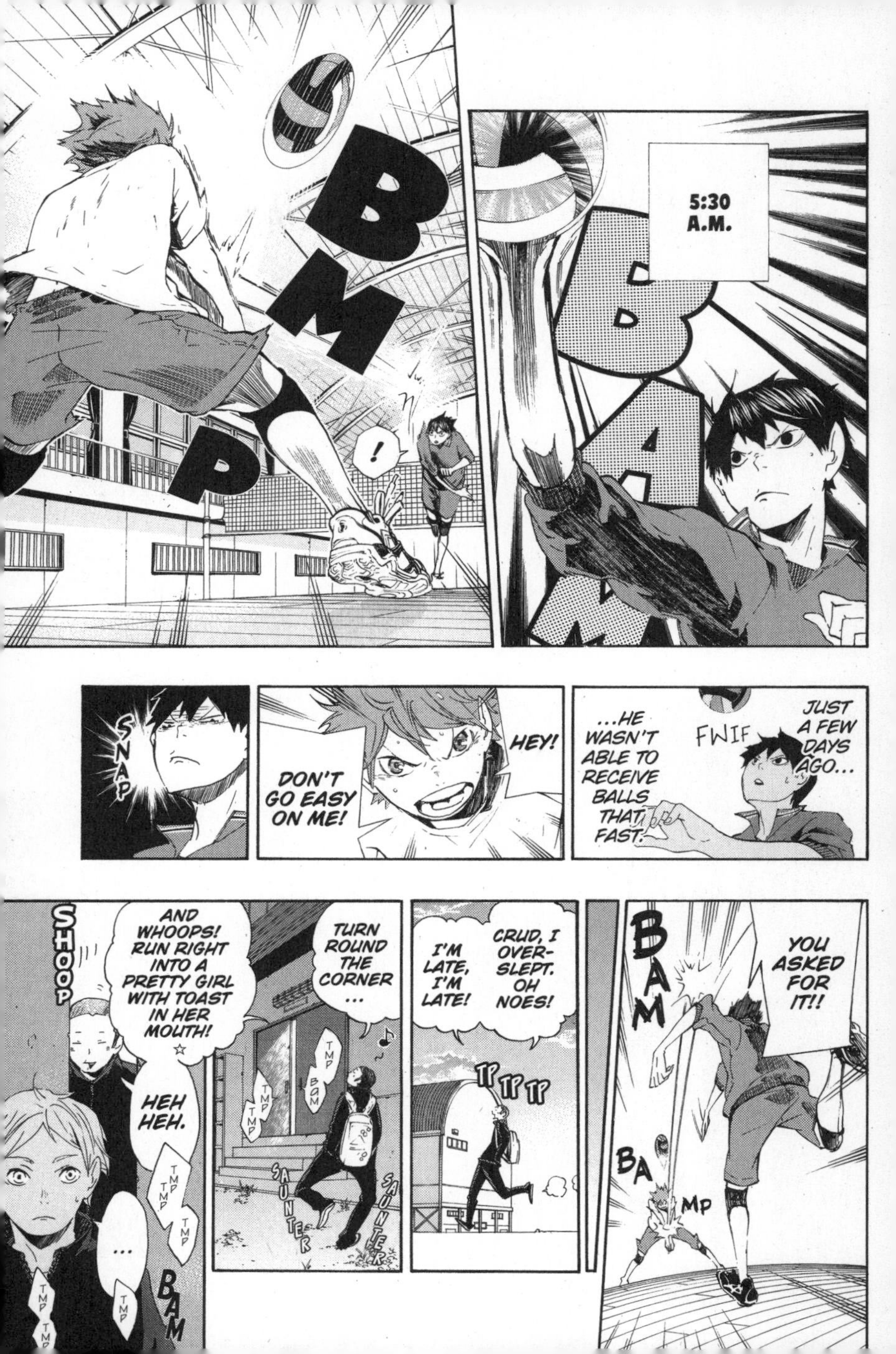

5:30 A.M.
BMP
!
JUST A FEW DAYS AGO…
FWIF
…HE WASN'T ABLE TO RECEIVE BALLS THAT FAST.
HEY!
DON'T GO EASY ON ME!
SNAP
BAM
YOU ASKED FOR IT!!
BA MP
CRUD, I OVER-SLEPT. OH NOES!
I'M LATE, I'M LATE!
TP TP TP
TURN ROUND THE CORNER …
TMP TMP BAM
SAUNTER
SAUNTER
SHOOP
AND WHOOPS! RUN RIGHT INTO A PRETTY GIRL WITH TOAST IN HER MOUTH! ☆
HEH HEH.
…
TMP
BAM

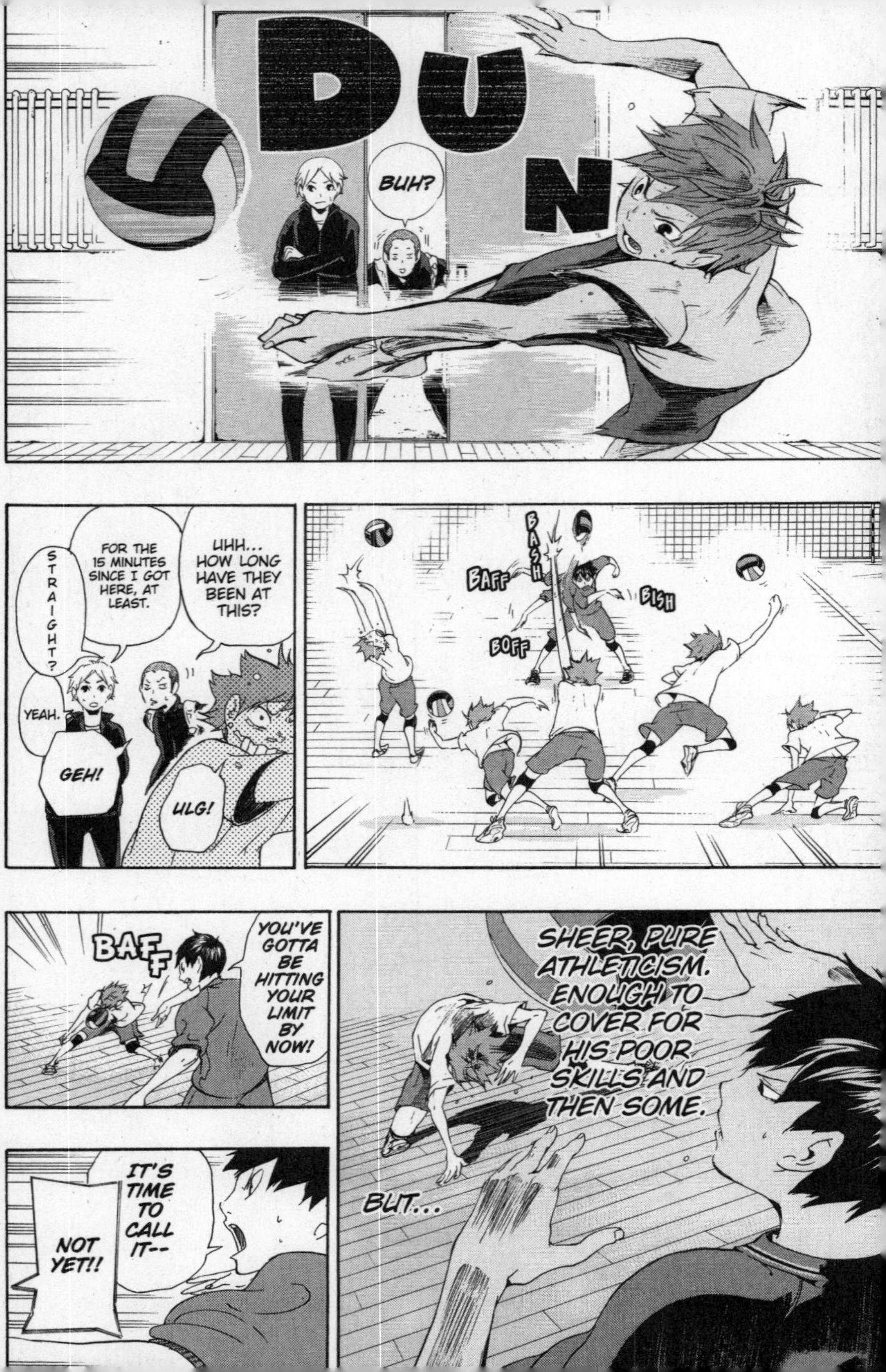
DUN
BUH?
BASH
BAFF
BISH
BOFF
UHH... HOW LONG HAVE THEY BEEN AT THIS?
FOR THE 15 MINUTES SINCE I GOT HERE, AT LEAST.
STRAIGHT?
YEAH.
ULG!
GEH!
SHEER, PURE ATHLETICISM. ENOUGH TO COVER FOR HIS POOR SKILLS AND THEN SOME.
BUT...
YOU'VE GOTTA BE HITTING YOUR LIMIT BY NOW!
BAFF
IT'S TIME TO CALL IT--
NOT YET!!

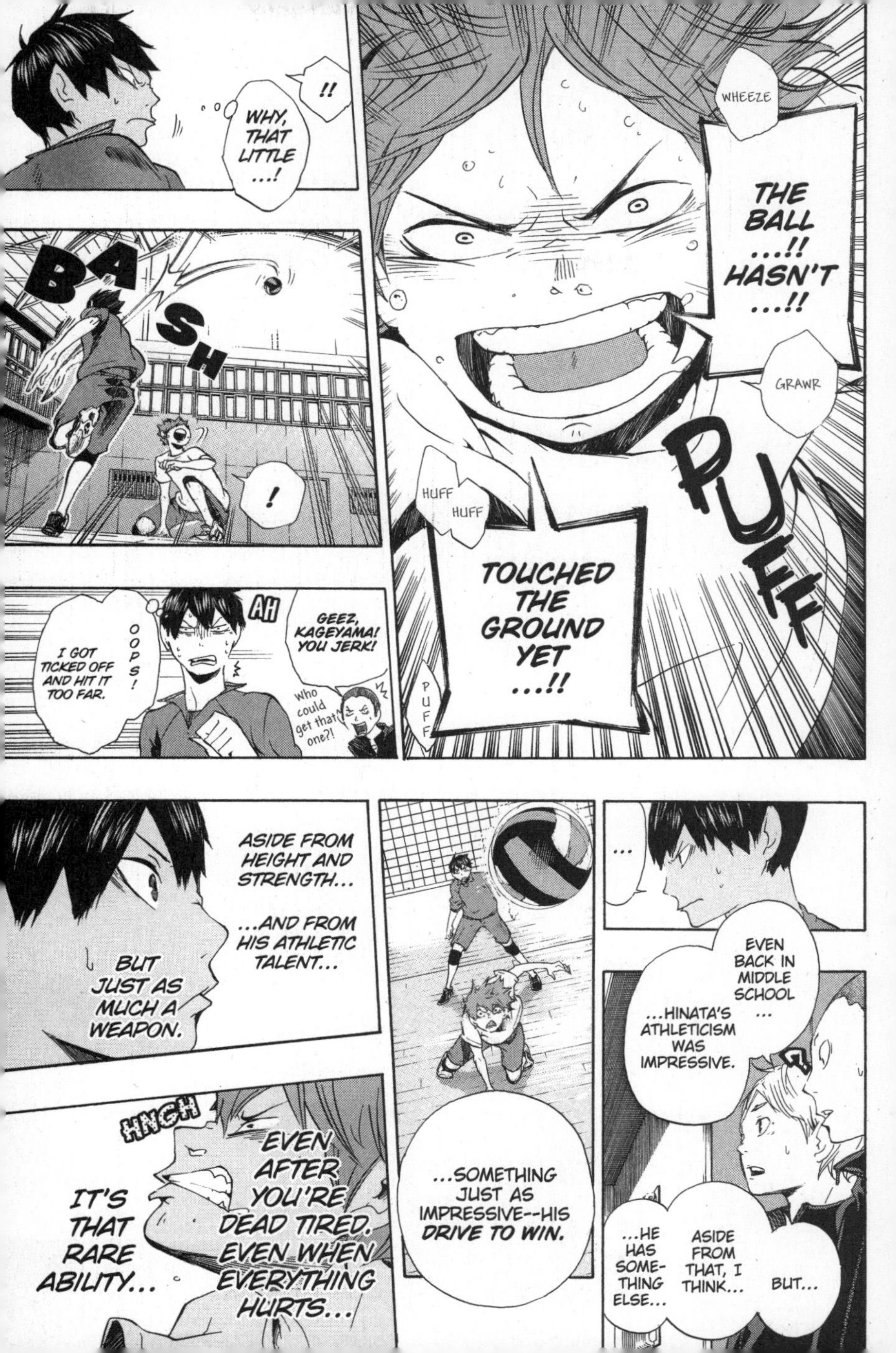
WHEEZE
THE BALL ...!! HASN'T ...!!
GRAWR
PUFF
TOUCHED THE GROUND YET ...!!
HUFF HUFF
PUFF
!!
WHY, THAT LITTLE ...!
BASH
!
AH
GEEZ, KAGEYAMA! YOU JERK!
who could get that one?!
OOPS!
I GOT TICKED OFF AND HIT IT TOO FAR.
...
EVEN BACK IN MIDDLE SCHOOL ...
...HINATA'S ATHLETICISM WAS IMPRESSIVE.
BUT...
ASIDE FROM THAT, I THINK...
...HE HAS SOMETHING ELSE...
...SOMETHING JUST AS IMPRESSIVE--HIS DRIVE TO WIN.
ASIDE FROM HEIGHT AND STRENGTH...
...AND FROM HIS ATHLETIC TALENT...
BUT JUST AS MUCH A WEAPON.
HNGH
EVEN AFTER YOU'RE DEAD TIRED. EVEN WHEN EVERYTHING HURTS...
IT'S THAT RARE ABILITY...

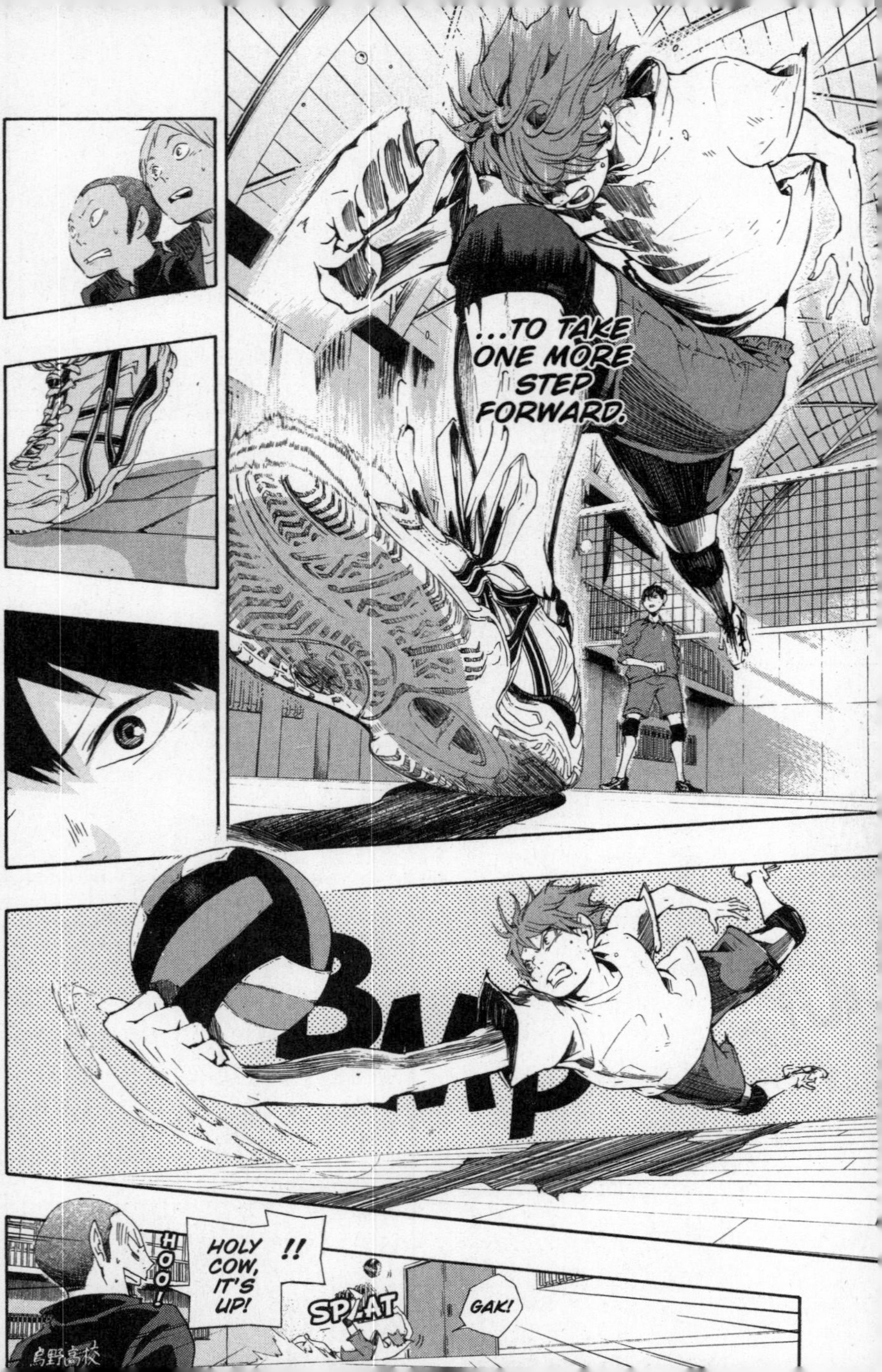
...TO TAKE ONE MORE STEP FORWARD.
BMP
GAK!
SPLAT
HOLY COW, IT'S UP!!
HOO!
烏野高校

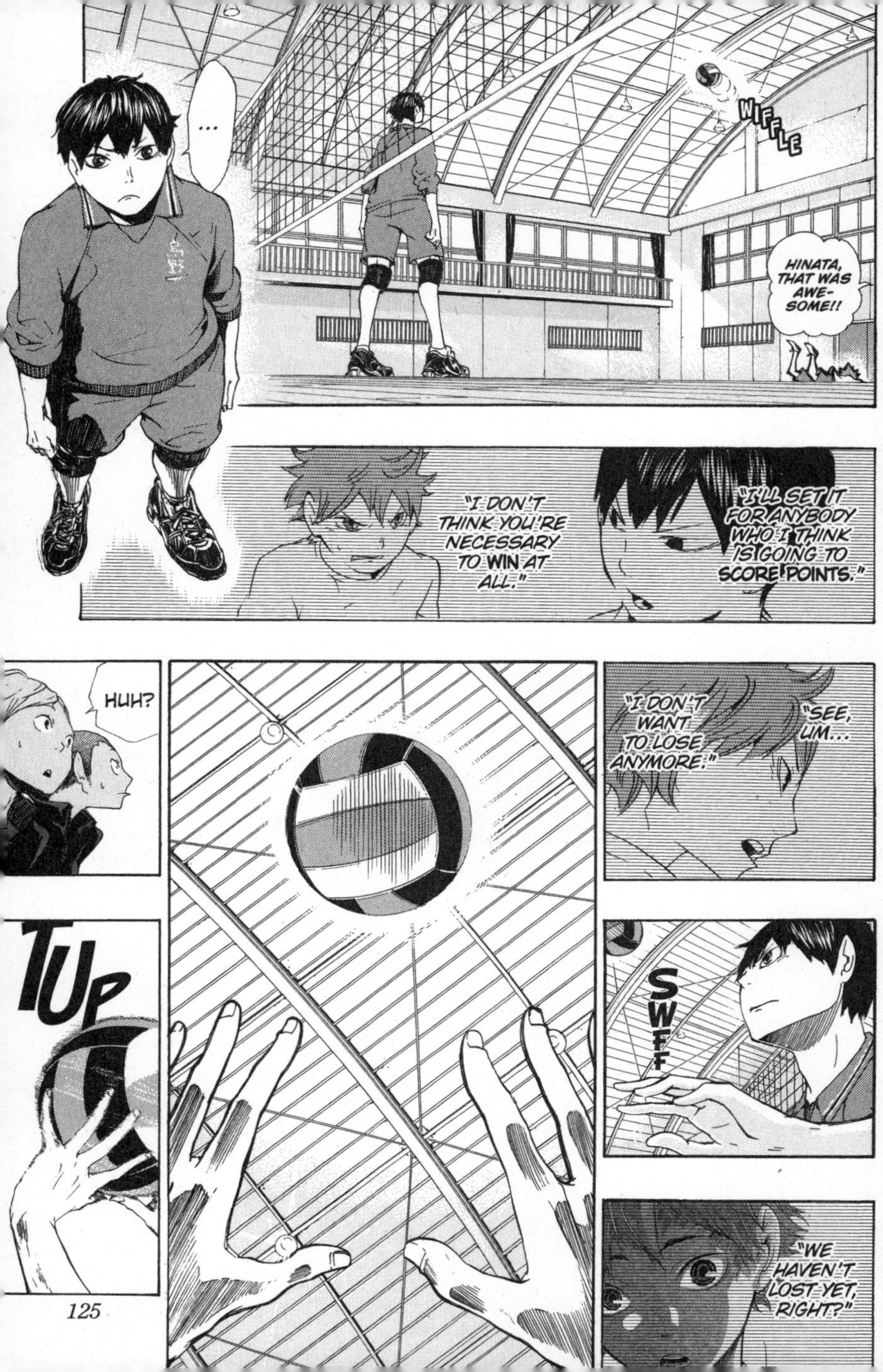

WIFFLE
HINATA, THAT WAS AWE-SOME!!
...
"I'LL SET IT FOR ANYBODY WHO I THINK IS GOING TO SCORE POINTS."
"I DON'T THINK YOU'RE NECESSARY TO WIN AT ALL."
"SEE, UM...
"I DON'T WANT TO LOSE ANYMORE."
SWFF
"WE HAVEN'T LOST YET, RIGHT?"
HUH?
TUP

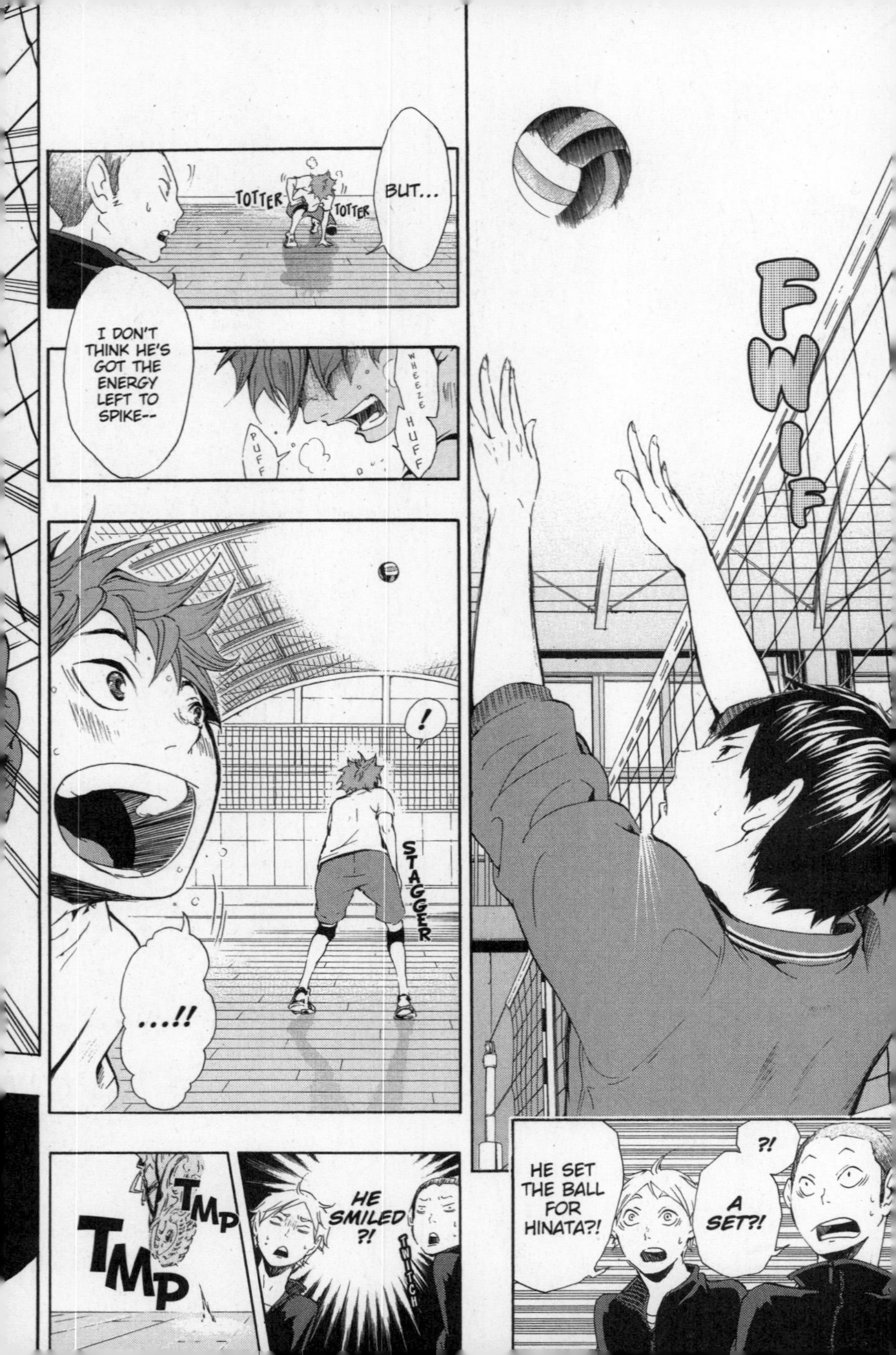
FWIF
BUT...
TOTTER
TOTTER
I DON'T THINK HE'S GOT THE ENERGY LEFT TO SPIKE--
WHEEZE
HUFF
PUFF
!
STAGGER
...!!
?!
A SET?!
HE SET THE BALL FOR HINATA?!
HE SMILED?!
TWITCH
TMP
TMP

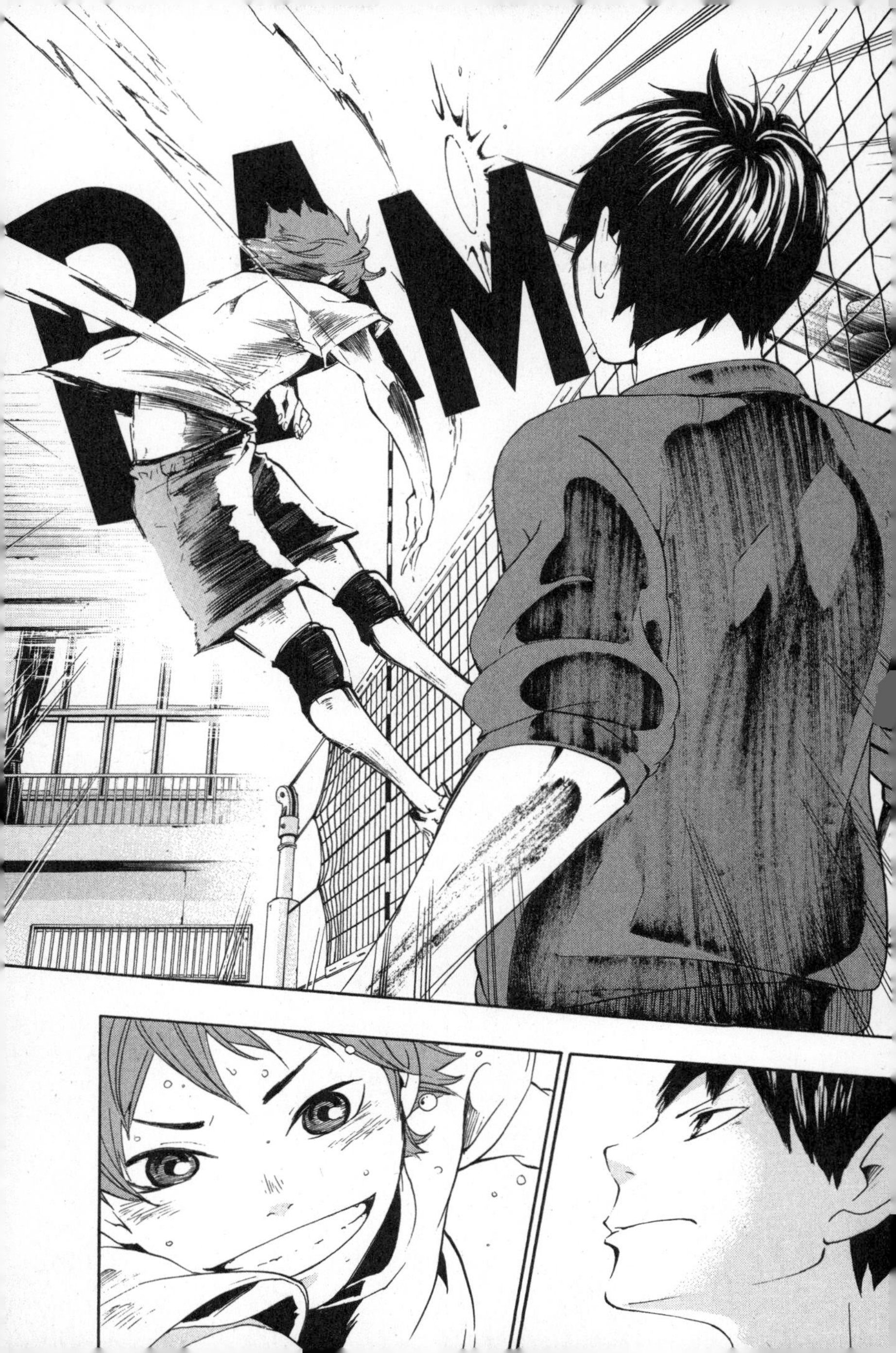
BAM

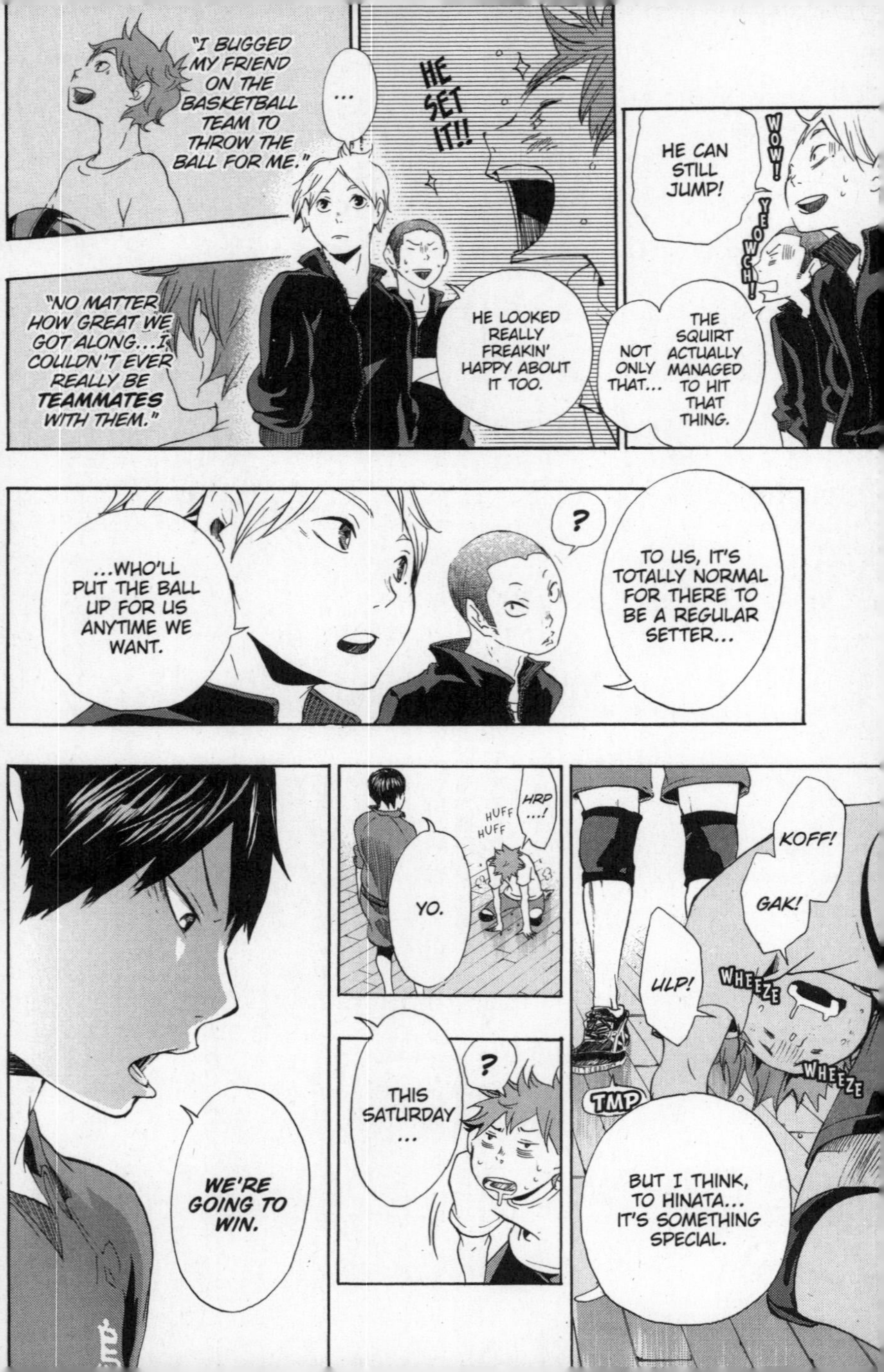
HE SET IT!!
HE CAN STILL JUMP!
WOW!
YEOWCH!
NOT ONLY THAT...
THE SQUIRT ACTUALLY MANAGED TO HIT THAT THING.
HE LOOKED REALLY FREAKIN' HAPPY ABOUT IT TOO.
...
"I BUGGED MY FRIEND ON THE BASKETBALL TEAM TO THROW THE BALL FOR ME."
"NO MATTER HOW GREAT WE GOT ALONG...I COULDN'T EVER REALLY BE TEAMMATES WITH THEM."
TO US, IT'S TOTALLY NORMAL FOR THERE TO BE A REGULAR SETTER...
?
...WHO'LL PUT THE BALL UP FOR US ANYTIME WE WANT.
KOFF!
GAK!
WHEEZE
ULP!
WHEEZE
TMP
BUT I THINK, TO HINATA... IT'S SOMETHING SPECIAL.
HRP ...!
HUFF HUFF
YO.
?
THIS SATURDAY ...
WE'RE GOING TO WIN.

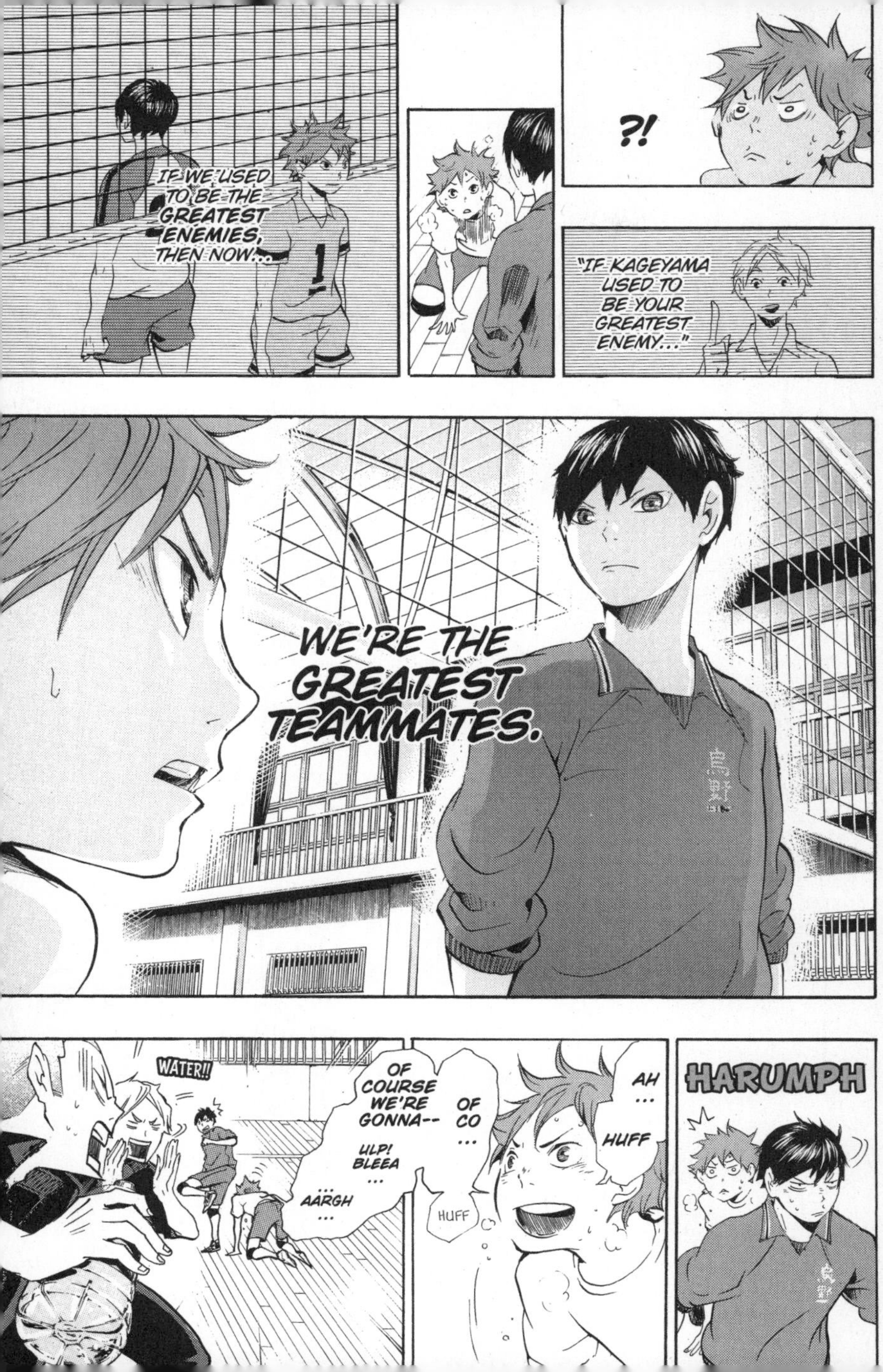
?!
"IF KAGEYAMA USED TO BE YOUR GREATEST ENEMY..."
IF WE USED TO BE THE GREATEST ENEMIES, THEN NOW...
WE'RE THE GREATEST TEAMMATES.
HARUMPH
AH ...
HUFF
OF CO ...
OF COURSE WE'RE GONNA--
HUFF
WATER!!
ULP! BLEEA ...
... AARGH ...

HEY YOU! YEAH _____ GUY
WHO SAID MY LAST _____ DIRT--
C'MON! CO_____ _____ EHIND
THE GYM! _____ _____CHA!

RYUNOSUKE TANAKA

**KARASUNO HIGH SCHOOL
CLASS 2-1**

POSITION: WING SPIKER

**HEIGHT: 5'10"
WEIGHT: 151 LBS.
(AS OF APRIL, 2ND YEAR
IN HIGH SCHOOL)**

BIRTHDAY: MARCH 3

**FAVORITE FOOD:
MELON-SHAPED BREAD**

**CURRENT WORRY:
HE WENT TO HELP A
FIRST-YEAR GIRL WHO
LOOKED LOST, AND SHE
STARTED CRYING.**

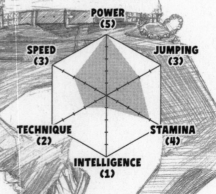

**ABILITY PARAMETERS
(5-POINT SCALE)**

POWER
(5)

SPEED
(3)

JUMPING
(3)

TECHNIQUE
(2)

STAMINA
(4)

INTELLIGENCE
(1)

CHAPTER 5

"THE VOLLEYBALL PLAYER IS NOT A SOLOIST BUT A MEMBER OF AN ORCHESTRA... WHEN THE PLAYER BEGINS TO THINK, 'I AM SPECIAL,' THAT PLAYER IS FINISHED."

--COACH BERNARDO REZENDE,
COACH OF THE BRAZILIAN MEN'S VOLLEYBALL TEAM,
THE #1 RANKED VOLLEYBALL TEAM IN THE WORLD

FROM THE BOOK THE MAN AND THE SYSTEM THAT MADE BRAZILIAN VOLLEYBALL THE BEST, *BY NORIKO YONEMUSHI.*

PUBLISHED BY TOHO PUBLISHING CO., LTD.

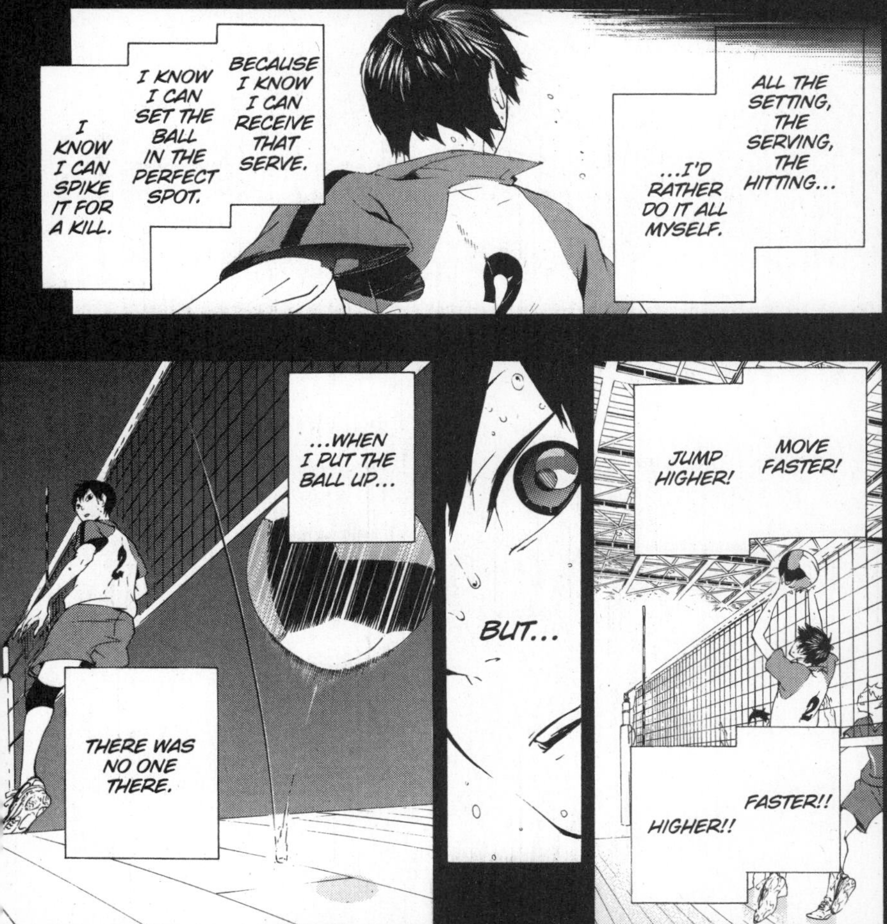
ALL THE SETTING, THE SERVING, THE HITTING...
...I'D RATHER DO IT ALL MYSELF.
BECAUSE I KNOW I CAN RECEIVE THAT SERVE.
I KNOW I CAN SET THE BALL IN THE PERFECT SPOT.
I KNOW I CAN SPIKE IT FOR A KILL.
MOVE FASTER!
JUMP HIGHER!
FASTER!!
HIGHER!!
BUT...
...WHEN I PUT THE BALL UP...
THERE WAS NO ONE THERE.

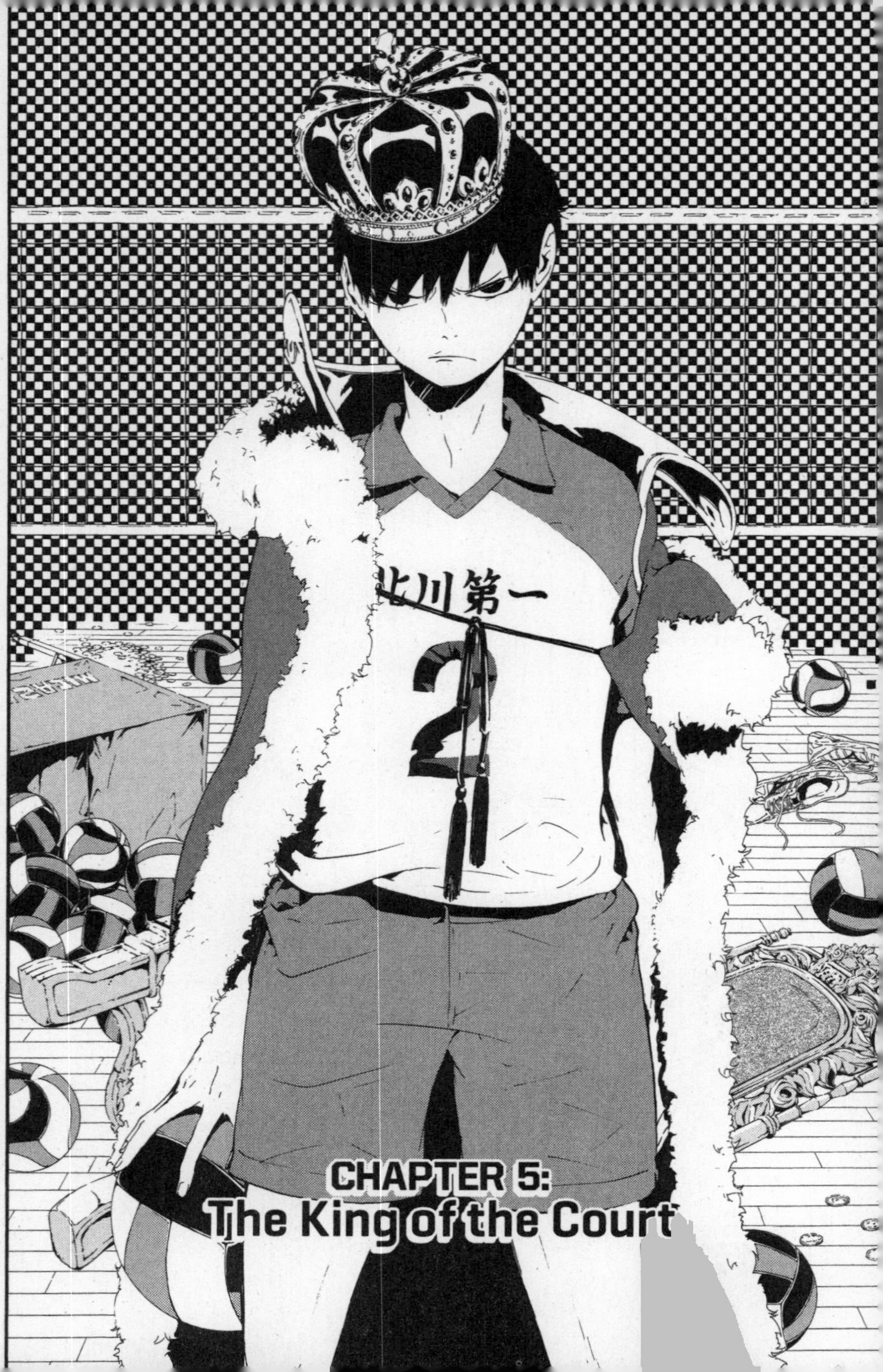
北川第一
2
CHAPTER 5:
The King of the Court

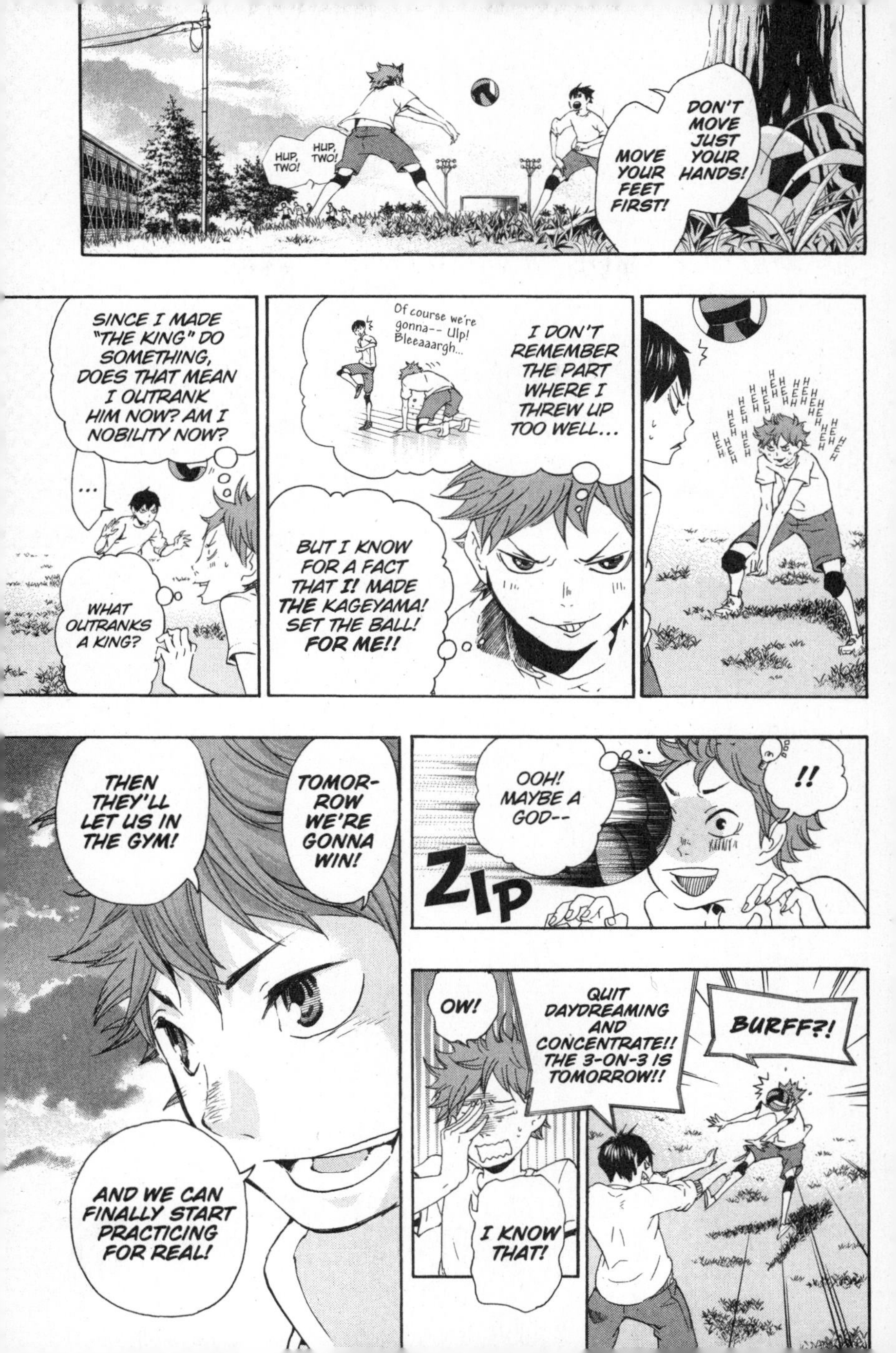
DON'T MOVE JUST YOUR HANDS!
MOVE YOUR FEET FIRST!
HUP, TWO!
HUP, TWO!
HEH HEH HEH HEH
I DON'T REMEMBER THE PART WHERE I THREW UP TOO WELL...
Of course we're gonna-- Ulp! Bleeaaargh...
BUT I KNOW FOR A FACT THAT I! MADE THE KAGEYAMA! SET THE BALL! FOR ME!!
SINCE I MADE "THE KING" DO SOMETHING, DOES THAT MEAN I OUTRANK HIM NOW? AM I NOBILITY NOW?
...
WHAT OUTRANKS A KING?
!!
OOH! MAYBE A GOD--
ZIP
BURFF?!
QUIT DAYDREAMING AND CONCENTRATE!! THE 3-ON-3 IS TOMORROW!!
OW!
I KNOW THAT!
TOMORROW WE'RE GONNA WIN!
THEN THEY'LL LET US IN THE GYM!
AND WE CAN FINALLY START PRACTICING FOR REAL!

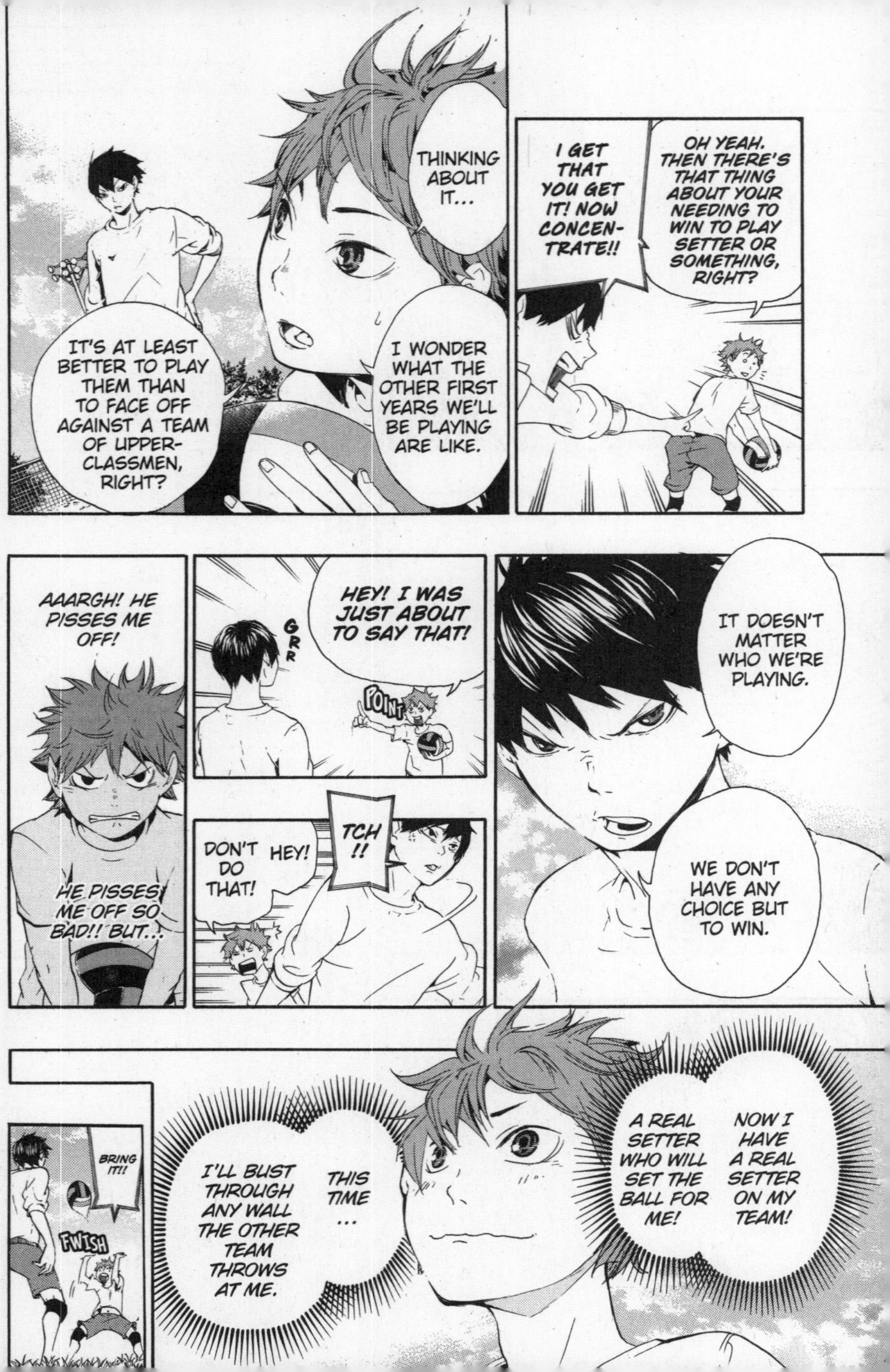
OH YEAH. THEN THERE'S THAT THING ABOUT YOUR NEEDING TO WIN TO PLAY SETTER OR SOMETHING, RIGHT?
I GET THAT YOU GET IT! NOW CONCENTRATE!!
THINKING ABOUT IT...
I WONDER WHAT THE OTHER FIRST YEARS WE'LL BE PLAYING ARE LIKE.
IT'S AT LEAST BETTER TO PLAY THEM THAN TO FACE OFF AGAINST A TEAM OF UPPERCLASSMEN, RIGHT?
IT DOESN'T MATTER WHO WE'RE PLAYING.
WE DON'T HAVE ANY CHOICE BUT TO WIN.
HEY! I WAS JUST ABOUT TO SAY THAT!
GRR
POINT
TCH!!
HEY!
DON'T DO THAT!
AAARGH! HE PISSES ME OFF!
HE PISSES ME OFF SO BAD!! BUT...
NOW I HAVE A REAL SETTER ON MY TEAM!
A REAL SETTER WHO WILL SET THE BALL FOR ME!
THIS TIME...
I'LL BUST THROUGH ANY WALL THE OTHER TEAM THROWS AT ME.
BRING IT!!
FWISH

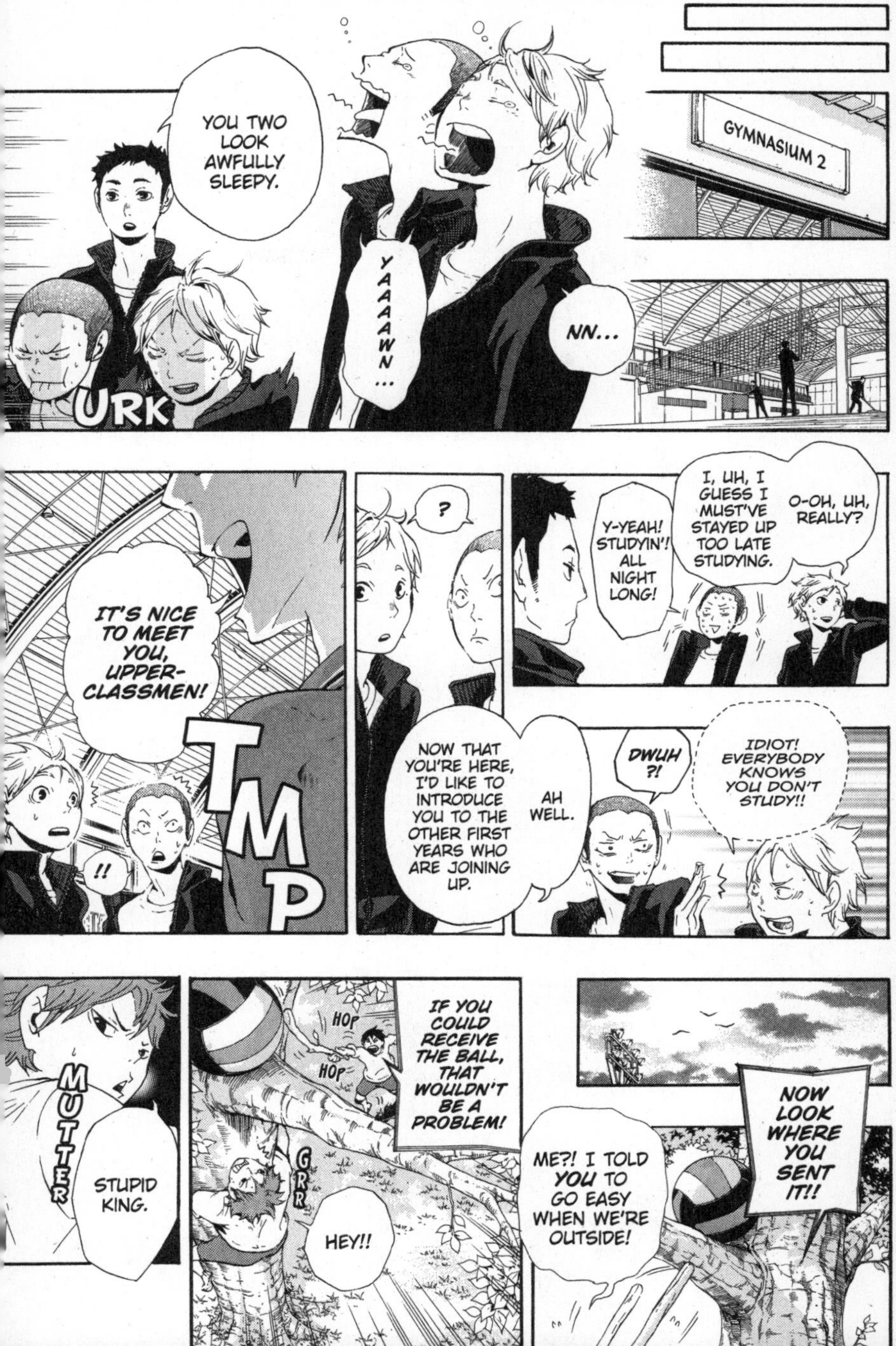
GYMNASIUM 2
NN...
YAAAAAWN...
YOU TWO LOOK AWFULLY SLEEPY.
URK
O-OH, UH, REALLY?
I, UH, I GUESS I MUST'VE STAYED UP TOO LATE STUDYING.
Y-YEAH! STUDYIN'! ALL NIGHT LONG!
IDIOT! EVERYBODY KNOWS YOU DON'T STUDY!!
DWUH ?!
AH WELL.
NOW THAT YOU'RE HERE, I'D LIKE TO INTRODUCE YOU TO THE OTHER FIRST YEARS WHO ARE JOINING UP.
?
IT'S NICE TO MEET YOU, UPPER-CLASSMEN!
TMP
!!
NOW LOOK WHERE YOU SENT IT!!
ME?! I TOLD YOU TO GO EASY WHEN WE'RE OUTSIDE!
IF YOU COULD RECEIVE THE BALL, THAT WOULDN'T BE A PROBLEM!
HOP
HOP
GRR
HEY!!
MUTTER
STUPID KING.

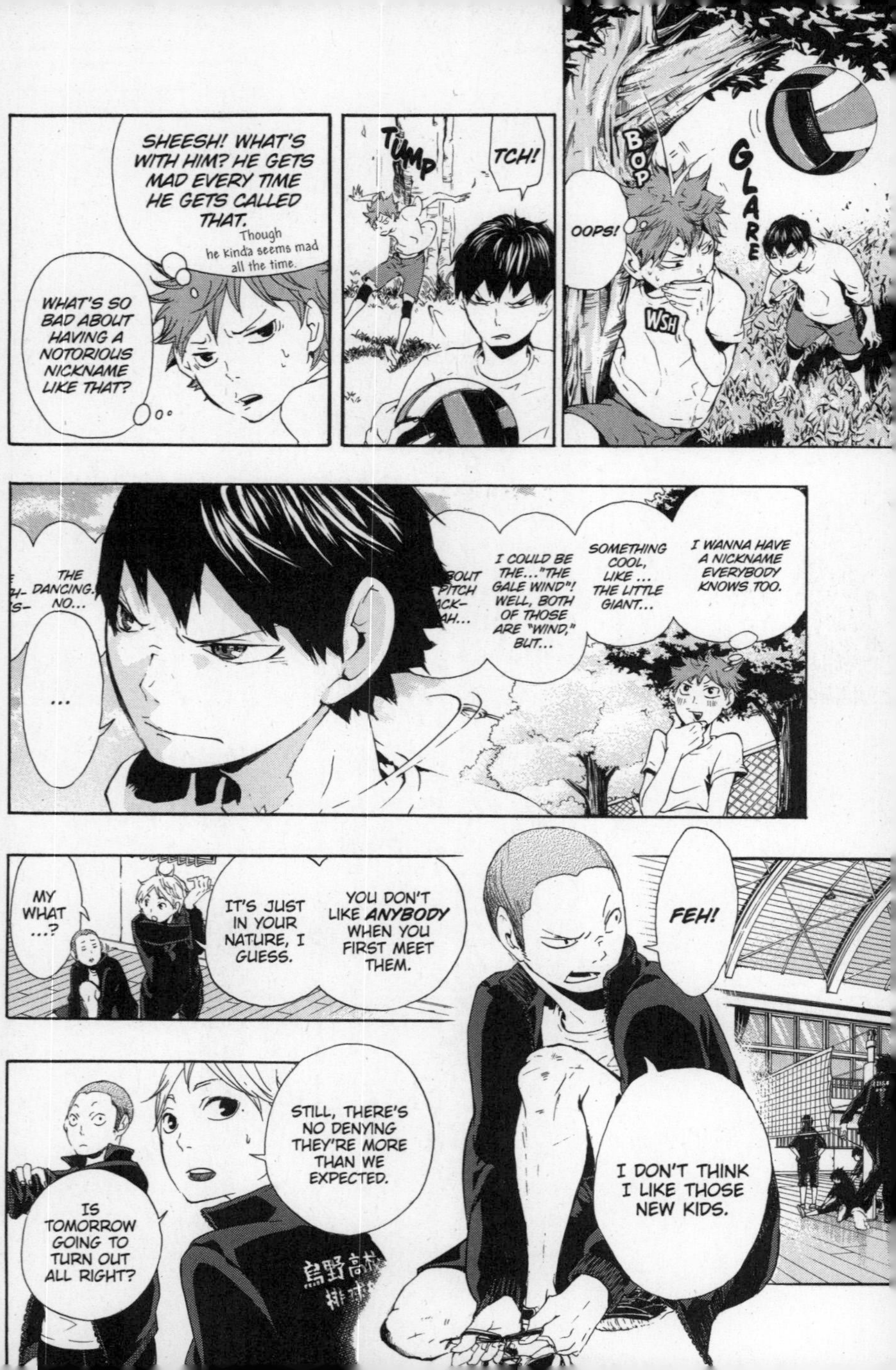
BOP
GLARE
OOPS!
TUMP
TCH!
SHEESH! WHAT'S WITH HIM? HE GETS MAD EVERY TIME HE GETS CALLED THAT.
Though he kinda seems mad all the time.
WHAT'S SO BAD ABOUT HAVING A NOTORIOUS NICKNAME LIKE THAT?
I WANNA HAVE A NICKNAME EVERYBODY KNOWS TOO.
SOMETHING COOL, LIKE... THE LITTLE GIANT...
I COULD BE THE..."THE GALE WIND"! WELL, BOTH OF THOSE ARE "WIND," BUT...
...
FEH!
I DON'T THINK I LIKE THOSE NEW KIDS.
YOU DON'T LIKE *ANYBODY* WHEN YOU FIRST MEET THEM.
IT'S JUST IN YOUR NATURE, I GUESS.
MY WHAT ...?
STILL, THERE'S NO DENYING THEY'RE MORE THAN WE EXPECTED.
IS TOMORROW GOING TO TURN OUT ALL RIGHT?

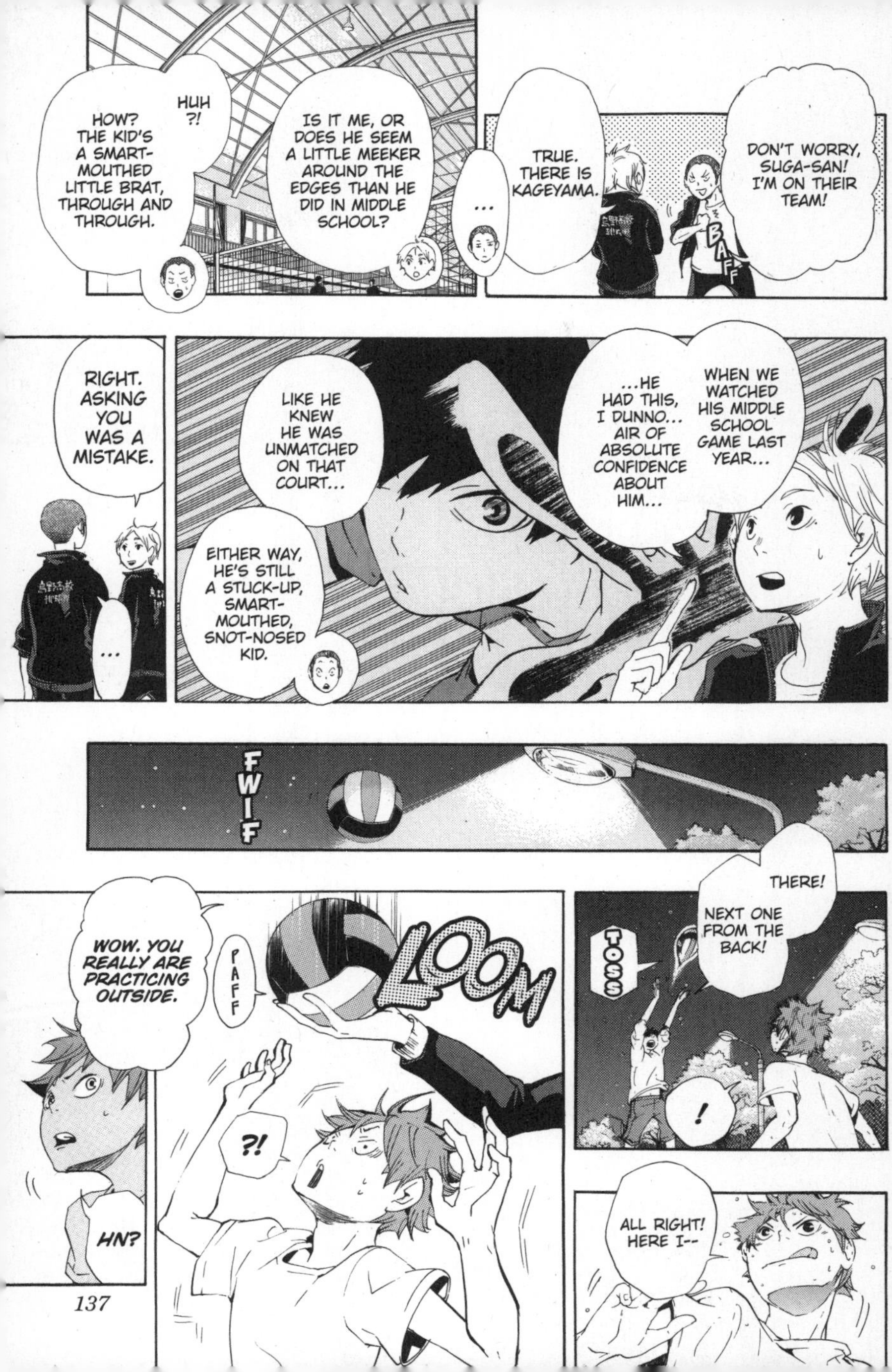
DON'T WORRY, SUGA-SAN! I'M ON THEIR TEAM!
BAFF
TRUE. THERE IS KAGEYAMA.
...
IS IT ME, OR DOES HE SEEM A LITTLE MEEKER AROUND THE EDGES THAN HE DID IN MIDDLE SCHOOL?
HUH ?!
HOW? THE KID'S A SMART-MOUTHED LITTLE BRAT, THROUGH AND THROUGH.
WHEN WE WATCHED HIS MIDDLE SCHOOL GAME LAST YEAR...
...HE HAD THIS, I DUNNO... AIR OF ABSOLUTE CONFIDENCE ABOUT HIM...
LIKE HE KNEW HE WAS UNMATCHED ON THAT COURT...
EITHER WAY, HE'S STILL A STUCK-UP, SMART-MOUTHED, SNOT-NOSED KID.
RIGHT. ASKING YOU WAS A MISTAKE.
...
FWIF
THERE!
NEXT ONE FROM THE BACK!
TOSS
!
ALL RIGHT! HERE I--
WOW. YOU REALLY ARE PRACTICING OUTSIDE.
PAFF
LOOM
?!
HN?

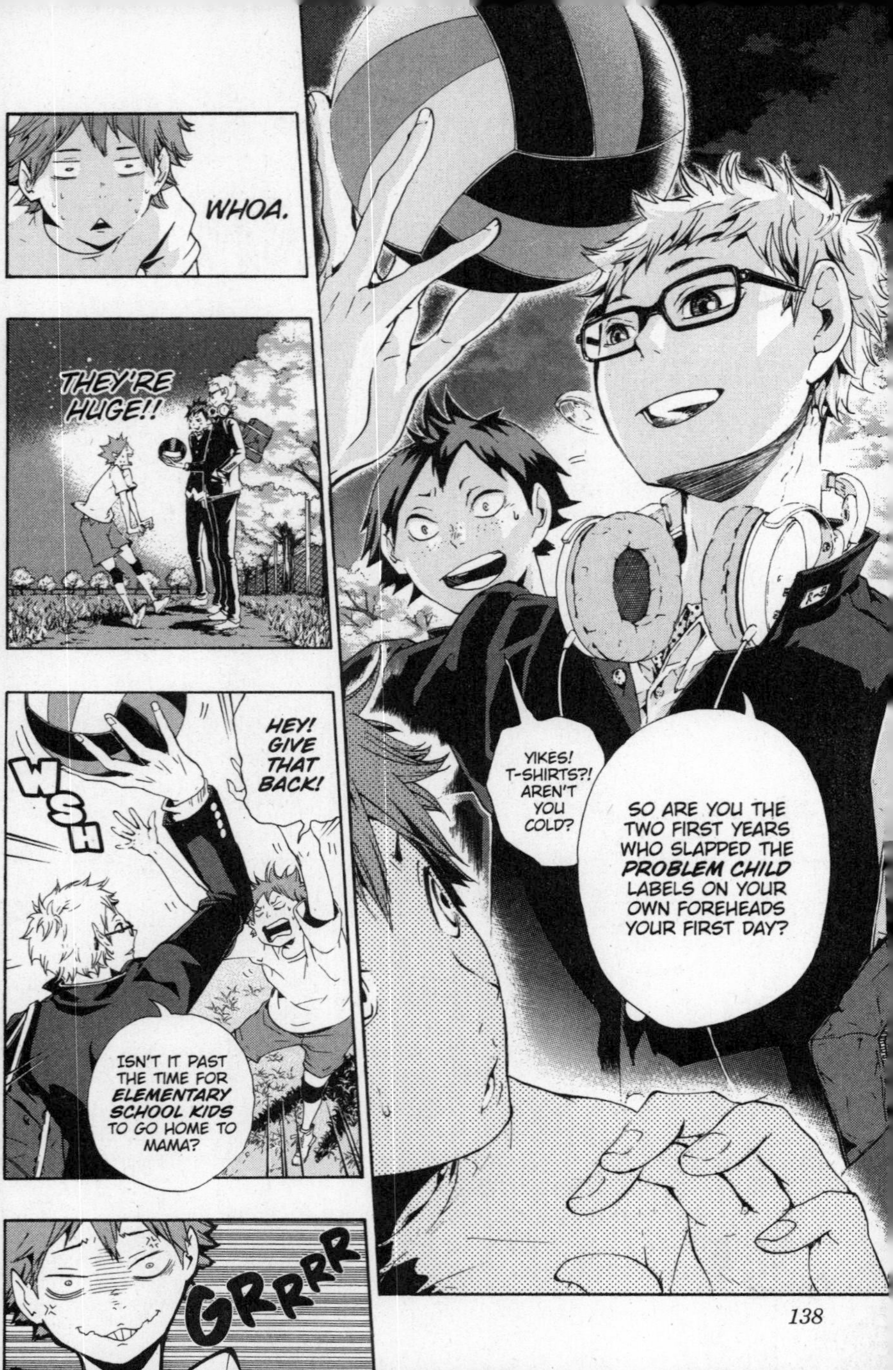

SO ARE YOU THE TWO FIRST YEARS WHO SLAPPED THE PROBLEM CHILD LABELS ON YOUR OWN FOREHEADS YOUR FIRST DAY?
YIKES! T-SHIRTS?! AREN'T YOU COLD?
WHOA.
THEY'RE HUGE!!
HEY! GIVE THAT BACK!
WSH
ISN'T IT PAST THE TIME FOR ELEMENTARY SCHOOL KIDS TO GO HOME TO MAMA?
GRRRR

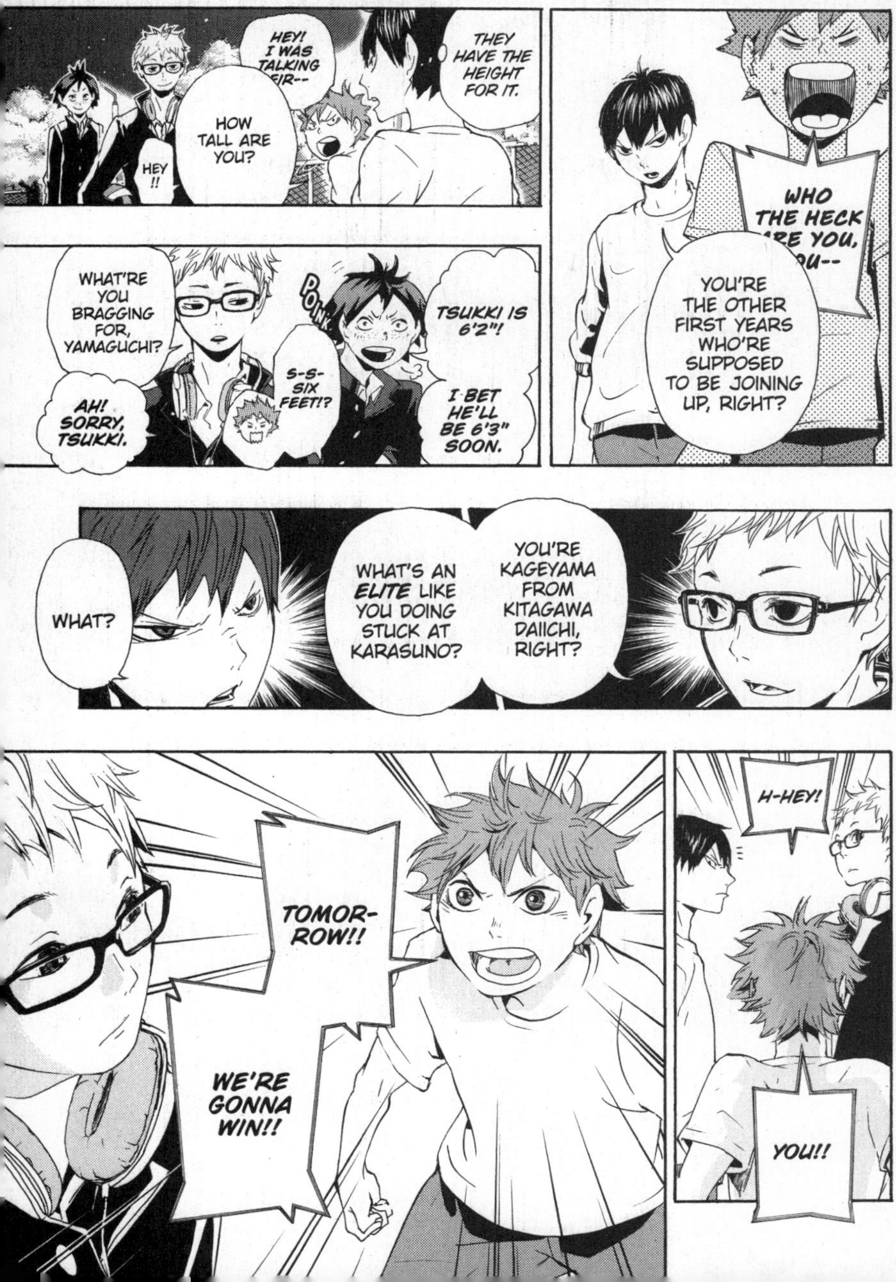
WHO THE HECK ARE YOU, YOU--
YOU'RE THE OTHER FIRST YEARS WHO'RE SUPPOSED TO BE JOINING UP, RIGHT?
THEY HAVE THE HEIGHT FOR IT.
HEY! I WAS TALKING FIR--
HOW TALL ARE YOU?
HEY !!
TSUKKI IS 6'2"!
I BET HE'LL BE 6'3" SOON.
POINK
S-S-SIX FEET!?
WHAT'RE YOU BRAGGING FOR, YAMAGUCHI?
AH! SORRY, TSUKKI.
YOU'RE KAGEYAMA FROM KITAGAWA DAIICHI, RIGHT?
WHAT'S AN ELITE LIKE YOU DOING STUCK AT KARASUNO?
WHAT?
H-HEY!
YOU!!
TOMOR-ROW!!
WE'RE GONNA WIN!!

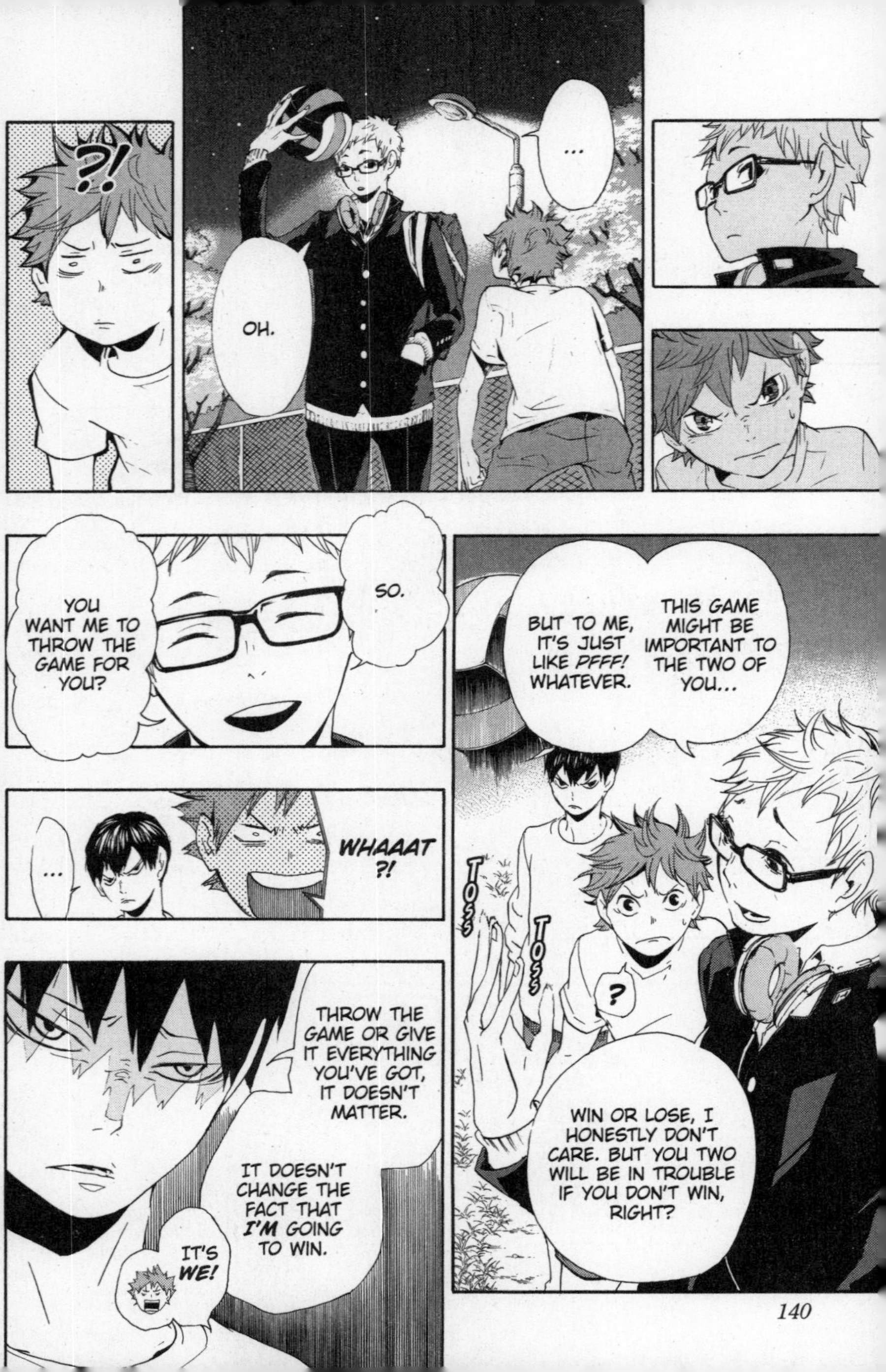
...
OH.
?!
THIS GAME MIGHT BE IMPORTANT TO THE TWO OF YOU...
BUT TO ME, IT'S JUST LIKE *PFFF!* WHATEVER.
TOSS
TOSS
?
WIN OR LOSE, I HONESTLY DON'T CARE. BUT YOU TWO WILL BE IN TROUBLE IF YOU DON'T WIN, RIGHT?
SO.
YOU WANT ME TO THROW THE GAME FOR YOU?
WHAAAT?!
...
THROW THE GAME OR GIVE IT EVERYTHING YOU'VE GOT, IT DOESN'T MATTER.
IT DOESN'T CHANGE THE FACT THAT ***I'M*** GOING TO WIN.
IT'S ***WE!***

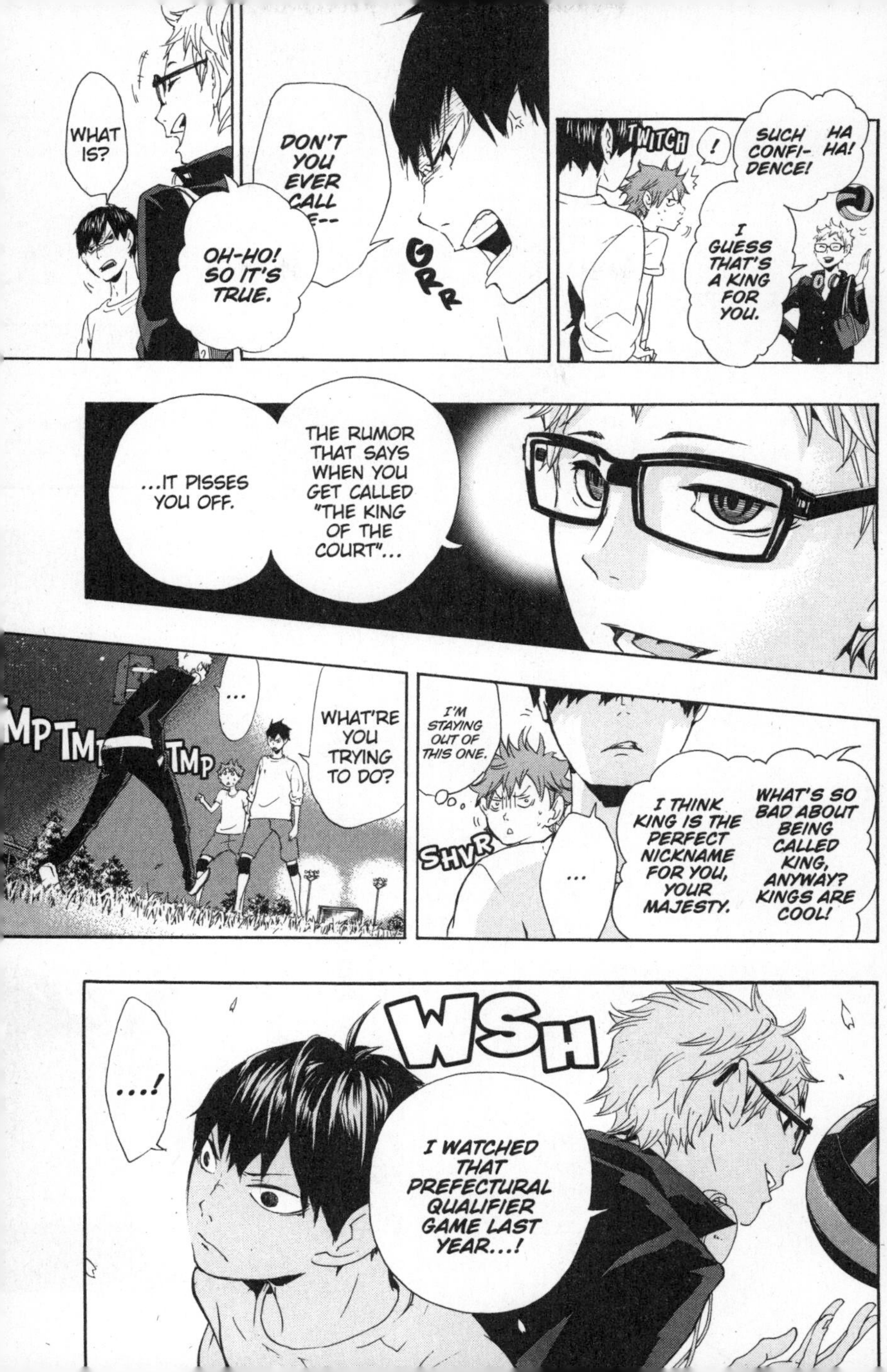
HA HA!
SUCH CONFI-DENCE!
I GUESS THAT'S A KING FOR YOU.
!
TWITCH
DON'T YOU EVER CALL
GRR
OH-HO! SO IT'S TRUE.
WHAT IS?
THE RUMOR THAT SAYS WHEN YOU GET CALLED "THE KING OF THE COURT"...
...IT PISSES YOU OFF.
WHAT'S SO BAD ABOUT BEING CALLED KING, ANYWAY? KINGS ARE COOL!
I THINK KING IS THE PERFECT NICKNAME FOR YOU, YOUR MAJESTY.
...
I'M STAYING OUT OF THIS ONE.
SHVR
WHAT'RE YOU TRYING TO DO?
...
TMP
WSH
I WATCHED THAT PREFECTURAL QUALIFIER GAME LAST YEAR...!
...!

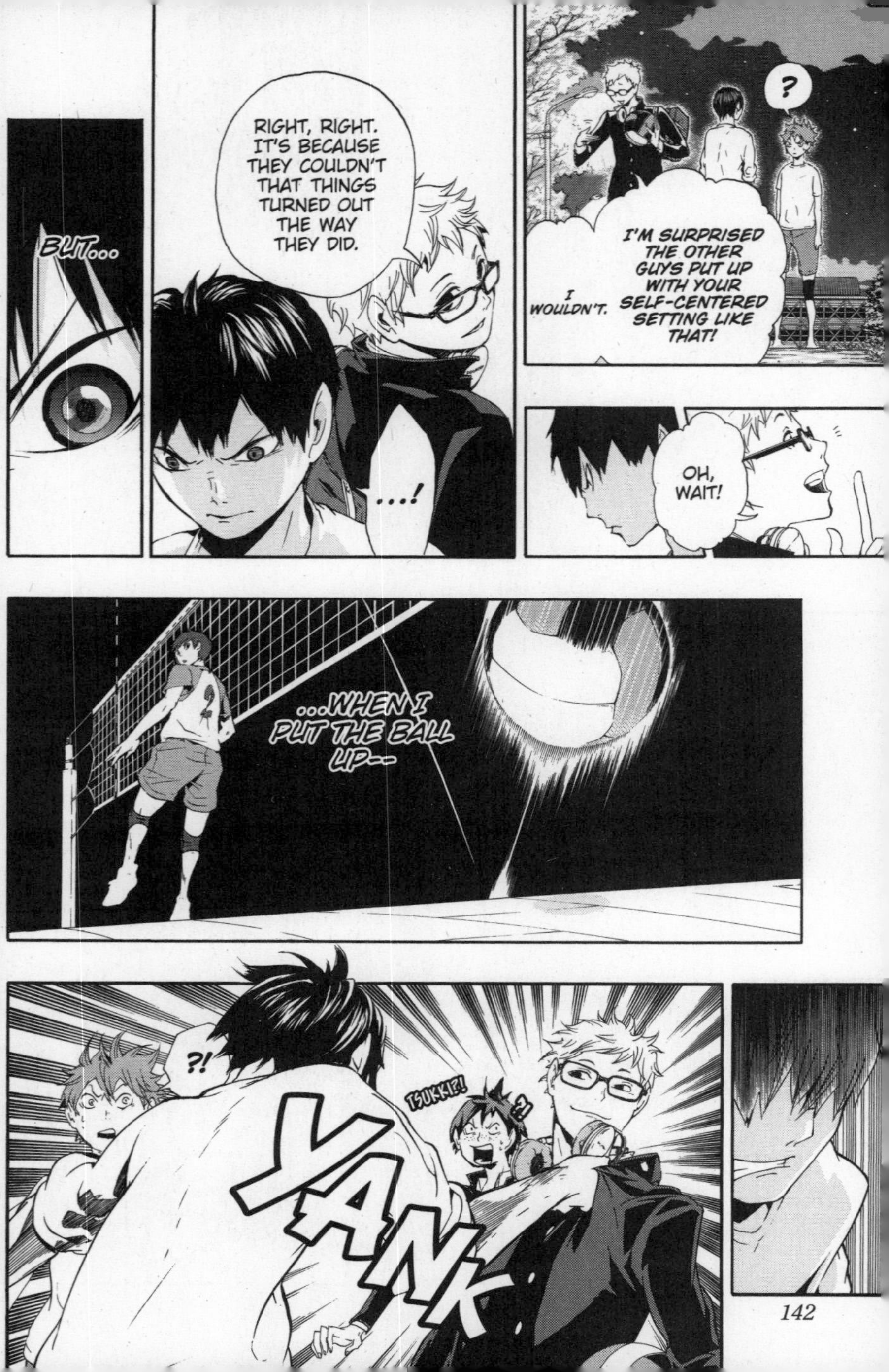
?
I'M SURPRISED THE OTHER GUYS PUT UP WITH YOUR SELF-CENTERED SETTING LIKE THAT!
I WOULDN'T.
OH, WAIT!
RIGHT, RIGHT. IT'S BECAUSE THEY COULDN'T THAT THINGS TURNED OUT THE WAY THEY DID.
...!
BUT...
...WHEN I PUT THE BALL UP--
TSUKKI!?!
?!
?!
YANK

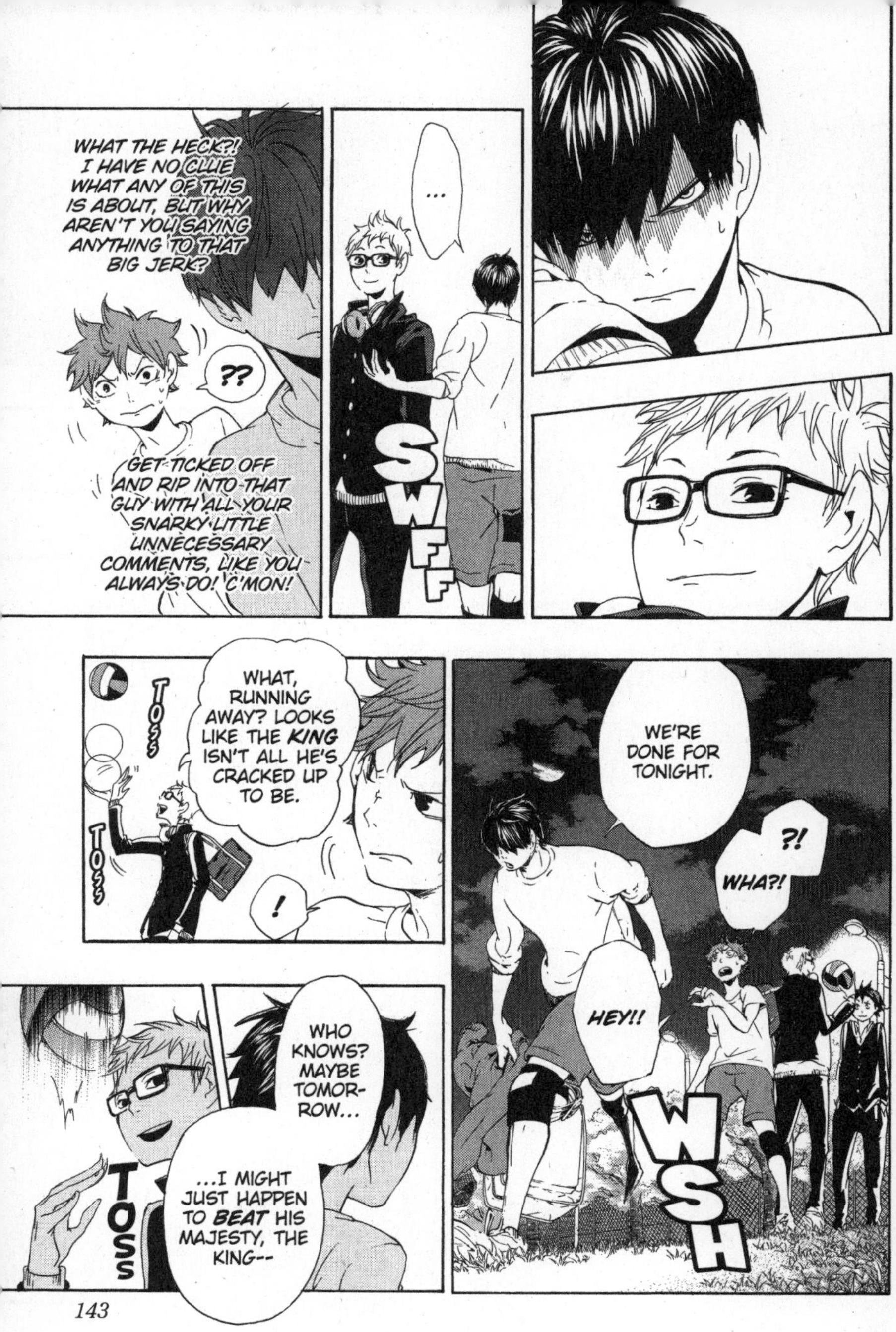
...
SWFF
WHAT THE HECK?! I HAVE NO CLUE WHAT ANY OF THIS IS ABOUT, BUT WHY AREN'T YOU SAYING ANYTHING TO THAT BIG JERK?
??
GET TICKED OFF AND RIP INTO THAT GUY WITH ALL YOUR SNARKY LITTLE UNNECESSARY COMMENTS, LIKE YOU ALWAYS DO! C'MON!
WE'RE DONE FOR TONIGHT.
?!
WHA?!
HEY!!
WSH
TOSS
TOSS
WHAT, RUNNING AWAY? LOOKS LIKE THE ***KING*** ISN'T ALL HE'S CRACKED UP TO BE.
!
WHO KNOWS? MAYBE TOMORROW...
...I MIGHT JUST HAPPEN TO ***BEAT*** HIS MAJESTY, THE KING--
TOSS

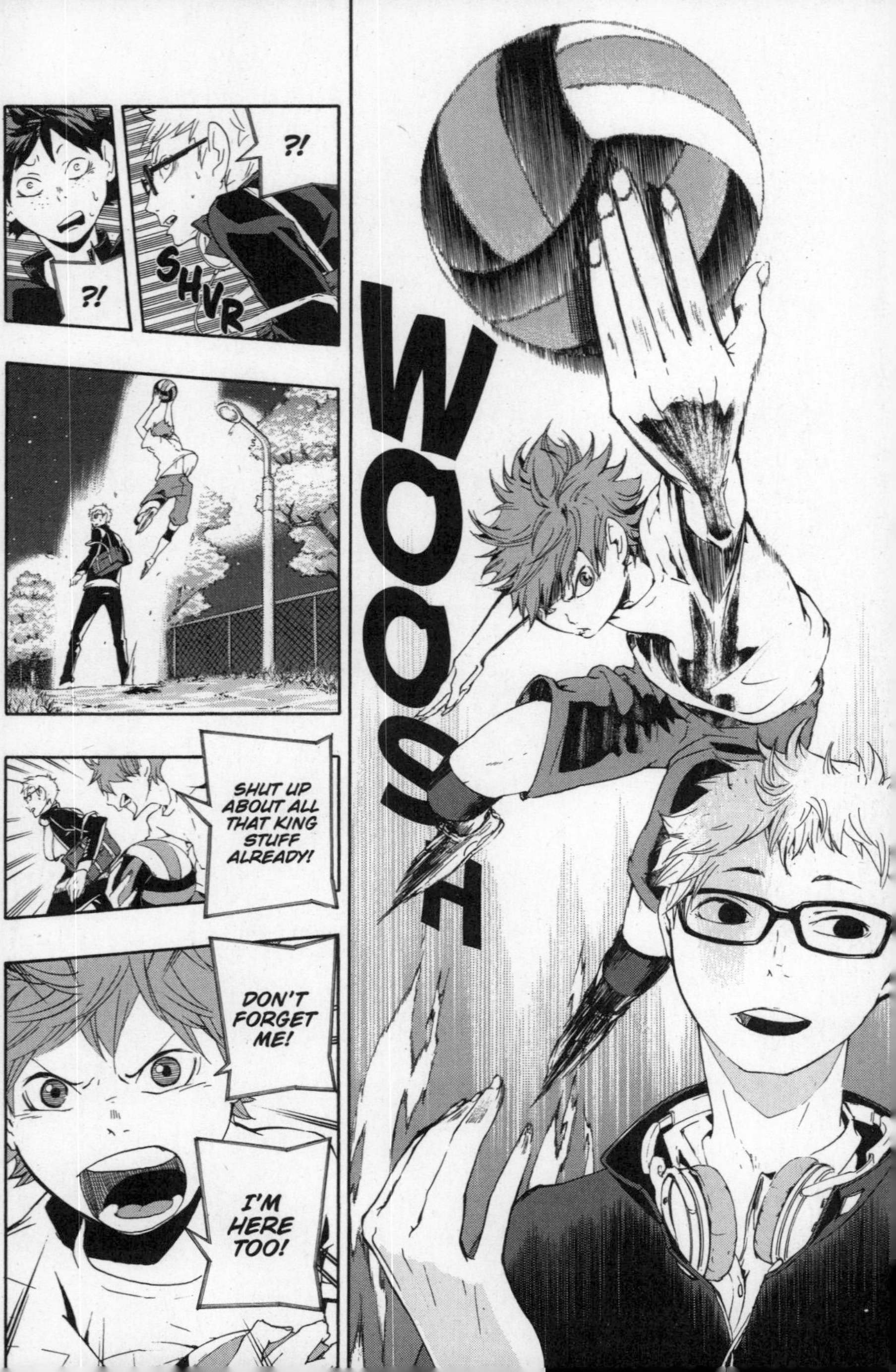
WOOSH
?!
SHVR
?!
SHUT UP ABOUT ALL THAT KING STUFF ALREADY!
DON'T FORGET ME!
I'M HERE TOO!

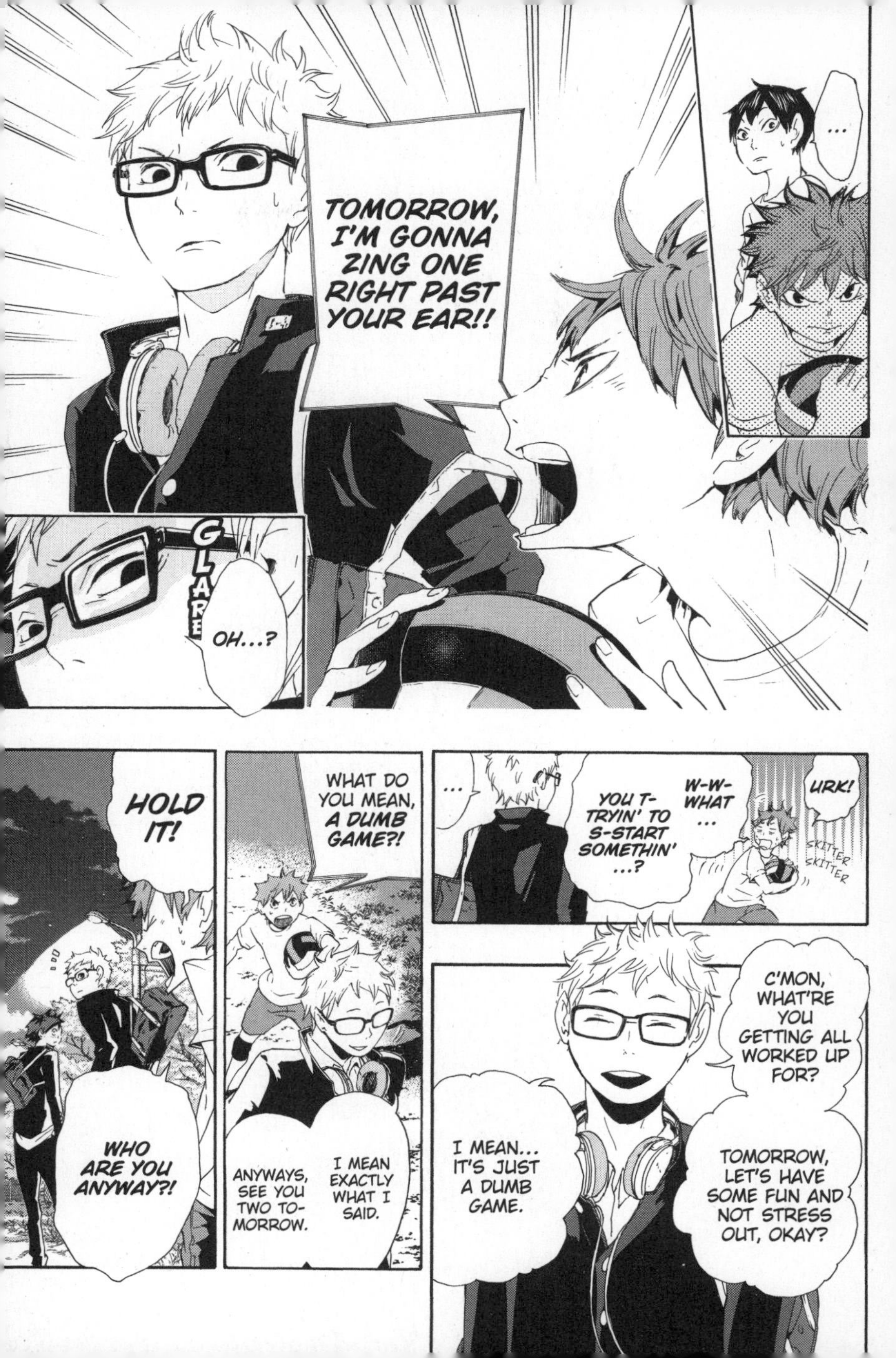
...
TOMORROW, I'M GONNA ZING ONE RIGHT PAST YOUR EAR!!
GLARE
OH...?
URK!
W-W-WHAT...
YOU T-TRYIN' TO S-START SOMETHIN' ...?
...
SKITTER SKITTER
C'MON, WHAT'RE YOU GETTING ALL WORKED UP FOR?
TOMORROW, LET'S HAVE SOME FUN AND NOT STRESS OUT, OKAY?
I MEAN... IT'S JUST A DUMB GAME.
WHAT DO YOU MEAN, A DUMB GAME?!
I MEAN EXACTLY WHAT I SAID.
ANYWAYS, SEE YOU TWO TO-MORROW.
HOLD IT!
WHO ARE YOU ANYWAY?!

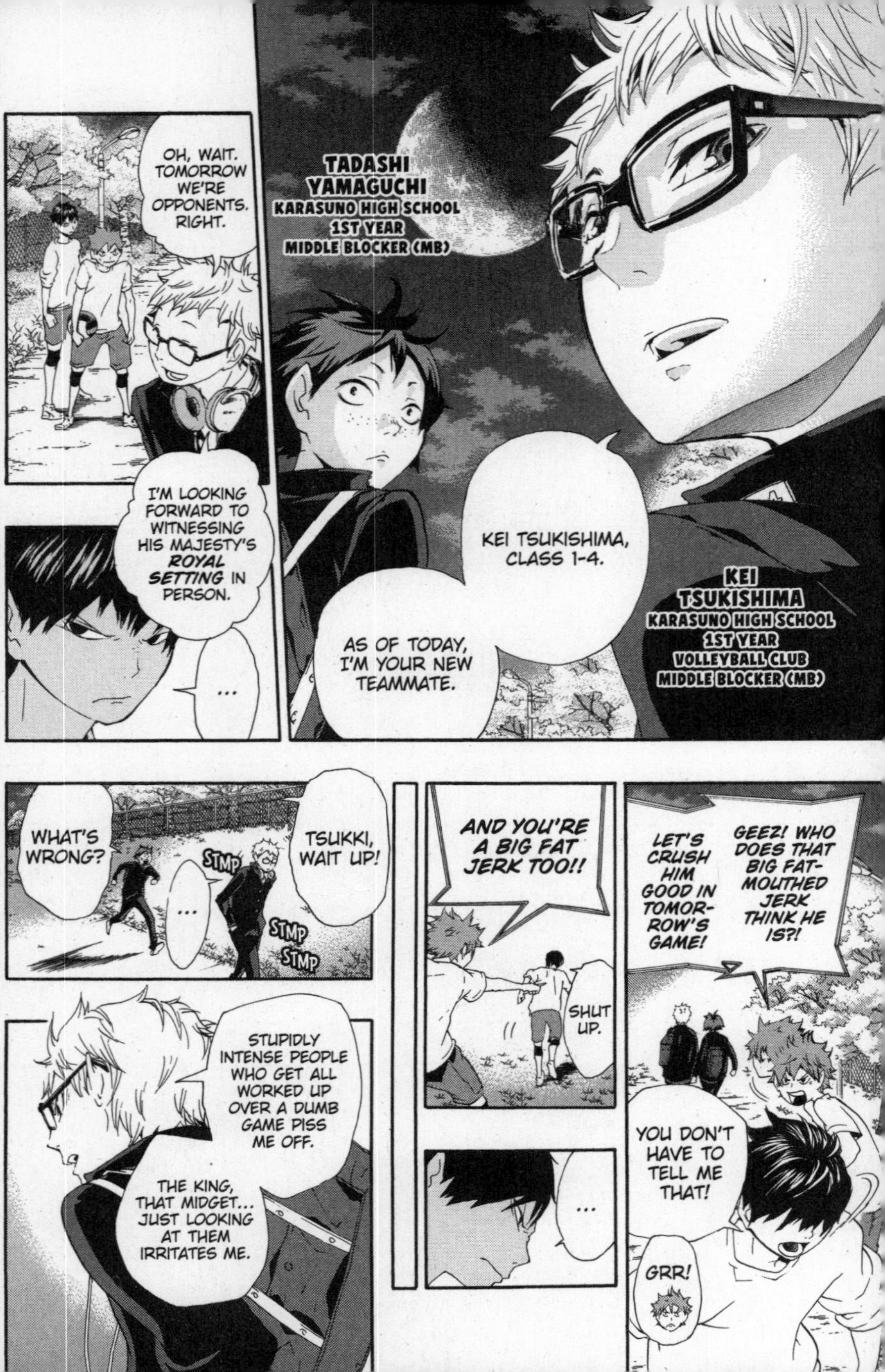

KEI TSUKISHIMA, CLASS 1-4.
AS OF TODAY, I'M YOUR NEW TEAMMATE.
KEI TSUKISHIMA KARASUNO HIGH SCHOOL 1ST YEAR VOLLEYBALL CLUB MIDDLE BLOCKER (MB)
TADASHI YAMAGUCHI KARASUNO HIGH SCHOOL 1ST YEAR MIDDLE BLOCKER (MB)
OH, WAIT. TOMORROW WE'RE OPPONENTS. RIGHT.
I'M LOOKING FORWARD TO WITNESSING HIS MAJESTY'S *ROYAL SETTING* IN PERSON.
...
GEEZ! WHO DOES THAT BIG FAT-MOUTHED JERK THINK HE IS?!
LET'S CRUSH HIM GOOD IN TOMORROW'S GAME!
YOU DON'T HAVE TO TELL ME THAT!
GRR!
AND YOU'RE A BIG FAT JERK TOO!!
SHUT UP.
...
TSUKKI, WAIT UP!
WHAT'S WRONG?
...
STMP
STMP
STMP
STUPIDLY INTENSE PEOPLE WHO GET ALL WORKED UP OVER A DUMB GAME PISS ME OFF.
THE KING, THAT MIDGET... JUST LOOKING AT THEM IRRITATES ME.

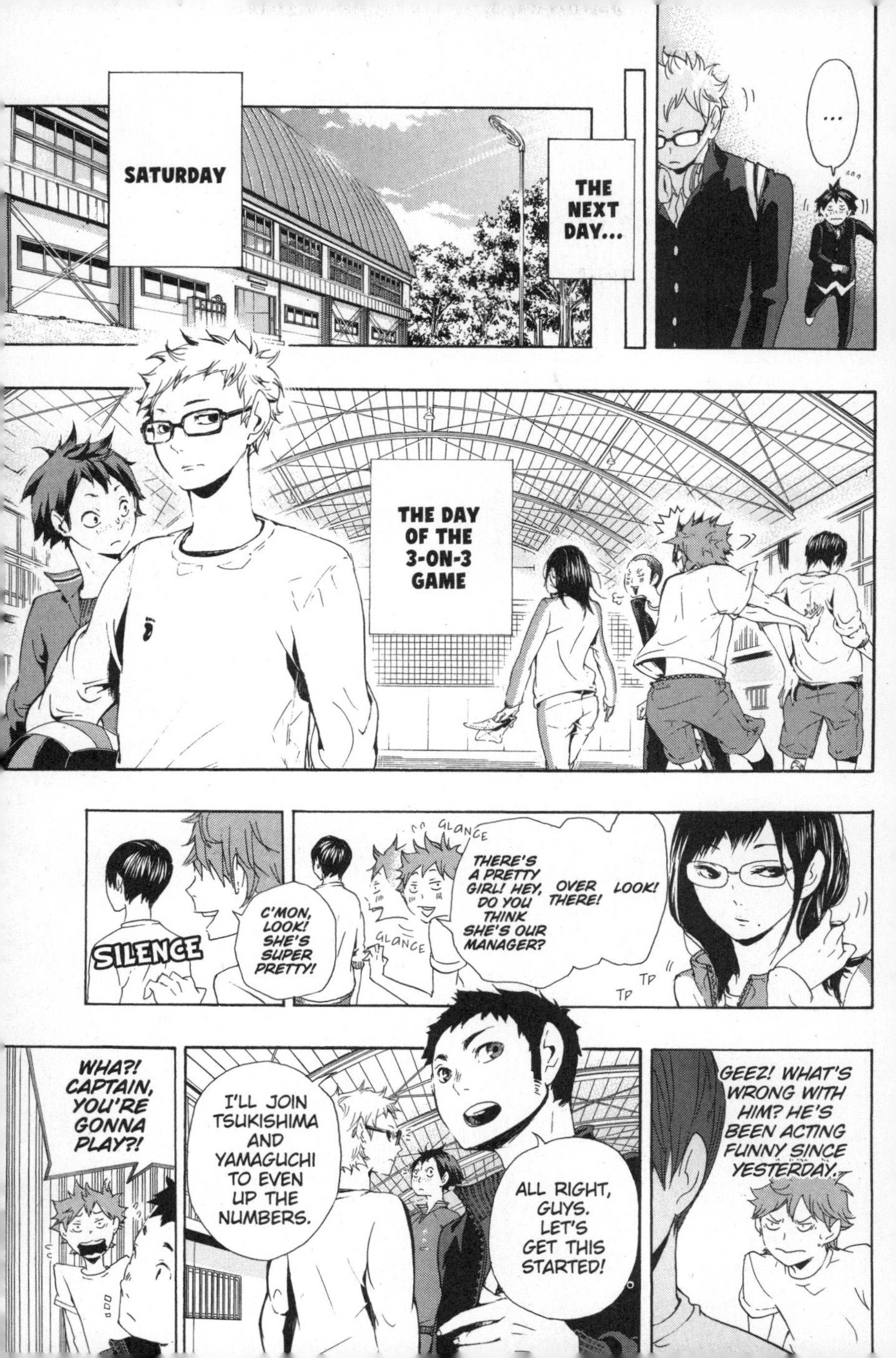
...
THE NEXT DAY...
SATURDAY
THE DAY OF THE 3-ON-3 GAME
LOOK!
OVER THERE!
THERE'S A PRETTY GIRL! HEY, DO YOU THINK SHE'S OUR MANAGER?
GLANCE
TP TP
C'MON, LOOK! SHE'S SUPER PRETTY!
GLANCE
SILENCE
GEEZ! WHAT'S WRONG WITH HIM? HE'S BEEN ACTING FUNNY SINCE YESTERDAY.
ALL RIGHT, GUYS. LET'S GET THIS STARTED!
I'LL JOIN TSUKISHIMA AND YAMAGUCHI TO EVEN UP THE NUMBERS.
WHA?! CAPTAIN, YOU'RE GONNA PLAY?!

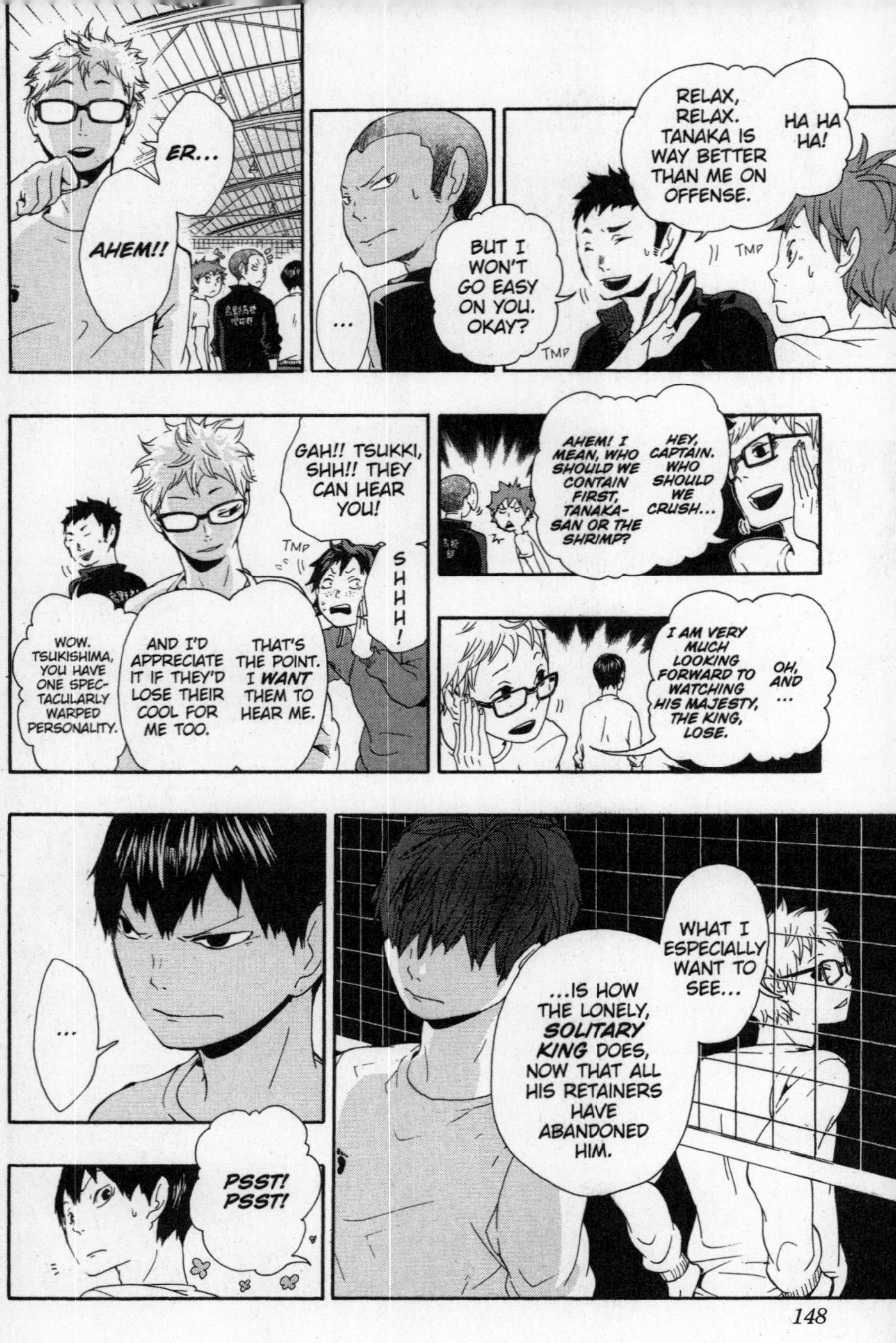
RELAX, RELAX. TANAKA IS WAY BETTER THAN ME ON OFFENSE.
HA HA HA!
TMP
BUT I WON'T GO EASY ON YOU. OKAY?
TMP
...
ER...
AHEM!!
HEY, CAPTAIN. WHO SHOULD WE CRUSH...
AHEM! I MEAN, WHO SHOULD WE CONTAIN FIRST, TANAKA-SAN OR THE SHRIMP?
OH, AND ...
I AM VERY MUCH LOOKING FORWARD TO WATCHING HIS MAJESTY, THE KING, LOSE.
GAH!! TSUKKI, SHH!! THEY CAN HEAR YOU!
TMP
SHHH!
THAT'S THE POINT. I WANT THEM TO HEAR ME.
AND I'D APPRECIATE IT IF THEY'D LOSE THEIR COOL FOR ME TOO.
WOW. TSUKISHIMA, YOU HAVE ONE SPECTACULARLY WARPED PERSONALITY.
WHAT I ESPECIALLY WANT TO SEE...
...IS HOW THE LONELY, SOLITARY KING DOES, NOW THAT ALL HIS RETAINERS HAVE ABANDONED HIM.
...
PSST! PSST!

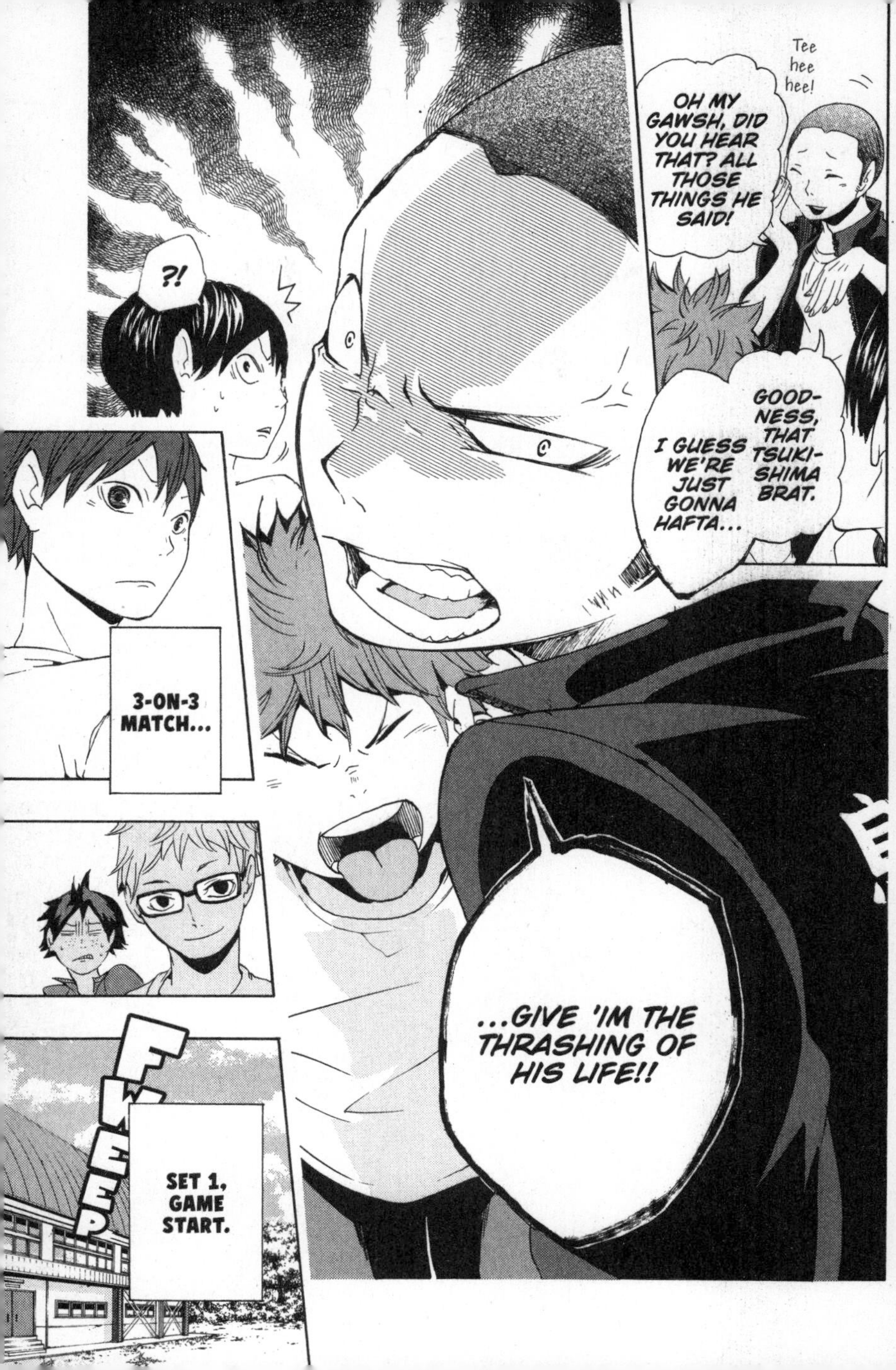
Tee hee hee!
OH MY GAWSH, DID YOU HEAR THAT? ALL THOSE THINGS HE SAID!
GOODNESS, THAT TSUKISHIMA BRAT.
I GUESS WE'RE JUST GONNA HAFTA...
...GIVE 'IM THE THRASHING OF HIS LIFE!!
?!
3-ON-3 MATCH...
FWEEP
SET 1, GAME START.

DAICHI SAWAMURA

KARASUNO HIGH SCHOOL
CLASS 3-4

VOLLEYBALL CLUB CAPTAIN

POSITION: WING SPIKER

HEIGHT: 5'10"
WEIGHT: 154 LBS.
(AS OF APRIL, 3RD YEAR IN HIGH SCHOOL)

BIRTHDAY: DECEMBER 31

FAVORITE FOOD:
SOY-SAUCE RAMEN

CURRENT WORRY:
HE IS BEING PLAGUED BY NIGHTMARES OF THE VICE PRINCIPAL'S TOUPEE FLYING OFF OVER AND OVER AGAIN.

ABILITY PARAMETERS
(5-POINT SCALE)

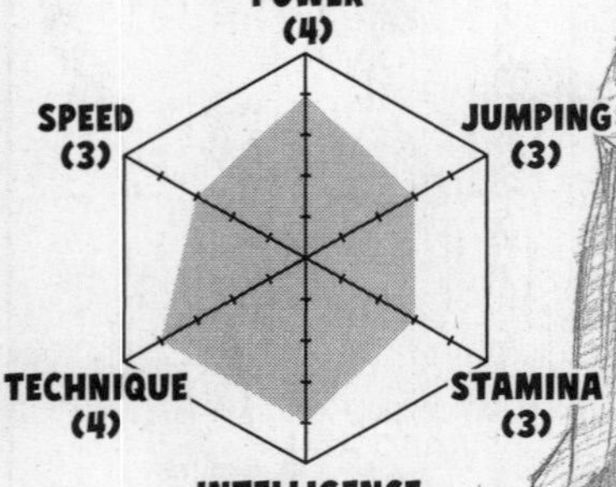
POWER (4)
JUMPING (3)
STAMINA (3)
INTELLIGENCE (4)
TECHNIQUE (4)
SPEED (3)

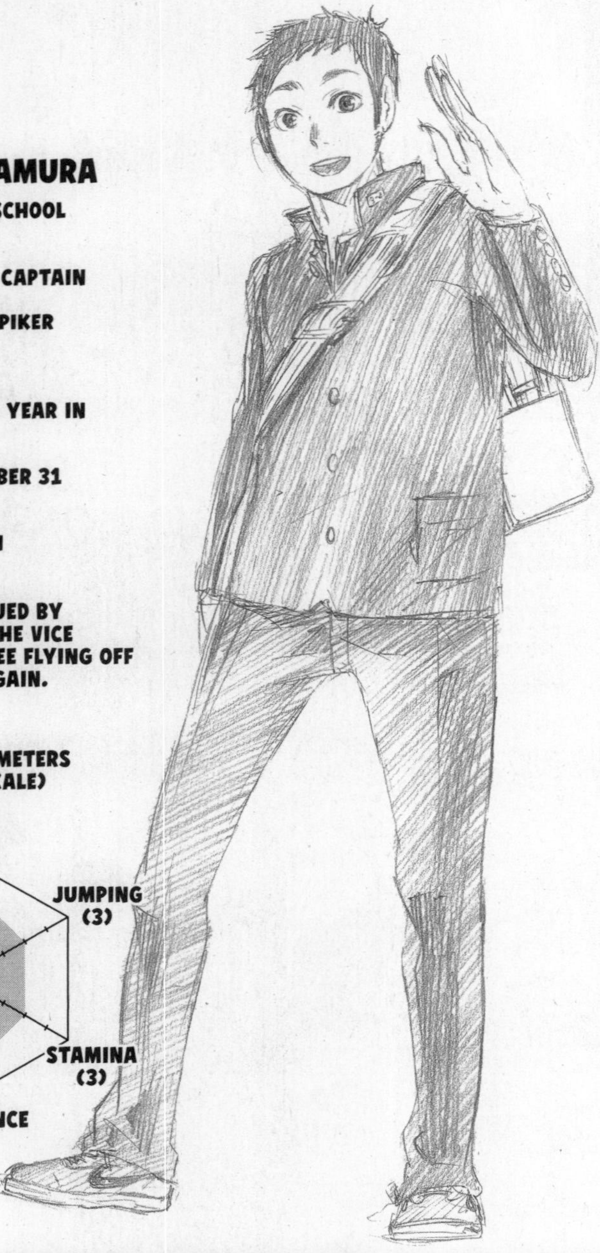

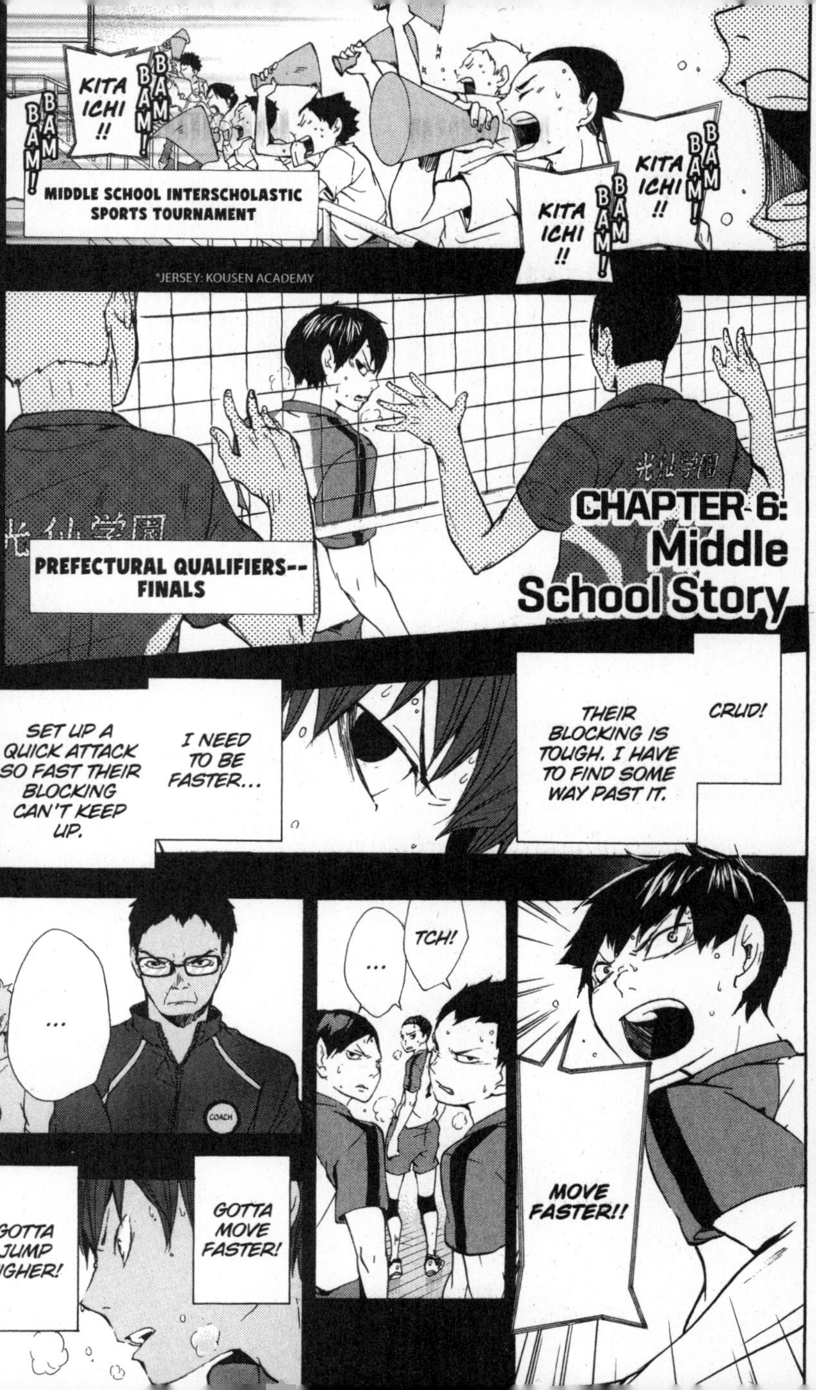
BAM BAM BAM!
KITA ICHI!!
BAM BAM BAM!
KITA ICHI!!
BAM BAM BAM!
KITA ICHI!!
BAM BAM BAM!
MIDDLE SCHOOL INTERSCHOLASTIC SPORTS TOURNAMENT
*JERSEY: KOUSEN ACADEMY
CHAPTER 6: Middle School Story
PREFECTURAL QUALIFIERS-- FINALS
CRUD!
THEIR BLOCKING IS TOUGH. I HAVE TO FIND SOME WAY PAST IT.
I NEED TO BE FASTER...
SET UP A QUICK ATTACK SO FAST THEIR BLOCKING CAN'T KEEP UP.
MOVE FASTER!!
TCH!
...
...
GOTTA MOVE FASTER!
GOTTA JUMP HIGHER!

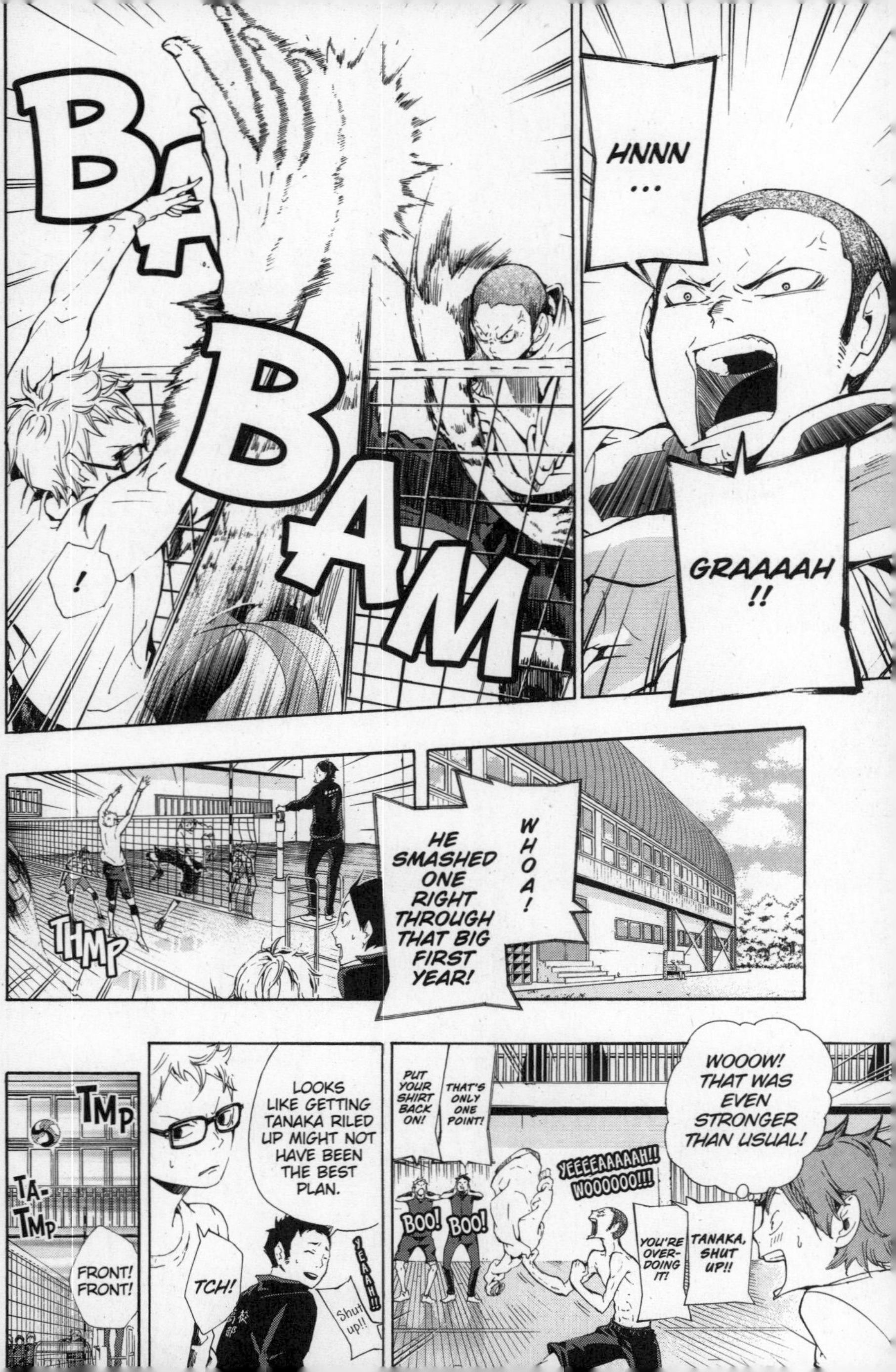
HNNN...
GRAAAAH!!
BAM
!
WHOA!
HE SMASHED ONE RIGHT THROUGH THAT BIG FIRST YEAR!
THMP
WOOOW! THAT WAS EVEN STRONGER THAN USUAL!
TANAKA, SHUT UP!!
YOU'RE OVER-DOING IT!
YEEEEAAAAAH!!! WOOOOOO!!!
THAT'S ONLY ONE POINT!
PUT YOUR SHIRT BACK ON!
BOO!
BOO!
LOOKS LIKE GETTING TANAKA RILED UP MIGHT NOT HAVE BEEN THE BEST PLAN.
YEAAAH!!
Shut up!!
TCH!
TMP
TA-TMP
FRONT! FRONT!

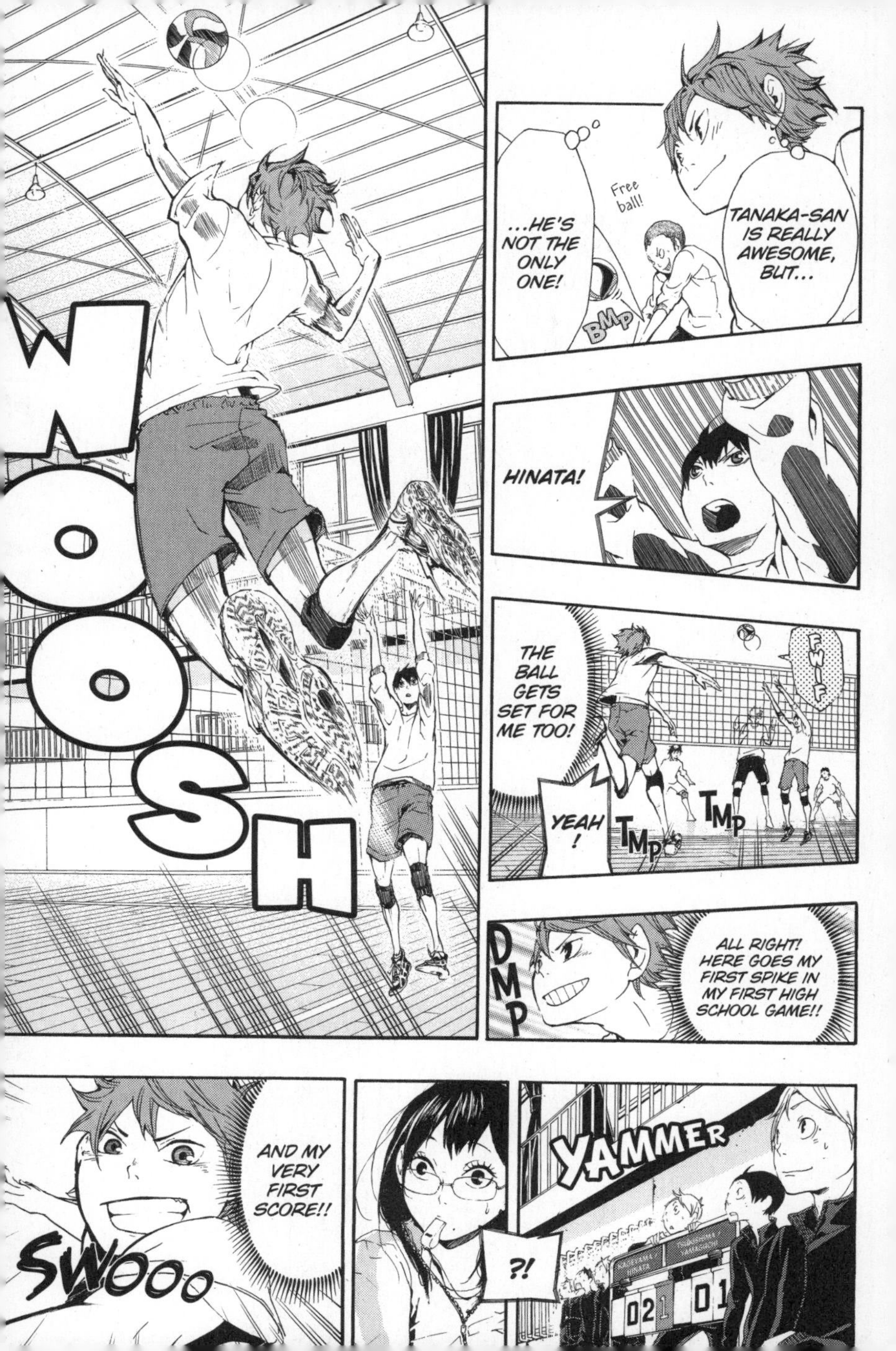

TANAKA-SAN IS REALLY AWESOME, BUT...
Free ball!
...HE'S NOT THE ONLY ONE!
BMP
HINATA!
FWIF
THE BALL GETS SET FOR ME TOO!
YEAH!
TMP
TMP
ALL RIGHT! HERE GOES MY FIRST SPIKE IN MY FIRST HIGH SCHOOL GAME!!
DMP
WHOOSH
YAMMER
02
01
?!
AND MY VERY FIRST SCORE!!
SWOOO

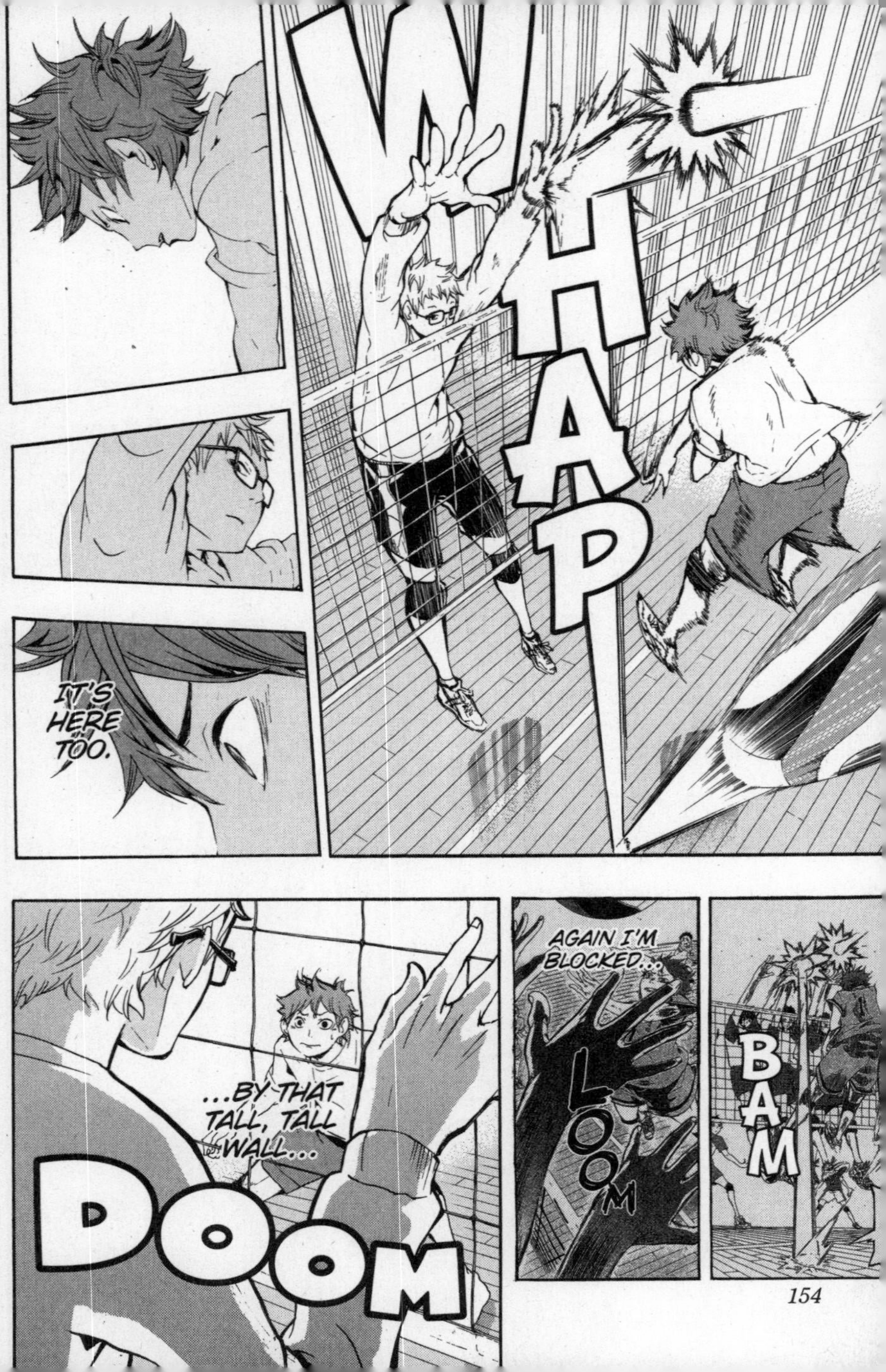
WHAP
IT'S HERE TOO.
BAM
AGAIN I'M BLOCKED...
LOOM
...BY THAT TALL, TALL WALL...
DOOM

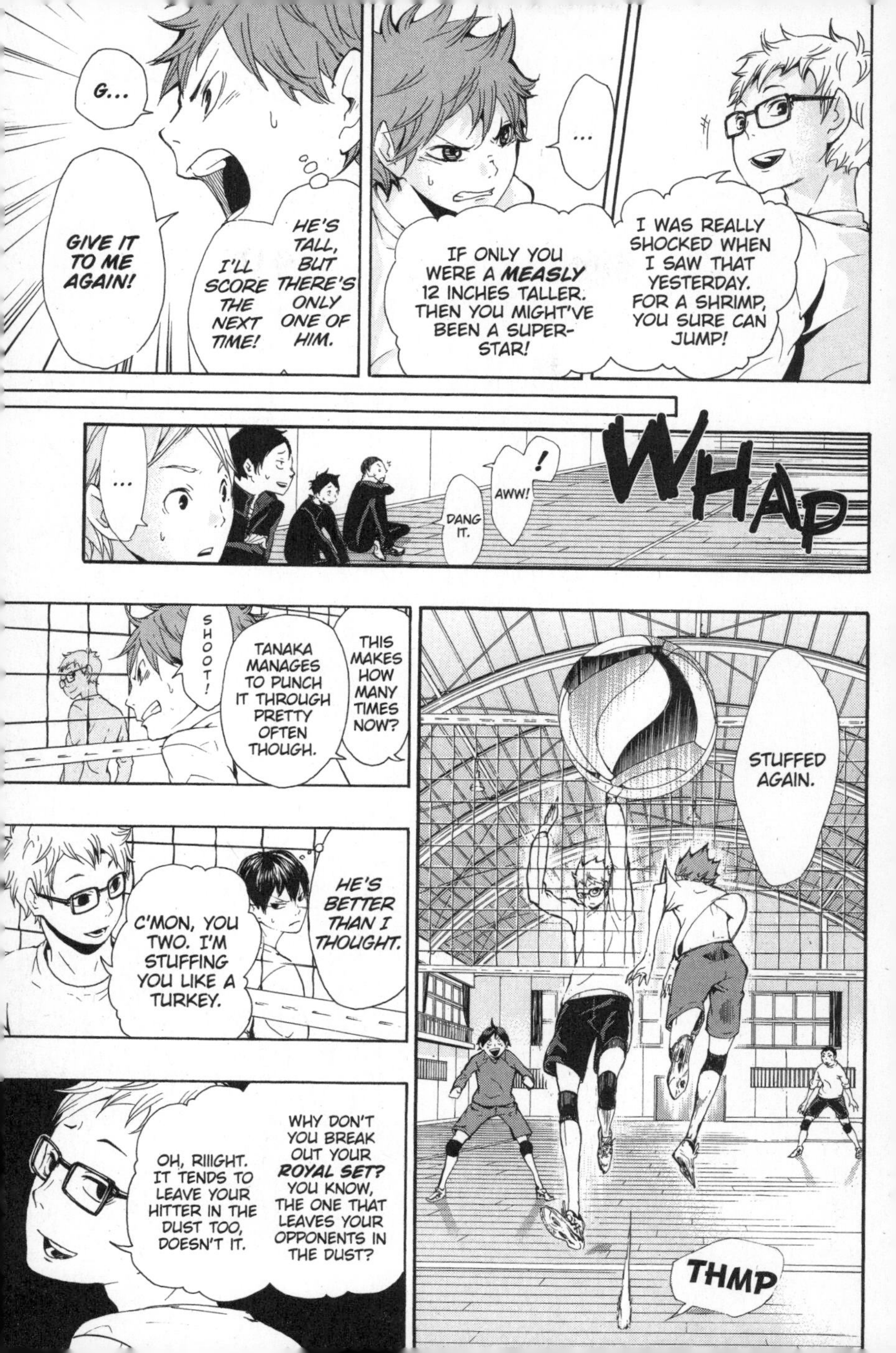

I WAS REALLY SHOCKED WHEN I SAW THAT YESTERDAY. FOR A SHRIMP, YOU SURE CAN JUMP!
IF ONLY YOU WERE A **MEASLY** 12 INCHES TALLER. THEN YOU MIGHT'VE BEEN A SUPER-STAR!
...
G...
HE'S TALL, BUT THERE'S ONLY ONE OF HIM.
I'LL SCORE THE NEXT TIME!
GIVE IT TO ME AGAIN!
WHAP
!
AWW!
DANG IT.
...
STUFFED AGAIN.
THMP
THIS MAKES HOW MANY TIMES NOW?
TANAKA MANAGES TO PUNCH IT THROUGH PRETTY OFTEN THOUGH.
SHOOT!
HE'S BETTER THAN I THOUGHT.
C'MON, YOU TWO. I'M STUFFING YOU LIKE A TURKEY.
WHY DON'T YOU BREAK OUT YOUR ***ROYAL SET?*** YOU KNOW, THE ONE THAT LEAVES YOUR OPPONENTS IN THE DUST?
OH, RIIIGHT. IT TENDS TO LEAVE YOUR HITTER IN THE DUST TOO, DOESN'T IT.

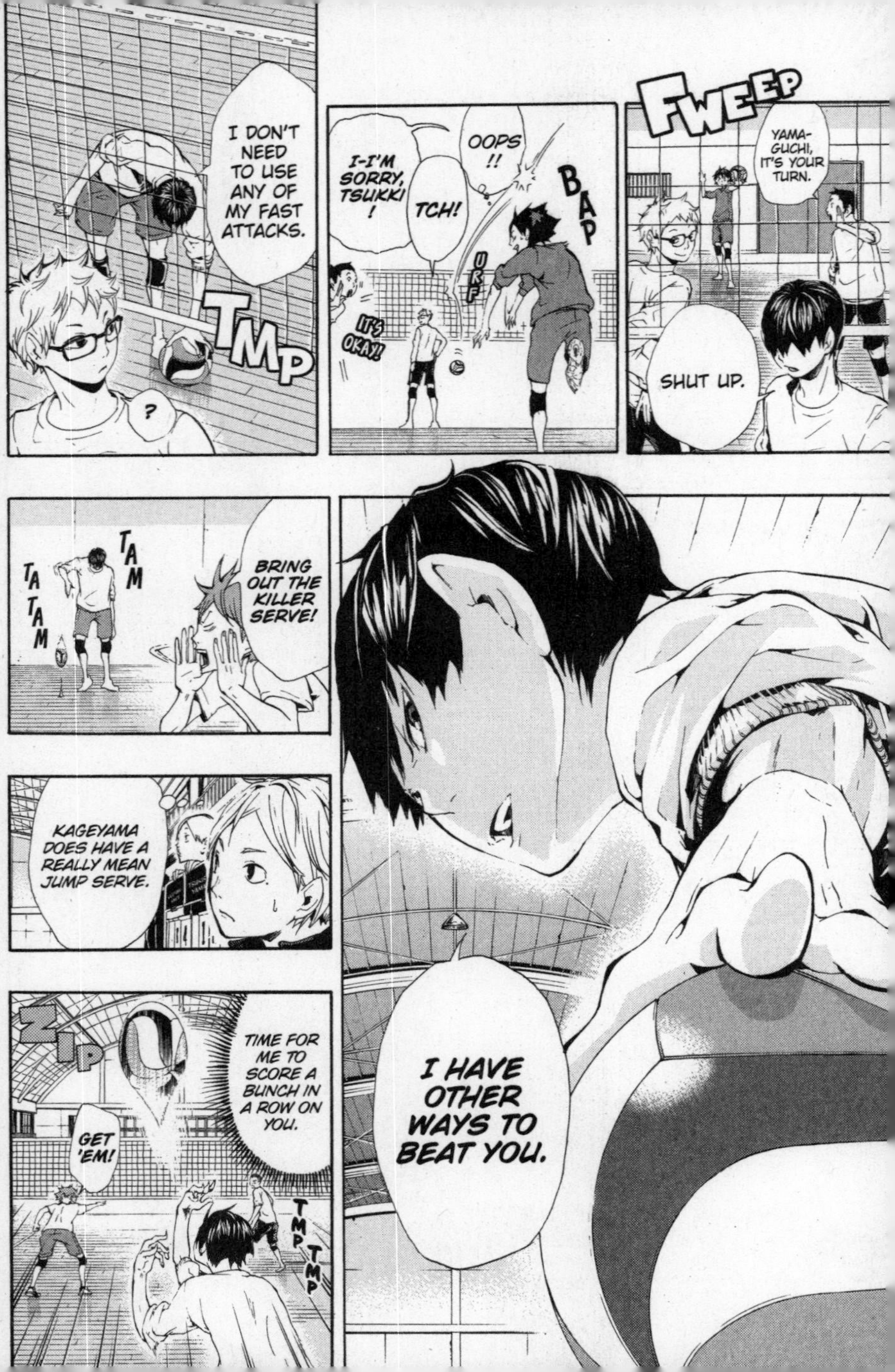
FWEEP
YAMA-GUCHI, IT'S YOUR TURN.
SHUT UP.
BAP
OOPS !!
TCH!
I-I'M SORRY, TSUKKI !
URF
IT'S OKAY!
I DON'T NEED TO USE ANY OF MY FAST ATTACKS.
TMP
?
I HAVE OTHER WAYS TO BEAT YOU.
BRING OUT THE KILLER SERVE!
TAM
TA TAM
KAGEYAMA DOES HAVE A REALLY MEAN JUMP SERVE.
TIME FOR ME TO SCORE A BUNCH IN A ROW ON YOU.
ZIP
GET 'EM!
TMP TMP

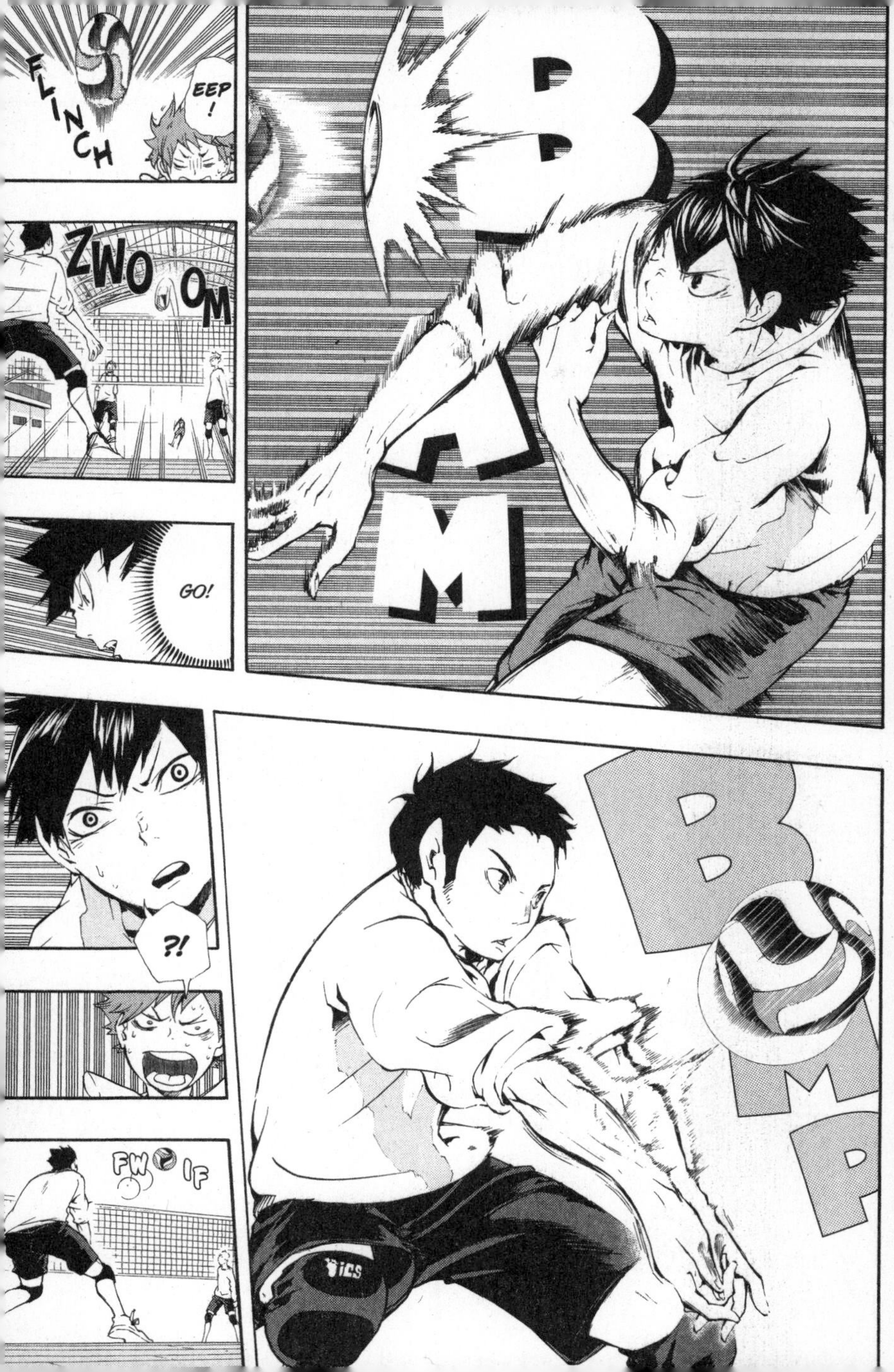
BUM
FLINCH
EEP!
ZWOOOM
GO!
BUMP
?!
FWOIF

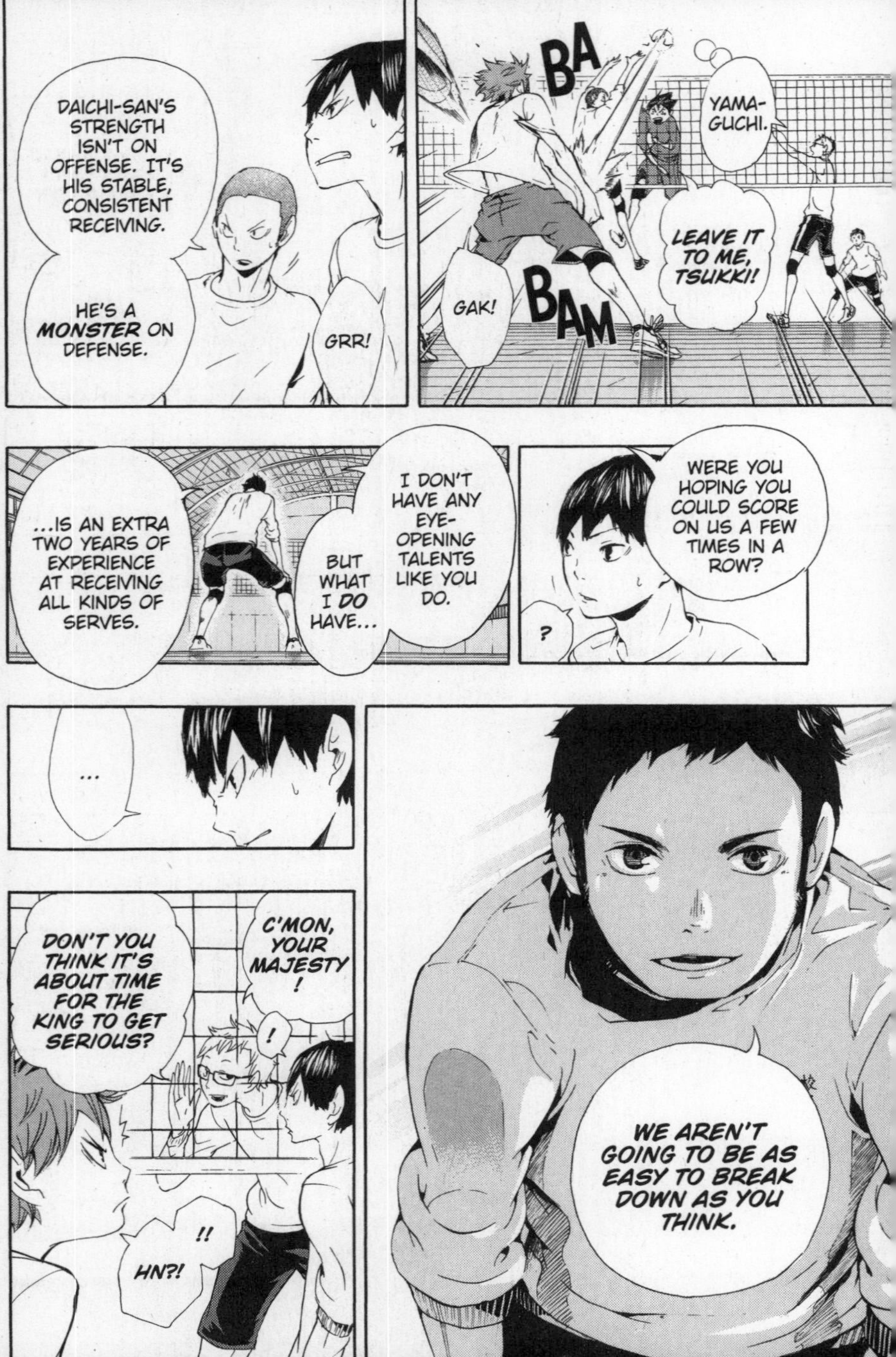
YAMA-GUCHI.
LEAVE IT TO ME, TSUKKI!
BA
BAM
GAK!
DAICHI-SAN'S STRENGTH ISN'T ON OFFENSE. IT'S HIS STABLE, CONSISTENT RECEIVING.
HE'S A MONSTER ON DEFENSE.
GRR!
WERE YOU HOPING YOU COULD SCORE ON US A FEW TIMES IN A ROW?
?
I DON'T HAVE ANY EYE-OPENING TALENTS LIKE YOU DO.
BUT WHAT I DO HAVE...
...IS AN EXTRA TWO YEARS OF EXPERIENCE AT RECEIVING ALL KINDS OF SERVES.
WE AREN'T GOING TO BE AS EASY TO BREAK DOWN AS YOU THINK.
...
C'MON, YOUR MAJESTY!
DON'T YOU THINK IT'S ABOUT TIME FOR THE KING TO GET SERIOUS?
!
!!
HN?!

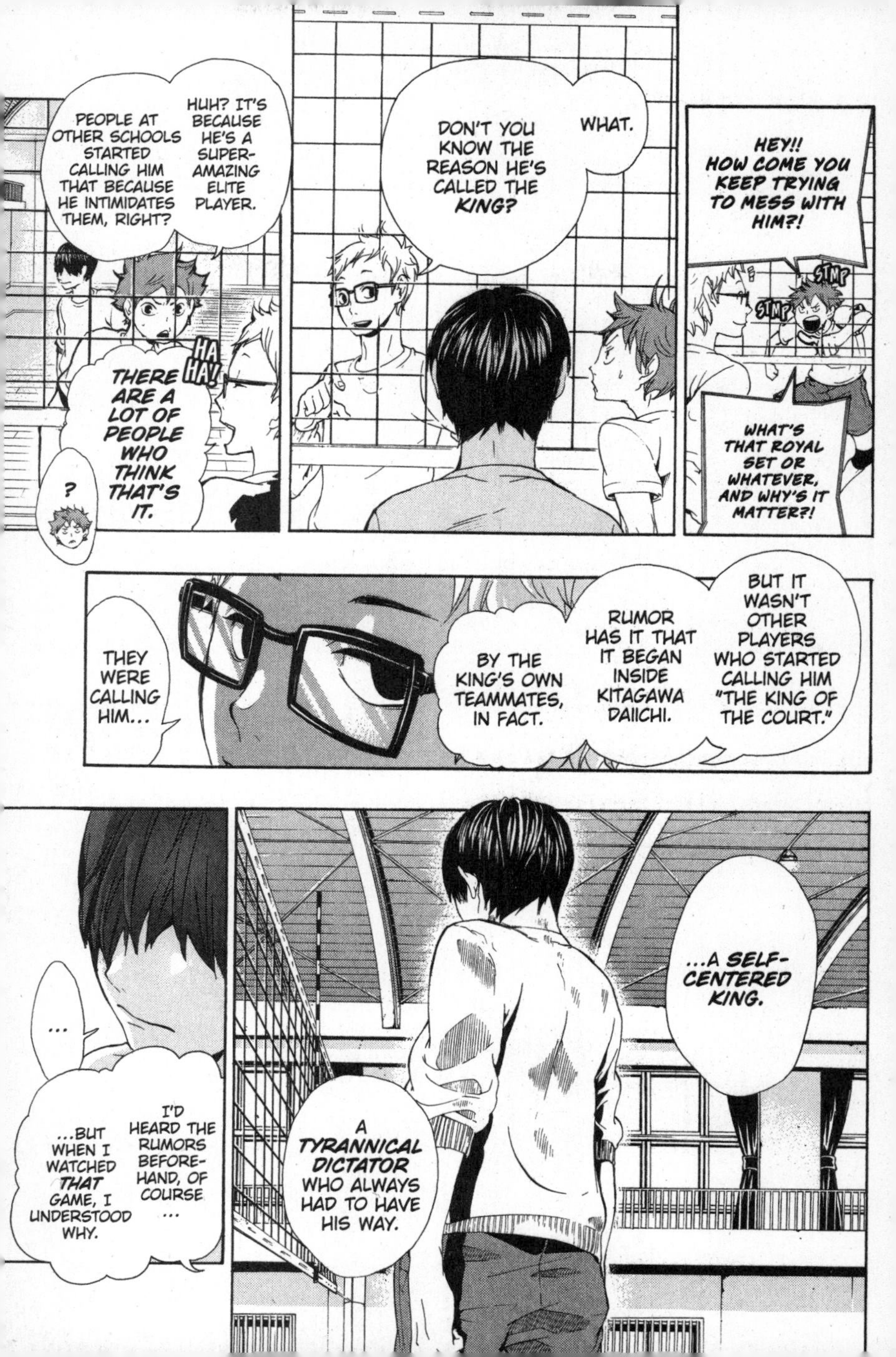
HEY!! HOW COME YOU KEEP TRYING TO MESS WITH HIM?!
STMP
STMP
WHAT'S THAT ROYAL SET OR WHATEVER, AND WHY'S IT MATTER?!
WHAT.
DON'T YOU KNOW THE REASON HE'S CALLED THE KING?
HUH? IT'S BECAUSE HE'S A SUPER-AMAZING ELITE PLAYER.
PEOPLE AT OTHER SCHOOLS STARTED CALLING HIM THAT BECAUSE HE INTIMIDATES THEM, RIGHT?
HA HA!
THERE ARE A LOT OF PEOPLE WHO THINK THAT'S IT.
?
BUT IT WASN'T OTHER PLAYERS WHO STARTED CALLING HIM "THE KING OF THE COURT."
RUMOR HAS IT THAT IT BEGAN INSIDE KITAGAWA DAIICHI.
BY THE KING'S OWN TEAMMATES, IN FACT.
THEY WERE CALLING HIM...
...A SELF-CENTERED KING.
A TYRANNICAL DICTATOR WHO ALWAYS HAD TO HAVE HIS WAY.
...
I'D HEARD THE RUMORS BEFOREHAND, OF COURSE...
...BUT WHEN I WATCHED THAT GAME, I UNDERSTOOD WHY.

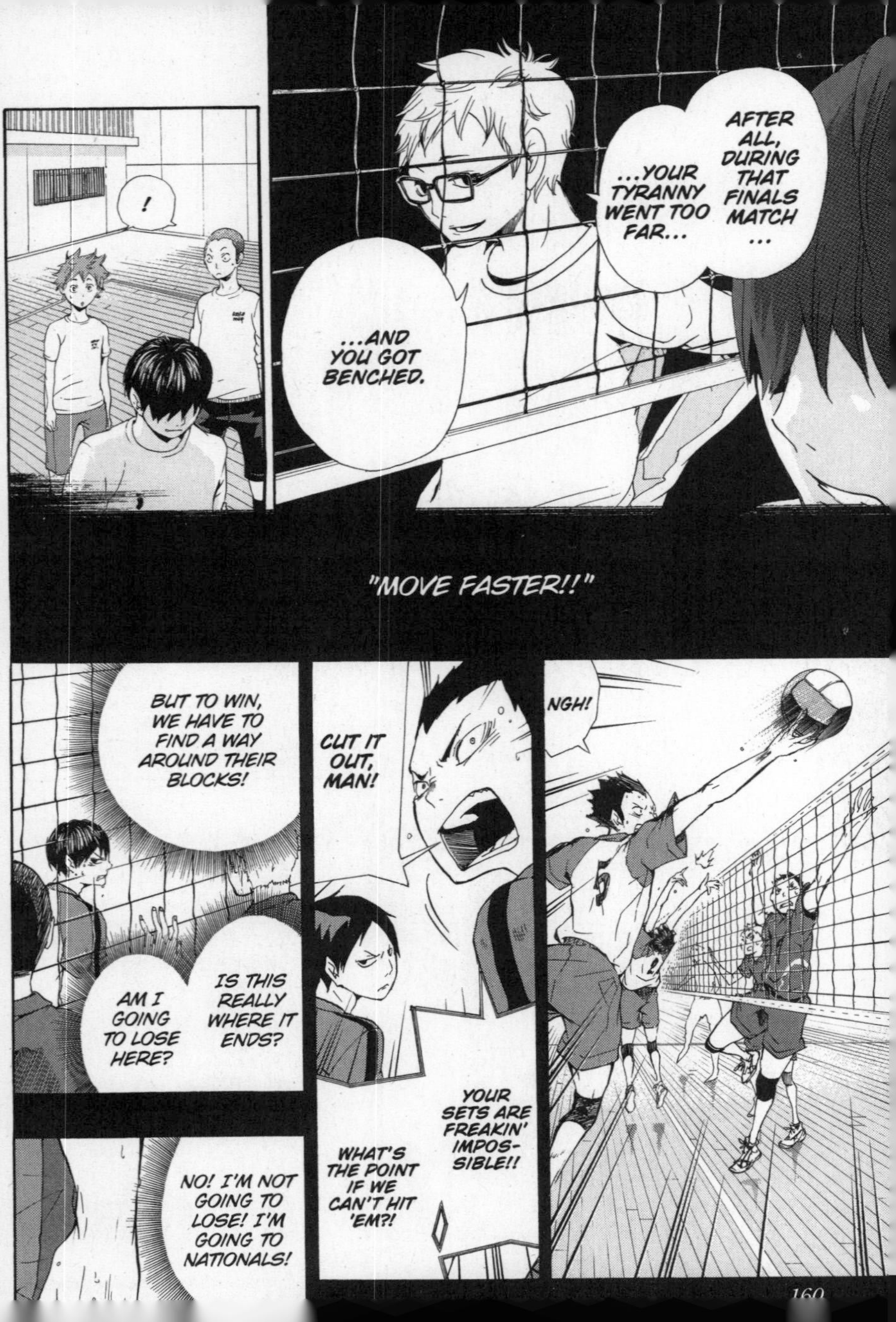
AFTER ALL, DURING THAT FINALS MATCH...
...YOUR TYRANNY WENT TOO FAR...
...AND YOU GOT BENCHED.
!
"MOVE FASTER!!"
NGH!
CUT IT OUT, MAN!
YOUR SETS ARE FREAKIN' IMPOSSIBLE!!
WHAT'S THE POINT IF WE CAN'T HIT 'EM?!
BUT TO WIN, WE HAVE TO FIND A WAY AROUND THEIR BLOCKS!
IS THIS REALLY WHERE IT ENDS?
AM I GOING TO LOSE HERE?
NO! I'M NOT GOING TO LOSE! I'M GOING TO NATIONALS!

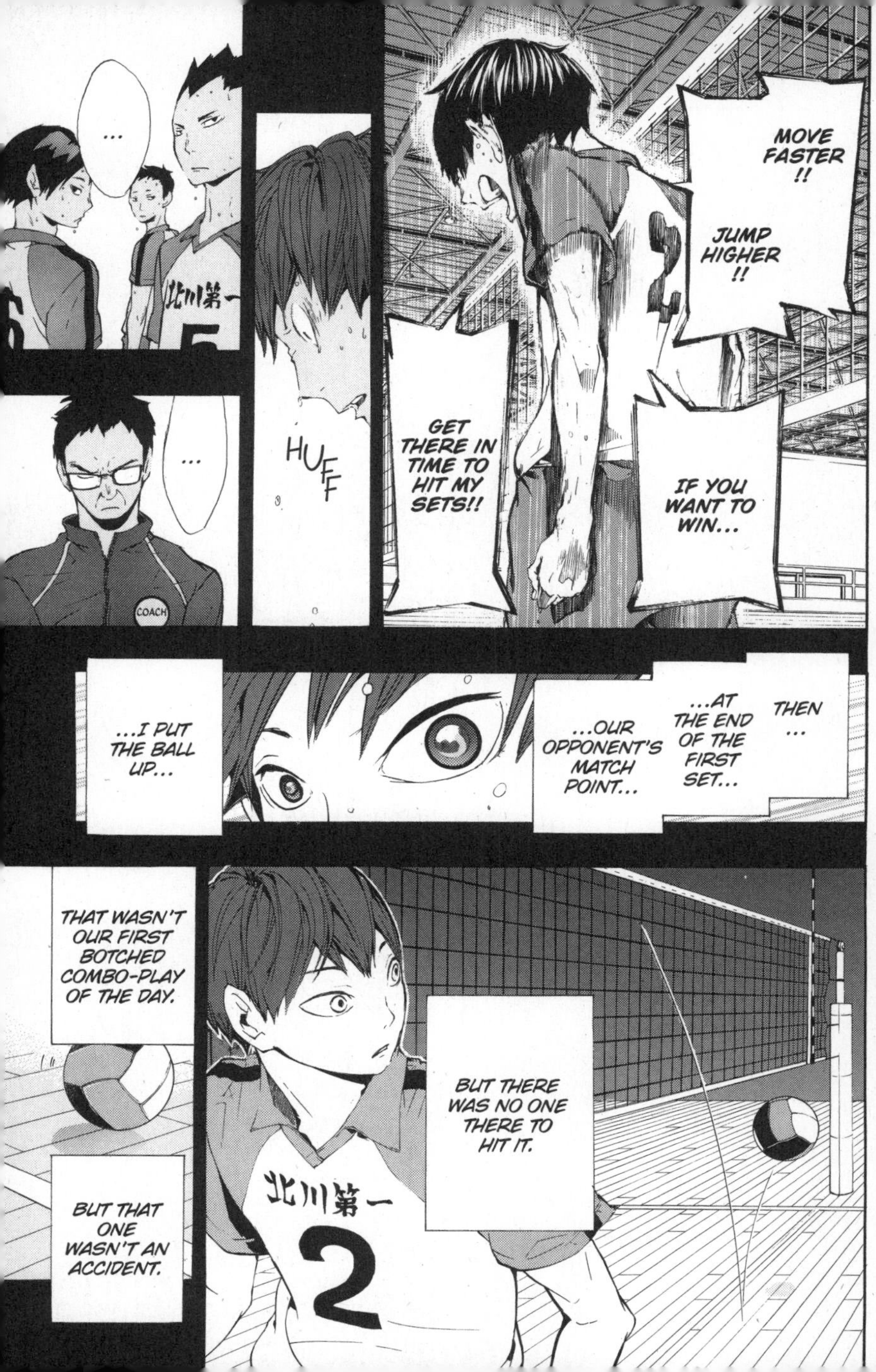
MOVE FASTER !!
JUMP HIGHER !!
IF YOU WANT TO WIN...
GET THERE IN TIME TO HIT MY SETS!!
HUFF
...
...
THEN ...
...AT THE END OF THE FIRST SET...
...OUR OPPONENT'S MATCH POINT...
...I PUT THE BALL UP...
BUT THERE WAS NO ONE THERE TO HIT IT.
THAT WASN'T OUR FIRST BOTCHED COMBO-PLAY OF THE DAY.
BUT THAT ONE WASN'T AN ACCIDENT.

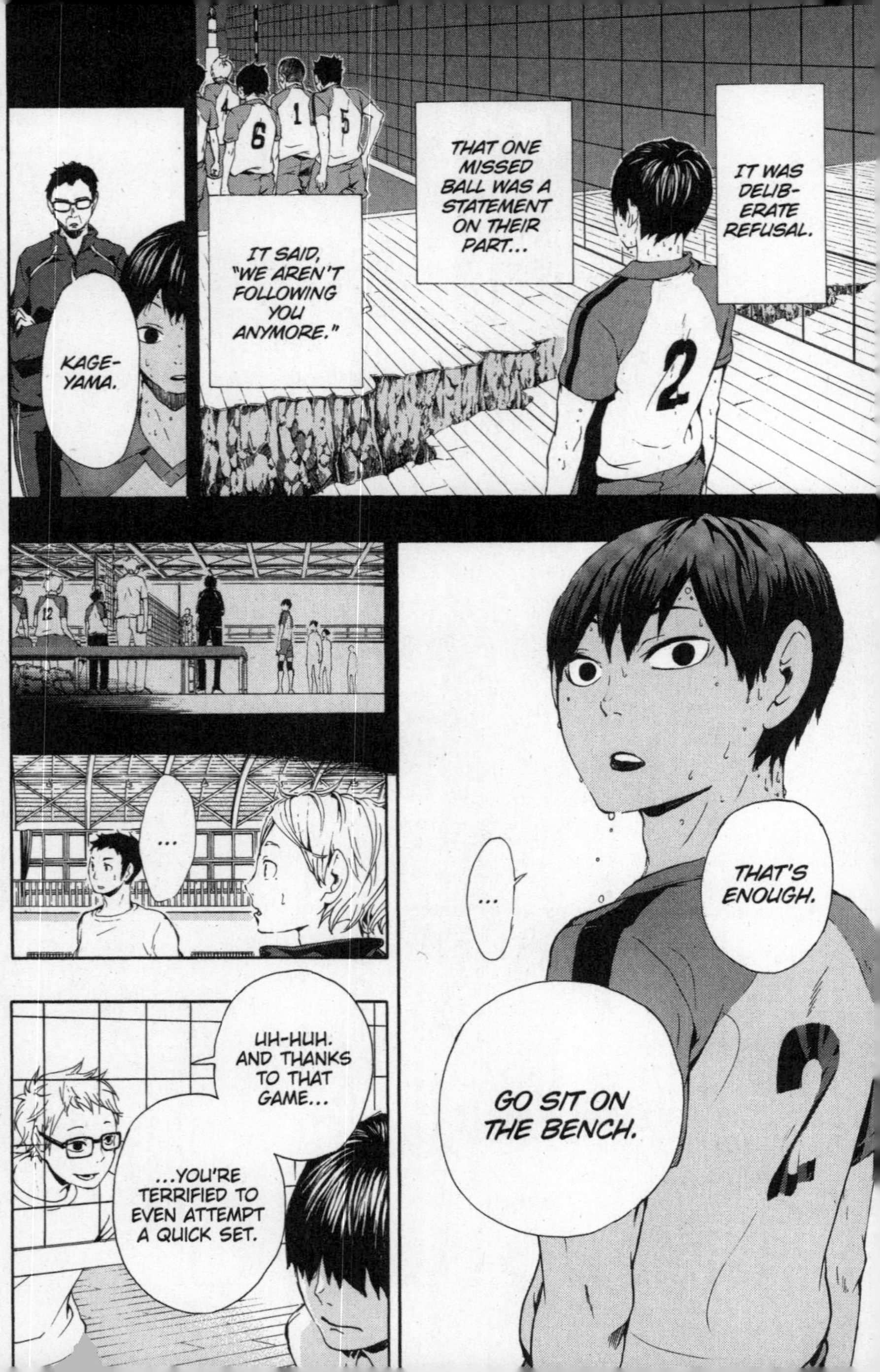
IT WAS DELIB-ERATE REFUSAL.
THAT ONE MISSED BALL WAS A STATEMENT ON THEIR PART...
IT SAID, "WE AREN'T FOLLOWING YOU ANYMORE."
KAGE-YAMA.
THAT'S ENOUGH.
...
GO SIT ON THE BENCH.
...
UH-HUH. AND THANKS TO THAT GAME...
...YOU'RE TERRIFIED TO EVEN ATTEMPT A QUICK SET.

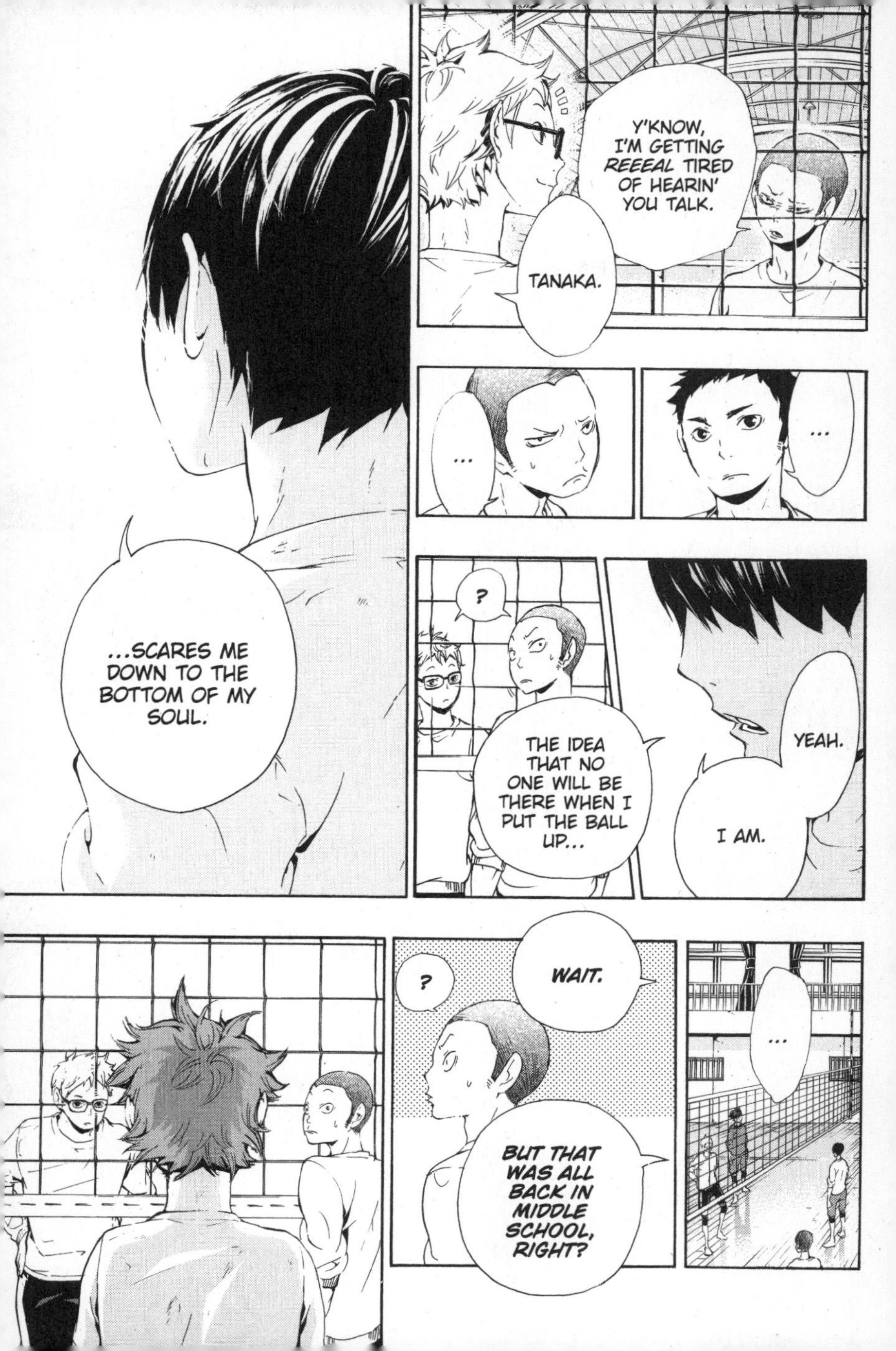

Y'KNOW, I'M GETTING REEEAL TIRED OF HEARIN' YOU TALK.
TANAKA.
...
...
YEAH.
I AM.
?
THE IDEA THAT NO ONE WILL BE THERE WHEN I PUT THE BALL UP...
...SCARES ME DOWN TO THE BOTTOM OF MY SOUL.
...
WAIT.
?
BUT THAT WAS ALL BACK IN MIDDLE SCHOOL, RIGHT?

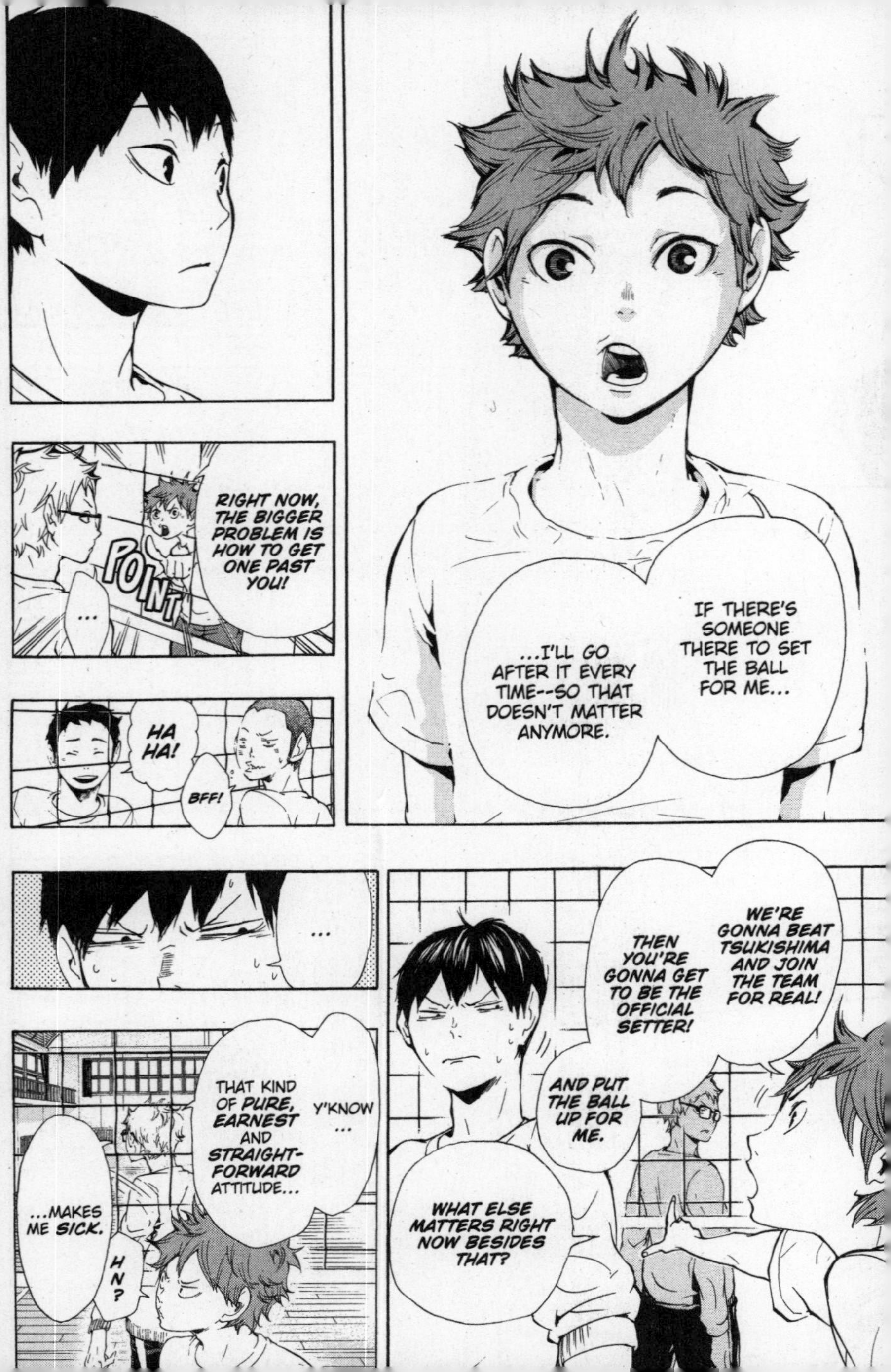
IF THERE'S SOMEONE THERE TO SET THE BALL FOR ME...
...I'LL GO AFTER IT EVERY TIME--SO THAT DOESN'T MATTER ANYMORE.
RIGHT NOW, THE BIGGER PROBLEM IS HOW TO GET ONE PAST YOU!
POINT
...
HA HA!
BFF!
WE'RE GONNA BEAT TSUKISHIMA AND JOIN THE TEAM FOR REAL!
THEN YOU'RE GONNA GET TO BE THE OFFICIAL SETTER!
AND PUT THE BALL UP FOR ME.
WHAT ELSE MATTERS RIGHT NOW BESIDES THAT?
...
Y'KNOW...
THAT KIND OF PURE, EARNEST AND STRAIGHTFORWARD ATTITUDE...
...MAKES ME SICK.
HN?

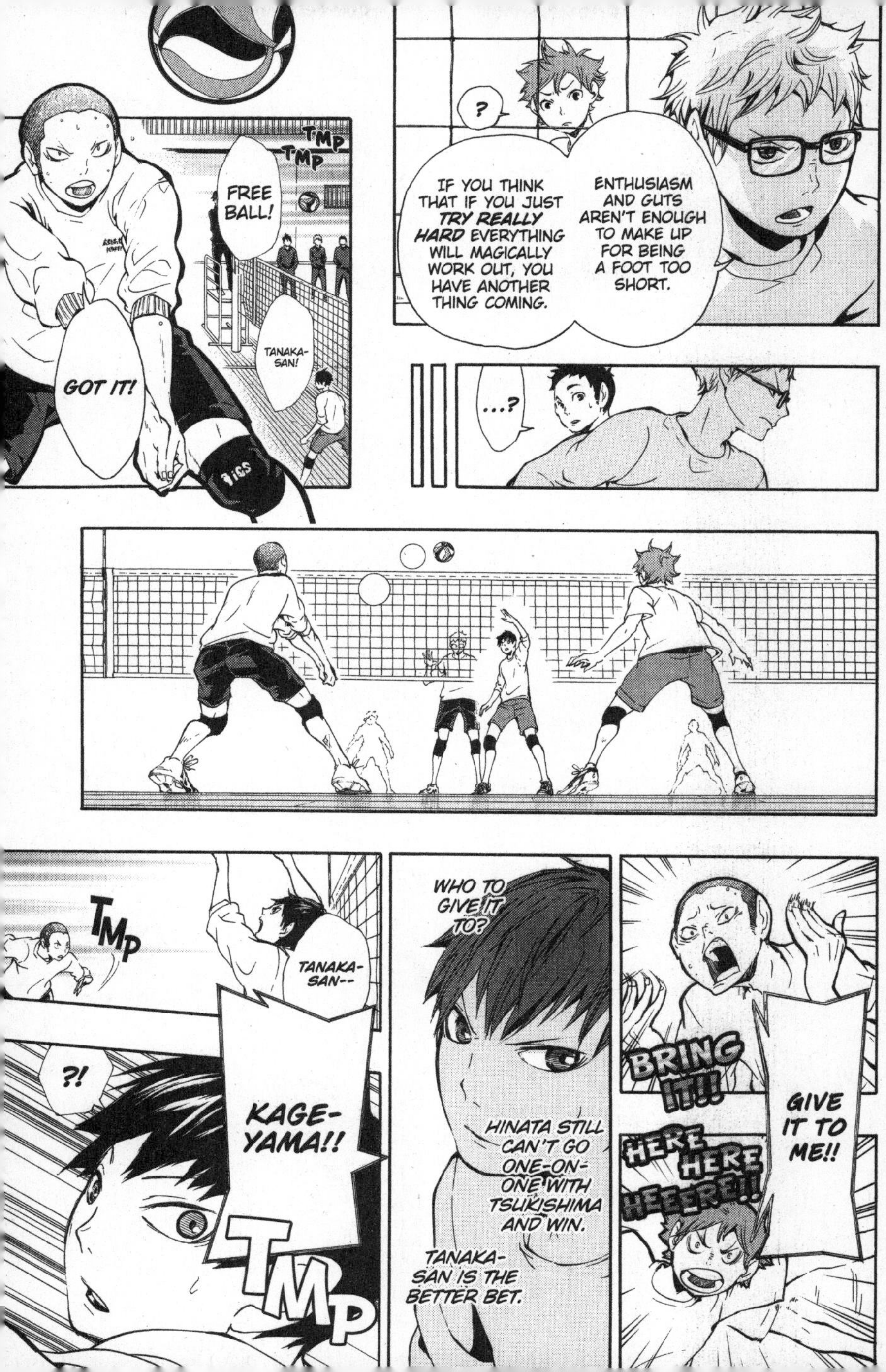
?
ENTHUSIASM AND GUTS AREN'T ENOUGH TO MAKE UP FOR BEING A FOOT TOO SHORT.
IF YOU THINK THAT IF YOU JUST TRY REALLY HARD EVERYTHING WILL MAGICALLY WORK OUT, YOU HAVE ANOTHER THING COMING.
...?
TMP
TMP
FREE BALL!
TANAKA-SAN!
GOT IT!
BRING IT!!
GIVE IT TO ME!!
HERE HERE HEEERE!!
WHO TO GIVE IT TO?
HINATA STILL CAN'T GO ONE-ON-ONE WITH TSUKISHIMA AND WIN.
TANAKA-SAN IS THE BETTER BET.
TANAKA-SAN--
TMP
KAGE-YAMA!!
?!
TMP

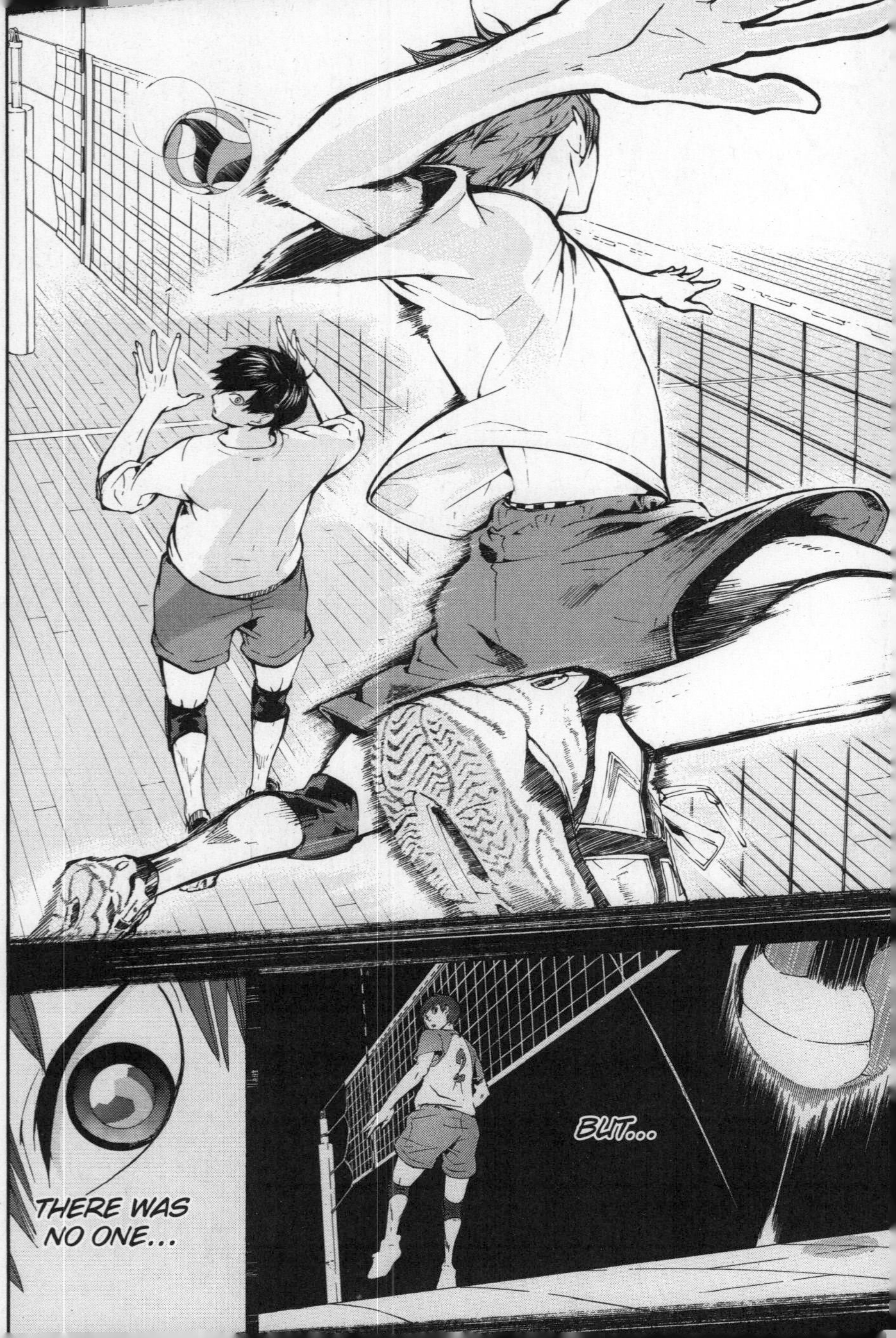
BUT...
THERE WAS
NO ONE...

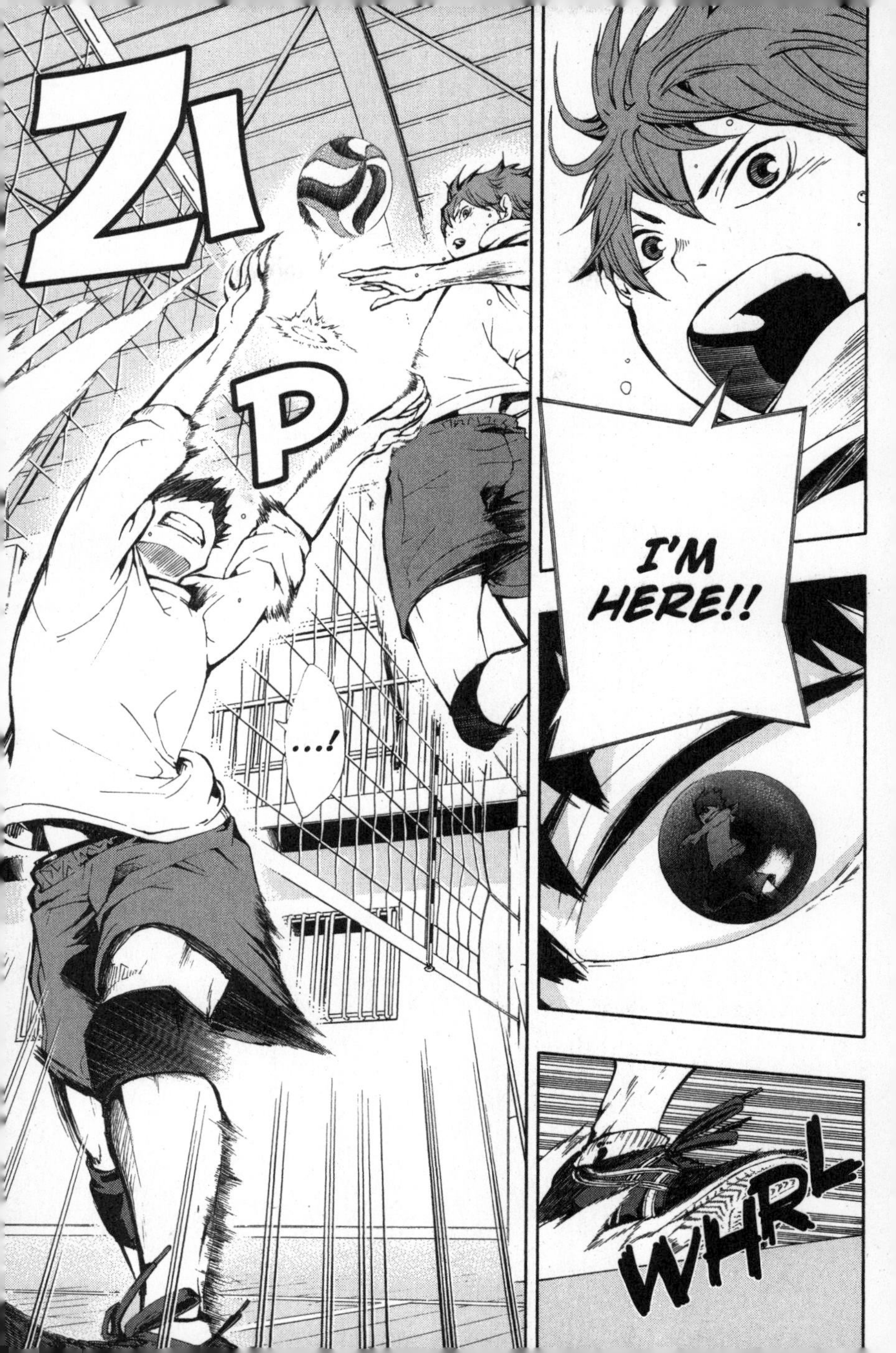
I'M HERE!!
WHRL
ZIP
...!

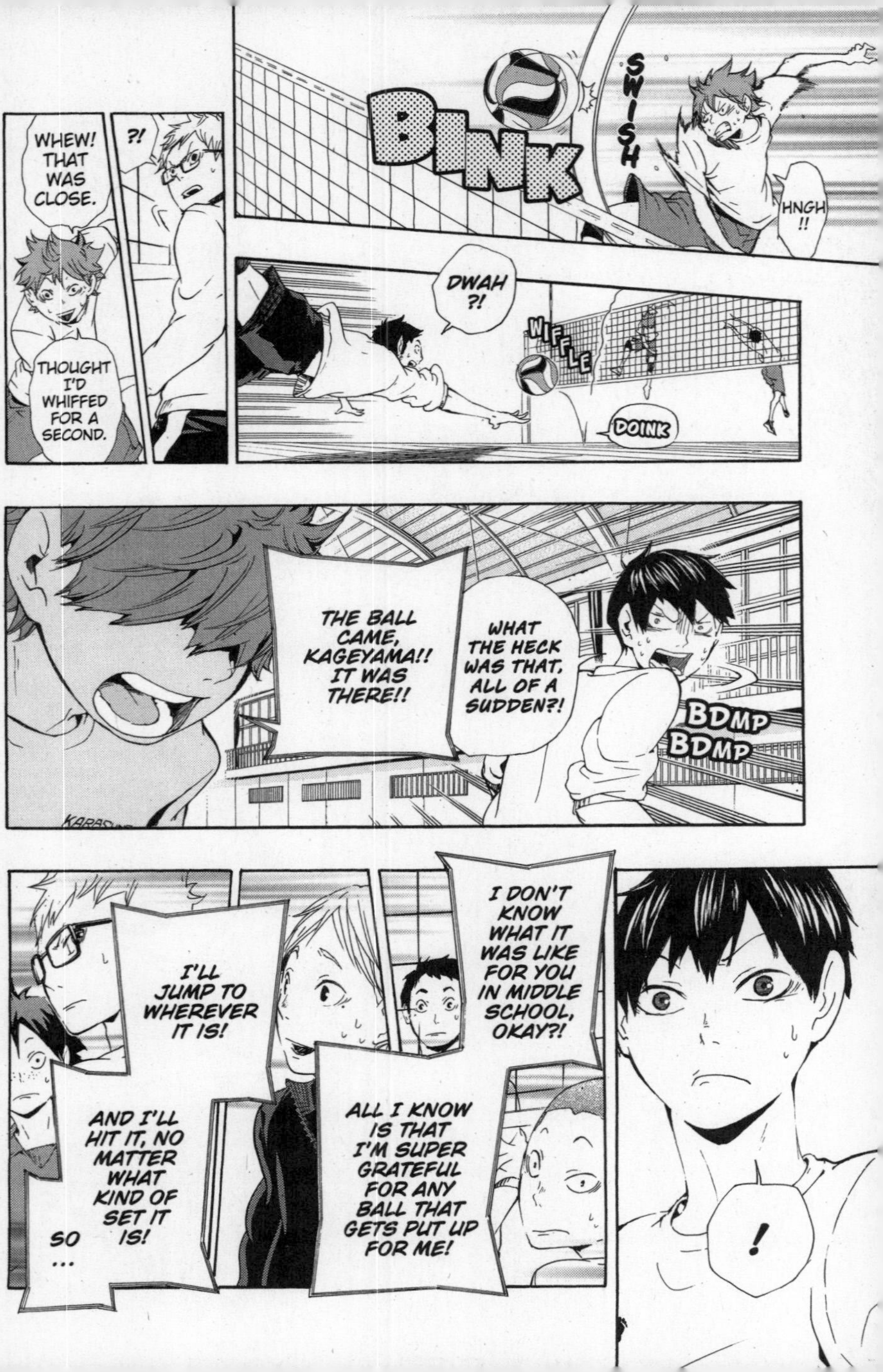
SWISH
BLINK
HNGH!!
DWAH?!
WIFFLE
DOINK
?!
WHEW! THAT WAS CLOSE.
THOUGHT I'D WHIFFED FOR A SECOND.
BDMP BDMP
WHAT THE HECK WAS THAT, ALL OF A SUDDEN?!
THE BALL CAME, KAGEYAMA!! IT WAS THERE!!
!
I DON'T KNOW WHAT IT WAS LIKE FOR YOU IN MIDDLE SCHOOL, OKAY?!
ALL I KNOW IS THAT I'M SUPER GRATEFUL FOR ANY BALL THAT GETS PUT UP FOR ME!
I'LL JUMP TO WHEREVER IT IS!
AND I'LL HIT IT, NO MATTER WHAT KIND OF SET IT IS!
SO...

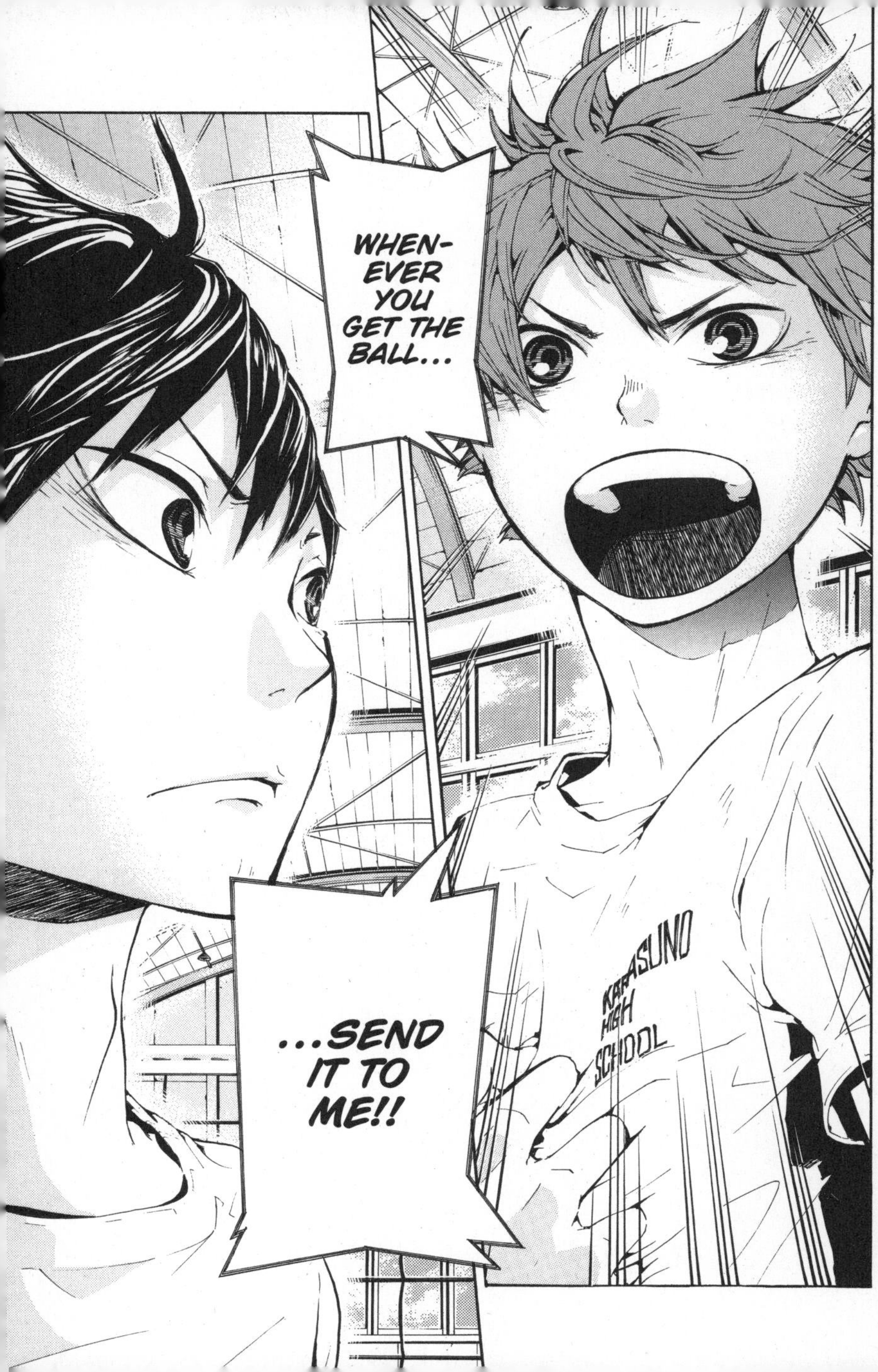
WHEN-EVER YOU GET THE BALL...
...SEND IT TO ME!!

KOUSHI SUGAWARA

KARASUNO HIGH SCHOOL
CLASS 3-4

VOLLEYBALL CLUB
VICE CAPTAIN

POSITION: SETTER

HEIGHT: 5'9"
WEIGHT: 140 LBS.
(AS OF APRIL, 3RD YEAR OF HIGH SCHOOL)

BIRTHDAY: JUNE 13

FAVORITE FOOD:
SUPER-SPICY MAPO TOFU

CURRENT WORRY:
A LOT OF THE TEAM'S UNDERCLASSMEN ARE TALLER THAN HIM.

ABILITY PARAMETERS
(5-POINT SCALE)

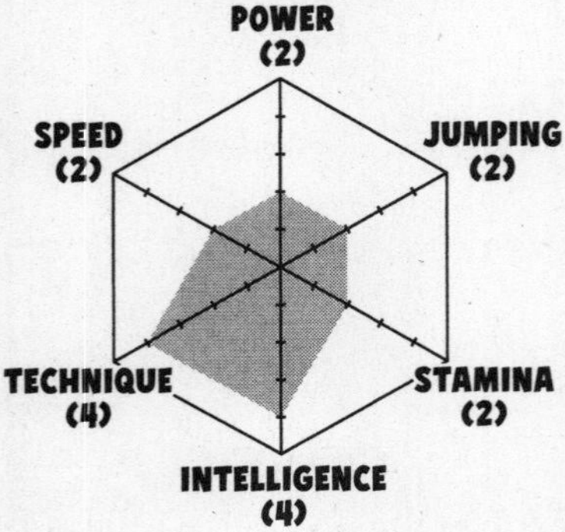
POWER (2)
JUMPING (2)
STAMINA (2)
INTELLIGENCE (4)
TECHNIQUE (4)
SPEED (2)

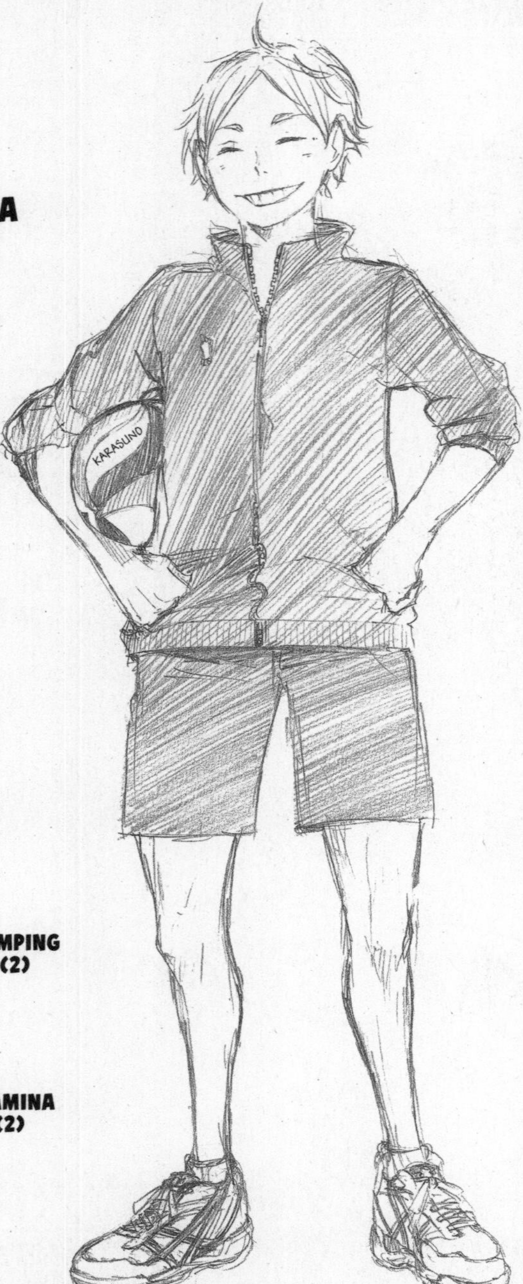
KARASUNO

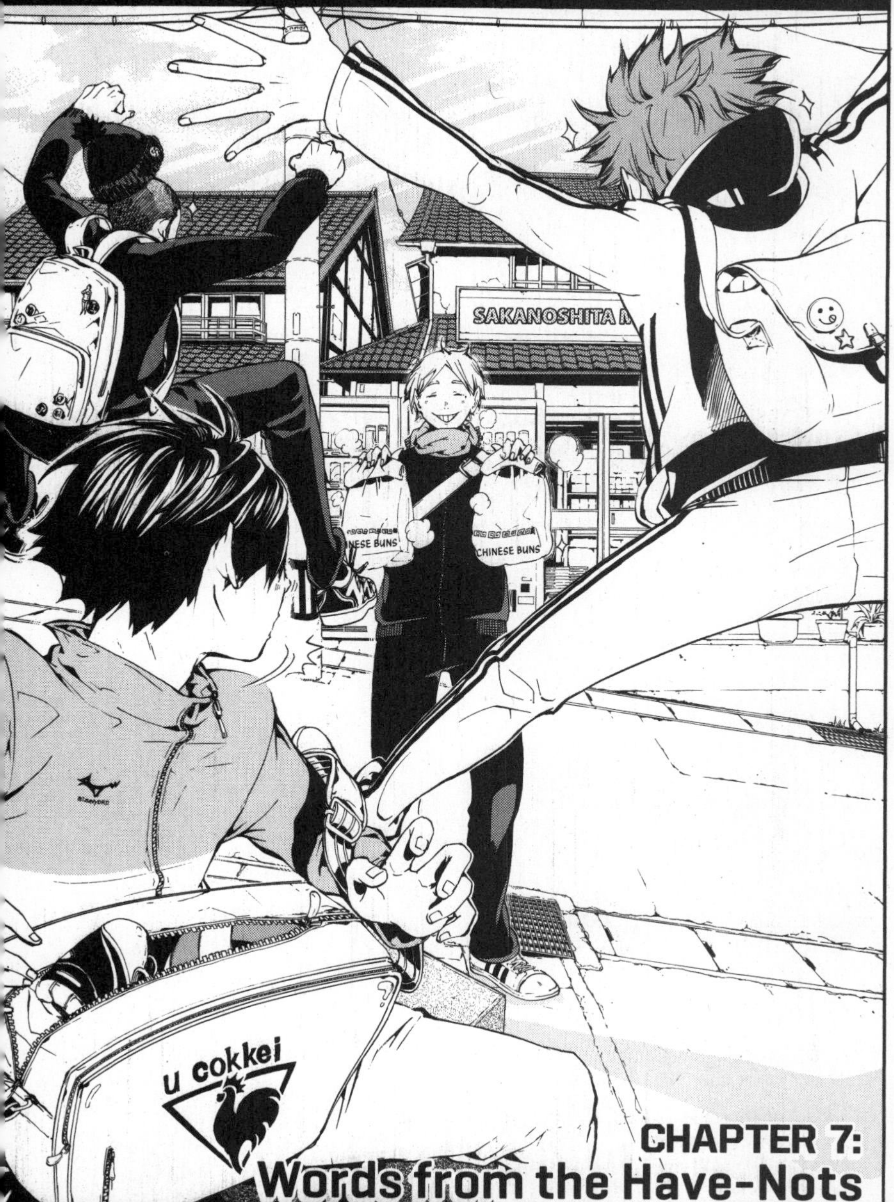
SAKANOSHITA M
NESE BUNS
CHINESE BUNS
u cokkei
CHAPTER 7:
Words from the Have-Nots

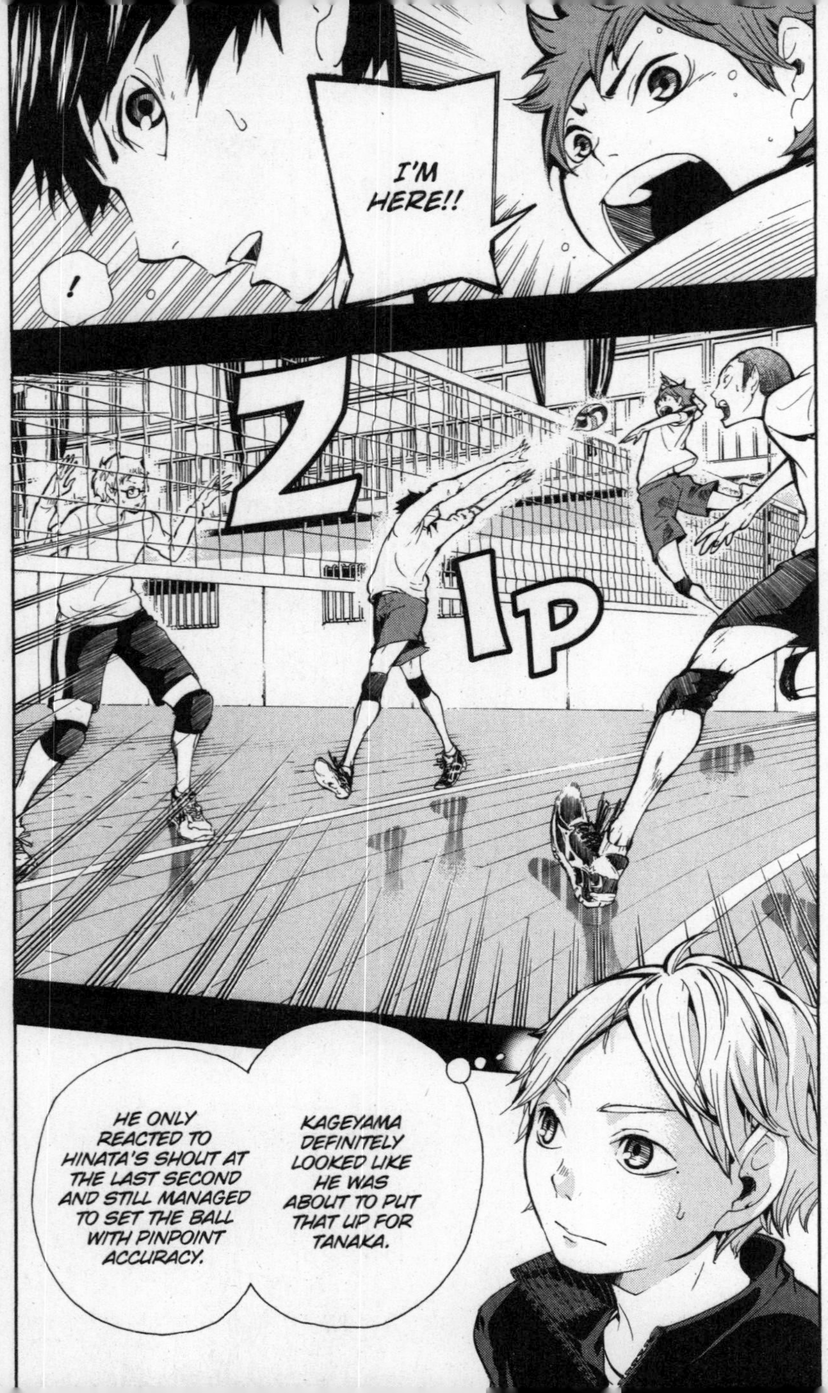
I'M HERE!!
!
ZIP
KAGEYAMA DEFINITELY LOOKED LIKE HE WAS ABOUT TO PUT THAT UP FOR TANAKA.
HE ONLY REACTED TO HINATA'S SHOUT AT THE LAST SECOND AND STILL MANAGED TO SET THE BALL WITH PINPOINT ACCURACY.

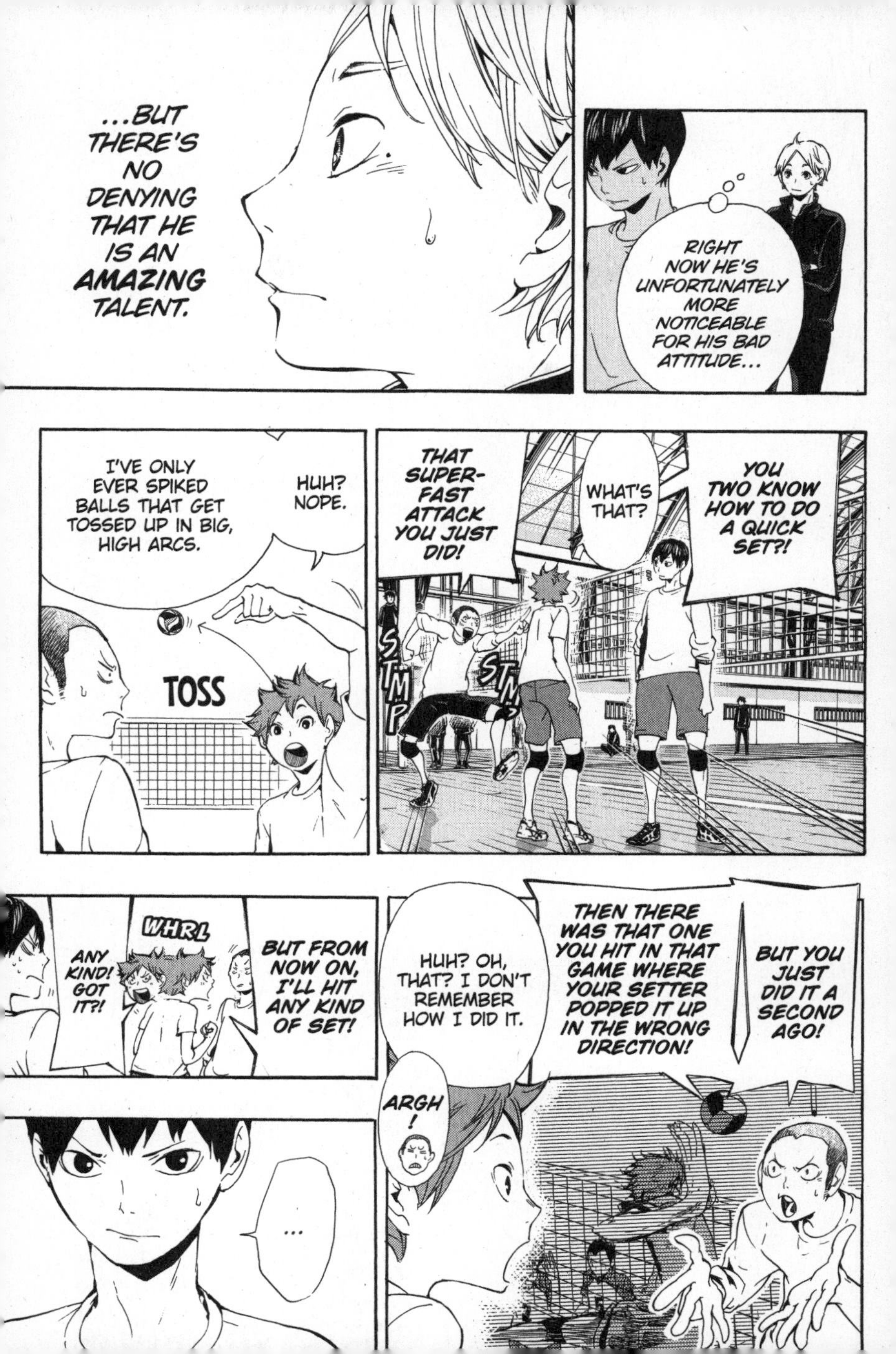

RIGHT NOW HE'S UNFORTUNATELY MORE NOTICEABLE FOR HIS BAD ATTITUDE...
...BUT THERE'S NO DENYING THAT HE IS AN AMAZING TALENT.
YOU TWO KNOW HOW TO DO A QUICK SET?!
WHAT'S THAT?
THAT SUPER-FAST ATTACK YOU JUST DID!
STMP
STMP
HUH? NOPE.
I'VE ONLY EVER SPIKED BALLS THAT GET TOSSED UP IN BIG, HIGH ARCS.
TOSS
BUT YOU JUST DID IT A SECOND AGO!
THEN THERE WAS THAT ONE YOU HIT IN THAT GAME WHERE YOUR SETTER POPPED IT UP IN THE WRONG DIRECTION!
HUH? OH, THAT? I DON'T REMEMBER HOW I DID IT.
ARGH!
BUT FROM NOW ON, I'LL HIT ANY KIND OF SET!
WHRL
ANY KIND! GOT IT?!
...

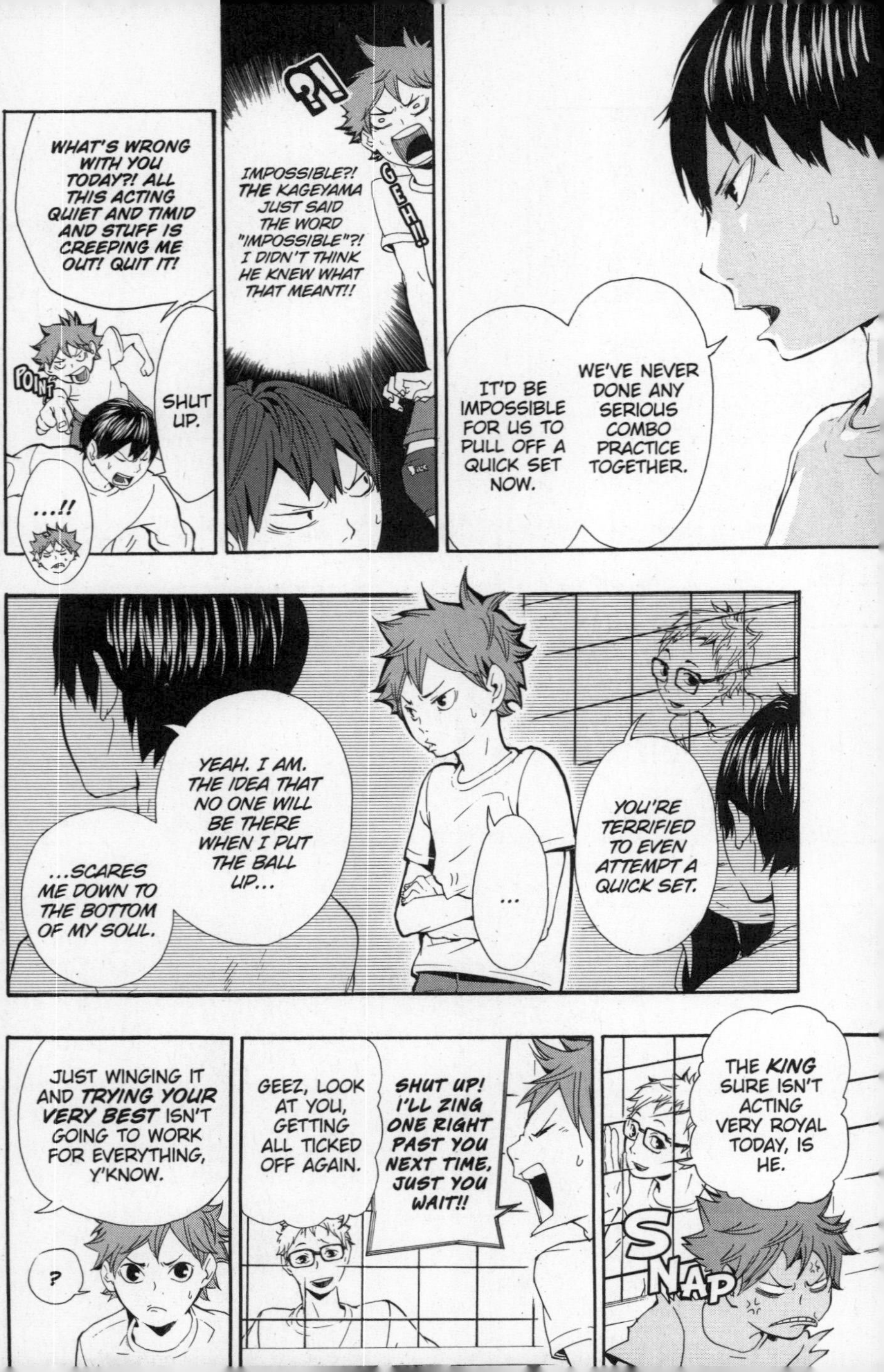
WE'VE NEVER DONE ANY SERIOUS COMBO PRACTICE TOGETHER.
IT'D BE IMPOSSIBLE FOR US TO PULL OFF A QUICK SET NOW.
?!
IMPOSSIBLE?! THE KAGEYAMA JUST SAID THE WORD "IMPOSSIBLE"?! I DIDN'T THINK HE KNEW WHAT THAT MEANT!!
GEH!!
WHAT'S WRONG WITH YOU TODAY?! ALL THIS ACTING QUIET AND TIMID AND STUFF IS CREEPING ME OUT! QUIT IT!
POINT
SHUT UP.
...!!
YOU'RE TERRIFIED TO EVEN ATTEMPT A QUICK SET.
...
YEAH. I AM. THE IDEA THAT NO ONE WILL BE THERE WHEN I PUT THE BALL UP...
...SCARES ME DOWN TO THE BOTTOM OF MY SOUL.
THE KING SURE ISN'T ACTING VERY ROYAL TODAY, IS HE.
SNAP
SHUT UP! I'LL ZING ONE RIGHT PAST YOU NEXT TIME, JUST YOU WAIT!!
GEEZ, LOOK AT YOU, GETTING ALL TICKED OFF AGAIN.
JUST WINGING IT AND TRYING YOUR VERY BEST ISN'T GOING TO WORK FOR EVERYTHING, Y'KNOW.
?

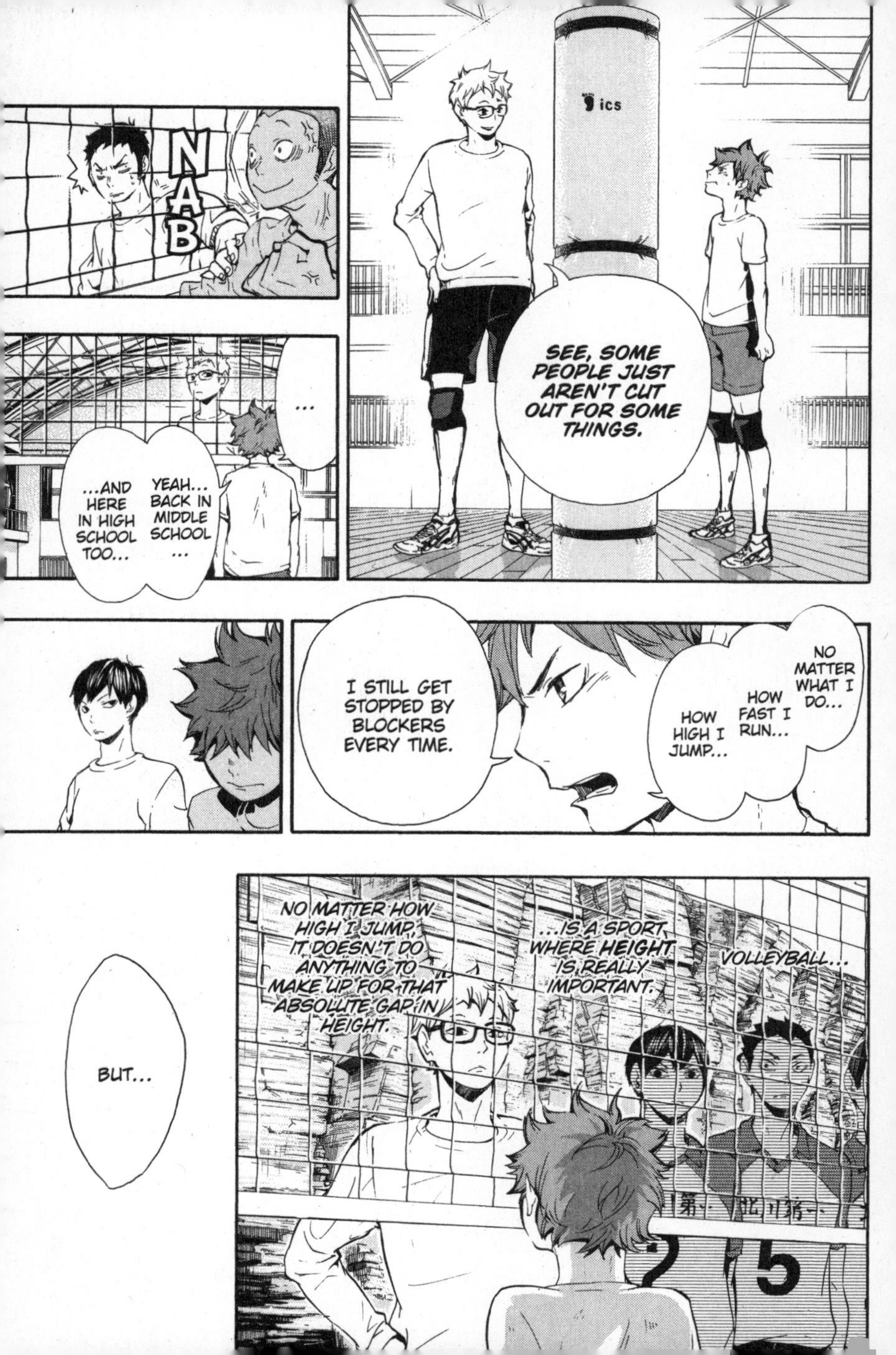
ics
SEE, SOME PEOPLE JUST AREN'T CUT OUT FOR SOME THINGS.
NAB
...
YEAH... BACK IN MIDDLE SCHOOL ...
...AND HERE IN HIGH SCHOOL TOO...
NO MATTER WHAT I DO...
HOW FAST I RUN...
HOW HIGH I JUMP...
I STILL GET STOPPED BY BLOCKERS EVERY TIME.
VOLLEYBALL...
...IS A SPORT WHERE HEIGHT IS REALLY IMPORTANT.
NO MATTER HOW HIGH I JUMP, IT DOESN'T DO ANYTHING TO MAKE UP FOR THAT ABSOLUTE GAP IN HEIGHT.
5
BUT...

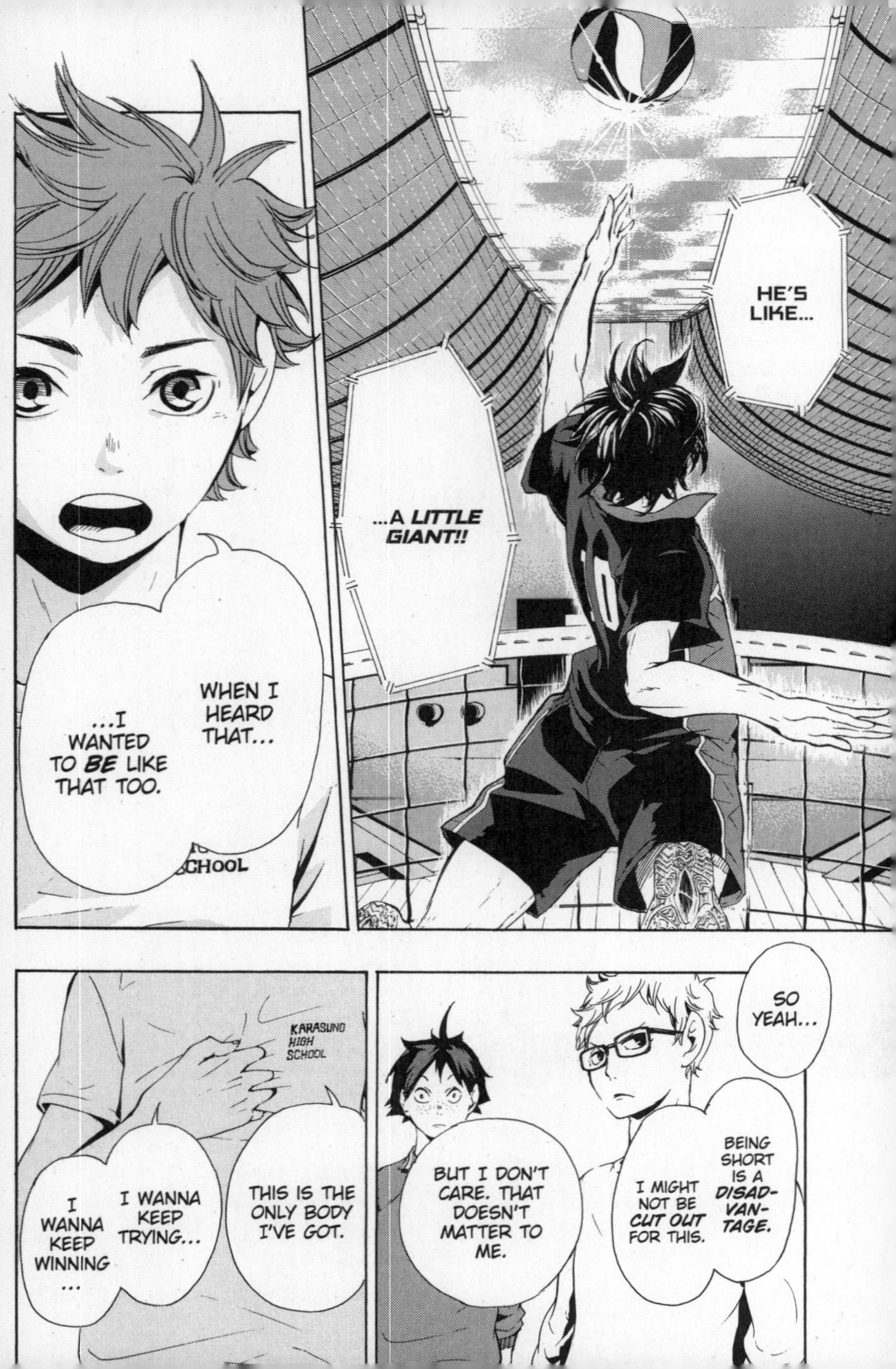
HE'S LIKE...
...A *LITTLE GIANT!!*
WHEN I HEARD THAT...
...I WANTED TO ***BE*** LIKE THAT TOO.
SCHOOL
SO YEAH...
BEING SHORT IS A ***DISADVANTAGE.***
I MIGHT NOT BE ***CUT OUT*** FOR THIS.
BUT I DON'T CARE. THAT DOESN'T MATTER TO ME.
KARASUNO HIGH SCHOOL
THIS IS THE ONLY BODY I'VE GOT.
I WANNA KEEP TRYING...
I WANNA KEEP WINNING...

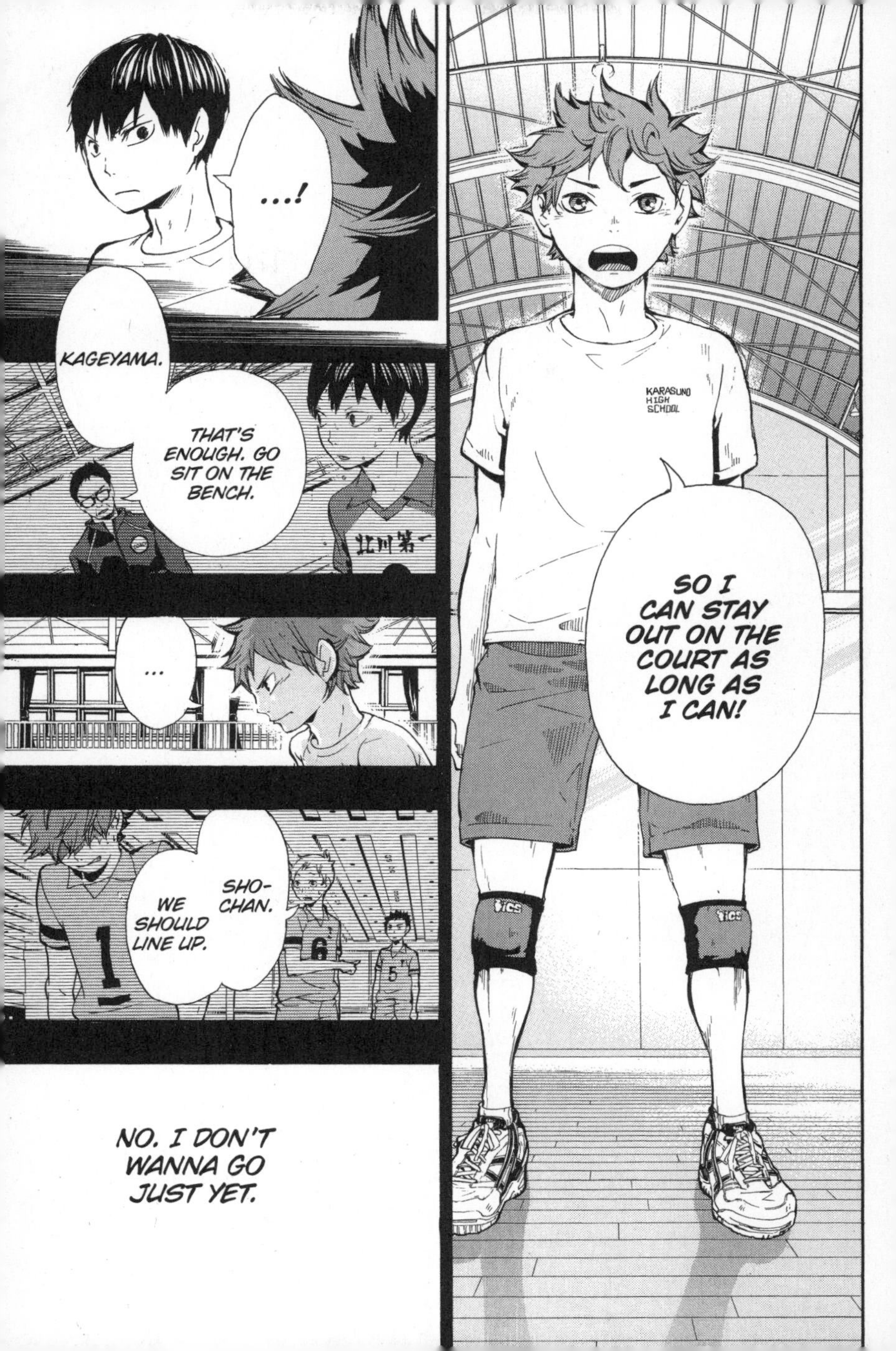
KARASUNO HIGH SCHOOL
SO I CAN STAY OUT ON THE COURT AS LONG AS I CAN!
...!
KAGEYAMA.
THAT'S ENOUGH. GO SIT ON THE BENCH.
北川第一
...
SHO-CHAN.
WE SHOULD LINE UP.
NO. I DON'T WANNA GO JUST YET.

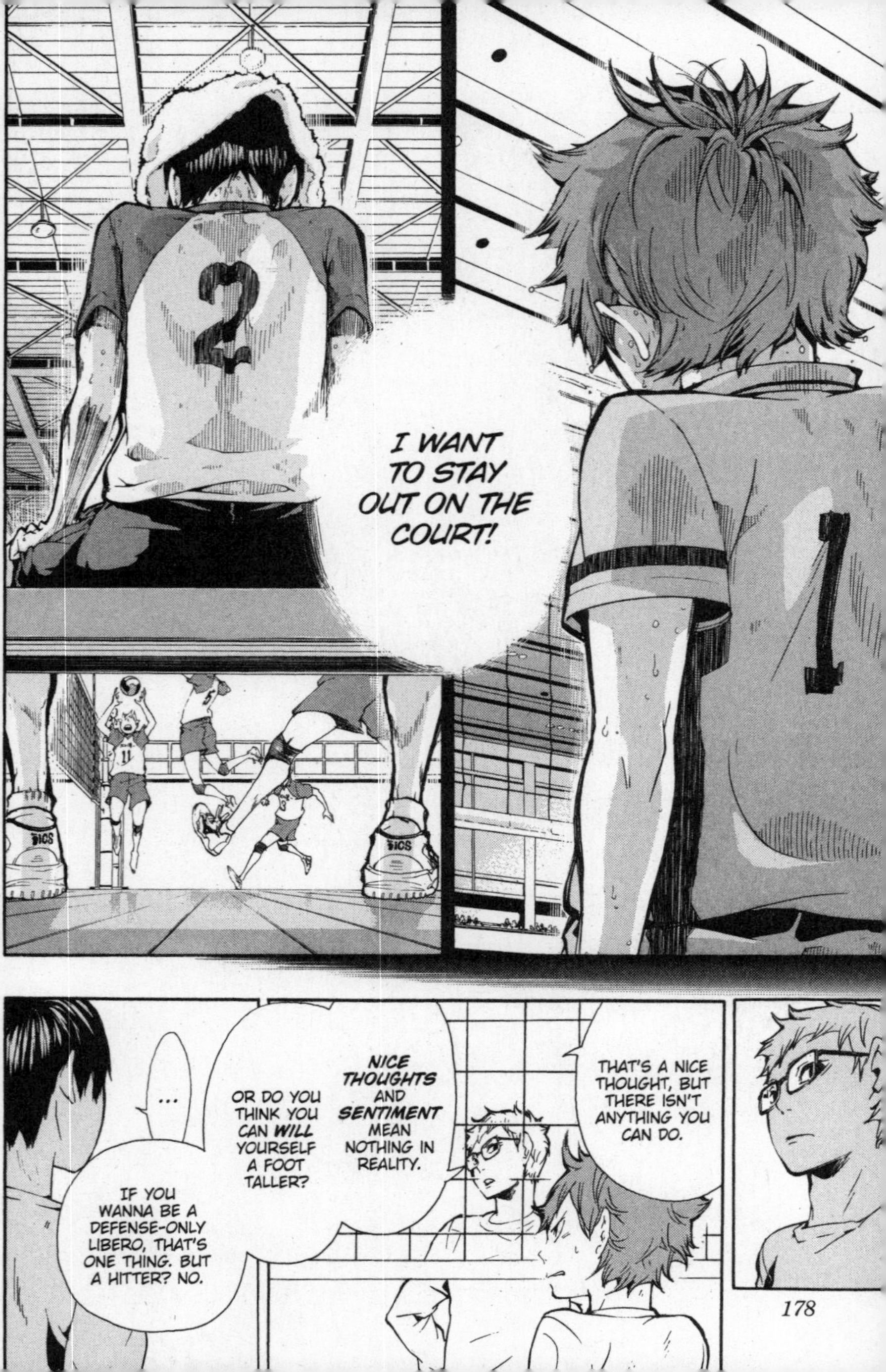
I WANT TO STAY OUT ON THE COURT!
THAT'S A NICE THOUGHT, BUT THERE ISN'T ANYTHING YOU CAN DO.
NICE THOUGHTS AND SENTIMENT MEAN NOTHING IN REALITY.
OR DO YOU THINK YOU CAN WILL YOURSELF A FOOT TALLER?
...
IF YOU WANNA BE A DEFENSE-ONLY LIBERO, THAT'S ONE THING. BUT A HITTER? NO.

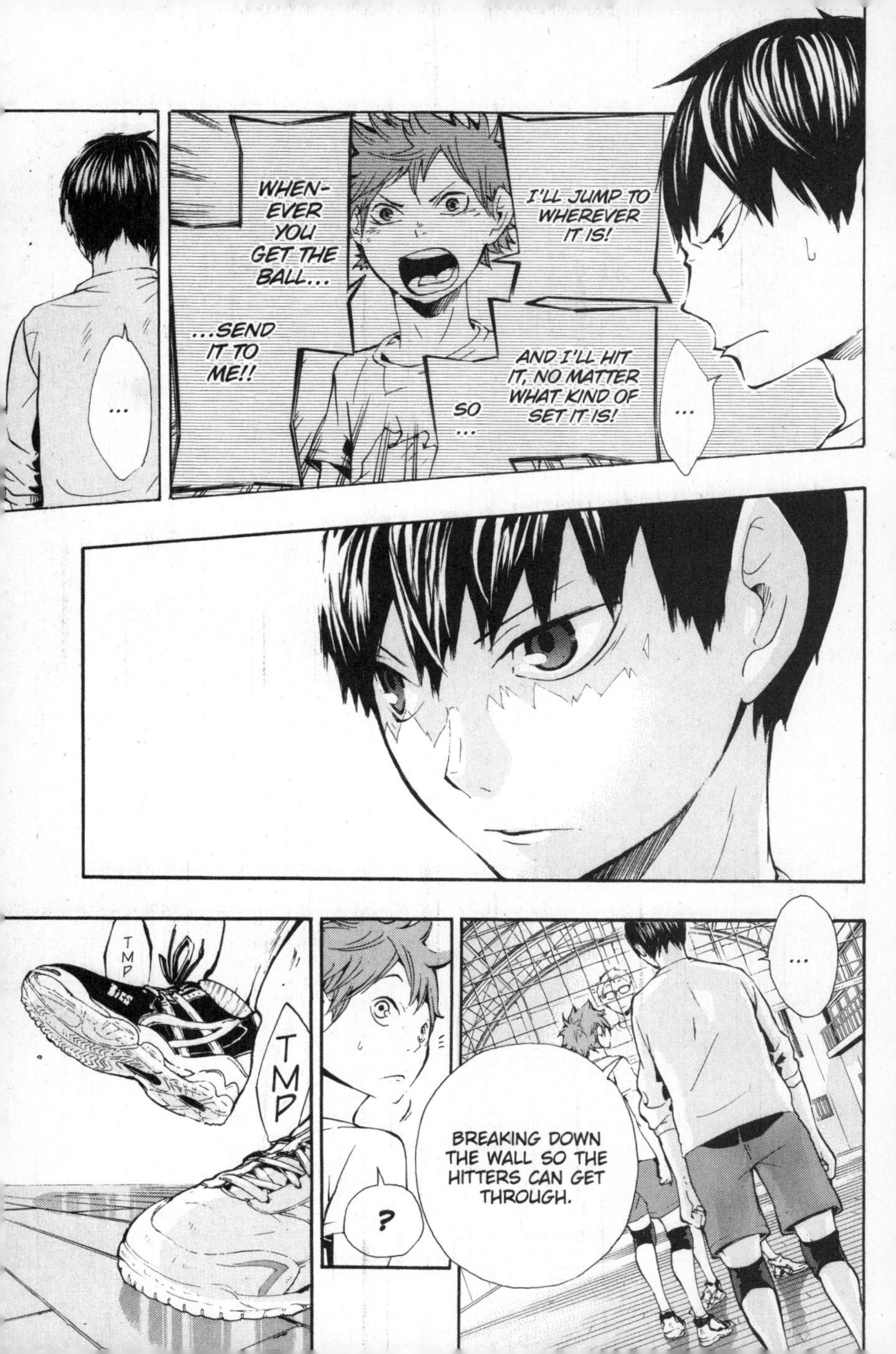
...
WHEN-EVER YOU GET THE BALL...
I'LL JUMP TO WHEREVER IT IS!
AND I'LL HIT IT, NO MATTER WHAT KIND OF SET IT IS!
SO...
...SEND IT TO ME!!
...
...
BREAKING DOWN THE WALL SO THE HITTERS CAN GET THROUGH.
?
TMP
TMP

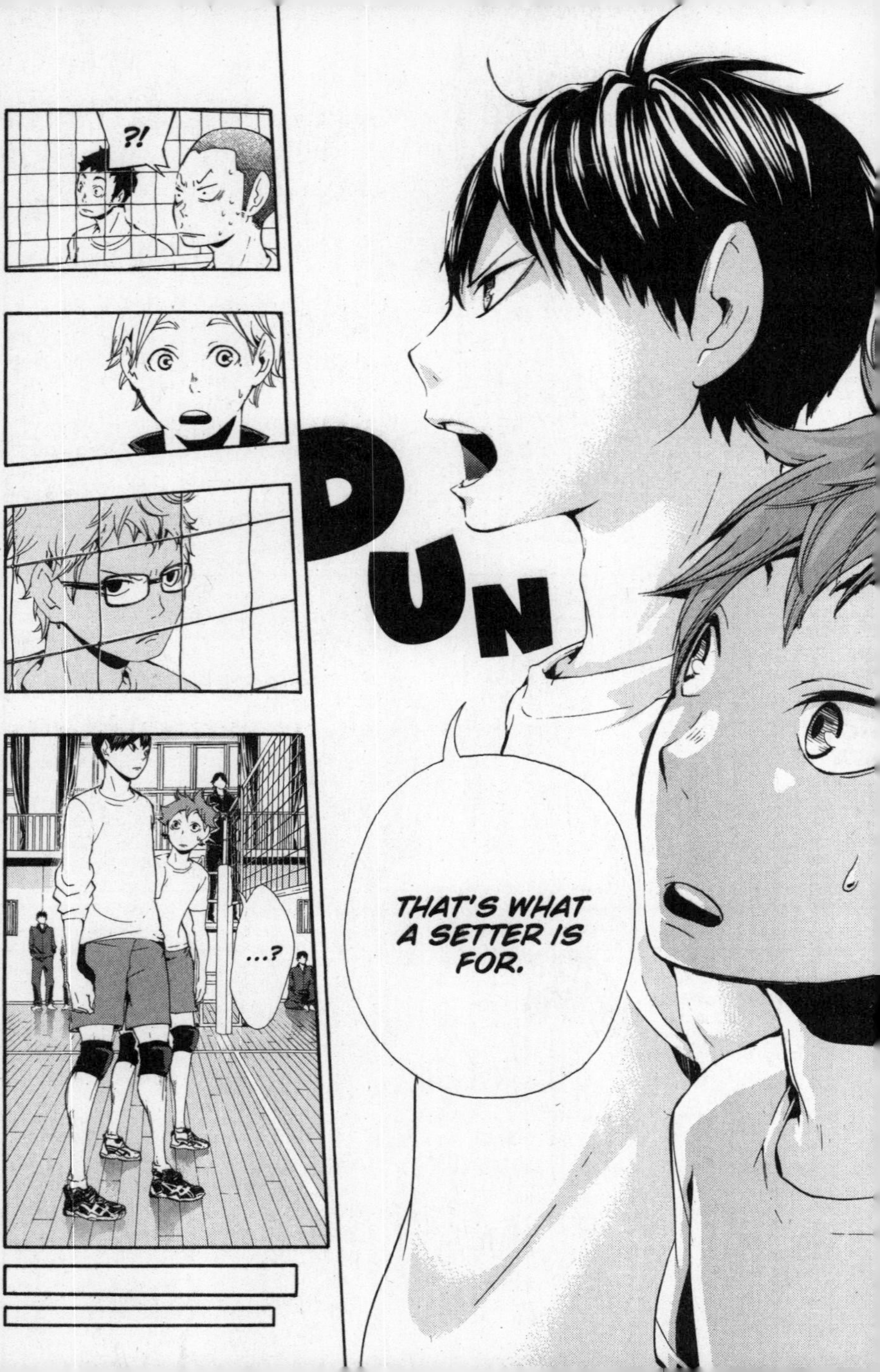
DUN
THAT'S WHAT A SETTER IS FOR.
?!
...?

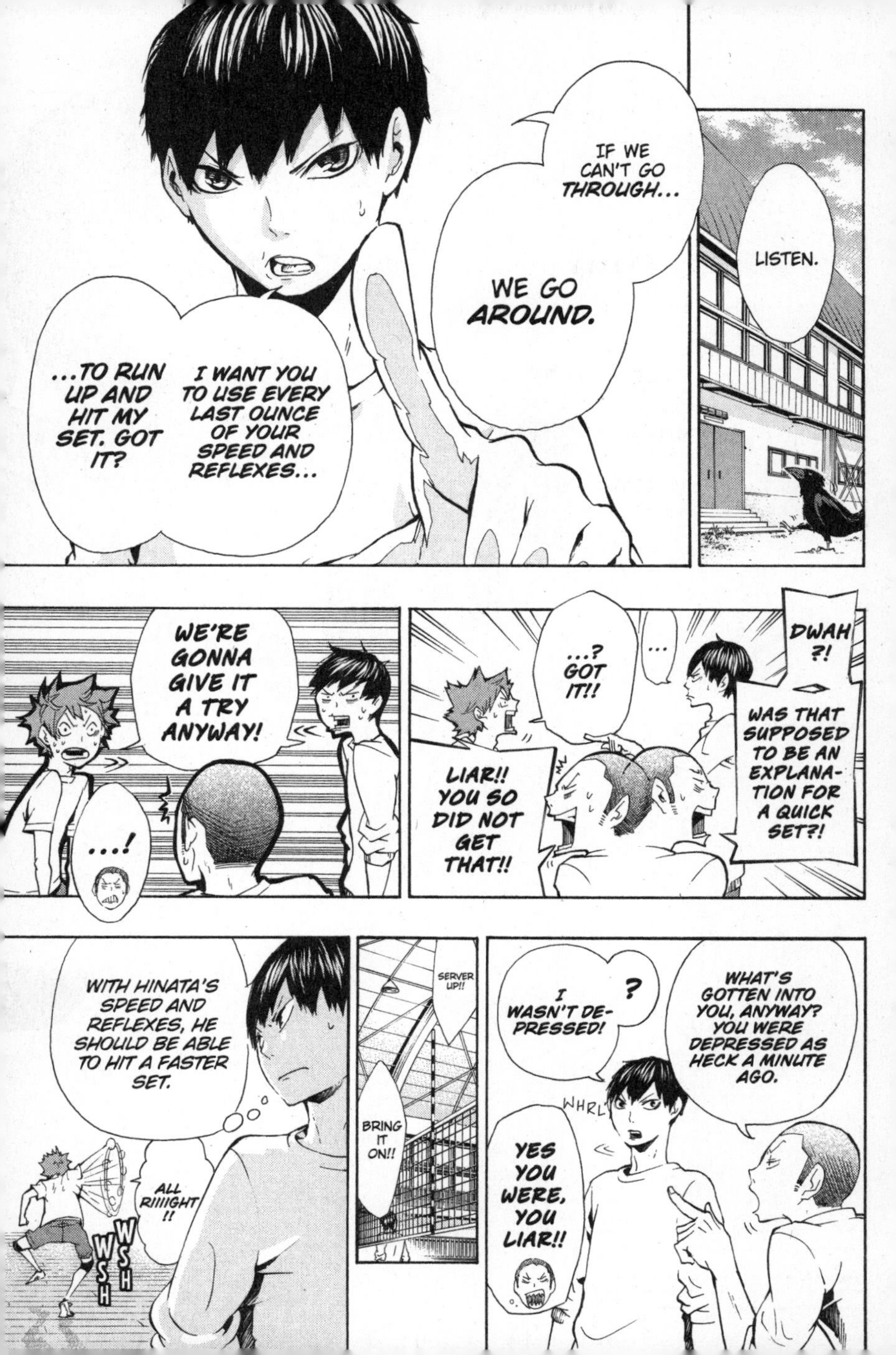
LISTEN.
IF WE CAN'T GO THROUGH...
WE GO AROUND.
I WANT YOU TO USE EVERY LAST OUNCE OF YOUR SPEED AND REFLEXES...
...TO RUN UP AND HIT MY SET. GOT IT?
DWAH?!
WAS THAT SUPPOSED TO BE AN EXPLANA-TION FOR A QUICK SET?!
...
...? GOT IT!!
LIAR!! YOU SO DID NOT GET THAT!!
WE'RE GONNA GIVE IT A TRY ANYWAY!
...!
WHAT'S GOTTEN INTO YOU, ANYWAY? YOU WERE DEPRESSED AS HECK A MINUTE AGO.
WHRL
?
I WASN'T DE-PRESSED!
YES YOU WERE, YOU LIAR!!
SERVER UP!!
BRING IT ON!!
WITH HINATA'S SPEED AND REFLEXES, HE SHOULD BE ABLE TO HIT A FASTER SET.
ALL RIIIGHT!!
WSH
WSH

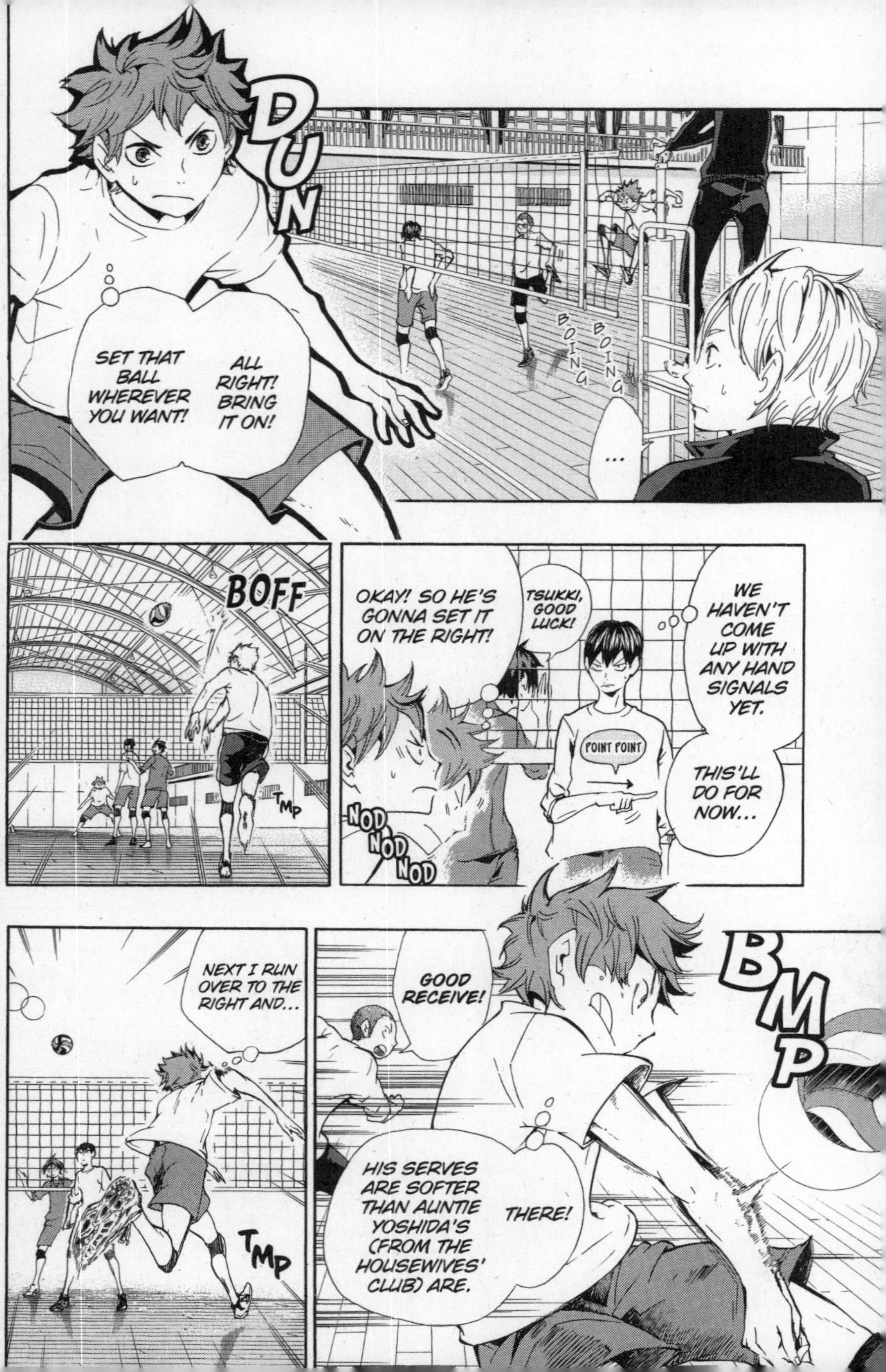
...
BOING
BOING
DUN
SET THAT BALL WHEREVER YOU WANT! ALL RIGHT! BRING IT ON!
WE HAVEN'T COME UP WITH ANY HAND SIGNALS YET.
THIS'LL DO FOR NOW...
TSUKKI, GOOD LUCK!
OKAY! SO HE'S GONNA SET IT ON THE RIGHT!
POINT POINT
NOD NOD NOD
BOFF
TMP
BMP
GOOD RECEIVE!
THERE!
HIS SERVES ARE SOFTER THAN AUNTIE YOSHIDA'S (FROM THE HOUSEWIVES' CLUB) ARE.
NEXT I RUN OVER TO THE RIGHT AND...
TMP

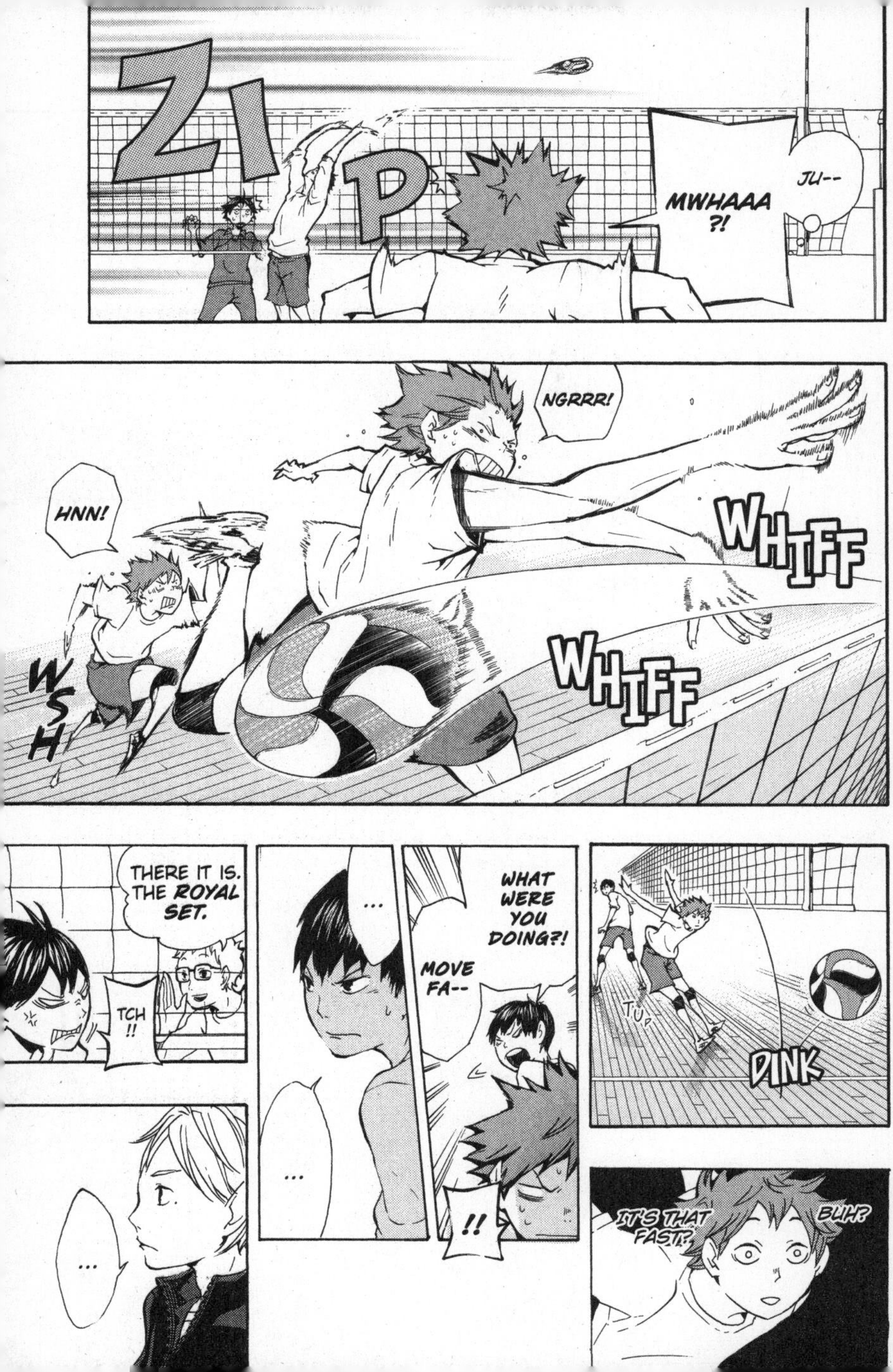
JU--
MWHAAA ?!
ZIP
NGRRR!
WHIFF
WHIFF
HNN!
WSH
TUP
DINK
BUH?
IT'S THAT FAST?
WHAT WERE YOU DOING?!
MOVE FA--
!!
...
...
THERE IT IS. THE *ROYAL* SET.
TCH !!
...

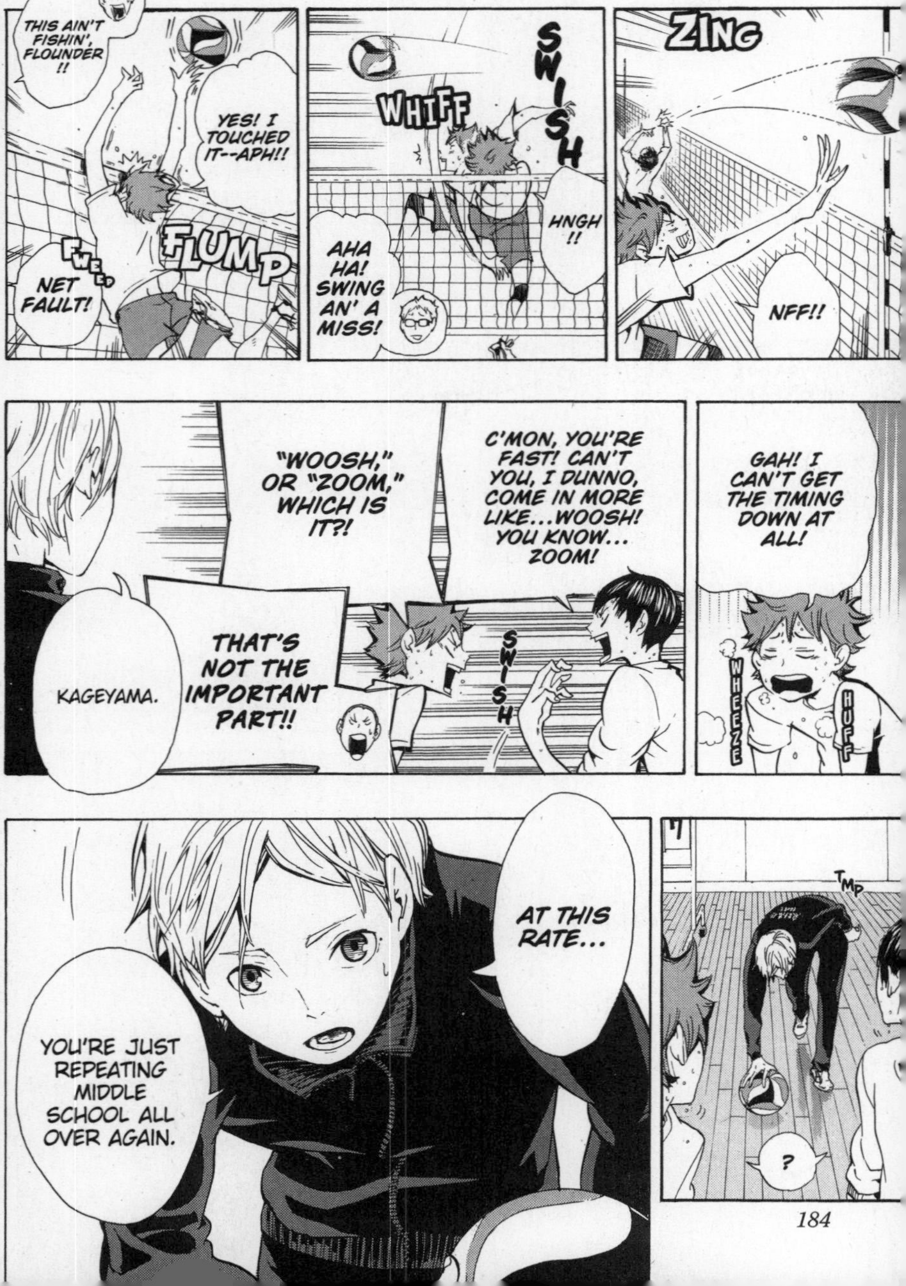

ZING
NFF!!
SWISH
WHIFF
HNGH!!
AHA HA! SWING AN' A MISS!
THIS AIN'T FISHIN', FLOUNDER!!
YES! I TOUCHED IT--APH!!
FLUMP
FWEEP
NET FAULT!
GAH! I CAN'T GET THE TIMING DOWN AT ALL!
WHEEZE
HUFF
C'MON, YOU'RE FAST! CAN'T YOU, I DUNNO, COME IN MORE LIKE...WOOSH! YOU KNOW... ZOOM!
"WOOSH," OR "ZOOM," WHICH IS IT?!
SWISH
THAT'S NOT THE IMPORTANT PART!!
KAGEYAMA.
TMP
?
AT THIS RATE...
YOU'RE JUST REPEATING MIDDLE SCHOOL ALL OVER AGAIN.

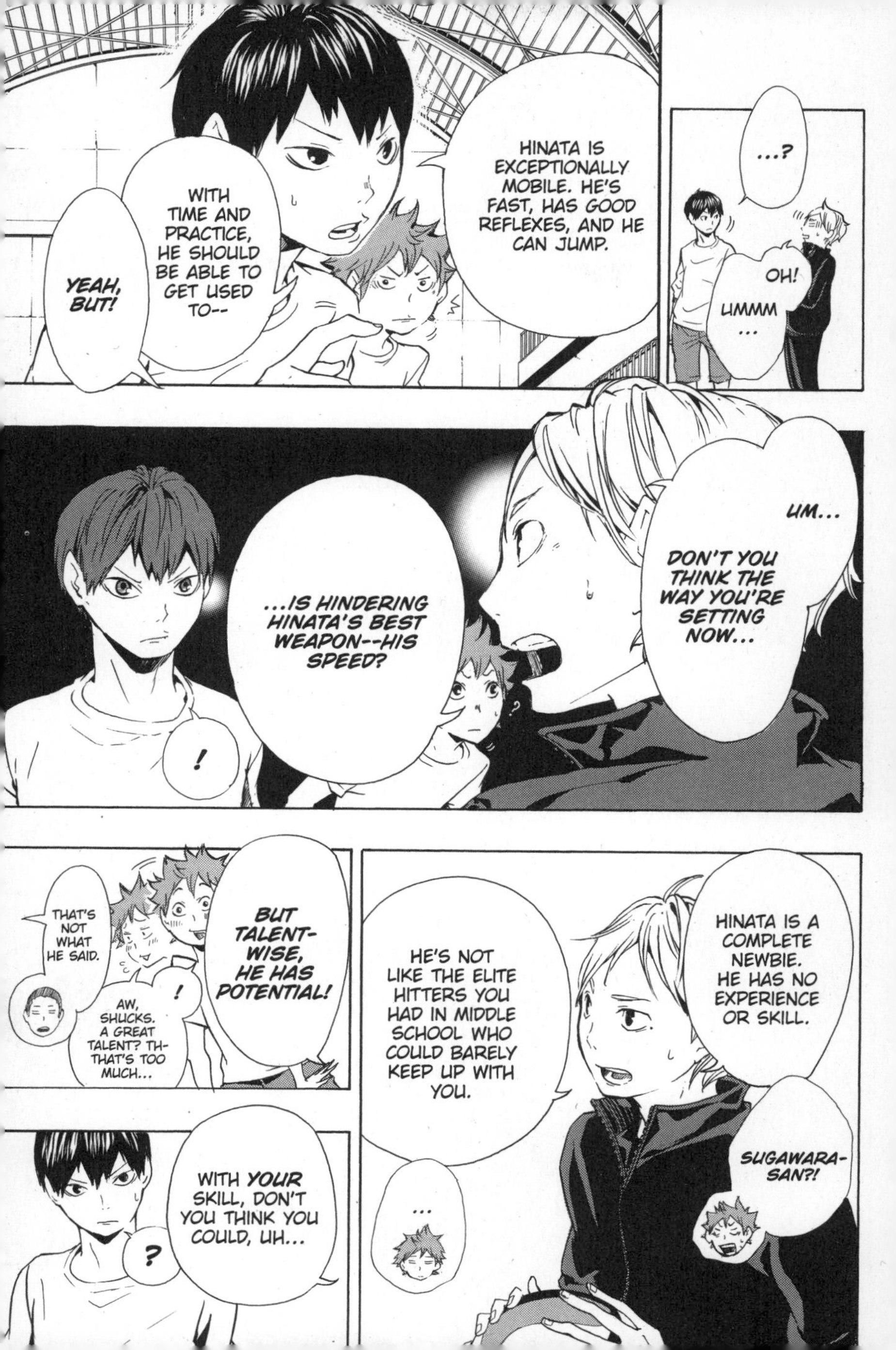
...?
OH! UMMM...
HINATA IS EXCEPTIONALLY MOBILE. HE'S FAST, HAS GOOD REFLEXES, AND HE CAN JUMP.
WITH TIME AND PRACTICE, HE SHOULD BE ABLE TO GET USED TO--
YEAH, BUT!
UM...
DON'T YOU THINK THE WAY YOU'RE SETTING NOW...
...IS HINDERING HINATA'S BEST WEAPON--HIS SPEED?
!
HINATA IS A COMPLETE NEWBIE. HE HAS NO EXPERIENCE OR SKILL.
HE'S NOT LIKE THE ELITE HITTERS YOU HAD IN MIDDLE SCHOOL WHO COULD BARELY KEEP UP WITH YOU.
SUGAWARA-SAN?!
...
BUT TALENT-WISE, HE HAS POTENTIAL!
!
THAT'S NOT WHAT HE SAID.
AW, SHUCKS. A GREAT TALENT? TH-THAT'S TOO MUCH...
WITH YOUR SKILL, DON'T YOU THINK YOU COULD, UH...
?

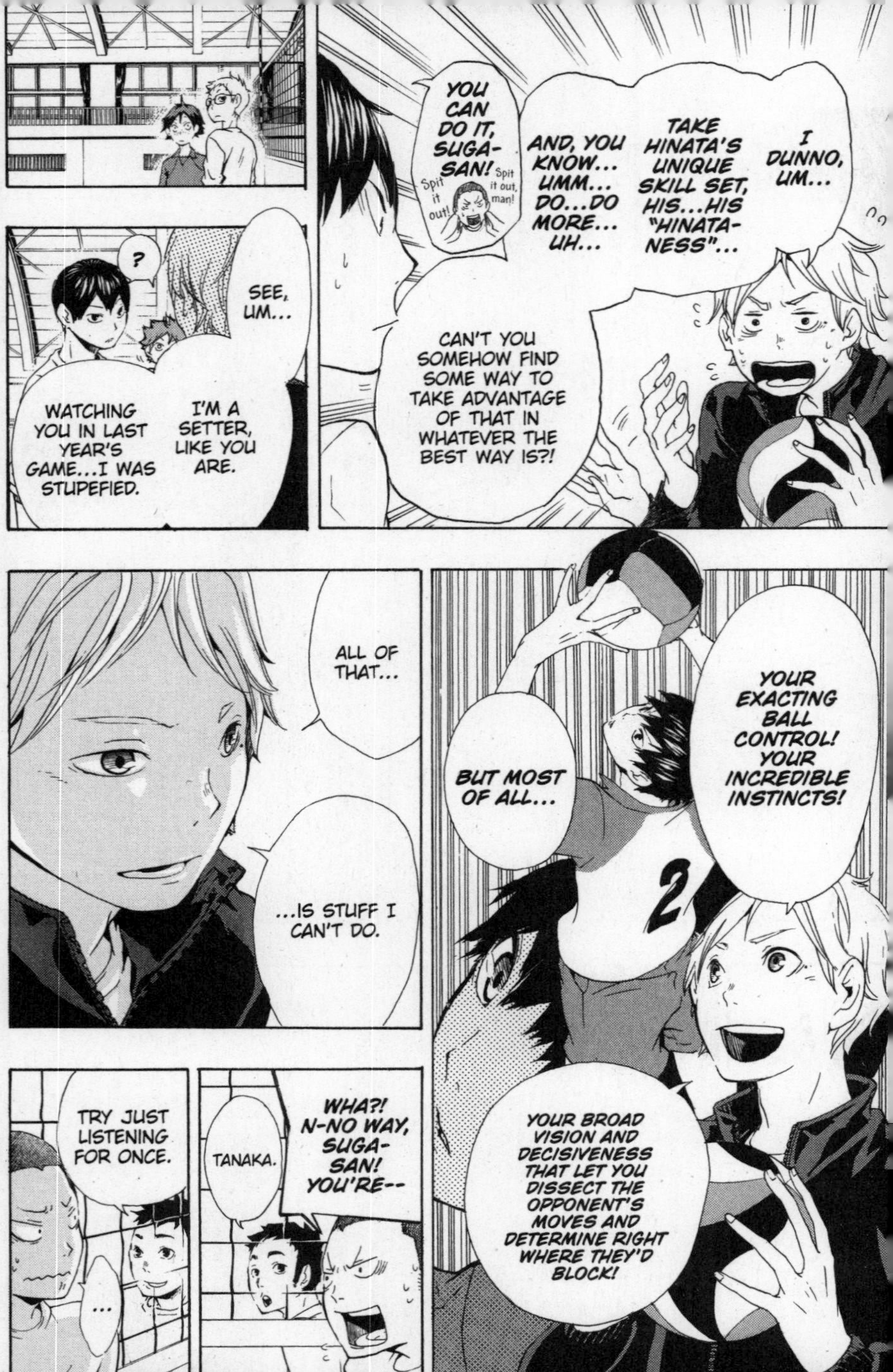
I DUNNO, UM...
TAKE HINATA'S UNIQUE SKILL SET, HIS...HIS "HINATA-NESS"...
AND, YOU KNOW... UMM... DO...DO MORE... UH...
YOU CAN DO IT, SUGA-SAN!
Spit it out, man!
Spit it out!
CAN'T YOU SOMEHOW FIND SOME WAY TO TAKE ADVANTAGE OF THAT IN WHATEVER THE BEST WAY IS?!
?
SEE, UM...
I'M A SETTER, LIKE YOU ARE.
WATCHING YOU IN LAST YEAR'S GAME...I WAS STUPEFIED.
YOUR EXACTING BALL CONTROL! YOUR INCREDIBLE INSTINCTS!
BUT MOST OF ALL...
YOUR BROAD VISION AND DECISIVENESS THAT LET YOU DISSECT THE OPPONENT'S MOVES AND DETERMINE RIGHT WHERE THEY'D BLOCK!
ALL OF THAT...
...IS STUFF I CAN'T DO.
WHA?! N-NO WAY, SUGA-SAN! YOU'RE--
TANAKA.
TRY JUST LISTENING FOR ONCE.
...

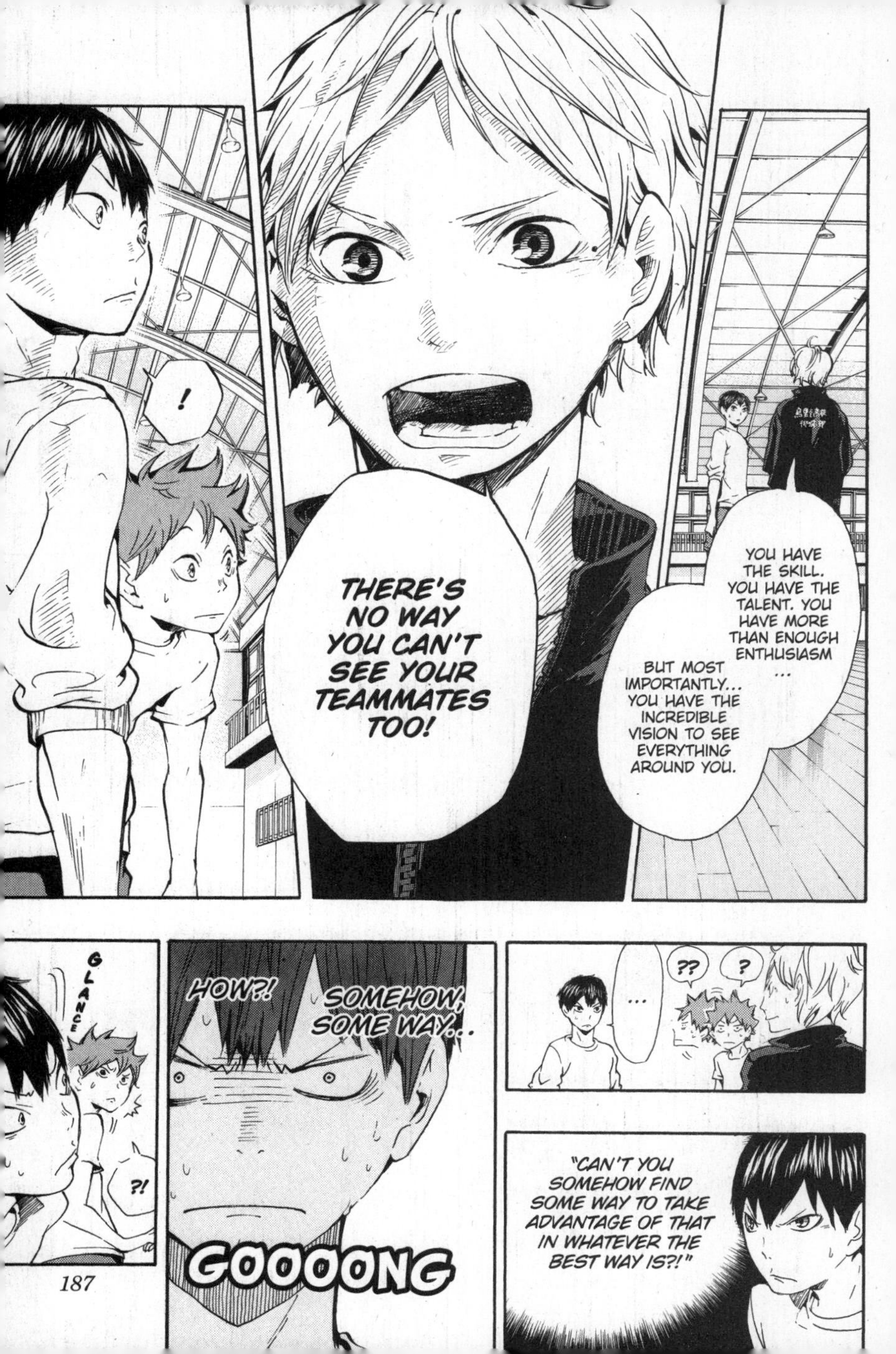
YOU HAVE THE SKILL. YOU HAVE THE TALENT. YOU HAVE MORE THAN ENOUGH ENTHUSIASM ...
BUT MOST IMPORTANTLY... YOU HAVE THE INCREDIBLE VISION TO SEE EVERYTHING AROUND YOU.
THERE'S NO WAY YOU CAN'T SEE YOUR TEAMMATES TOO!
!
?
??
...
"CAN'T YOU SOMEHOW FIND SOME WAY TO TAKE ADVANTAGE OF THAT IN WHATEVER THE BEST WAY IS?!"
SOMEHOW, SOME WAY...
HOW?!
GOOOOONG
GLANCE
?!

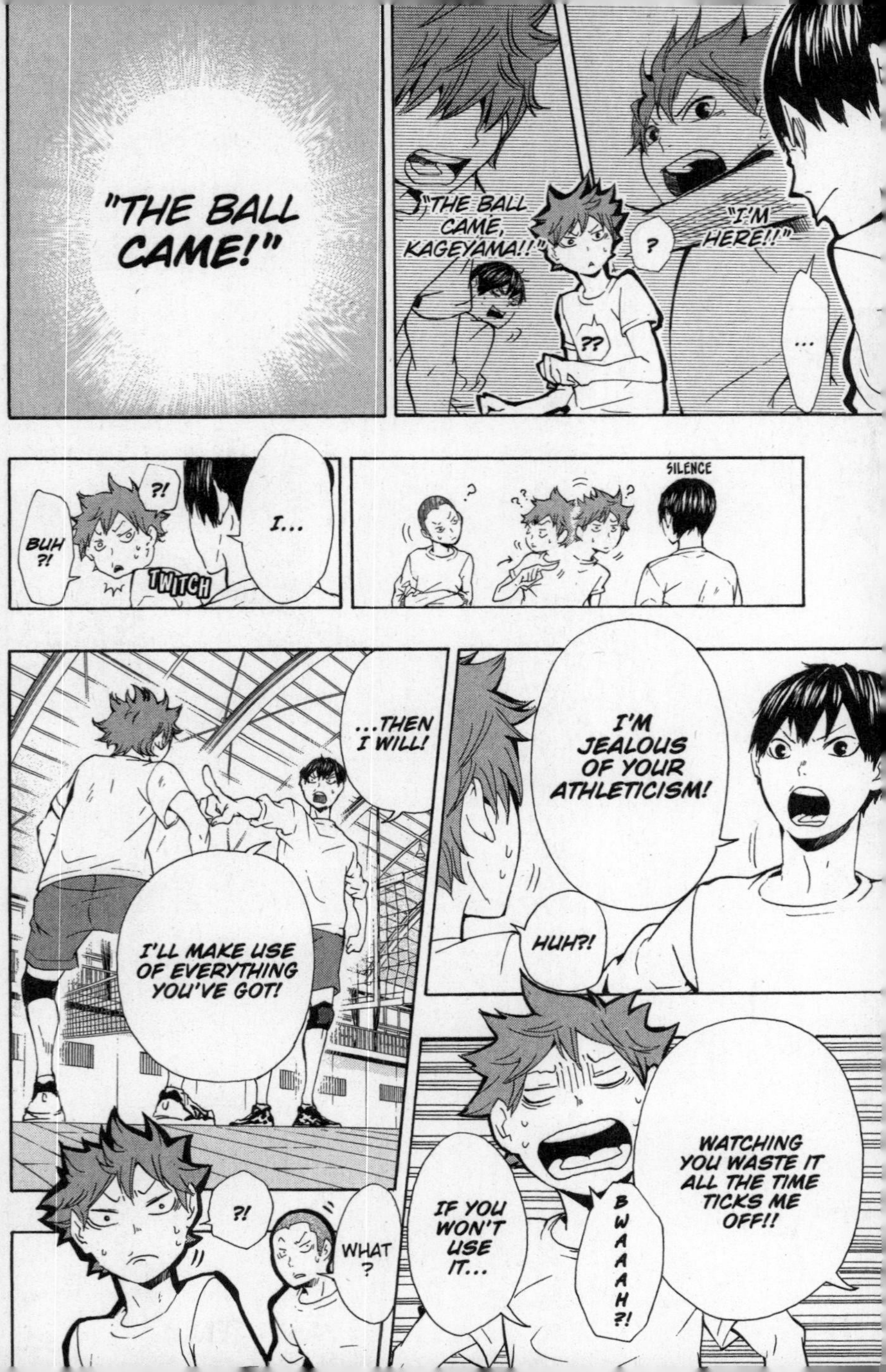
"I'M HERE!!"
...
?
"THE BALL CAME, KAGEYAMA!!"
??
"THE BALL CAME!"
SILENCE
?
??
?
I...
?!
TWITCH
BUH ?!
I'M JEALOUS OF YOUR ATHLETICISM!
HUH?!
WATCHING YOU WASTE IT ALL THE TIME TICKS ME OFF!!
BWAAAAH?!
IF YOU WON'T USE IT...
...THEN I WILL!
I'LL MAKE USE OF EVERYTHING YOU'VE GOT!
WHAT?
?!

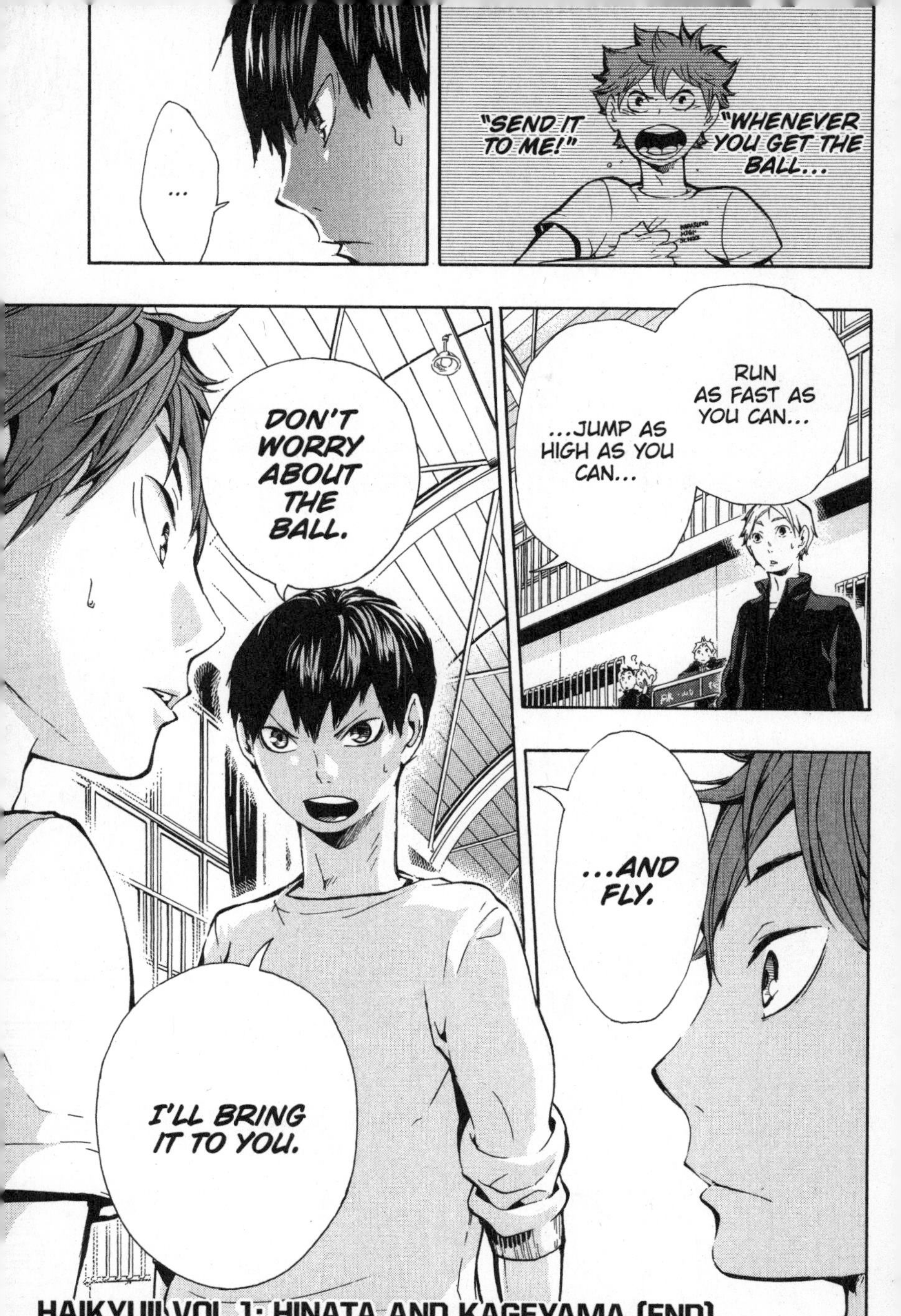
"WHENEVER YOU GET THE BALL...
"SEND IT TO ME!"
...
RUN AS FAST AS YOU CAN...
...JUMP AS HIGH AS YOU CAN...
...AND FLY.
DON'T WORRY ABOUT THE BALL.
I'LL BRING IT TO YOU.

HAIKYU!! VOL 1: HINATA AND KAGEYAMA (END)

EDITOR'S NOTES

The English edition of Haikyu!! maintains the honorifics used in the original Japanese version. For those of you who are new to these terms, here's a brief explanation to help with your reading experience!

When saying someone's name in Japanese, a suffix is often attached to indicate how familiar the speaker is with the person. Some are more polite and respectful, while others are endearing.

1 *-kun* is often used for young men or boys, usually someone you are familiar with.

2 *-chan* is used for young children and can be used as a term of endearment.

3 *-san* is used for someone you respect or are not close to, or to be polite.

4 *Senpai* is used for someone who is older than you or in a higher position or grade in school.

5 *Kohai* is used for someone who is younger than you or in a lower position or grade in school.

6 *Sensei* means teacher.

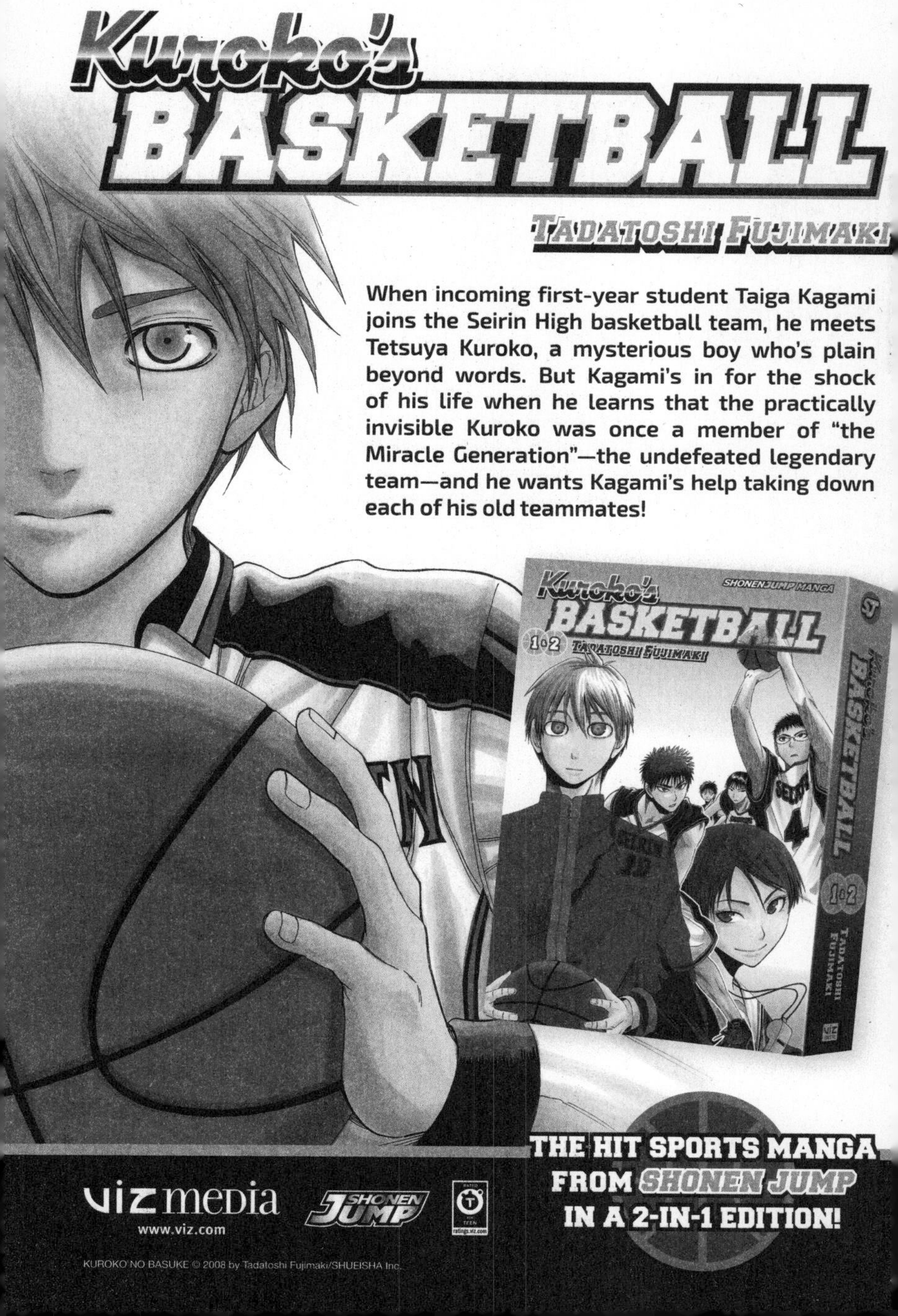
Kuroko's
BASKETBALL
TADATOSHI FUJIMAKI
When incoming first-year student Taiga Kagami joins the Seirin High basketball team, he meets Tetsuya Kuroko, a mysterious boy who's plain beyond words. But Kagami's in for the shock of his life when he learns that the practically invisible Kuroko was once a member of "the Miracle Generation"—the undefeated legendary team—and he wants Kagami's help taking down each of his old teammates!
Kuroko's BASKETBALL
SHONEN JUMP MANGA
1•2
TADATOSHI FUJIMAKI
THE HIT SPORTS MANGA
FROM SHONEN JUMP
IN A 2-IN-1 EDITION!
viz media
www.viz.com
SHONEN JUMP
RATED T FOR TEEN
ratings.viz.com
KUROKO NO BASUKE © 2008 by Tadatoshi Fujimaki/SHUEISHA Inc.

You're Reading the
WRONG WAY!

HAIKYU!! reads from right to left, starting in the upper-right corner. Japanese is read from right to left, meaning that action, sound effects and word-balloon order are completely reversed from English order.

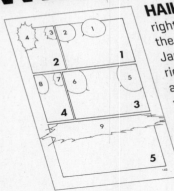